THE CAPITAL ORDER

THE CAPITAL ORDER

How Economists
Invented Austerity
and Paved the
Way to Fascism

CLARA E. MATTEI

The University of Chicago Press

Chicago and London

The University of Chicago Press, Chicago 60637
The University of Chicago Press, Ltd., London
© 2022 by The University of Chicago
Published 2022
Printed in the United States of America

31 30 29 28 27 26 25 24 23 22   1 2 3 4 5

ISBN-13: 978-0-226-81839-9 (cloth)
ISBN-13: 978-0-226-81840-5 (e-book)
DOI: https://doi.org/10.7208/chicago/9780226818405.001.0001

Library of Congress Cataloging-in-Publication Data

Names: Mattei, Clara E., author.
Title: The capital order : how economists invented austerity and
    paved the way to fascism / Clara E. Mattei.
Description: Chicago : University of Chicago Press, 2022. |
    Includes bibliographical references and index.
Identifiers: LCCN 2022005299 | ISBN 9780226818399 (cloth) |
    ISBN 9780226818405 (ebook)
Subjects: LCSH: Capitalism—Great Britain. | Capitalism—
    Italy. | Stagnation (Economics) | Fascism—Great Britain. |
    Fascism—Italy.
Classification: LCC HB501 .M38 2022 | DDC 330.12/2—dc23/
    eng/20220214
LC record available at https://lccn.loc.gov/2022005299

♾ This paper meets the requirements of ANSI/NISO z39.48-1992
(Permanence of Paper).

To Gianfranco Mattei and
revolutionaries everywhere—
past, present, future

Contents

Introduction

In March 2020, during the earliest days of the COVID-19 pandemic, the Democrat governor of New York, Andrew Cuomo, announced plans to slash Medicaid spending to hospitals by $400 million as part of his state budget. It was a shocking announcement: on the threshold of a pandemic, one of the country's most high-profile politicians was informing the public that he planned to underpay hospitals caring for New York's poorest and most vulnerable. "We can't spend what we don't have," Cuomo explained with a shrug in a press conference. These cuts were expected to go deeper in the following years, with similar cuts to come for the state's public schools.[1]

In October 2019, following an announced increase in the subway fare for citizens of Santiago, Chile, citizens flooded the streets in protest—not only because of transit concerns, but in response to the cumulative public toll of fifty years of privatization, wage repression, cuts in public services, and marginalization of organized labor that had fundamentally hollowed life and society for millions of Chileans. With hundreds of thousands demonstrating in the streets, Chile's government responded with dictatorship-style martial law, including a series of deeply unsettling displays of police force that spanned weeks.[2]

On July 5, 2015, 61 percent of voters in Greece passed a referendum to oppose a bailout plan from the International Monetary Fund and the European Union that was proposed to address Greece's sovereign debt crisis. Eight days later, and in spite of the public referendum, the Greek government signed an agreement anyway, settling on a three-year bailout loan that limited how the country could spend money on its people: Greece had to impose more pension reductions, increase its consumption taxes, privatize services and industries, and implement a pay cut for the country's public employees. Two years later, the Greek government privatized the country's ten main ports and put many of its islands up for sale.[3]

It is a trope of twentieth- and twenty-first-century life that governments faced with financial shortfalls look first to the services they provide their citizens when making cuts. Instances like these are innumerable and span every country in the world. When this happens, they produce highly predictable, uniformly devastating effects on societies. Call it *the austerity effect*: the inevitable public suffering that ensues when nations and states cut public benefits in the name of economic solvency and private industry. While austerity policies may not be identified by name, they underscore the most common tropes of contemporary politics: budget cuts (especially in welfare expenditures such as public education, health care, housing, and unemployment benefits), regressive taxation, deflation, privatization, wage repression, and employment deregulation. Taken together, this suite of policies entrenches existing wealth and the primacy of the private sector, both of which tend to be held up as economic keys that will guide nations to better days.

Americans have seen these policies repeated by governments at every level. Attacks on unions have decimated workers' collective bargaining rights; minimum wages languish at poverty levels; laws allow employers to enforce "non-compete clauses" that bar certain workers from changing jobs in pursuit of better pay;[4] welfare has transformed into "workfare," i.e., government assistance contingent upon low-wage work. Most tellingly, the country's regressive tax policies enforce inequitable sharing of public expenses: a larger share of tax revenue drawn from consumption taxes, which are shared across a society, paired with exorbitant tax cuts across top income brackets—91 percent during Eisenhower's presidency (1953–1961), 37 percent as of 2021—as well as a reduction in capital gains taxes and corporate taxes. (The Trump administration lowered the latter in 2017 from 35 percent to 21 percent, a remarkable shift from the 50 percent rate of the 1970s.) While wages in the US have been stagnant for decades, now, for the first time in history, the country's richest 400 families pay a lower overall tax rate than any other income group.[5]

Austerity is not new, nor is it a product of the so-called Neoliberal Era that began in the late 1970s. Outside, perhaps, of the less than three booming decades that followed World War II, austerity has been a mainstay of modern capitalism. It has been true throughout history that where capitalism exists, crisis follows. Where austerity has proven wildly effective is in insulating capitalist hierarchies from harm during these moments of would-be social change. Austerity is capitalism's protector, popular among states[6] for its effectiveness and billed as a means of "fixing" economies by increasing their "efficiency"—short-term readjustments for long-term gains.

In his famous book *Austerity: The History of a Dangerous Idea*, the political scientist Mark Blyth shows that although austerity has not "worked" in the sense of achieving its stated goals across history (e.g., reducing debt or boosting economic growth), it has nonetheless been employed by governments over and over again. Blyth refers to this pattern of compulsive repetition as a form of madness.[7] However, if we view austerity in this book's terms—as a response not just to economic crises (e.g., contraction of output and heightened inflation), but to crises of capitalism—we can begin to see method in the madness: austerity is a vital bulwark in defense of the capitalist system.

When I refer to a crisis of capitalism, I do not mean an economic crisis—say, a slowdown in growth or an uptick in inflation. Capitalism is in crisis when its core relationship (the sale of production for profit)[8] and its two enabling pillars (private property in the means of production and wage relations between owners and workers) are contested by the public, in particular by the workers who make capitalism run. As part of these expressions of unhappiness, people have historically demanded alternative forms of social organization. Indeed, and as this book will demonstrate, austerity's primary utility over the last century has been to silence such calls and to foreclose alternatives to capitalism. Mostly austerity serves to quash public outcry and worker strikes—not, as it is often advertised, to spontaneously improve a country's economic indicators by practicing greater economic discipline.

Austerity as we know it today emerged after World War I as a method for preventing capitalism's collapse: economists in political positions used policy levers to make all classes of society more invested in private, capitalist production, even when these changes amounted to profound (if also involuntary) personal sacrifices. In the early 1920s, austerity functioned as a powerful counteroffensive to strikes and other forms of social unrest that exploded on an unprecedented scale after the war—a period traditionally, and oddly, overlooked by political and economic scholars who study austerity. The timing of austerity's invention reflects its animating motivations. Of greater importance than austerity's purported economic efficacy was its ability to guard capitalist relations of production during a time of unprecedented social organizing and public agitation from working classes.

Austerity has been so widespread in its uptake over the last century that it has become largely undetectable: the economics of austerity, with its prescribed budgetary cuts and public moderation, is largely synonymous with today's economics. This makes a critical history of austerity, especially one rendered in class terms, profoundly challenging. But to the extent that we stop perceiving austerity as a sincere toolbox for managing an economy, and when we consider its history through the lens of class, it becomes clear that austerity preserves something foundational to our capitalist society. For capitalism to work in delivering economic growth, the social relation of capital—people selling their labor power for a wage—must be uniform across a society. In other words, economic growth presupposes a certain sociopolitical order, or *capital order*. Austerity, viewed as a set of fiscal, monetary, and industrial guardrails on an economy, ensures the sanctity of these social relations. The structural limitations it imposes on spending and wages ensure that, for the vast majority of those living in a society, "work hard, save hard" is more than just an expression of toughness; it's the only path to survival.

This book examines the history of how this system came to high fashion in the twentieth century, including its most powerful expression in the postwar economies of Britain and Italy. In both cases, austerity was a means for economists in power to reimpose capital order where it had been lost.

The story begins with the events of the Great War that triggered the most severe crisis of capitalism to date—the unprecedented wartime mobilizations within European countries that shattered capitalism's shield of inevitability. For most people living in these countries during and after the war, whether they feared or hoped for it, the abolition of capitalism loomed as the imminent outcome of the war's devastations and its showcasing of state economic planning. In the words of Willi Gallacher, the British shop steward leader, "the order of industry, which previous to the war seemed destined to last forever, is now tottering in every country of the world."[9] In Italy, the threat was likewise palpable to the famed liberal economist Luigi Einaudi: "it seemed that a shoulder shove would suffice to knock the so-called capitalist regime to the ground . . . the reign of equality seemed close to ensue." The words of the bourgeois professor were juxtaposed with the enthusiasm of Palmiro Togliatti, a leading member of the *Ordine Nuovo* ("new order") labor movement: "men recoil from the old order of things, they feel the need to place themselves in a new manner, to shape their community in a new form, of forging new living relations that allow for a construction of a wholly renewed social edifice."[10]

These new voices from the intellectual Left accelerated change in social relations. *L'Ordine nuovo*, based in the industrial Italian city of Turin and led by Togliatti and his comrade Antonio Gramsci, is crucial to this story because it embodies the most explicit antagonist to capitalist practice and its intellectual justifications. It represented a break from both hierarchical relations of society and top-down knowledge production.

The collective anti-capitalist awakening was facilitated by the extraordinary governmental measures during the war to temporarily interrupt capital accumulation by the owners of private industry. In order to confront the enormities of the war production effort, the governments of all warring nations were forced to intervene in what had been, until then, the untarnished realm of the market. As governments collectivized key industries—munitions, mines, shipping, and railways—they also employed workers and regulated the cost and supply of labor. State interventionism not only allowed the Allies to win the war; it also made clear that wage relations and the privatization of production—far from being "natural"—were political choices of a class-minded society.

After the war, emboldened by the new economic precedents of the mobilization effort, workers in Europe spoke with a stronger and more radical voice, and they expressed themselves in ways beyond the ballot box. They consolidated collective power through unions, parties, guilds, and rank-and-file institutions to control production. The extent of politicization among large chunks of the population meant that their public opinion on economic questions could no longer be ignored. As the famed British economist John Maynard Keynes well observed, "even if economists and technicians knew the secret remedy, they could not apply it until they had persuaded the politicians; and the politicians, who have ears but no eyes, will not attend to the persuasion until it reverberates back to them as an echo from the great public."[11]

In a moment of unparalleled democratic upheaval all over Europe, in the midst of mounting monetary inflation and revolutionary winds coming from Russia, Bavaria, and Hungary, economic experts had to wield their greatest weapons in order to preserve the world as they thought it should exist. Austerity was their most useful tool: it functioned—and still functions—to preserve the indisputability of capitalism.

The austerity counteroffensive successfully disempowered the majority. Austere governments and their experts implemented policies that either directly (through repressive pay and employment policies) or indirectly (through restrictive monetary and fiscal policies that depressed economic activity and raised unemployment) subjugated the majority to capital—a social relation in which a majority sells their capacity to work in exchange for a wage. Austerity shifted resources from the working majority to the saver/investor minority, and in so doing enforced a public acceptance of repressive conditions in economic production. This acceptance was further entrenched by experts whose economic theories depicted capitalism as the only and best possible world.

These events of the early 1920s, including the widespread bourgeois fear of the crumbling of capitalism, were a watershed moment. The antagonism of the political and economic establishment to the will of the public, and especially their interventions to quell such revolutionary sentiments, reestablished capital order in Europe and ensured the trajectory of the political economy for the rest of the century, a trajectory that has continued to this day.

Austerity, Then and Now

Part of what makes austerity so effective as a set of policies is that it packages itself in the language of honest, hardscrabble economics. Vague sentiments such as "hard work" and "thrift" are hardly novel; they have been extolled by economists since the days of Adam Smith, David Ricardo, and Thomas Robert Malthus, and their latter-day followers who cultivated these maxims as the stuff of personal virtue and good policy. These sensibilities were also reflected in 1821 with the institution of the gold standard, a policy whereby upstanding governments demonstrated their fiscal and monetary rigor by linking their currencies to their holdings of precious metals, both domestically and in colonies.[12] A closer history of austerity shows, however, that it was in its modern form something quite different from these earlier, moral exercises. Austerity as a twentieth-century phenomenon materialized as a state-led, technocratic project in a moment of unprecedented political enfranchisement of citizens (who had gained the right to vote for the first time) and mounting demands for economic democracy. In this way, austerity must be understood for what it is and remains: an anti-democratic reaction to threats of bottom-up social change. As this book will show, its modern form cannot be divorced from the historical context in which it was born.

In post–World War I Britain and in other liberal democracies where widespread political empowerment was historically extolled, the state

effectively wielded austerity as a political weapon against its own people. The British workers had fueled the nation's war effort, and in the
course of the wartime mobilization became aware that socioeconomic
relations were no natural givens and could be different. By imposing
austerity measures after the war, the British government effectively told
its working classes to return to the back of the line.

The public disgust for early austerity was its crucible: austerity was
rendered more antagonistic because it had to overcome—and indeed
tame—an incensed public. After World War I, with the gold standard
in pieces, the newly enfranchised European "great public" was not simply going to accept austere policies, and the experts knew it. Thus, they
devised austerity to conjoin two strategies: consensus and coercion.

Consensus implied a conscious effort to "awaken" the public to the
truth and necessity of reforms that favored economic stabilization,
even when it might hurt.[13] Recognizing that a restless public would be
unlikely to make the "correct" decision regarding this greater good,
experts complemented consensus with *coercion*. This took two forms.
First, austerity had within it the principle of excluding the general public from economic decision-making and instead delegating such decisions to technocratic institutions—especially the central banks, whose
setting of interest rates served as a hinge for public wages and unemployment. This preemption of decision-making by the expert class created a canvas for further policy decisions that propelled the installation
of austerity. Second, coercion lay not only in who made economic decisions, but also in the outcome of those decisions—that is, in the very
workings of austerity.

European governments and their central banks enforced the
"proper" (i.e., class-appropriate) behavior on the working classes in order to rescue capital accumulation by the wealthy. The three forms of
austerity policies—fiscal, monetary, and industrial—worked in unison
to exert a downward pressure on wages among the rest of society. Their
aim was to shift national wealth and resources toward the upper classes,
who, the economic experts insisted, were the ones capable of saving
and investing. Fiscal austerity comes in the form of regressive taxation
and cuts to "unproductive" public expenditures, especially on social

endeavors (health, education, etc.). While regressive taxation imposes thrift on the majority and exempts the saver-investor minority, budget cuts indirectly do the same: public resources are diverted from the many to the saver-investor few, in that budget cuts come with the stated priority of paying back the debt that rests in the hands of national or international creditors. Similarly, monetary austerity, meaning monetary revaluation policies (such as an increase in interest rates and reduction in money supply) directly protect creditors and increase the value of their savings. Meanwhile organized labor has its hands tied, since having less money in circulation depresses the economy and diminishes the bargaining power of the working class. Finally, industrial austerity, which takes the form of authoritarian industrial policies (layoffs of public employees, wage reductions, union- and strike-busting, etc.), further protects vertical wage relations between owners and workers, fostering wage repression in favor of the higher profit of the few. This book will study these three forms of austerity—what I call the austerity trinity—and how they at once require and advance one another. This historical inquiry, examining a moment in which capitalism was very much on the ropes, enlightens many vital connections that economists overlook when discussing austerity today.

First, austerity policies cannot be reduced to mere fiscal or monetary policies from central government institutions. Industrial policies, public and private, that create favorable conditions for profit and discipline workers are central to austerity as well. Indeed, as the book will show, our experts' fixation on debt repayment, balanced budgets, foreign exchanges, and inflation reveals a more fundamental purpose: taming class conflict, which is essential for the continued reproduction of capitalism.

Second, this inquiry clarifies that austerity is more than just economic policy; it is an amalgamation of policy and theory. Austerity's policies thrive because they sit atop a set of economic theories that inform and justify them. This book examines the threading of a certain kind of theory within policy making, including how the resulting technocracy—government controlled by technical experts—is central to protecting modern capitalism from its threats. There are no better candidates to illustrate this entanglement than the characters in the post–World War I story, who were among the most influential technocrats of the 1920s.

Technocracy and "Apolitical" Theory, Then and Now

Technocracy dominates governmental policy making on multiple fronts. One is the historical convention of economists advising people who govern. The other is epistemic, a form whereby these economists frame economics—including the economic arguments they themselves posited—as having achieved a standpoint above class interests or partisanship. Economics, economists argue, constitutes value-free truths about capitalism—natural facts of this world rather than constructed (or at least political) positions.

The technocracy that facilitated austerity's rise in the twentieth century can be attributed to the British economist Ralph G. Hawtrey, who authored the texts and memoranda that would serve as the guidelines for British austerity after World War I. As is the nature of technocracy, Hawtrey had help. Working at his side were the charismatic Sir Basil Blackett and Sir Otto Niemeyer, both powerful senior Treasury officials who closely advised the chancellor of the exchequer, Britain's minister in charge of economic and financial policies.

In Rome, the school of academic Italian economics that led the country's austerity policies was presided over by Maffeo Pantaleoni, who directed a group of economists under the Italian Fascist government that was codified in 1922 under "The Duce," Benito Mussolini. The prime minister granted Pantaleoni's pupil Alberto De Stefani exceptional powers to apply austerity in De Stefani's role as minister of finance. The Italian economists took advantage of this rare opportunity to explore the reaches of what they considered "pure economics," a school of economics-as-natural-law that aligned with austerity. They enjoyed an unprecedented advantage in governance in that they could directly implement economic models without the encumbrance of democratic procedures—and sometimes, thanks to Mussolini, with the help of tools of political oppression.

This book delves into the writings and public comments of these two sets of economic experts, men who designed austerity policies and wrangled consensus for their brute-force implementations. While their voices were central to the formulation of austerity after World War I, their role in this insidious counterrevolution has not been studied or explicated elsewhere. What their stories make clear, and what remains true today, is that in order to persist, austerity requires experts willing to speak to its virtues. That relationship remains true today, albeit with an ever-refreshed cast of technocratic figures.

After World War I, economists in Britain and Italy—both capitalist nations, but dramatically different otherwise—enjoyed unprecedented roles in shaping and implementing public policy to guide their nations' postwar reformations. In both cases, economists leaned heavily on the principles of what they thought of as "pure economics"—then an emerging paradigm, but one still foundational to today's mainstream economics, or what we sometimes refer to as the neoclassical tradition.

The "pure economics" paradigm successfully established the field as the politically "neutral" science of policies and individual behavior. By dissociating the economic process from the political one—i.e., by presenting economic theory and conceptualizing markets as free from social relations of domination—pure economics restored an illusion of consent within capitalist systems, allowing these relations of domination to masquerade instead as economic rationality. Indeed, technocracy's strength rested in this power to frame austerity's most fundamental objectives—reinstating capitalist relations of production, and subjugating the working class into accepting the inviolability of private property and wage relations—as a return to an economy's natural state.

These economists' "apolitical" theory was centered on an idealized caricature of an economic being: the rational saver. This broad-stroke characterization had a dual result: first, it created the illusion that anyone could be a rational saver, provided they worked hard enough and no matter their material conditions and endowments; and second, it discredited and devalued workers, who went from being understood as productive members of society to being seen as social liabilities based on their inability to practice virtuous economic behaviors. (Note: it was, and remains, exceedingly challenging for people to save money they don't have.) Accordingly, workers after the war lost all the agency that the theories and actions of the *Ordinovista* movement had won for them. Because through the economists' lens, the productive class in a society was not the working class, but the capitalist class—the people who could save, invest, and thus contribute to the private accumulation of capital. Economic theory was no longer a tool for critical thought and action; it was a mold for imposing passive consent and maintaining a top-down status quo.

Austerity's capacity to divert attention from systemic problems also helped foster collective passivity. Economists attributed postwar economic crises to the excesses of citizens, who were thereby delegitimized in their socioeconomic needs and expected to redeem themselves through economic sacrifices, restraint, hard work, and wage curtailment—all essential preconditions for capital accumulation and international economic competitiveness.

Austerity policies in the spirit of "pure economics" were a disaster for most people living in Britain and Italy in the 1920s. Thus, the book delves into the paradox of a doctrine that presents itself as apolitical but has as its central purpose the "taming of men," as the Italian academic and economist Umberto Ricci crudely put it in 1908. Under a veneer of apolitical science, technocrat economists were undertaking the most political action of all—bending the working classes to the wills and needs of the capital-owning classes for the enrichment of a small minority.

The story of austerity is also an origin story for the rapid ascent and awesome political power of modern economics. It is true today, but was not after World War I, that capitalism is the only show in town: mainstream economic theory flourishes because our societies rely almost entirely on the coercion of people who have no alternative but to sell their labor power to the propertied few in order to survive. (As the economist Branko Milanović notes in his 2019 book *Capitalism, Alone*, "the fact that the entire globe now operates according to the same economic principles is without historical precedent."[14]) Rather than acknowledging and studying the odd homogeneity of this reality, mainstream economics works to conceal it. Class conflict and eco-

nomic domination are supplanted by a supposed harmony between individuals in which those at the top are seen as those who exhibit greater
economic virtue and whose quest for profit is beneficial to all. In this
way economic theory thwarts critiques of vertical relations of production, justifies capitalism, and counsels public compliance.

Capitalism's ubiquity today can make criticizing or even observing
capitalism seem quaint. After all, we have internalized its teachings to
the point that our values and beliefs are largely aligned with those that
are functional to capital accumulation. It is all so embedded that today
a majority of American workers can live paycheck to paycheck with
little to no social insurance and still largely accept that their position
is one they deserve; the country's wealthy, meanwhile, benefit from
a seeming national allergy to any form of even mild tax reform that
would shift more tax burden to the wealthy. The current landscape is
quite different from the one technocrats were confronting in 1919, but
the two are most certainly connected.

Indeed, even an economic expert like Keynes, usually understood as
the most vocal critic of austerity,[15] in 1919 was of a very different opinion. He shared with colleagues at the British Treasury a sense of terror
around the threatened breakdown of the capital order—and surpris-
ingly enough, he also shared their austere solution to the capitalist crisis. As the 1920s progressed, Keynes's economic theory of how best to
avoid crises *did* change; what *did not* change was his fundamental concern to preserve capital order—what he described as the "thin and precarious crust of civilization"[16] that required protection. This existential
anxiety remains a cardinal feature of Keynesianism to this day.[17] Even
though Keynes is not a central figure in this story, his intellectual bond
with several of austerity's principals remains essential to fully understanding the nature and impetus of the so-called Keynesian Revolution
later in the twentieth century.

Liberalism and Fascism, Then and Now

The story of austerity's counteroffensive against the upstart lower class
began at two international financial conferences, first in Brussels in

1919 and then in Genoa in 1922. These two conferences constituted landmark events in the rise of the first global technocratic agenda of austerity. Their agendas found swift, direct application throughout Europe, most notably in Britain and Italy—two socioeconomic settings that were poles apart. At one end, Britain, a solid parliamentary democracy led by well-established institutions and orthodox Victorian values, was an empire whose centuries-long world economic-financial hegemony was now being contested by an ascendant United States. At the other end was Italy, an economically backward country that was reeling from fresh revolutionary surges and civil war. Italy lacked self-sufficiency and was highly dependent on foreign imports and capital. By October 1922 Mussolini's Fascism had seized Italy's reins.

This book narrates the parallel and intertwined stories of austerity's triumphs in Britain and Italy after World War I. I choose to focus on these nations because the disparities of their political-institutional realities facilitate identification of the fundamental elements of austerity and the capitalist mode of production across places and through time. Britain, the cradle of classical liberalism, and Italy, the birthplace of fascism, are unquestioningly understood to represent opposite ideological worlds. However, once austerity becomes our historical focus, the lines of division start to blur. Austerity transcends all ideological and institutional differences, barreling toward a similar goal within dissimilar countries: the necessity to rehabilitate capital accumulation in settings where capitalism has lost its innocence and been revealed in its classist tendencies.

This story also reveals how British liberalism and Italian Fascism fostered similar environments for austerity to thrive. These similarities went beyond the shared sacrifices of British and Italian citizens, or the fact that both countries' agendas of austerity were rationalized by similar economic theories. It is also evident that the original formation of Italy's Fascist dictatorship required the support of the Italian liberal elite as well as the support of the Anglo-American financial establishment, both of which Mussolini was able to secure by implementing— often with force—austerity policies. Tellingly, the years 1925 to 1928 correspond to the peak of both the Fascist regime's consolidation and of American and British financial investments in Italian government bonds. Fascist Italy's austerity economy provided these liberal countries with a profitable place to park their capital, much to their expressed satisfaction.

When it came to dealing with Mussolini and Fascist Italy, the liberal axis of Britain and the United States constructed a practical dissonance: they looked past the country's unsavory politics, which after 1922 were grounded in state-sponsored political violence, while taking advantage of the opportunities in Italy's stabilized economy. To the liberal financial establishment, a country with revolutionary fervor like Italy's required a strong state to reinstate order; that Italy veered all the way to an authoritarian state would just accelerate the subjugation of a radicalized working class to austerity. As this story demonstrates, both Fascist and liberal economists agreed on this point.

While the Italian economists' anti-democratic views were more explicit—Pantaleoni called democracy "the management of the state and its functions by the most ignorant, the most incapable" (Pantaleoni 1922, 269)—the British technocrats also recognized that, even in Britain, economic institutions required exemption from democratic control in order to proceed optimally. Indeed, the Brussels and Genoa conferences formalized central bank independence as a crucial step to this end. The famed British economist Ralph Hawtrey described the advantage of situating a central bank free from "criticism and pressure," noting that the bank could follow the precept "Never explain; never regret; never apologise" (Hawtrey 1925a, 243).

Throughout these pages an interesting theme will come to the fore: economic experts, whether Fascist or liberal, recognized that in order to secure economic freedom—i.e., the market freedom of the "virtuous" saver/entrepreneur—countries had to forgo, or at minimum marginalize, political freedoms. This was apparent especially in Italy during the country's "red years" of 1919 to 1920, when the majority of the country's workers demonstrated their unwillingness to accept a notion of economic freedom that presupposed their subordination to hierarchical relations of production. These workers fought for the liberation of the majority and espoused an understanding of economic freedom that was antithetical to that of experts, one that presupposed the over-throw of private property and wage labor in favor of shared means and democratic control of production. The fate of capitalism, for our econ-omists, hung in the balance. A sweeping counteroffensive—one that transcended party lines—was underway.

The Italian case exposes a repressive drive that was only latent in the British case and persists today in countries across the world. While in Italy industrial austerity directly subordinated labor through the ban-ning of strikes and unions (except Fascist unions—a contradiction in terms, seemingly), Britain's monetary austerity caused an economic downturn[18] that indirectly achieved the same ends: unprecedented un-employment (up to 17 percent of the insured laborers in 1921), which weakened workers' bargaining power and lowered wages, and an ensu-ing reduction in government revenues that tied the state's hands and precluded any public response to workers' needs or demands.

That the British experts were willing to tolerate such high unem-ployment, ostensibly in the service of controlling inflation, is part of the "madness" to which Blyth refers. However, this madness makes sense if we recognize that high unemployment functions to suppress the threat that workers' demands posed to capitalism. What the British economist A. C. Pigou called the "inescapable fact" of unemployment is that it not only killed the political enthusiasm of the working classes, but also forced workers to accept lower pay—in the postwar case of Britain, a 41 percent nominal wage drop from 1920 to 1923 that allowed for the profit rate to recover swiftly from its immediate postwar trou-bles.[19] In this way, it is clear that the primary advantage of the economic downturn was the unequivocal restoration of the capitalist class struc-ture. Rather than exercising direct political and economic coercion, as Italy did, Britain relied on seemingly apolitical technocrats at the heads of its Treasury and the Bank of England, who achieved similar ends through monetary deflation and budget cuts; the structural violence of macroeconomic policy could do the same as the physical violence of Fascist militias. These dire social consequences were evident to po-litical observers. In 1923, Labour MP Dr. Alfred Salter's words echoed through the British Parliament: "Unfortunately the question of wages has returned to the position of ten years ago with a vengeance. . . . You have even got the extraordinary spectacle of able-bodied men in full employment . . . receiving wages at such a low level that they are obliged to have recourse to the Poor Law. . . . It is a most astounding state of things."[20]

The close connection between austerity and technocracy, and the success of early efforts to build consensus around its coercive policies, remain a vivid reality today. Despite repeated economic crises, economists are still relied upon to devise the solution when a new crisis emerges, and their solutions continue to require that workers absorb the lion's share of hardship through lower wages, longer workdays, and welfare cuts.[21]

Wage Repression, Then and Now

Some economists have referred to austerity as a simple "policy mistake," a technical miscalibration that produced suppression of domestic demand and tightening of labor markets. This view dramatically underestimates the impacts of austerity, the success and legacy of which remain indelible to this day. After all, the combination of fiscal, monetary, and industrial policies in the austerity playbook have dealt a lasting blow to the working classes and their expectations for a different socioeconomic system. The rehabilitation of hierarchical wage relations—in which the majority of people cannot make their living in any other way than by selling their labor power as a commodity on the market, and by doing so, renounce their right to have a say in how this commodity is consumed by the employer who purchases it—is perhaps austerity's defining characteristic. In doing so, and as chapter 9 details, it also produces an increase in the rate of exploitation for workers and a surge in profits for owners.

In political economy, the concept of capitalist exploitation refers to the dynamic in which an employee exerts a greater amount of labor than she receives in compensation. In other words, the capitalist class appropriates a surplus value (its profits), as well as other forms of surplus value, such as rents and interest (see Foley 1986). The rate of exploitation can be measured by comparing the amount of national income that goes to profits (profit share) as compared to wages (wage share); another way is to compare labor productivity to wages paid. In both measures, Italy and Britain saw increasing exploitation across the 1920s. Mapping this against political events, the conclusions about austerity's effects on workers become clear: exploitation plummeted during the "red years" of 1918–1920, as nominal daily wages of workers quadrupled (Britain) or even quintupled (Italy) compared to the prewar years. This trend changed immediately with the introduction of austerity.

A century later, exploitation due to wage stagnation—what I show to be the most intractable legacy of austerity[22]—persists as the main driver of a global inequality trend in which a country like Italy (which suffers far less inequality than the United States) has seen the wealth of its richest 6 million increased by 72 percent in the last ten years. The country's poorest 6 million have had their wealth diminished by 63 percent over the same period. The official data tells that in 2018, 5 million people (8.3 percent of the Italian population) lived in absolute poverty, i.e., were deprived of the necessary means to live with dignity.[23] The numbers in 2020 worsened: 5.6 million people, 9.4 percent of the population, live in absolute poverty. In Britain the situation is no less gloomy: 30 percent of the country's children (4.1 million) lived in relative poverty in 2017–2018, and 70 percent of these children lived in working families. As of 2020, the number of poor children has increased to 4.3 million.[24]

In a 2020 macroeconomic analysis of the US economy, the economists Lance Taylor and Özlem Ömer showed that in the preceding forty years, the profit share of the nation's output rose substantially, while the labor share of that same output correspondingly went down. The relationship between owner profit and worker loss was symmetrical; one was taking from the other. An increase in exploitation was also evident, with real wages grossly lagging behind labor productivity.[25] Once the reader is acquainted with the story in this book, the inner workings of such dynamics will become familiar, and hopefully clear.

Today, as in the 1920s, the winners under austerity remain an affluent minority: the richest 1 percent of the population subsists primarily on profit-related incomes tied to existing wealth (e.g., dividends, interest). The rest of the population—those who rely on income from labor alone, or the bottom 60 percent who rely on a combination of low wages and social benefits—has lost (Taylor and Ömer 2020). It is a defeat so thorough and so striking that the median American male worker in 2019 actually earned less in real terms than what he did in 1973. Since that year, structural inequality has robbed American workers of $2.5 trillion each year, money that flowed directly into the hands of the few.[26]

Warren Buffet, the renowned investor and as of 2020 the fourth richest person on earth, was quoted in 2006 as observing: "There's class warfare, all right, but it's my class, the rich class, that's making war, and we're winning."[27] This book shows how the biggest victory of all, and the one that paved the way for all the winning that followed, was the fight that took place a century ago.

Methods and Sources

Tracing the origin story of austerity began in 2013 at the archives of the Library of the Bank of Italy and the Bank's De Stefani Archive, both located in Rome. Here I spent years studying the works of the Italian economists who would become central to my story.

The main challenge in piecing together this history was to avoid the compartmentalization of its characters' different lives—their personal, academic, and political trajectories—and to integrate and study the connections between the economists' theoretical writings, political interventions, and public commentaries. As I did so, a coherent austerity agenda—an agenda that was at once theory and practice—came into stark relief. Much of the archival material that informed this process finds its first translation in the pages of this book.

The same approach guided my research in the British National Archives, the archives of the Bank of England, and the Churchill Archives Center: uncovering and contextualizing the worldviews of the experts at the British Treasury who drove Britain's austerity movement. The study of Ralph Hawtrey's theory was long and hard: the man was prolific both in his academic publications and in the memoranda he wrote for his colleagues at the Treasury. His thoughts were often opaque. However, as I put the pieces of the puzzle together, a holistic picture of austerity emerged. As this book will detail, it was a design heeded and realized by the work of his senior colleagues, Sir Basil Blackett and Sir Otto Niemeyer. Unearthing the activities of these men from dusty Treasury files, I was riveted by the evidence of Hawtrey's persuasion of the other two, and in turn how the two bureaucrats, neither one a trained economist, came to be missionaries in campaigns to export the British austerity agenda to other countries around the globe.

To understand and to develop a chronology of the class conflicts in Britain and Italy during and after the war, I immersed myself in the journalism of the period—left, right, and center; working class and bourgeois. This included the leftist Italian newspapers *L'Avanti* and *L'Ordine nuovo*, quoted often in this book, together with their British equivalents, *The Daily Herald* and the labor pamphlets of the metallurgical shop stewards. Government archives were a crucial resource for reconstructing the voices of the British workers. Various bourgeois newspapers of the era (the *London Times*, the *Economist*, *La stampa*, *Il corriere della sera*) as well as transcripts of parliamentary debates provided a useful contrasting voice. I complemented this historical investigation with the dispatches from the British Embassy in Rome, housed within the Foreign Office files of the National Archives; these are among the most telling voices in the book.

A discomfort in telling a new history is the potential that it will be dismissed as a selective or even partisan telling. For this reason, and because I am an economist and cannot help myself, I have included a chapter at the end of the book that offers quantitative analysis to support the story I have otherwise told in archival and theoretical terms. For this penultimate chapter, chapter 9, I collected macroeconomic and financial data from the most up-to-date statistical sources to illustrate the economic changes in Britain and Italy that support my argument that austerity was, and remains, a tool of class control. If the history of the first eight chapters doesn't persuade readers, perhaps the economics of the final section will.

Part I

WAR AND CRISIS

The scale of the First World War reshaped Europe's capitalist economies. Many private industries became public ones, and governments suddenly functioned as both buyers and sellers in economies that were designed to meet basic needs at home and drive the war effort abroad. Whatever the old social order was, it appeared to be changing.

The change didn't last. With the end of the war, these same capitalist nations moved swiftly to revert their economies to their earlier states: top-down, capitalist, private. Wartime sentiments of egalitarianism were smothered; the power of organized labor was diluted. Capitalism was back.

Capitalism was more than a system of economy; it was a system of social order, too. If the war served as a brief, uncomfortable dalliance with the basic tenets of socialism—including a planned central economy and strong organized labor—then the postwar attempt to reverse all of that was a testament to the power and influence of capital over modern nations.

Capital is not, as its more recent usage suggests, mere wealth. Indeed, the accumulation of capital depends on two fundamental pillars: first, small groups or individuals own the means of production; second, they use those means for the accumulation of wealth through the hiring of wage workers. *Wage relations* are the primary social relationship in any capitalist system, and they can be observed wherever a worker sells her capacity to work to her employer in return for a wage—a relation that is called *capital*. Through this sale, the worker surrenders her agency over how her labor is used and what its products will be. For example, a person who works as a bank teller performs a set of required tasks, and for that she is paid a wage—not a share of the revenue she produces, which by design is greater than her wage. This condition is part of all types of wage-jobs in our society, from the least paid to the best paid. Most people regard it as a sort of natural order for modern societies.

This was not always the case. The capitalist system was subject to extensive political experimentation and legal formalization during the seventeenth century. By the mid-eighteenth century, capitalism had been refined to the point that its institutions could be considered *naturalized*. Private property and wage relations were no longer understood as historical institutions that evolved at the expense of other systems; they were the natural order of people and things. As part of this newly entrenched system, politics was understood as separate from the economy. Politics could evolve; the economy was self-governing, as God intended.[28]

In this view, an economy is "objective" because it is disciplined by the laws of markets, including the laws of supply and demand. In this objective realm, economic coercion is concealed because it acquires such an impersonal form: the majority of us are forced to sell ourselves on the labor market in order to survive in a society where, without money, we cannot obtain food or housing. In a capitalist society, people *depend* on the market.

Unlike in earlier class societies (i.e., slavery or feudalism), coercion under capitalism is peculiar in how impersonal it is: there is no overbearing figure to dictate the sale of our work. Whereas a serf would pay part of the product of his labor to a lord because of the lord's political clout and the threat of physical retaliation, a Starbucks employee "willingly" signs a work contract without any such personal pressure; the pressure she experiences comes from the alternative, destitution. Thus, in a capitalist society, she is inescapably bound by objective market forces, a form of coercion qualitatively different from that of pre-capitalist societies.

Politics, on the other hand, is the domain of states and governments, which means that *political* contestation may still occur under capitalism—but not in a way that challenges the economic system. For example, popular demands may include introducing a wealth tax or the bolstering of labor rights, but abolishing private wealth and wage labor is out of the question. The state therefore remains a neutral actor with respect to the market, and its role rests primarily in safeguarding private property and wage relations through the rule of law.

By the middle of the nineteenth century, with the establishment of the gold standard and the institutionalization of financial orthodoxy that emerged with it, capitalist class relations between owners and workers became more entrenched, and any scenario for redistributive demands in favor of the people was effectively blocked. The gold standard required states to secure a certain amount of gold in their coffers so as to be able to make good on their promise to convert the currency into gold at a fixed price. Hence, states' priority was to avoid the outflow of gold, a priority that implied tight fiscal and monetary policies. Running a trade surplus was the surest way to build up a country's gold reserves. Conversely, trade deficits led to an outflow of gold, since countries used gold to pay for their imports. Any extra public expenditure, or any easing of credit—the bases for redistributive policies—would result in gold flights and were therefore nonstarters.

A tight fiscal budget, on the other hand, could bolster trade surpluses by lowering domestic demand. And higher rates of interest (which promised higher returns on capital while deterring imports as they slowed the domestic economy) would draw gold bullion back into the country. Hence, the imperative of fiscal and monetary rigor was normalized.

Prior to the First World War, this "natural" order of things found its sturdiest practice in Britain, the capitalist empire *par excellence* for more than two hundred years, as well as in younger nation-states such as Italy. But the war's demand for domestic production quickly produced a complete subversion of such entrenched foundations—suddenly capitalism did not appear to be so natural after all. There ensued a collapse of the divide between the economic and the political that entailed the dwindling of the unchallenged status of the two pillars.

During the war, the state demolished its former boundaries of action. Faced with the choice between life or death, victory or defeat, war governments were forced into implementing economic practices that were unheard of—or better, unimaginable—until that moment. The self-regulating capacities of the market had proved inadequate for the unprecedented productive necessities of the war struggle.

As will be discussed in chapter 1, British and Italian states were compelled to take a major role as producers: key war industries were put under their control. This included not just munitions, but also strategic energy and transport sectors like coal, shipping, and railways. In this respect, the once firm boundary between private property and public property, between entrepreneurs and bureaucrats, lost its semblance of immovability. Through war collectivism, states broke the glass on the sanctity of the private organizations of production. For the first time, these states also subordinated the priority of private economic profit to that of political need. The collapse of the gold standard that followed served to facilitate these novel political priorities. With it, spaces for financial alternatives emerged that had not previously been thought of.

Meanwhile, a second fundamental boundary was also broken: the states began to heavily regulate the labor market (including facets like labor mobility, working conditions, and wages) across all key war industries, even those that it did not directly control. In doing so, the state threatened the second capitalist pillar, wage relations. In the face of these developments, workers facing lower wages and harsher discipline were shown that their burdens were the result not of impersonal market forces, but of explicit governmental decisions. The political intervention on industrial relations, a necessity of the war, exposed how relations of production could be a front for political activism and historical change.

States had disrupted their neutral positions with respect to the market, and in doing so they broke with earlier notions of the market's inviolability. Once the traditional boundary between the economic and the political faltered, the rule of private property and wage relations toppled: popular contestation of old norms emerged more than ever. In 1919 this crisis of capitalism was on, and it was unprecedented.

Most economic historians of World War I and the interwar period focus on the "economic problems" facing countries because of the monetary and financial outcomes of war: soaring inflation and mounting debt had compromised countries' creditworthiness, creating deep uncertainty and threatening capital flight. But looking deeper at these dynamics, it emerges that economic uncertainty was only a part of the problem. Part of what this book will explore is how economic uncertainty in these postwar countries had a political basis—indeed, how the economic and political crises were inseparable, with the former imposed by the latter. The postwar financial crisis was a crisis of legitimacy for capital order and its social relations.

The general public was noticing that state intervention within the economy was not a neutral act in the name of the good of the whole, but rather an authoritarian force to ensure the profit of the ruling classes. Chapter 2 explores how pressure from below pushed states to extend welfare measures in an attempt to appease their restless citizens. However, while these measures were reformist in intention, they were not so in their outcome. Indeed, they triggered further demands to fundamentally eradicate the very capitalist pillars that states set out to protect.

Put simply: the new, historic conditions of the war effort and the interwar period allowed citizens, especially those in the working class, to see that society could be different. The self-rationalizations of the system were breaking down, and with their deterioration came proposals for radical alternatives that could overcome them. Chapters 3 and 4 explore the political strikes and the movement for workers' control that reached their climaxes after the war and became central to labor's charge in both Britain and Italy. In aggregate, these workers demanded an overhaul of their economies, a replacement for the capitalist industrial system that moved toward a new social order in which associations of workers would control industries, either partially or completely. In this sense, emancipated work would replace capitalist exploitation, and public service and production *for use* would replace production *for profit*.

The popular struggles in the two countries examined here exemplified the wide-ranging courses of action: from union campaigns that successfully pierced the establishment, to the effective operation of British building guilds that produced "for need" within the capitalist market, all the way to Italian factory occupations that were led by revolutionary workers' councils.

In sum, the degree of state intervention during the war and the heightening of class antagonism that it engendered constituted a great revolutionary rupture from 1918 to 1920. It was the largest crisis in the history of capitalism, embodied in the unprecedented popular mobilization of strikes, alternative policy proposals, and alternative organizations of production. The logic of austerity can only be understood as a dramatic reaction to this landscape.

CHAPTER 1

The Great War and the Economy

As the military struggle developed in scope and intensity, and the necessity of concentrating national efforts on the war became more pressing, section after section of industry was taken over, and in wages, prices and profits, from raw material to finished product, was placed under Government control. The process of extending State control, taking over more works and applying it to an always "widening" range of products continued unbroken. . . .

The War Cabinet Report for the Year 1917 (His Majesty's Stationery Office 1918a, 130)

World War I was primarily an industrial war: military victory vitally depended on the production apparatus of the belligerent countries and their technical-industrial efforts. Indeed, once expectations of a short war faltered, an escalation of production was a prerequisite to survive the conflict. The "home front" gained decisive strategic weight.

In this context, Britain and Italy faced a similar problem, albeit from completely different positions. Britain was the world's first industrial power; Italy was still a largely agricultural country that had only recently begun industrializing, and its young capitalism was still highly dependent on foreign capital and imports. On the eve of the war, Italy's GDP (only a quarter of which was industrial) was less than half of Britain's. In 1913 Britain produced nine times more steel than Italy, and for other raw materials the disproportion was even greater.[1]

Notwithstanding these major differences, the war effort brought about similar structural changes in the relationships between these countries' states and markets—changes that fueled profound political contention in each. This chapter looks at the novel governmental interventions in two economic spheres: production and labor. It also explores the voices of contemporaries involved—both bureaucrats and workers—to show how this epochal break from the past set the scene for a full-blown crisis of capitalism.

A Remarkable Transformation

By the time the armistice that ended fighting in World War I arrived in November 1918, the orthodox relationship between markets and states across Europe had been wholly upset. There had been nothing like it before: the practice of laissez-faire capitalism[2] had to be dismantled for nations to survive the war.

Britain went to war convinced of the power of what Adam Smith described as the invisible hand: relying upon private enterprise and the law of supply and demand to secure the most efficient outcomes, even in war. E. M. H. Lloyd, a civil servant employed in the British war office, described the British establishment's approach to the war effort: "the doctrine implicitly acted upon was that the higher the price and the greater the freedom allowed to the private contractor, the greater would be the increase in the supply; it followed that if only the Government paid high enough prices and left private firms to their own devices, munitions would be forthcoming in abundance" (Lloyd 1924, 23). Before long, business as usual did not deliver. By 1916 the failure of laissez-faire and the free price mechanism was unmistakable. Increased government demand and price increases led to profiteering, but did not bring increased supplies. While the country suffered supply shortages and inflation, private businesses diverted resources to the more profitable business lanes of the moment—luxury goods and exports.

The faith in the market took a while to dissipate. As British parliamentary secretary to the Ministry of Shipping Leo George Chiozza Money wrote, only once "we had been brought to the edge of the abyss" did the State give up "[d]octrinaire individualism" (Chiozza Money

1920, 44, viii). The case of British shipping was exemplary, since, as the British War Cabinet reported to Parliament, "if shipping failed we could neither continue in the war nor maintain our population" (His Majesty's Stationery Office [hereafter HMSO] 1918a, 106). Once the war broke out, the contrast between public needs and private interest plainly surfaced: it was highly profitable to sell British ships to foreigners, and the British nation lost enormous tonnage (see Chiozza Money 1920, 73). By February 1917, private shipowners sold ships abroad at such a rate that "the fate of Britain literally hung in the balance" (Hurwitz 1949, 194). There were not even sufficient ships to import the bare necessities of a nation at war.

Reluctantly, British bureaucrats had to rethink their priorities, and the words of civil servant Lloyd echoed this conversion: "National organization and centralized control were found to be more effective than high prices and *laissez-faire* in stimulating supply" (Lloyd, 1924, 23). Through "a series of fits and starts, improvisations and experiments" (Cole 1923, xi–xii), the British state took charge of the vast range of the nation's economic activity and gradually developed an organic system of controls.[3] Its power reached into "almost every aspect of national life" (Armitage 1969, 1). By 1918, "direct or indirect control of industry and agriculture was virtually all-pervasive" (Pollard 1969, 47).

The shipping industry was again at the forefront of this shift. Once a competent ministry was established, it requisitioned the entirety of British merchant tonnage at Blue Book rates,[4] meaning that the state would pay the merchants a fixed freight rate. Hence, ships were nationalized as to use, and the government allocated tonnage according to the priorities of import needs, privileging shorter trade routes that would secure faster imports. In the meantime, state-owned shipyards took on the task of construction (HMSO 1918a, 110–14). In the words of the historian R. H. Tawney, "the Government was by that time master of the whole field of land and sea transport" (Tawney 1943, 2).

Of course, war collectivism did not emerge from thin air, but from dramatic financial gymnastics. World War I required a break from the laissez-faire tradition of balanced budgets that for more than two centuries had been "regarded by all except a tiny minority as part of the natural order of life" (Morgan 1952, 34).[5] It fell in parallel with its equivalent international policy, the gold standard. Until then, the gold standard had tied the hands of governments and prohibited engaging in any fiscal or monetary expansion that would have produced an outflow of gold.[6] Once the constraints of the gold standard were suspended, novel and unorthodox financial techniques—including loan-financed investments and expansionary credit policies[7]—became the order of the day. Interventionist monetary policies could now yield resources hitherto unthinkable.

In Italy, the same dynamics emerged: war collectivism was characterized by improvisation and gradualism, all in a framework of generalized skepticism toward breaking from laissez-faire. Soon, sweeping state intervention became inescapable. Italy had to secure arms, military equipment, food, raw material, and industrial labor force in a moment when international trade was dim and the majority of workers had been sent to the front.

Observers at the time remarked on the country's stark transition to a "collectivist" state, a central planner of the national economy—or as the Italian economist (and later, in 1948, president of the Republic) Luigi Einaudi liked to put it, the emergence of an *economia associata*, or associated economy. In 1915, the economist Riccardo Bachi wrote: "The State as a war entrepreneur has become the center, the pivot, the engine of the entire economy" (Bachi 1916, viii). The Italian government had initiated mild forms of interventionism to promote industrialization through subsidies and infrastructure beginning in the late nineteenth century (Zamagni 1990, 213–15). It was the unprecedented scale of this practice during the war that shocked contemporaries. Prior to the war the country's real expenditures were 17 percent of nominal GDP; they shot up to 40 percent in 1918 (Ciocca 2007, 172). While private consumption grew by 6 percent from 1913 to 1918, the numbers for public consumption were unheard of: rising by almost 500 percent.

As the Italian government intervened to promote capital accumulation, it also transformed. First, it shouldered a major bureaucratic expansion. The new administrative state apparatus mirrored the increased

economic commitment, multiplying in both ministries and public employees. The second major shift was toward a *stronger* state: executive
power grew to the detriment of the legislative (to meet the need for
rapid decisions, with no obstacles from political opposition)[8] and it executed sweeping repressive practices over the population to annihilate
political dissent. This phenomenon in Italy reached extents that were
unknown in other parliamentary democracies (Procacci 1999, 13). With
the royal decree against defeatism of October 1917 (known as the Sacchi
decree), the state criminalized all freedom of opinion and thought, and
citizens lived in terror of being prosecuted—even for a mere complaint
about the high price of bread (see Procacci 2013, 107–33). It was a historic turn within the Italian state toward authoritarianism, and much of
its legislation would be reanimated later by the Fascist regime.

State Control over Private Property and Production

During the war, the apparatus of governments' industrial control was
broad and diverse. In most instances, states directly seized the means
of production in key war industries. This was the case for breweries,
national shipyards, and most importantly the arms sector, where the
government owned purpose-built national shell and munition factories
to make all types of munitions equipment, including airplanes, high
explosives, and tear gas. In Britain, by spring 1918, there were more
than 250 national factories, mines, and quarries (Tawney 1943, 2). Public investment was impressive; it dramatically reshaped the landscape
to the point that "a whole country-side, as in the case of [the Southern
Scottish town] Gretna, became a factory" (Wolfe 1923, 65; on Gretna see
also Chiozza Money 1920, 62–64).

Likewise, the Italian state owned 60 munitions factories; by 1917 it
had seized the right to requisition plants and take direct control of the
production process in cases of inefficient private management. This
legislation was preceded by other actions that expropriated private
property, even without consent. Such expropriations included government seizure of industrial patents in order to orient them toward

national security. The same was true for all goods and services considered necessary for war purposes (see De Stefani 1926a, 412–13 and Miozzi 1980, 41–42).

Most common, in both Britain and Italy, was the model of directly managing firms still under private ownership, an arrangement in which the state imposed and controlled outputs and fixed prices.[9] The British Munitions Act of July 2, 1915, gave the Ministry of Munitions power to control any private establishment essential to war production and to limit the establishments' profits at 20 percent above prewar levels.[10] In Italy, a royal decree of June 26, 1915 (Royal Decree 997, in GU 177 [June 26, 1915]) on industrial mobilization empowered the government to classify as "*stabilimenti ausiliari*" [auxiliary factories] all private industries that were involved in producing necessary war supplies, or industries that had the potential to produce war material (see Article 13, reprinted in Franchini 1928, 96–97). Clearly, these categories were extremely broad and could include private establishments in all sectors of the economy. Italy had 221 auxiliary factories in 1915; by the end of the war it had 1,976. In Britain, factories under the Ministry of Munitions' control numbered about 20,000 (Tawney 1943, 2). In both countries, government-controlled businesses encompassed coal—"the blood which coursed through British [and Italian] industry"[11]—as well as important transportation sectors (shipping, railways), mining, quarrying, clothing, paper, wood, leather, agriculture, public utilities, metallurgy, textiles, and chemicals.

The complexity of the state-control system mirrored the interconnectedness of the capitalist economy, which was itself blurred by markets' monetary transactions. Let me elaborate through an example. In a capitalist monetary economy, a person goes to the market and buys a woolen jacket in exchange for money—a simple transaction. Such a monetary exchange, however, is only what occurs at the surface. It hides the heterogenous inner workings of production: the making of the woolen jacket requires workers to extract coal (necessary to transport wool), to rear the sheep, to weave, etcetera.[12] In capitalist economies before the war and today, the relationship between money and commodities hides the underlying social relationships of production. Accordingly, under capitalism, relationships between people are expressed as relationships between things. War collectivism brought these social interconnections into view. In the example of wool (which was important for clothing both civilians and the army), the government took on all stages of its production, including those that were hidden under capitalism.

The reach of both the British Ministry of Munitions and its Italian counterpart, the Ministry of War and Munitions, illustrate the states' central roles in co-opting their countries' industrial mobilization. Their operations were akin to an octopus with tentacles reaching across entire economies. Control of munitions production soon led to control of essential raw materials, factory space, and sources of power and labor (see Wrigley in Burk 1982, 46). These ministries also developed research departments for technical innovations and conducted experiments in chemistry, physics, electronics, and other fields.[13]

In the Italian case, production took place through a chain of centralized directives disseminated via regional committees.[14] These seven (later eleven) regional committees were the first organs of "industrial planning" [programmazione economica]; they directed the production process of the auxiliary factories, collected technical information, distributed electric energy and raw material, and (notably) disciplined the labor force.

Italian manufacturing during the war was fueled by state-run agriculture; the state mandated the farming of certain crops and decided on the use of the country's land. The department of agrarian mobilization [reparto di mobilitazione agraria] under the Ministry of Agriculture became the main superintendent of these matters.[15] It controlled the production and distribution of fertilizers, and purchased machines to mechanize production. The ministry also requisitioned seeds and private agricultural machines for use all over the country.

In 1917 the British Cultivation of Lands Order gave local authorities the power to seize private land, even without owners' consent, for the creation of allotments to supplement farm production (Hurwitz 1949, 216). These requisition practices for national productive and distributive needs—visibly encroaching on the sanctity of private property—

were complemented by national laws that granted citizens the right to occupy lands and facilities. The measures were crucial to hasten social appeasement, satisfy the subsistence needs of the population, and avoid the worst forms of social unrest. In 1917 the Italian government granted cooperatives of peasants the right to occupy land in the case of noncompliant [*inadempienti*] landowners.[16] As we shall investigate in chapters 3 and 4, these reforms actually sparked a political movement advocating for "land to the peasants" that reached its peak immediately after the war.

Even with these modest measures of appeasement, Italy saw widespread protests brought about by a grave lack of basic foodstuffs, especially in the cities (bread in Turin; rice in Lombardy; oil in Livorno). After much uncertainty and delay, in 1916 the state repealed the free-market mechanism for household supplies and inaugurated "a vast nationalization of food commerce" (Bachi 1926, 158) that included the state purchase and distribution of food; price caps; requisitions (for example of cereal and livestock); and rationing.[17] In Britain too, by 1918, the Ministry of Food was buying and selling over four-fifths of all food consumed by civilians. It fixed the maximum prices of over nine-tenths of the population's food.

States' interventions in the economy promoted a public sense that basic necessities were now an inalienable right—and that the government was obliged to secure them. The priorities of the economy had radically shifted, from profit for a few to securing the needs of the many. In Italy, "rationing was practiced for many commodities, at times also for non-general consumption-goods, bringing about the perhaps unwanted result of acquainting to certain consumption habits certain social classes to whom they were previously almost unknown" (Bachi 1926, 165). These measures escalated aspirations for a better standard of life after the war (ibid., 166–67).

International markets were also subject to breach by state intervention. Given the heavy dependence of Britain and Italy on foreign goods, both governments had to take control of the importing and distribution of raw material, commodities, and foodstuffs.[18] Each government became its country's greatest importer, and bulk purchases on the international markets allowed governments to fix prices at lower rates.[19]

In sum, in all the ways discussed above—from industrial production to land cultivation and price-fixing—the British and Italian states barged into the realm of the economic. For the first time, capitalism witnessed a threat to the inviolability of private property. Private property had to subordinate its prerogatives to a political and national interest and even to people's basic needs. In this way the state shook one of the supposedly unshakeable pillars of capital accumulation. The tremors in laissez-faire capitalism did not stop here, however, reverberating to another fundamental pillar: wage relations.

State Control over Wage Relations

A market economy requires a pool of unemployed workers who are ready to be hired to meet increased production demands. Within a capitalist society, these people are structurally competing with one another. The presence of these individuals guarantees lower labor costs (because workers are replaceable) and "naturally" disciplines the workers, who have an incentive to keep their jobs and paychecks. Under normal conditions, the reserve army of labor is replenished by the very process of capital accumulation: in their competition to lower commodity prices, capitalists constantly seek out new technological innovation, which in turn expels a segment of the working class from the process of production. The reserve army is further replenished by mechanization, in which the process of production is simplified or automated, and skilled workers are made expendable.

World War I caused a shift in the power relations between capital and labor. As the demand for labor soared with the intensification of war production, employers were confronted with a labor shortage: the draft and voluntary enlistment had depleted the reserve army of labor.[20] In Britain, for example, a third of the male labor force was enlisted. This meant that the mechanism of the free market could no longer effectively distribute labor where it was most needed.

To add to the woes of the market, reaching voluntary agreements between capital and labor was a lengthy process, often involving disputes and labor stoppages that tended to intensify in moments of labor strength, disrupting efficient war production. It followed that the prewar tradition of self-regulation and industrial autonomy had to be abandoned in favor of forceful state regulation. As observed by Humbert Wolfe, controller of the labor-regulation department at the British Ministry of Munitions, "[l]abour ceased to be a commodity to which the laws of supply and demand applied" (Wolfe 1923, 102).

In Britain, almost 5 million workers were employed by 1918 in firms operating under the Munitions Act, accounting for roughly half of the available male labor force.[21] The purpose of the legislation was to tackle the major obstacles to efficient output, summarized by Wolfe, who fathered the scheme, as "interruptions of work by stoppages, failure to put forth the full amount of energy during work, either owing to Trade Union restriction or to indiscipline, doubt as to wages, resentment against employers' profits, opposition to dilution of labour, and the tendency of labour not to stay where it was most actively required or to desert important work for less important work more highly paid" (1923, 101).

The Italian state took over the labor market with the same purpose and with means that closely resembled those in Britain, but it went much further in exercising its repressive sway on the workforce. The implicit coercion of the laws of the capitalist market was now replaced with unprecedented political coercion.[22] This was to a great extent the expression of the state's crude reaction to a labor force that was firmly anti-statist and pacifist; suffice to say that the Italian state did not enjoy the wartime support of its public majority. Indeed, Italy was the only European country that went to war without the official support of any working-class party or any union. The disgruntled rank and file shared the opinion that "the horrendous war is the fatal outcome of the capitalist system, which, born in violence deludes itself by finding in violence the solution of its crisis."[23] As General Dallolio, head of the Ministry of War and Munitions, spelled out, the work of Italy's regional committees had as a priority to tackle "the very delicate problem of maintaining control on the working class, whose union and political organizations had openly manifested an aversion for war intervention."

By June 1915 the Italian state had taken direct control of almost one million workers (902,000) working in two thousand industrial businesses—the great majority of the industrial apparatus.[24] In both countries state control consisted of regulation in three large domains: supply of labor (both its increase and its mobility); cost of labor; and efficiency of labor. What follows is a very brief exploration of each.

DISCIPLINING LABOR

Increasing productivity required disciplined workers. During the war, the Italian government replaced private capitalists as the main guarantor of labor discipline.

In doing so, the Italian government came up with a drastic measure: the militarization of the labor force—a form of extreme duress that the British trade unions successfully opposed. This meant that once a firm was declared auxiliary, all personnel from head technicians to workers, including "women, the elderly, and children [*i fanciulli*]," fell under military jurisdiction (Einaudi 1933, 111). Hence, the advent of the phenomenon of "factory-barracks," as the union leader Bruno Buozzi described them. Indeed, workers were formally equated to soldiers; they surrendered to forced labor, and were subjected to a rigid work regimen based on the penal code and enforced by military agents.[25] Unauthorized absence from work was often likened to desertion.

It is noteworthy that some private capitalists *aspired* to achieve the status of auxiliary factories, as it would guarantee the submission of the workers "to a rigorous discipline of military nature, the suppression of strikes and workers upheavals" (Einaudi 1933, 105). Collective organization of workers, insubordination, obstructionism, and sabotage were especially punished. The state was strict with its workers: by the end of the war 50 percent of Italian workers had been fined at some point. Other common penalties that especially impacted militants and union leaders were dismissal, prison, confinement to marginal areas, and, in the case of enlisted workers, a return to the front (see Procacci 1999 and 1983).[26]

In Britain, even if repression was not overtly militaristic, the Ministry of Munitions removed many disciplinary powers from employers to directly enforce a draconian order of work regulation.[27] Not only were strikes outlawed; the Ministry also prosecuted misconduct such as drunkenness, gambling, or absence from work without permission. Cases of bad timekeeping were not exempt from discipline, and were officially attributed to "indifference" and "temperamental laziness" (memo of Ministry of Munitions, reprinted in Rubin 1987, 179–80).

To achieve desired outcomes, governments used the parallel strategy of softening the antagonism with labor. The British War Cabinet Report recognized that accelerated mechanization during the war had "aggravated" the feeling "that industry was becoming dehumanised" (HMSO 1918a, 100). The worker "[w]anted more individual consideration and some voice in the determination of the conditions under which he should work" (ibid.). Coercive methods had to be integrated alongside policies that would elicit consent and promote cooperation. Hence, in the report of the following year, the War Cabinet championed the intention to satisfy "the public mind," which had been "prepared for a new order of things in industry after the war," a new order that would offer a "more democratic basis, if there is to be lasting peace in the industrial world" (HMSO 1919a, 145, 149).

To codify these promises, the Ministry of Labour approved the 1917 recommendation to establish Whitley councils (named after MP J. H. Whitley) to represent both employers and trade unions and to discuss not only wages and work conditions but also job security, technical education, and improvements in management. By September 1920, sixty-one councils were in operation representing over 3,500,000 workers (Miller 1924, 17). However, the radical rank and file agitated strongly against the Whitley councils on the grounds that the scheme was an attempt to lure workers into accepting class collaboration that would work to the advantage of the employer class. Workers attacked the state's move in favor of Whitley councils as "a red herring to draw the workers away from the real struggle for workers control in industry," also claiming that the councils "perpetuated the class division in society and left the whole profit-making system of capitalism intact" (Hannington 1941, 72).

As the war dragged on, protests among workers in Italy mounted, and fears of a revolutionary rupture emerged. It became increasingly obvious to officials that law and order alone might not suffice to mollify workers. Following the British model, the government offered a semblance of involvement of workers in industrial mobilization. For example, within the Regional Industrial Committees, the representatives of the industrialists nominated by the Ministry were joined by an equal number of labor representatives, often union members such as Buozzi, who joined the Committee of the Lombardy region.

Most importantly, in both countries internal factory committees took on an increasingly representative role. These were grievance committees elected by union members within a factory to handle everyday problems of discipline, arbitration, and the like. The war boosted the development of workers' assemblies to elect their representatives in the committees,[28] increasing union membership within the unskilled rank and file (see Tomassini in Menozzi et al. 2010, 43–44; see also Bezza 1982). In this way, in both countries, the seeds of workers' self-organization were planted during the war. As will be detailed in chapter 4, by 1919 these committees would grow into a concrete alternative to the capitalist mode of production.

COPING WITH A SMALL LABOR SUPPLY

Wartime states seized control of the supply of labor to tackle the problem of manpower shortages. A basic step in this direction was to expand the pool of available workers through the process of dilution: i.e., the introduction of unskilled labor, including women, in jobs formerly reserved for skilled men. As mentioned, dilution is integral to capitalist production where the competition among capitalists and the pressure from workers induces the capitalist constantly to cut costs by technological innovation and more efficient reorganization of the labor process. During the war, countries greatly boosted this tendency through increased mechanization of production, which broke the work process into simple stages that less skilled workers could manage. As the British Women's Employment Committee confirmed, women "have replaced men in iron and steel works, in chemical works, in brickyards and in gasworks . . . sub-division, sectionalisation, and above all, the introduction of mechanical assistance has enabled their employment on work previously regarded as beyond their strength" (Ministry of Reconstruction 1919, Cd. 9239, p. 14).

To increase the pool of labor, Italy removed its limits on worker age and on women's labor. By August 1918, Italian women represented 22 percent of the labor force (198,000 women), while children accounted for 6.5 percent (60,000 children).[29]

With the war, then, came the birth of a "new working class" that was widely expanded and unskilled, composed of a large number of peasants, artisans, women, and adolescents. This new social component was foreign to the hierarchical dynamics of organized labor, and thus potentially more insubordinate—and prone to radicalization.

An alternative to expanding the pool of available labor was to increase the extraction of surplus value from the employed workers by intensifying the production process and extending the working day.[30] The Italians put both measures into widespread practice.[31] The government extended the operating schedules of "auxiliary" establishments by abolishing hour limits and Sunday rests. Regional committees' meeting minutes document incessant work activity, with almost no breaks, that could easily reach 15 or 16 hours a day (Camarda and Peli 1980, 158–59). Overtime work became compulsory. The government even suspended the prohibition on night work for women and children in cases where it "was deemed necessary for the works in the interest of the state and for other absolute needs of public interest" (De Stefani 1926a, 22). The unparalleled strain on Italian and British workers was mirrored by the growth of accidents in the workplace and by the multiplication of absences—often a matter of survival.[32] In a moment where workers were not substitutable, there was a thin line between overexploitation and collapse of productivity due to exhaustion. This realization pushed the British government to establish a Health and Munitions workers committee that investigated overwork and advocated for the decrease of working hours and the abolition of night work.[33] Although no such committee was established in Italy, as we shall see in chapter 2, the government did implement provisions to improve health conditions to assure the reproduction of the labor force.

Piecework—or payment based on result—was rare before the war. The state generalized it so as to make it the decisive part of workers' wages, and it was understood as the best incentive to increase productivity. In both countries, initially, this meant greater compensation for the unskilled relative to the skilled, as the latter's specialized work normally delivered less in the same amount of time.[34] Notwithstanding the initial grievances among skilled workers (see Cole 1923, 165–66), the levelling and flattening of wages had the important political consequence of setting the basis for a class unity amongst workers that did not exist prior to 1914.

Beyond the expansion of the pool of workers and their greater exploitation, the government had to undertake a number of planning tasks to compensate for the inability of the laws of the market to distribute labor power efficiently among industries. Political control over labor mobility allowed the government to shift work wherever it deemed necessary.

The role of employment exchanges, or public employment agencies, grew exponentially in both countries.[35] They undertook the delicate task of adjusting supply and demand through central analysis of the labor supply and a "scientific classification of man-power" (Wolfe 1923, 69). In Italy, for example, by 1918 a central office of employment coordinated all public employment agencies. It collected data regarding the labor market, while studying optimal allocative solutions (De Stefani 1926a, 17).[36]

On the other hand, limits were also imposed on the mobility of labor. In Britain, section 7 of the Ministry of Munitions Act prevented workers from transferring freely from one job to another by requiring workmen to obtain a leaving certificate before engaging in alternative employment. This harsh provision had a twofold motive. First, the depletion of the reserve army of labor gave workers enhanced bargaining power, which forced employers to bid up wages in order to attract available labor, especially skilled labor. By imposing a political limit on such mobility, the government could ensure a cap on wages. Second, these certificates also prevented the constant turnover of labor, which hampered the production process. These leaving certificates were highly unpopular (Hurwitz 1949, 107), and were fiercely contested as a slavery clause. The rank and file all over the country revolted against a measure that tied the hands of the employee but not the employer, who was left free to fire his workers and was not compelled to issue a certificate even once he fired them. Through union bargaining, the certificates were repealed in October 1917.

In Italy there was no public pushback powerful enough to inhibit the political assault on the bargaining power of workers. The military-state apparatus broke the resistance capacity of the skilled workers' unions, especially FIOM (Federazione Impiegati e Operai Metallurgici), the union of the metal and steel workers.[37] Dismissals, resignations, and transfers of personnel from one industry to another could occur only with the written authorization of the Regional Committees (CRMI), which had full decision-making power on the matter and observed much stricter criteria than applied to the leaving certificates in Britain (Franchini 1928, 99). Workers' anger mounted against a state that forbade any benefit from the war, "to the point that, notwithstanding the enormous demand for labor their [workers'] pay has not increased during the war not even in the same proportion as the cost of living" (Buozzi, in Bezza 1982, 84).

SETTING THE PRICE OF LABOR

Under laissez-faire capitalism, wages were mainly settled through local bargains between labor and capital; governments had no say in the process. This changed during the war: industrialists competed for scarce labor through wage increases, while mounting worker mobilizations (to cope with the concurrent increases in cost of living) also pushed for higher wages. Here the state did intervene, acting promptly against this threat to capital accumulation by taking control of wage contracts. The words of the historian Samuel Hurwitz hold true for both countries: "it would be a mistake to think that on the whole the British worker was better off because of Government intervention. State interference in wage settlements 'acted to keep the level of wages rather lower than would have otherwise been the case'" (Hurwitz 1949, 129).

The state also worked to simplify and unify wage rates and avoid the lengthy and disruptive processes of wage disputes that hindered capital accumulation and thus war output.[38] Toward these goals the Italian and British government established mandatory arbitration tribunals that mediated between workers and employers in lieu of strikes and lock-outs. It was a significant leap: "from this time labour could not (if the law were obeyed) enforce a wages demand, or an objection to a work-man's dismissal, or an alteration in workshop conditions, by a strike" (Wolfe 1923, 102).

In Britain, the newly founded Committee on Production quickly developed into the principal arbitration tribunal for the settlement of labor disputes.[39] It was a body of government officials, later joined by certain employers and trade union representatives, that pioneered the use of the cost-of-living index for the purpose of fixing wages and war bonuses. The complaints of an employer published in the *Glasgow Herald* articulated the economic power of this governmental body: "at the present time, the payer of wages has hardly any voice in the fixing of them. This is done, for the most part, without any reference to employ-ers by a [Government] Committee on Production" (*Glasgow Herald*, September 25, 1917, reprinted in Rubin 1987, 22).

In fact, as employers knew, even during the conflict the state was often pressured to safeguard against excessive exploitation of unskilled labor. In Britain, for example, in 1916 organized workers forced the government to amend the Munitions Act to stipulate that unskilled workers—when employed in place of the skilled—could not receive lower pay.

Meanwhile, the newly established Ministry of Labour[40] enacted pro-visions to regulate Britain's "ill-organised and ill-paid industries"—to establish some minimal working standards (HMSO 1918a). The minis-try was engaged in "making enquiry as to wages and conditions" and had the power to establish trade boards at a rapid pace, through a spe-cial order not subject to parliamentary scrutiny. The boards extended to a wide range of non-unionized industries, and were responsible for setting minimum wages and improving the conditions of work.

As for Italy, mandatory arbitration was in the hands of the regional

committees, which, in case of failed agreement among the employers and workers, would decide by ordinance.[41] In reality, the country's
adoption of the principle of equal treatment was an embellishment: in
auxiliary factories the state froze wages at their prewar level until three
months after the end of the war (sanctioned by Royal Decree 1277, August 22, 1915, in De Stefani 1926a, 420). As a practical matter, workers
had no choice but to take on an increasing amount of overtime work
to compensate for soaring food prices. This hard reality was very much
at odds with the polemic on high wages that was vocally mounted by
the bourgeoisie during the last years of the war (see Frascani 1975, 69).

In sum, the war brought about an unprecedented degree of state
control over labor. In setting the price of labor, disciplining it, and controlling its supply, the Italian and British governments had exposed the
profoundly political nature of the capitalist economy. No longer was
surplus extraction a matter of mere economic coercion executed by
the impersonal laws of the market; exploitation was now enforced by
state intervention. This meant that surplus extraction became explicitly
political, emblematically represented by the fact that Italian workers
who refused to sell their labor power would be condemned to prison
or to the front. The basis was set for those who were living through
these changes to gain awareness of the link between economic power
and political power. The full consequences were cropping up: if economic power is political, it means there is nothing natural about economic power, and the systems by which it is distributed *can* be changed
through struggle. As we shall see in greater detail in chapter 4, anti-
statism and anti-capitalism went hand in hand.

The Consequences of a Remarkable Transformation

THE VISION OF THE BUREAUCRATS

The impact of the Great War could not have been imagined before it
actually happened. Britain—the major capitalist economy up until the
war—experienced extensive nationalization of the means of production, and young capitalist countries like Italy followed in its footsteps.

The unprecedented political control over private property and wage relations had groundbreaking social consequences with potential to change the face of free-market capitalism, or even abolish it completely. These consequences could be felt all around the world.

Inside the government apparatus, many bureaucrats, politicians, and prominent intellectuals had been converted to belief in the benefits of nationalization and envisaged it as a long-lasting structural change. The war, many felt, "marked the end of an epoch"; there was no "returning to the uncovenanted mercies of pre-war individualism" (Tawney 1943, 11). The involvement of the state exposed the irrationality of the market—that it was "wasteful" and "anti-social"—and showed the possibility that it might be overcome.

In 1918 the British War Cabinet noted that "[t]he nation today is far better organized and far more productive than it has ever been before" (HMSO 1918a, xvi). And indeed, the controlled economy delivered beyond anyone's expectations. Despite a dearth of material, losses at sea, and the shortage of manpower, the total output of British industry had hardly declined at all during the war (Pollard 1969, 53–54).[42]

Against deep-seated market beliefs, the methods of scientific pricing and national organization were far from ineffective; in fact they had rationalized nationwide systems of production and distribution.[43] Food control had successfully responded to high food prices to the point that total consumption in terms of calories per adult male fell only very slightly, and distribution was "much more equitable in war than in peace" (Pollard 1969, 51). Moreover, the Ministry of Munitions left quite an impression on contemporaries for its administrative successes, especially in its capacity to invest and transmit innovative technology and management practices to the firms under its control (Wrigley, in Burk 1982, 47–49).

In his 1920 pamphlet *The Triumph of Nationalization*, the British economist Leo George Chiozza Money asked why, if the principles of national organization had proven so successful to win the war, they should not be expanded in peacetime. "The foundation for a new and better order had been well and truly laid" (Chiozza Money 1920, 137–38). These thoughts echoed those expressed in the official British War

Cabinet documents: "Reconstruction," it was insisted, "is not so much a question of rebuilding society as it was before the war, but of moulding a better world out of the social and economic conditions which have come into being during the war" (HMSO 1918a, xix).

Such words were not outliers: they represented a common sentiment widely present within the British public debate. The opening speech of incumbent prime minister Lloyd George at the November 1918 coalition election campaign was eloquent: "We cannot return to the old conditions. (Cheers.) War is like a ploughshare and a harrow. It has turned up and rent the soil of Europe. You cannot go back."[44]

Nationalization *seemed* like a permanent path forward. At a campaign stop in Dundee in December 1918, even the liberal Winston Churchill advocated nationalization of the railways, endorsing the proposal of the railway nationalization society that the government acquire the railway stocks.[45] After the armistice, the Ministry of Reconstruction presented wide-ranging plans for public spending while, as we shall see in chapter 3, the British government called the Sankey committee to discuss the permanent nationalization of coal.

In Italy, the same was true. Notwithstanding the exorbitant costs, corruption, and managerial problems—much of which the enquiry on war expenditures exposed for all to see[46]—the Italian war effort proved impressive: within just a few years of nationalization, the country was equipped with a military arsenal that was not much inferior to the other belligerent powers (Romeo 1972, 116), even producing more cannons than Britain itself (7,709 vs. 6,690) and exporting military equipment. In those years, northern Italy completed the industrial transformation that had been initiated at the beginning of the century.

Wartime documents of the Italian Ministry of Arms and Munitions reveal that many leaders envisioned the role of the regional and central committees not as an exception for the war effort, but rather as a more long-lasting economic turn (see Zaganella 2017, 192–94). The monthly bulletins of the central committee were inundated with tributes. War mobilization was lauded as "a really grandiose phenomenon"—"an instruction" for the future.[47]

The praise was not ubiquitous. As we will see in the second part of this book, enemies to national control were powerful and very worried. Men of the British Treasury, along with many in the British[48] and Italian liberal elite and its professional economists, formed a united front against "state socialism."[49] Their worries were indeed justified: all around them, opposition was being sown to challenge the once immovable institutions of private property and wage relations.

THE VISION OF THE WORKERS

As chapters 2–4 will explore in depth, the interwar challenge to the pillars of capitalism came primarily from the working classes, people who had witnessed firsthand how capitalist relations of production—and their exploitative nature—were no longer governed by impersonal "laws of the market," but rather resulted from explicit political choices.

The rhetoric of "the equality of sacrifice" appeared empty in the face of soaring profits of industrial capital and speculation on the one end, and insufficient wages to cope with the mounting prices of basic living necessities on the other. Headlines from the *Daily Herald*, the independent daily of the British Left, denounced what workers widely saw as criminal political choices: "Merciless Exploitation: Labour Calls on Government to Reduce Cost of Living or Resign" (July 10, 1919) and "Penalty of Being Poor: How Workers Struggle Daily to Exist Under Present High Prices. Forced to Work Overtime" (August 26, 1919).[50]

The August 1919 article went on: "A constant struggle, not to live, but to merely exist, is the penalty of being poor during the era of the profiteer. From various parts of the country reports are coming to us showing clearly and conclusively how the workers are suffering from the high prices." A day prior, the description was even more disheartening: "The margin between income and expenditure is so narrow that the purchase of other household sundries . . . has to be met with a reduction, or the absolute denial of necessary food. . . . I have spoken to many working-class women, who have told me that they have not bought any new clothing for many months, and their appearance was adequate proof of the statement. Not for a longer period had they had as much amusement as even a cheap seat in a cinema theatre. The traditional indulgence of a glass of beer is rapidly becoming a thing of the past."[51]

While it is true that the British imposed caps on sale prices and limits on profits,[52] these measures did not antagonize private capital. Rather, private capital had cooperated, securing for itself guaranteed fixed dividends and substantial economic advantages. Moreover, the windfall opportunities that came with compelling trade unions to abandon their restrictive practices (for example, on work hours and wage flexibility) and a license to impose tighter factory discipline outweighed any disadvantage of the modest profit limitation (Rubin 1987, 19). The British government also footed the bill for the reproduction of the labor force through welfare measures.[53] In other words, these costs were transferred from the private capitalists to the community at large—i.e., a process of socialization of the cost of reproduction. As embattled British labor leaders would declaim, the government was "compelled to drop its mask of impartiality and appear in its true character as an instrument of class domination" (Gallacher and Campbell 1972, 6).

In Italy, as in Britain, during the war the state assisted capitalists with deference. It became the main supplier and client of industry; it procured raw material, acted as guarantor of bank credits and as discipliner of the labor force; and it provided subsidies and coordinated effort (see De Stefani 1926a, 144–55).[54] During the war Italian capitalists gained exponentially more; unlike in Britain, the Italian state had no ceiling on profits. Industrialists ably justified price increases while the government lacked any serious tool to account for their production costs, ultimately accepting and buying at inflated prices. Purchasing contracts were often made informally, and negligence, abuse, and fraud were the ordinary state of things.[55] The state granted tax breaks to abet the capitalists further (Segreto 1982, 42–43). The metallurgical and mechanical sector especially benefited. Large industries like Fiat, Ilva, and Ansaldo had increased their workforce tenfold (Zaganella 2017, 190).[56] Fiat alone was producing fifteen times more vehicles in 1918 than in 1914 (more than 90 percent of which were for the Italian government). Overall, the automobile sector increased its revenue from 32 million in

1913 to 160 million in 1918.[57] The surge in profits confirmed the expectation of many Italian capitalists who had strongly supported war intervention as an opportunity to get out of the overproduction trap while minimizing their dependence on foreign capital (Porisini 1975, 8).

No one could deny that the state was intervening not as a universal benevolent actor but rather as the promoter of the "best" conditions for capital accumulation, which implied the subordination of workers and the concentration of exorbitant profits in a few hands. The ideology of national unity—so fundamental for the sanctity of capitalism—was crumbling, thereby providing an unprecedented boost to social antagonism and ideas of radical change.

This was especially true in Italy, where the population had never been fully ideologically incorporated within the state. This gulf between the spirit of the people and the Italian state had grown even greater over the course of World War I. The fact that the decision to enter the war had been taken by King Vittorio Emanuele III and a few others without parliamentary consultation diffused among the people a sense of being "deceived and violated" (*ingannato e violentato*, Tasca 1965, 11). This deception was palpable as real wages shrank by 20 percent during the war years. Indeed, just between 1917 and 1918 the cost-of-living index increased by 40 percent (Frascani 1975, 60)—gravely worsening the living standards of the working classes, both in industry and agriculture and in public administration.[58]

The impulse for change, however, was also percolating in Britain, a country enmeshed in bourgeois values where, despite greater exploitation, some sections of the working classes improved their living standards during the war.[59] The 1919 British official report on labor unrest read: "throughout the war the workers have been led to expect that the conclusion of hostilities would be followed by a profound revolution in the economic structure of society" ("Memorandum on the Causes of and Remedies for Labour Unrest," February 27, 1919; reprinted in Cole 1920a, 247).

In Britain there was growing consensus that the old order should not return, or at least that it should not continue unchanged. Such widespread conviction was as much a reaction to the classist nature of economic intervention as it was the outcome of workers' newly acquired power. In fact, interventionist British policies during the war had required constant mediation with the representatives of labor in order to secure their collaboration.[60] In this manner, the state acknowledged the newly empowered union bodies that were elevated "to a new sort of status: from interest groups they became 'governing institutions'" (Middlemas 1979, 20). In Britain, during the war, labor representatives not only constantly participated in governmental committees; they also participated as ministers and officials in the state apparatus itself.[61]

In Italy, industrial mobilization had not been the product of an agreement with unions—their voices were muffled compared to those of their British counterparts. However, FIOM did partake in certain state commissions,[62] and for the first time the union directly confronted industrialists on the general productive strategies of the country. Thus, war collectivism marked the beginning of Italian collective bargaining at a national level (Bezza 1982, 99) and the beginning of a climate of industrial relations in which workers believed they could demand more.

This pressure for change was ever more pronounced from below. In fact, war collectivism prompted a great divide within the labor movement that would characterize the immediate postwar years: a moderate political project within bourgeois institutions versus a call for a fundamental break with the past through economic democracy. The Clydeside region in Britain and the city of Turin in Italy are both emblematic of this politicization process: the working rank and file in both places viewed their union leadership with hostility, believing leaders were collaborating with the "servile state." The two regions were the beating hearts of their respective countries' metallurgical industries and, importantly, the identities of each nation's working-class protest: illegitimate strikes spread like wildfire, especially after 1917 and the galvanizing effect of the Russian Revolution.[63] Both governments brutally repressed strikes and sentenced radical leaders to jail. The repression, however, had only a temporary deterrent effect. British shop stewards formed a powerful Clyde Workers Committee, which led the formation of a National Workers Committee Movement, linking up unofficial leaders in factories throughout the country. Meanwhile, self-governance in the Italian Factory Committees grew to the point of precipitating a movement of factory occupations in the summer of 1920.

Conclusion

During World War I, the political states of both Britain and Italy broke capitalist dogma and forcefully intervened in their countries' economies. For the political survival of each state, these interventions were necessary: they sought to promote the necessary capital accumulation to win the war, even while they sullied the sanctity of free-market capitalism in the process. This chapter studied the unfolding of this process, its reasons and its modalities, to set the scene for an exploration of the radical political consequences that followed.

Governments became their countries' main producers, both through the seizure of the means of production and the management of private industries—fixing output and prices while advancing capital and fostering technological innovation. The British and Italian governments dictated the crops that were to be grown, managed uncultivated land, fixed consumption prices, and determined distribution. They also entered the domestic and international markets as the main buyer of foodstuffs, raw materials, and commodities. These governments gained vast power to requisition land and goods while also setting limits on private profits. In other words, social production became political. The same was true of the labor market: to cope with a dwindling pool of labor, both governments intervened to discipline workers and control the supply of labor while also setting its price.

Most importantly, the British and Italian states' command over the two pillars of capitalist accumulation—private ownership of the means of production and wage relations—had the fundamental effect of politicizing their economies. Indeed, it exposed how relations of production could be a terrain of political contestation, thus prone to social change. The British and Italian workers were in the best position to grasp the full meaning of such an unprecedented turn of events. Their governments had tightened the exploitative grip on the workers; but unlike the grip of the invisible hand, the state's chokehold was visible and could thus be subverted. The workers—whose unions' contractual power had increased during the war—could now land heavy blows by demanding more social rights and different organizations of production. As we shall explore in chapter 2, immediately after the war the Italian and British governments were responsive to popular pressure— and even ready to enact substantive welfare measures in an attempt to appease popular demands for change.

CHAPTER 2

"A Wholly New School of Thought"

A crisis so tremendous as this drives even the least reflective mind to question those conventions, to penetrate beneath that surface where his questioning used to stop dead, to ask what purpose is served by this or that institution, this or that kind of life? . . . The mind soon ceases to be distressed by anything that seems inevitable, especially if the body that actually suffers belongs to someone else. Hence it needs a great shock to awaken a society to some fundamental change of outlook. Such a shock has come to England and to the world, and the defeat of Germany is not more important for mankind than the nature and the scale of the change of spirit that will result from it.

Jason [pseud.], *Past and Future* (1918, 3–4)

The significance of capitalist nations suspending their capitalist practices was not lost on the nations' people. Many, like the British journalist J. H. Hammond (who used the pseudonym Jason), observed these events as a fundamental crisis of society as it stood: "[the war] has shaken some millions of men out of the state of mind in which they accept the world as they find it" (Jason [pseud.] 1918, 9). These societies, awakened by war, questioned the purpose of the institutions of capital accumulation. Were they really as inevitable as they had seemed?

By 1919, a year after the war's end, a crisis of capitalism was underway. It proceeded on two fronts. The first was with workers, who focused on derailing or at least disfiguring capitalist social relations of production. The second was "reconstructionists"[1]—people within state

institutions or enlightened elite that agitated for a new set of social policies, and with these policies, for a more egalitarian society.

By the time the armistice came into force in November 1918, these
two groups were already moving in complement with one another.
On one side, the working rank and file were galvanized by their hope
for social reforms. State interventions to better these workers' material conditions had spurred the workers' sense of their rights, but also
deeply frustrated them—the reforms that passed never seemed to
match their emancipatory expectations. Reformists, meanwhile, were
growing in number and in ambition—they felt pressure from below
and were preoccupied with staving off a revolution. The more the workers demanded, the more the reconstructionists were ready to push for a
new social order. In turn, these greater social reforms heightened workers' aspirations to break from the system.

The "reconstructionist" forces within government posed a frontal
assault on capital accumulation in two main ways. The first, which
will be explored in chapter 3, is how the reconstructionist motivation
for social appeasement often, perhaps unavoidably, fueled the workers' revolutionary spirits. The second, and the focus of this chapter, is
how the reconstructionists themselves actually challenged the purity of
laissez-faire capitalism—and with it, the established identity of capitalist states. The unparalleled bluster of social reforms between 1918 and
1920—those called for and those enacted—reflect the existential nature
of this threat for capitalism. These social policies were the outcomes of
the postwar re-politicization of private property and wage relations—
the two pillars that during the war had been decoupled from market
forces. The glass had already been broken; the previously untouchable
economic institutions could now be molded toward unimaginable political ends.

The Great War had demonstrated the immense fiscal, monetary, and
industrial powers of the state, and accordingly how major redistributive reforms were concrete and viable—much more than conventional
economic thinking had allowed.[2]

Beyond "the Tyranny of Economic Creed"

The British civil servant Alfred D. Hall, describing the newfound re-constructionist spirit that had seized so many within the British and Italian establishments, characterized the moment as an enlightenment:

> Few can fail to feel the force of inspiration and experience which is be-ing born of the war, or to recognize the strength of the new hope with which the people are looking forward to the future. The nation [Britain] ardently desires to order its life in accordance with those principles of freedom and justice. . . . For no one can doubt that we are at a turning point in our national history. A new era has come upon us. We cannot stand still. We cannot return to the old ways, the old abuses, the old stupidities . . . the public not only has its *conscience aroused* and its heart stirred, but also has its mind open and receptive of *new ideas* to an un-precedented degree.[3]

This turning point was about ideas as much as practices—and how the two were ultimately inseparable when it came to change in society. A pamphlet written by two bureaucrats of the Italian Ministry of Military Assistance and War Pensions, Leo Pavoni and Diego Avarelli, echoed this same belief: "The war has been a war of ideas. Out of its miseries and catastrophes a luminous path has been traced for the ends of the State . . . [the war] has laid the foundations of the distinguished edifice of human solidarity" (Ministero per l'Assistenza Militare e le Pensioni di Guerra 1919, vi–vii).

The pamphlet continued by stressing a historical *aufhebung*: "The state of law that was considered the most elevated form of state before the war . . . has suddenly been overtaken and surpassed by the highest of conceptions: the *state of law and social welfare*" (ibid., 26). Doctor Michele Pietravalle, vice president of the Italian House, enthused: "the undelayable duty of the State" [*improrogabile dovere dello stato*] to safe-guard citizens' rights, especially those of the "underprivileged classes" [*classi diseredate*], was now "a categorical imperative" [*imperativo*

Table 2.1. Percentage of the active population of Italy and the UK covered by social welfare

Country	1910	1915	1920
Italy	4.8	4.8	27.3
United Kingdom (Great Britain)	17.5	36.3	43.3

Base = 1970 (the index value is set at 100 in the year 1970)

Source: Alber (1983, 220–21).

categorico] (Pietravalle 1919, 109–11). The law professor Filippo Vassalli went further: "The war has silently enacted a great revolution" embodied in the introduction of audacious legal principles that could even be named "state socialism" [*socialismo di stato*].[4]

Indeed, war had meant welfare.[5] In Britain, a minimal system of social guarantees had already been in place in the Victorian period, and the state had expanded social reforms through the early years of the twentieth century (see Peden 1985, 16–35).[6] However, the degree of state intervention during the war was unprecedented.[7] By 1918 local and national government expenditures on social services, expressed as a share of gross national product, had doubled (to around 8 percent—see Peden 1985, 57). The Italian case was even more impressive, since public welfare had barely existed prior to the war. By 1920 the country had performed the greatest leap in the extension of social welfare coverage of any European nation—increasing almost sixfold since 1915 (see table 2.1).

Reconstructionists aimed to concretize the social progress made during the war effort, which in their view represented a great stride toward a better society based on notions of social justice and redistribution. "There are all the indications of a wholly new school of thought which is laying hold of people,"[8] commented the former lord chancellor, Viscount Richard Haldane, a month after the armistice. This new school of thought reverberated among the leaders of government.

On November 23, 1918, British prime minister Lloyd George spoke to a crowd in Wolverhampton, and his tone was one of reconciliation leaning toward revolutionary: "What is our task? To make Britain a fit country for heroes to live in . . . [we] will lift those who have been living in the dark places to a plateau where they will get the rays of the sun."

These dark places included millions who were living under atrocious social conditions—"We mean to put these things right."[9]

Just as the British prime minister was certain that in this "new world" the workers "must be inexorable in their demands" (Tasca 1965, 18), so too on November 20, 1918, Italian prime minister Vittorio Orlando proclaimed that the war was "the greatest political-social revolution recorded by history" (ibid.). That same day, Antonio Salandra, Orlando's predecessor, reiterated, "The War is a revolution. . . . It is the hour of the youth. Let no one think that a peaceful return to the past will be possible after the storm" (ibid.).

The enlightened reconstructionist elite came from different professions (intellectuals, pastors, educators, professors) and governmental posts as well as from a variety of political backgrounds—from progressive liberalism to reformist socialism (Italy) or Labour (in Britain). Such a broad constituency was certainly not homogeneous, nor did its adherents aim to dismantle the hierarchical social order. They did, however, share a revulsion to competitive individualism and laissez-faire capitalism. The reconstructionists thus profoundly disputed the economic doctrine that for centuries had stood as the cornerstone of capital accumulation.

For Pietravalle, the member of the Italian House, the time had come to revise "material and moral values, and even to rethink, shake, break, knock down constitutions and institutions that once appeared as fundamental and sacred" (Pietravalle 1919, 103–6). The war experience, Hammond confirmed, "had emancipated and widened our imaginations" since it "removed the word 'impossible' from the language of politics," and "destroyed the superstition of the iron law which has checked and hampered all our hopes" (Jason [pseud.]1918, 35).

New social sensibilities overtook impersonal economic laws as the "universal arbit[ers]" of social relations. It entailed a breaking out of the "tyranny of a particular economic creed": human life could no longer be "subordinated" to the "imperious demand for the production of wealth."[10]

First, and most critically, emancipation from impersonal economic laws meant that social reforms could no longer be "delayed or refused sanction on the grounds of expense" (Addison 1918, 1). This was clear in the mind of the minister of reconstruction, Christopher Addison,[11] who in his determination emerged as a sort of living expression of the postwar reformist impulse.

The war had revealed to all—workers and bureaucrats alike—that economic priorities were actually political priorities, and thanks to unorthodox finance, the state could meet political objectives at any financial cost. Indeed, once the gold standard constraint was removed, the possibilities that emerged opened new horizons for social expenditure. Suddenly no expenditure—toward social measures that were within the society's resource capabilities—seemed beyond financial possibility.

In his memorandum on reconstitution finance to the government, Addison was adamant that "[i]t would be no defense to say that vital proposals were not enacted for want of money. *Nobody will believe it*" (ibid., 5, my italics). Eric Geddes, the minister of transport, also voiced the popular view: "You must be prepared to spend money on after-the-war problems as you did on during-the-war problems. That [money] must be found and added to our debt if necessary."[12]

While economic experts at the British Treasury were taking cover behind the priority of funding debt and curtailing inflation in support of creditor/investors (who were, in their minds, the sole sources of future capital accumulation and prosperity), the reconstructionists argued that such prosperity could actually be found via greater expenditure and new frontiers of social reform.[13]

Practical consensus among reconstructionists was grounded in faith in "human power" to change economic conditions through the interdependence between fiscal, monetary, and industrial policy. Progressive taxes and state spending had to go hand in hand with favorable credit policy and especially with industrial harmony achieved through forms of workers' industrial control or of industrial cooperation.[14] This "progressive trinity" of fiscal, monetary, and industrial policies would secure efficiency, high employment, and social justice.

Social Welfare for Social Peace

The postwar impulse to break away from economic orthodoxy was not, of course, spontaneous. Some of these sentiments had been percolating before the war began, and they were to a large extent a pragmatic response to social upheavals. Much of this pressure originated in organized labor.

For decades British and Italian unions and their working-class political parties had mobilized for social welfare.[15] During the war their demands became louder, reflecting a mounting distrust of governments and their classist policies. To promote national ideological cohesion, wartime states were thus pressured to experiment with various forms of welfare as a form of olive branch.[16] As the economist Arrigo Serpieri put it, the objective of social legislation was "winning the favor and quietude of the working masses," both in industry and in the countryside (Serpieri 1930, 343).

In Italy, it was only after the country's defeat in the Battle of Caporetto in November 1917—a massive loss of life that hollowed the spirit of the Italian people—that the state took on a central role as a social actor. It established the Ministry of Military Assistance and War Pensions, which would benefit citizens generally, and not just soldiers.[17]

The very fact that Italian social reforms were introduced by decree—an executive urgency procedure to overcome lengthy parliamentary debates—expressed the necessity of quick intervention for the sake of class appeasement and a recognition of popular demands. This remained vital even after the armistice, since the meager state-provided war welfare sparked additional discontent, its value regarded as laughable in the face of exploitation and inflation.

The Italian inflation crisis of the country's "red years" of 1919 and 1920 was marked by protests against the high cost of living and the predatory behaviors of "*i pescecani*" [literally, "sharks"]—a nickname for profiteers and speculators who embodied the iniquitous effects of inflation. Beginning on June 11, 1919, and continuing for almost a month, hungry and exasperated crowds dashed into stores throughout the country, taking food, clothing, and all manner of merchandise. Looting and chaotic riots began in the town of La Spezia, and then spread everywhere—from the northern towns of Liguria, Piedmont, Lombardy, and Veneto, to the central towns of Tuscany and Romagna, all the way to Rome and Palermo.[18] Journalists depicted vivid scenes of chaos and desperation with recurring patterns: spontaneous uprisings against the high cost of living were soon led by socialist organizations (especially *camere del lavoro*[19] and unions) who often called for social reform, general strikes, and assemblies. The red municipalities of Emilia—the epicenter of the uprisings—became home to assemblies that sat permanently (Maione 1975, 32). On July 6 the government rushed to pass a decree that authorized prefects and mayors to pass price controls with abatements up to 50 percent. Article 6 of the decree specified: "the just-price is determined on the basis of prices that are fixed locally by public bodies and consumer cooperatives." Prices were no longer determined by impersonal market forces; they were suddenly an output of democratic decision-making.

Many newspapers, even within the mainstream, supported these *prezzi politici* (political prices). *La Tribuna* of July 5, 1919, wrote in solidarity: "We don't feel like condemning these unrests of classes and masses . . . unrests are inevitable, even necessary. The history of politics in any time teaches us that the state institutions have the inclinations of falling asleep comfortably in their bureaucratic routine. . . . To awaken these high sleepers, there is a need for a little noise, and some noise in this sense never hurts" (Vivarelli 1967, 414–15). As the article made clear, pressure from below was an indispensable driver for reform.

Meanwhile, *The Times* and other British bourgeois publications observed the Italian scene with worried eyes. On its end, the leftist *Daily Herald* asked: "Will British workers, following the example of Italy, resort to violence in order to defeat the profiteers? Conan Doyle predicts that they will, unless something is done quickly and thoroughly" ("Will It End in Violence?" *Daily Herald*, July 10, 1919, 1).

The Italian workers, even more than their British counterparts, announced their indispensable role in society. Comprehensive social rights were no longer disputable. In the words of Rinaldo Rigola, textile worker and secretary of the Italian union General Confederation of Labour (CGdL), the worker was "the one without whom there would be nothing for nobody" (Rigola 1918, 7).

At the Turin congress of October 8, 1918, the Society for Mutual Aid and Cooperatives, in collaboration with the CGdL, spoke more formally: "The working class does not ask, nor intend to ask, for man-datory social insurance for sickness, disability, and old age as a phil-anthropic solution to the still-unresolved social problems—but as the *expression of rights* that have long matured though heretofore in vain, in the scathing and glorious field of labor and social production" ("Il congresso regionale piemontese per le assicurazioni sociali," *L'Avanti*, October 8, 1918).

The writing was on the wall: "the organized working class battles and intends to battle . . . not for fragmentary solutions . . . but for audacious solutions, extended, complete" (ibid.).

In a moment of unprecedented social tension, members of the state apparatus had no choice but to be receptive to these demands. In 1917, the economist Francesco Saverio Nitti, in his role as Treasury minister, had to publicly accept that the workers in the "trenches and fields" de-served "full rights of citizenship" and "no one could divert them."[20] The push gained momentum. Two years later, for example, Leonida Bissolati, upon his departure as head of the Ministry of Military Assistance and War Pensions, wrote in a note to his fellow civil servants, "Your work is far from done. . . . I vow the birth on a solid basis of the Ministry of State Assistance to unify the existing institutions for pension and social welfare. Such an institution would be a high social deed for democracy" (Ministero per l'Assistenza Militare e le Pensioni di Guerra 1919, 31).

Even for wealthy and propertied classes, the state responding in a way that avoided the worst possible break from the capitalist order was a clear necessity. In 1920, Vittorio Cottafavi, a wealthy property owner and MP of the Liberal Constitutional group, wrote to Nitti, who had become prime minister, to stress the strategic need to publicize the so-cial role of the state as an anti-revolutionary antidote:

> To draw near the workers to the state so that they can see in it a friend and a protector . . . in the endeavor of pacification . . . it would be very useful to familiarize the population with the great initiative of state-funded worker pensions, and with all that is currently being done on be-half of the working classes. Dispensing these healthy facts and brotherly propaganda would benefit public order.[21]

Some Italian workers' representatives looked up to Britain as an inspiration for their own reformist demands—since, as Rigola put it, it was evident that the British ruling classes "considered state social intervention as a duty" (Rigola 1918, 2). Indeed, similar political dynamics were at play in Britain—where, as we know, unions in combination with the Labour Party were much more influential than the Italian workers' organizations, even occupying ministerial posts. As we will further explore in the following chapters, unlike their Italian counterparts who flirted with revolution, the majority of British workers' leaders were explicitly reconstructionist in spirit—seeking to advance social good, but through governmental channels.

Founded in 1917 and active throughout the immediate postwar period, the British Ministry of Reconstruction[22] was a government entity charged with compensating the country's working classes for their war sacrifice. Central to this charge were programs for postwar social and economic improvement, including extensive plans for development in education, unemployment relief, and housing.

Housing was undeniably "the chief cause of the industrial unrest":[23] the unsanitary and unhealthy dwellings of the British workers were the most visible and outrageous marks of class difference and injustice. In a moment of global revolutionary fever, it had to be addressed no matter the economic impediments (which, following the financial outlay of the war, would not have been well received as excuses for inaction). In the words of the Labour leader and MP M. J. Davison: "Let me say quite frankly I am not concerned with the financial aspect of this problem. You did not hesitate to call upon the men to preserve this country from invasion. They protected your property and you did not consider for the moment whether it was going to cost a penny rate or a pound rate" (ibid., cc 1749).

Since construction of houses more or less stopped during the war, "at the lowest estimate there must have been a deficit of from 300,000 to 400,000 working-class houses by the end of 1918" (*Monthly Labour Review* 1921, 213). The lack of new housing was exacerbated by the lack of upkeep to existing housing, as during the war repairs and efforts to eliminate slums were forgone. Many dwellings were uninhabitable.[24]

This crisis was magnified by the higher cost of building in the postwar period, which resulted in higher rents and made it impossible for a considerable portion of the population to afford housing (ibid.). The growing strength of the Labour Party meant that the words of Davison pressuring parliament were to be taken seriously:

> We say that unless such a policy is adopted, unless the people of this country are housed in decency and in comfort, the Labour Party will take all the means at its disposal to endeavour to obtain a reversal of the verdict of the election of last December. If we care to do so, we can do it most effectively by a method which I would be the last man to advocate. . . . That is not said as a threat. (HC Deb 7 April 1919, vol. 114, cc 1748)

The Housing and Town Planning Act of April 1919 promised to build 500,000 new houses in three years.[25] This reform was "heroic" (Johnson 1968, 425) in its break from the past: it was the first official recognition of the political obligation of the state to house its citizens. A plurality of enlightened commissions under the Ministry of Reconstruction gave shape to the legislation and substantiated the widespread realization that private enterprise—responsible for approximately 95 percent of house-building prior to the war—was unable to grapple successfully and speedily with this social crisis.

Reformists in Action

THE AGENDA OF THE MINISTRY OF RECONSTRUCTION

The parliamentary debate around the housing bill in April 1919 demonstrated the determination and influence of the reconstructionists in British government. Liberal MP James Gilbert spoke for all: "It is very necessary that these houses should be built as soon as possible, because not only myself but every Member of this House is pledged to housing up to the hilt . . . this will mark a new era for the working classes of this country" (James Gilbert, HC Deb 7 April 1919, vol. 114, cc 1763).

The flames of a workers' revolution were doused with promises of "proper bathrooms, with a proper service of hot and cold water" (ibid., cc 1762). These new housing standards had been studied in scientific detail by the Tudor-Walters Committee under the Ministry of Reconstruction. The Committee was named after its chairman, a prominent architect and Liberal MP who collaborated with other renowned architects such as Frank Baines and Raymond Unwin. The most impressive recommendations, however, came from the "Women's Housing Sub-Committee" (also under the Ministry of Reconstruction). The all-women's committee, chaired by suffragette and feminist activist Mary Gertrude Emmott, took a very bottom-up approach. As the committee put it, its final report "embod[ied] only such improvements as are demanded by working women themselves" (Ministry of Reconstruction Advisory Council 1919, 20).

The women's committee's impressive scheme encompassed rules on windows, ventilation, and "labor-saving devices" for the housewife, such as the American "kitchen cabinet" that would save "unnecessary walking to and fro" (ibid., 9). Most importantly, the committee experimented with "wide possibilities of communal life"—gardens, playgrounds, social centers—since its members believed that "full attention should be given to the organisation of the resources available for social and intellectual development" (ibid., 20). The committee stressed the material conditions for women's emancipation. A section of the report titled "Communal Holiday Homes" confronted "the difficulty experienced by working women in obtaining a real rest and holiday." The plan envisaged "(1) Houses in which mothers could, without anxiety, leave their young children . . . (2) Large houses in seaside or country places to which groups of working people might go for a holiday" (ibid., 13).

The Women's Cooperative Guild[26] led another sweeping campaign to recognize and compensate a woman's unpaid labor of child bearing and rearing. In the words of the suffragette public intellectual Maude Royden: "motherhood is a service which entitles a woman to economic independence" (Pedersen 1993, 146). The Family Endowment Committee asked the government to fund all mothers from pregnancy until the child reached the age of five. Even *The Times* published supportive accounts for this demanding budgetary measure ("Saving the Children," *The Times*, February 25, 1919, 7). Unfortunately, with the resurgence of austerity in the 1920s, this agenda never saw the light of day.

In those early postwar years, all of these committees gave voice to a larger working-class constituency that aimed to develop the foundations for a revolution in social life based on "co-operative buying and selling" and especially "the spread of communal living" (Ministry of Reconstruction Advisory Council 1919, 14).

Within the state apparatus the enlightened bourgeoisie and the representatives of labor joined hands to deliver on the promise of a new and more just society through unprecedented social reforms—"intimately and immediately connected to one another"[27] (Ernest Pretyman, HC Deb 7 April 1919, vol. 114, cc 1773).

The Adult Education Committee was active for more than two years. Prominent reconstructionists including the politician Ernest Bevin, the unionist Frank Hodges, and the economist R. H. Tawney, under the chairmanship of the Oxford Don A. L. Smith, joined forces to produce a visionary final report in October 1919.

Galvanized by the August 1918 Education Act—which abolished all fees in public elementary schools, raised the ending age for compulsory education from 12 to 14, and required local authorities to provide for part-time continuation schools for 14-to-16-year-olds[28]—the Committee called for a profound democratization of economic and political decisions.

Its members honored the newly acknowledged centrality of labor with a groundbreaking commitment written in capital letters that is still an unmet ideal today: "ADULT EDUCATION IS A PERMANENT NATIONAL NECESSITY, AN INSEPARABLE ASPECT OF CITIZENSHIP, AND THEREFORE SHOULD BE BOTH UNIVERSAL AND LIFELONG."[29]

A "systematic," "continuous," and "social" education, as the "duty of the community," would satisfy workers' widespread "appetite for knowledge" and overcome "work without thought" (Ministry of Reconstruction 1919b, 36–37). This non-vocational type of adult education was the opposite of a top-down process or of an indoctrinating exercise on the part of the state.[30] Rather, it was a timely response to a mounting popular educational movement.[31]

Indeed, the Committee envisioned a "considerable increase in financial contributions from the State" (ibid., 117) to assist all forms of "voluntary organizations," such as the Workers' Educational Association. That association provided a "network" of classes and reading circles over many districts, uniting "some 2,555 societies, including 952 Trade Unions, Trades Councils and branches, 388 Co-operative Societies, and other organisations in a popular educational movement" (ibid., 38–39). Other hubs that built workers' consciousness through a variety of critical courses, including those on the history and economics of capitalism and socialist theory, were to be the beneficiaries of state grants. The likes of London's Working Man College, Ruskin College, and Labour College expressed "the belief of organized labour in the importance of bringing higher education within reach of the younger generation of trade unionists" (ibid., 39).[32]

The insight on the theory-practice connection—between "knowledge and effective action"—was spreading: "It is significant, indeed, of the growing belief in the value of study that movements and organizations whose main purpose is a practical one have come more and more in recent years to encourage it among their members by organizing lectures, classes and reading circles or by supplying them with books" (ibid., 39–40). *L'Ordine nuovo* movement in Italy of those years would develop these thoughts to their full revolutionary consequences (as we shall see in chapter 4).

The Adult Education Committee envisioned the spread of critical economic knowledge to the rural areas. It remarked: "it is certain that with the growth of trade unionism amongst agricultural workers, there will be a demand for economic history and economics from the point of view of the workers' experience and interests" (ibid., 146). This vision of cultural empowerment gave rise to ambitious schemes of public transport and urban planning, for example to build a Village Institute—"a living nucleus of communal activity" that included "a hall large enough for dances, cinema shows, concerts, plays, public lectures, and exhibitions," as well as "a public library and local museum" (ibid., 142–43).

THE REACH OF RECONSTRUCTION

The year 1919 was a year of nationalization projects that favored the working classes of Britain. This included not only the coal sector (as we will see in the next chapter), but also the transportation and health sectors.

The Ministry of Transport was conceived as a body with the power to nationalize any transport undertaking (roads, railways, canals, and docks) and to control the supply of electricity.[33] These nationalization schemes, especially for railways, caused uproar within the conservative establishment, with the chairman of the Council of the Chamber of Commerce describing the bill as a "revolution by Act of Parliament" ("Ways and Means Communication," *The Times*, March 4, 1919, 12). Yet even *The Times* endorsed its progressive appeal, understanding the government's "transport revolution" as "one of their most important weapons in the new war which is just beginning against obsolete and inefficient industrial and social conditions" ("Commons and Transport Bill," *The Times*, March 6, 1919, 6).

Similarly, the Ministry of Health was created in 1919 to centralize health governance and "ultimately abolish the Poor Law" (Charles Sitch, HC Deb 26 February 1919, vol. 112, cc 1878).[34] MPs spoke of "the nationalisation" of "the very greatest asset which any nation or any individual may possess, namely, the nationalisation of the health of the people of this country" (ibid., Major Alexander Farquharson, cc 1878).

Elected officials hailed the health bill as "a splendid thing" (ibid., Captain Walter Elliot, cc 1891). It gained "unanimous support from all quarters of the House" (ibid., Major Waldorf Astor, cc 1909).[35] MPs spoke about a society where the "rigid distinction between the words 'prevention' and 'cure'" was surpassed (ibid., Major Alexander Farquharson, cc 1880). If criticisms were raised, they were in the direction of asking for more. Many in the House stood in favor of reinforcing the power of action of the Ministry—especially concerning mental health and funds for medical research. Unfortunately, as we will see in the second part of the book, universal national health care was doomed to be a victim of postwar austerity.

Italian reconstructionists within government had similar ambitions for a national health service. One commission, the Abbiate Commission, proposed a universalist welfare reform—"insurance is to be extended to all citizens"—that took much from the demands of the popular Italian union CGdL and the Socialist Party.[36] As in the case of Britain, the project was to centralize and simplify social provision under a single insurance: covering healthcare against illness, accident protection, and maternity coverage.[37] Pietravalle and his colleagues on the Commission were directly inspired by the British reforms when they campaigned for a Ministry of Health that would guide "under one directive mind" (Pietravalle 1919, 108) the extensive "newborn, more promising and higher tasks" of public health (ibid., 110). The leaders of CGdL pushed for an even more comprehensive and "less rigid plan," one that would include more categories of workers at lower ages, and guarantee higher subsidies, especially for the workers with lower wages (Rigola 1918, 4).

Emancipatory projects regarding healthcare were put on the back burner by the Liberal postwar governments and later drowned by the Fascist austerity campaign. After this setback, the universal national health system would not become a reality in Italy until 1978. And in the early 1990s, the resurgence of austerity again began chipping away at these government programs.

In 1919, though, the high season of social reform was in full throttle—to the point that, by that December, the Liberal Democrat Mario Cermenati, undersecretary of the Ministry of Military Assistance, could commend his country for rising "from last place" to occupy "the vanguard for social insurance," and for its "will to do even more."[38] To substantiate Cermenati's optimism, it is enough to mention the three most important reformist victories.

In April 1919, the state declared insurance against disability and old age[39] mandatory and extended it to cover all private sector workers.[40] It inaugurated an early form of a cross-class redistributive system that benefited some 12 million workers, including tenant farmers, *mezzadri* (sharecroppers), white-collar workers, and shopkeepers with low incomes (Pavan 2019, 851). Augusto Ciuffelli, the minister of agriculture, industry, and commerce, presented the provision to Parliament invoking Italy's "awareness of her duties to her people" and the legislation's "great task of peace and social justice" (ibid., 850).

The wave of reform continued with the effective institution in 1919 of mandatory insurance against accidents for agricultural workers[41] (originally introduced in Regent's Law Decree 1450, August 23, 1917, in GU, 1917 General Index of Subjects, 47). This law, strongly favored by Socialist trade unions, overwhelmed the opposition of landowners and the Chamber of Commerce, who worried that state intervention— especially centralized public management of accident insurance through the newly instituted *Cassa Nazionale Infortuni* (CNI)—would irrevocably alter class hierarchies. A January 1918 Chamber of Commerce manifesto opposed the law and warned: "the decree would have a major impact on relations between workers and owners, both politically and owing to its financial repercussions."[42]

For the first time, this law made insurance for accidents in agriculture public and mandatory, applying the modern principle of an automatic right to compensation that was not linked to the contribution of the employer. With this reform, 9 million farm workers gained social protection, joining the industrial workers. In a 1921 decree, Prime Minister Giolitti would further extend the law's scope by lowering the barrier to eligibility. Mussolini's austerity axe of 1923, however, made sure to immediately gut Giolitti's decree (Royal Decree Law 432, February 11, 1923, in GU 64 [March 17, 1923], 2286).

Finally, Italy had become a front runner in its unemployment reform, another means to quell high working-class demands. Apart from the Soviet laws of 1917, the Italian scheme was the first one to introduce a large-scale system of obligatory unemployment insurance (covering industrial and agricultural workers and white-collar employees of both sexes, aged fifteen to sixty-five).[43] This 1919 scheme was even more inclusive than its British counterpart of 1920.[44]

Reformism: Pacification or Polarization?

The postwar creation of the Italian Ministry of Labour and Social Welfare, which closely resembled the British Ministry of Labour (established in 1916), reveals the double-edged significance of the reconstructionist project.[45] On the one hand, the explicit objective of the Nitti government was to strengthen state intervention for the protection of the working classes. On the other, this reform constituted an attempt to harmonize productive relations and thus guarantee the survival of a fragile capitalist system.

Since the beginning of the century, the Socialist party, the CGdL, and the national leagues of cooperatives had been calling for a ministry "to deal with the problems of labor" [che provveda ai problemi del lavoro].[46] The prewar Liberal governments avoided this project—there was overwhelming opposition to a ministry understood as "a class ministry" [un ministero di classe].[47] After the war, however, things were different. The war dynamics ushered in new priorities, and no imperative was stronger than assimilating the working classes and defusing their rejection of the capitalist state. The government sought social peace through social and labor reform. Indeed, the collaborative relation between labor and the state was a pillar of Nitti's "productivist reformism"—a creed that largely overlapped with that of many British reconstructionists.[48] The reader may thus discern the fundamental ambivalence of reconstructionism: even in its construction of safety nets, the welfare state still performs a function of social control. Workers have less incentive to break from a system that provides them with greater labor rights and social benefits.[49]

Notably, even in such an explosive social moment, most social reforms were not actually so reformist in their results. Rather than appeasing workers, the "enlightened agenda" stimulated higher expectations for a better future. Cracks between reformers and radicals emerged.

For example, while the CGdL campaigned for insurance against disability and old age, the rank and file began mobilizing against the payment of insurance quotas.[50] In the summer of 1920 workers at the Bianchi workshop in Milan organized a strike that was supported by the Chamber of Labour of Bologna and Turin: "What purpose do these social insurances have when we are on the verge of revolution? Why pay if we will soon have all the power?" (Tasca 1920, 124). These cracks became fault lines, and in 1920 an ascendent Benito Mussolini wrote in an article for *Il popolo d'Italia* that it was not only the Liberal state that was in grave crisis, but the reformist attitude of the unions themselves.[51]

The reformist governments' lack of toehold was painfully clear to the governments themselves. In January 1921, an Italian parliamentary commission made plain that in the new Ministry of Labour "the workers see by now the supreme organ of protection of their interests and from it they expect further reforms directed to the material and moral elevation of the worker."[52]

The Italian reconstructionist project's desperation for social peace failed, ultimately ushering in the 1922 Fascist regime. As we shall explore, Fascist austerity abruptly broke the season of reforms and inaugurated a return of the most uncompromising ruling classes. Emblematic of this newly found strategy of "appeasement" was the dismantling of the Ministry of Labour in 1923.[53]

Rather than advancing national unity, reconstructionism had polarized society. On the one side stood workers and their revolutionary practices, whose vilification by the state would later give rise to austerity policies. On the other side was the reactionary bourgeoisie, supported by influential economists—the protagonists of the second part of the book—who initiated a powerful campaign against the "paternalistic bureaucratic" state and unleashed the weapon of austerity. Austerity operated as a defense mechanism not only against revolutionary upsurges but also against the very principles of postwar welfare capitalism and its potential expansion.

Certainly Britain represented a less explosive scenario, but this was only a difference in degree, not in kind. Even if it is true that in a mature capitalist economy the workers' representatives were more profoundly integrated into the state apparatus, social polarization was still an insidious reality. The struggles of the miners we will explore in chapter 3 are indicative of how social reforms amplified demands to take over production. As Lord Sankey noted in the official 1919 coal commission report, there was in the coalfields much more than "a desire for the material advantages of higher wages and shorter hours." Workers expressed "to an ever-increasing extent, a higher ambition of taking their due share and interest in the direction of the industry to the success of which they, too, are contributing" (Great Britain, Royal Commission on Coal Industry 1919b, vii). To halt the threats to the old order, a vocal "anti-waste" campaign against public expenditure burst through the seams and found strong institutional support in the austerity crusade of the experts at the British Treasury.

Conclusion

During the Great War, the British and Italian governments employed social welfare as a powerful strategy of political cohesion on an unprecedented scale. In a moment when laissez-faire capitalism was revealing its classist bias, the states intervened as redistributive actors to stave off the system's internal combustion. In the war's immediate aftermath, the reconstructionists propelled this strategy further: equitable reform could moderate popular discontent and placate workers, who would now have something to lose from breaking away from the bourgeois socioeconomic order. Appeasing the collective involved an ambitious reconstruction of society on a socially inclusive basis, nowhere better expressed than in the British Ministry of Reconstruction and its numerous enlightened committees or in the Italian Ministry of Labour and Social Welfare—the symbols of workers' voice within the state apparatus.

There is no doubt that at its root the impulse toward reconstruction was a matter of existential preservation: reforms were the antidote to any immediate deracination of the bourgeois social contract. Paradoxically, however, what was required for its preservation was in itself a threat to capitalism, or at least a grave threat to "pure" laissez-faire capitalism.

Indeed, with postwar reconstruction, the priorities of the economic system dramatically shifted: from satisfying the individual profit motive to satisfying the collective social need. Resources were transferred away from private capital to the collective. This meant, for example, that tax revenues and newly created credits were used for programs of public health and education instead of being channeled back into the pockets of savers-investors.

After the war, many rejected the "old economic creed" in favor of "a progressive trinity"—expansionist fiscal and monetary policies and inclusive industrial agendas that outmuscled the impersonal laws of the market. In affirming human agency, reconstructionists refused to bow to budgetary constraints as an "economic limit" to policies of social distribution. These plans for a "new society" reached for high emancipatory goals—from the spread of communal living that empowered women to the funding of workers' schools that taught about labor rights and socialist theory.

Ultimately, economic orthodoxy had to contend with two sets of enemies. First was the reconstructionists, who—through their vision of increasing social redistribution to the detriment of private capital— represented an important enemy of capitalism in its pure laissez-faire form. But an arguably greater enemy emerged at the same time, one that challenged the very foundations of capitalism and was emboldened by reconstructionist reforms: people's revolutionary ambitions. Rather than being appeased by social redistribution, workers were galvanized by it. The years 1919–1920 were marked by vast mobilizations toward an alternative socioeconomic system which entailed the overcoming of private ownership of the means of production and wages themselves.

The mutually enhancing relation between reforms and working-class consciousness proved to be an explosive synergy. Ironically, the reformists, who had bent the iron laws of the market to avoid a revolution, had actually contributed to sparking another one. These radical embers that charred capitalism are the subject of chapter 3.

CHAPTER 3

The Struggle for Economic Democracy

Economic movements have a rapidly growing tendency to become also political, not only because the workers possess a greatly increased power and are far more conscious of it, but also because their economic claims are animated by a steadily deepening hostility to the whole capitalist order of society. Not only do the workers feel stronger, they have also a growing feeling that capitalism is insecure.

G. D. H. Cole, *Chaos and Order in Industry* (1920a, 8–9)

Capitalism's crisis of legitimacy was born from its undressing during World War I: state interventions in national economies expanded the limits of what was possible, politically, and in doing so opened up spaces for greater political imagination around the organization of socioeconomic relations. Put simply, the very conditions created by state control during the war caused the breakdown of the commonsense rationality that had justified the system up to that point. Chapter 2 detailed how such a breakdown was manifested in the postwar reconstructionist spirit and its attempts at appeasement via social reforms. Now we examine how the loss of legitimacy for capitalist governments went much deeper: it opened the question of the profit motive—the core of capitalism—as well as its two fundamental pillars, private ownership of the means of production and wage relations.

Following the war, pockets of workers from across Europe were drawn to modes of organization in which production was intended for use rather than profit; communal property was favored over private property; freedom was valued above the commodification of labor. The strength and revolutionary significance of the Italian and especially British labor movements after the war have been downplayed by many labor historians in the decades that followed; G. D. H. Cole, the political theorist and economist who wrote this chapter's epigraph, wrote in his 1958 *A History of Socialist Thought, Vol. 4*, "I have tried to make plain that there was no point at all at which there was any possibility of a British Revolution" (Cole 1958, 449). This was a departure from his dispatches from the period itself, including a 1919 testimony that read in part, "[f]or I do sincerely believe that the present economic order is breaking down, and that its definite collapse is a matter not of decades, but of years" (Cole 1920a, 24). He observed that what had held capitalism together until that point, that is, "the widespread conviction that capitalism was inevitable" (ibid., 8), was collapsing.

Indeed, during the red years of 1919–1920, collective imagination was fired by events happening elsewhere in Europe. The writings of the reformist-socialist Pietro Nenni reveal the interconnected and transnational nature of the crisis: "The fall of the Hohenzollern in Germany, the dissolution of the Habsburg empire and the flight of its last emperor, the Spartacist movements in Berlin, the Bolshevik revolution in Hungary, the Soviet in Bavaria . . . fired the imaginations and inspired the hope that the old world was on the point of crumbling and that humanity was on the verge of a new era of a new social order" (Nenni 1946, 6).[1]

If one is to argue that capitalism was crumbling during this period—as I do—then the unparalleled surges of industrial action in Britain and Italy are exhibits A and B. These postwar industrial actions sought new relations of production to construct democratic societies.

Labor movements were grounded in demands for workers' control, i.e., the substitution of a new industrial order that replaced the capitalist industrial system, partially if not completely. Cole, in his earlier voice, explains: "But, when Labour asks for control, it is not with profits or profit-sharing that it is primarily concerned, but with the democratisation of the actual management of industry, and the securing for the organised workers of a real measure of control over the conditions under which they work. Labour's remedy for the curse of profiteering is not a share in profits for itself, but the public ownership of industry combined with a system of democratic control" (Cole 1920b, Preface, vx). A campaign as radical as one for workers' control required the deployment of multiple strategies. This chapter details three: the struggles of the British miners for nationalization; the rise of Italian cooperatives; and the proliferation of the British guilds.

Labor Storms the Stage of History

In 1918, new electoral laws enfranchised men regardless of property qualifications and, in Britain, also women, subject to constraints.[2] This meant that workers' concerns now shaped the political landscape.

In Britain, the change in the electoral base (which grew from 5.2 to 12.9 million with the new law) granted center stage to the Labour Party, which dethroned the Liberal Party as the main rival to the Tories. The Labour Party won 4.5 million votes—eight times more than in prewar years. Regardless of our judgment on the authenticity of the party's lofty ambitions to seize the means of production—as declared in their constitutional manifesto of 1918[3]—the characterization of this period in the British historian Eric Hobsbawm's observations are undeniable: "For the first time in history, a proletarian party became and remained a major alternative government party, and the fear of working-class power and expropriation now haunted the middle classes, not so much because this is what the Labour leaders promised or performed, but because its mere existence as a mass party threw a faint red shadow of potential Soviet revolution across the country" (Hobsbawm 1999, 187).

The November 1919 Italian electoral results were even more challenging to capital accumulation: the Socialist Party and the Popular Party[4] gained the majority in the Chamber of Deputies—256 of the 508 total seats. The Socialists alone obtained 1,840,600 votes and seated 156 representatives (32 percent of the entire parliament), while the traditional Liberal party all but disappeared. By 1920 the Socialist Party counted 4,367 local sections, and governed a third of all municipalities (around

2,800 *comuni*) and more than a third of the provincial councils.[5] Socialists also directed 8,000 cooperatives. This was no ordinary feat, and
was partly incited by the party's radicalization since the time of war.[6]
Its immediate agenda targeted "the socialization of financial capital, the
suppression of state debt, the socialization of housing, means of transportation and of big agrarian property and of the big industrial and
commercial business" (*L'Avanti*, August 8, 1919).

More dramatically, the Socialist Party also rejected any form of
parliamentarism. It fought fights in electoral terms and with a clear-
eyed revolutionary set of objectives. This most intense dissemination
of communist principles was meant to "facilitate the abolition of the
institutions of bourgeois domination" (Tasca 1965, 95). Elections were
thus understood as a barometer to measure the shift of power toward
labor and as a powerful means of cultivating class consciousness. While
the proletarian parties were growing in strength, so too were workers'
unions—with the two organizations being structurally interconnected
in both countries.

In Britain, the industrial capital of the world, between 1914 and 1918
trade union membership rose from 4 million people to 6.5 million
people, and eventually reached a record figure of almost 8.4 million in
1920. In just six years, unionization had doubled: 40 percent of the total
working population joined the unions. In Italy, the escalation was just
as impressive. The thrust of trade unionism into the urban and rural
proletariat escalated like never before: almost 3.8 million workers—
five times the prewar total—participated in organized labor protests.
What's more, the socialist workers' federation surpassed all others in
popularity. The CGdL grew impressively: in just the two postwar years
participation climbed eightfold, reaching 2 million members by 1920.[7]
Especially combative were its adherent organizations: FEDERTERRA,
the "red league" of agrarian workers, and FIOM, the "red union" of the
metal workers.

The surge in union membership was primarily the result of the wartime onboarding of new workers (and new kinds of workers): women,
the unskilled, and the semi-skilled.[8] The war had given birth to a "new
and much more embattled working class" that had very little to lose. As

we know from chapter 1, these workers had been deeply politicized by war collectivism, and were seemingly disinclined to watch their own subjugation. Direct industrial action was the most vivid expression of this burgeoning politicization.

Strikomania

In Britain after the war, class tensions soared and strikes doubled compared to 1912, the prewar year with the largest outburst of strikes. The peak of this trend was 1919, in which almost 35 million working days were lost to strike action—six times as many as the previous year—and an average of 100,000 workers were on strike every day.[9] Not just coal miners, railway men, transport workers, and dockers, but also police officers, soldiers, ex-servicemen, journalists, painters, teachers, farm workers, cotton spinners, and many other groups of workers took to the streets against their employers or the state.

Flipping through the pages of the *Daily Herald* of the years 1919–1920, one encounters countless reports of direct action undertaken by the country's workers, giving substance to the idea that "[n]o one can doubt the existence in the United Kingdom at the present time of the most widespread and deep-seated unrest that has ever been known in this country."[10]

In July 1919 alone, coal miners were striking throughout the country, bakers were preparing a national strike against night labor, and police officers were about to take to the streets. The latter fought to obtain unionization, identifying themselves strongly as workers and spreading political insecurity: the forces of law and order were not going to support the government.[11] The Liverpool police strike of August 1919 found solidarity among workers of other industries, leading to heavy rioting and the intervention of troops.[12] In the meantime, carpenters, tailors, chefs, steel workers, soldiers, and builders were fighting to gain control over the conditions of their labor, or at least to improve them.

The "strikomania" [*scioperomania*], as it was branded, did not spare Italy. In 1919, the number of recorded strikes in Italy had more than doubled relative to the prewar years, and as in Britain, had increased more than sixfold during the transition from war to peacetime. In 1919 the workdays lost to labor disputes in agriculture and industry topped 22 million, and in 1920 rose to almost 31 million.[13] The number of strikes kept growing in 1920, involving nearly 2,314,000 workers (1,268,000 industrial and 1,045,732 agricultural workers)—that is, around 50 percent of the labor force in the capitalist-productive sectors, including industry, construction, agriculture, mining, etcetera.[14]

Just as the reports in the *Daily Herald* provided a vivid picture of strikes across Britain, so too did the Italian *L'Avanti*, the socialist newspaper that saw its subscriptions among Italian workers and peasants boom after the war. On April 2, 1920, under the headline "The Fierce Battles of the Working Class" [*le aspre lotte della classe lavoratrice*], the paper chronicled the national strike among public employees, which lasted almost a month (see *L'Avanti*, April 28); the strike of the agricultural workers in the Padania region; the strike of the bread-makers in Brescia; the strike of the construction workers in Bergamo; the strike of the railway men in Casale Monferrato; the strike of the telegraphic workers in Milan; and the metallurgical stoppages in Turin, Florence, Pavia, etcetera. On the following day *L'Avanti* ran a headline "Daily Battles of the Working Proletariat" [*le quotidiane battaglie del proletariato lavoratore*] and reported the strike of 30,000 paper manufacturers; the strike of the stonemasons in Mantua; the strike of the gas workers in Monza; the mobilization of the farmers in Forlì; and the final accords for the increase in wages of the textile workers of Milan after a harsh stoppage of labor. During that month of April alone, Italy recorded 195 strikes, with 229,960 participants and 2,454,012 workdays lost.[15] Women participated in high numbers, even leading the charge in many sectors, including the textile industry, where the strike was among the most combative and where women strikers outnumbered men three to one (in 1919, for example, 148,832 women participated compared to 44,991 men).[16]

The news reports depicted not only workers' struggles, but their unprecedented successes: across the country, workers gained economic and representational rights.[17] By 1921, average Italian nominal daily industrial wages quintupled (around a 400 percent increase) compared to their prewar levels (Scholliers and Zamagni 1995).[18] Such gains were absolutely unheard of: during the twenty years of industrial development (1890–1910) the aggregate "natural" increase of average nominal wages had only been 53 percent. By 1920, nominal weekly wages for British manual workers had soared 178 percent with respect to their prewar levels—a high of £3.70 compared to £1.26 in 1910 (Scholliers and Zamagni 1995, table A.23, 261). To give a sense of these gains, consider that for an entire century before the war, the incremental increase of average British weekly earnings from one year to the next never exceeded more than £0.10.[19] During the red years, Italian and British workers fought for, and secured, a standardization of the eight-hour workday. *L'Avanti* hailed the event triumphantly as "a conquest without precedent . . . an unheard victory in the history of the world proletarian movement" (*L'Avanti*, February 21, 1919, 2, Milan edition).

Strikes Get Political

As worker demonstrations proliferated, their goals evolved. What began as direct actions in the expression of industrial interests became political—and on an international scale.

In both Britain and Italy, workers mobilized in solidarity with Russian and Hungarian workers to counter the anti-Soviet attacks that had been waged by international wealthy interests. The most acclaimed example in Britain was the *Jolly George* episode, where British dockers sabotaged the government's support of the Polish war against Soviet Russia by refusing to arm a supply ship:[20]

> [T]he episode of the *Jolly George*, a vessel under charter to carry arms to Poland from Harwich [Essex], acquired world-wide celebrity when the dockers successfully refused to load its cargo, and it became clear that any attempt to defeat the boycott by the use of blackleg labour would result in a widespread sympathetic strike. . . . In Russia it was even reported, and for a time believed, that the Revolution had broken out in Great Britain. There was indeed a sudden wave of feeling among the British workers, for whom the affair of the *Jolly George*, small though it

was in itself, had a symbolic significance as standing for international solidarity in support of the Russian Revolution against its capitalist-imperialist enemies. (Cole 1958, 427–28)

A month later, July 20–21, 1919, CGdL and the Italian Socialist Party organized a general strike, calling on workers across the country to march in solidarity with their struggling Russian comrades. Later, in June 1920, Italian soldiers and workers in the city of Ancona took control of the military barracks and refused to depart for Albania, which was then under Italian occupation (see *L'Avanti*, June 30, 1920). This action precipitated solidarity strikes and popular uprisings throughout Italy, where the people opposed arms production and called for repatriation of all Italian soldiers. The movement ultimately contributed to the full recognition of Albanian independence and the cessation of deployment of Italian soldiers. However, after the war, the politicization of strikes meant something more than direct confrontation with the state on foreign affairs: economic movements *themselves* had become deeply political.

What had previously registered as strictly economic demands, such as hours and wage increases, were now considered as part of more systematic demands that directly involved the state (which had become the de facto employer). The direct intervention of the state in production meant that industrial struggles against the employers immediately developed into political struggles against the state—and thus to demands that state power be used to bring social production under democratic control (Clarke 1988, 199). As James Sexton, a British dock laborer, commented: "there was considerable difficulty, if it was not almost impossible, to dissociate political and industrial questions" (Labour Party 1919, 119).

Moreover, unrest was no longer occurring primarily as an intervention for immediate economic benefits. Quite the contrary: a large motivating factor was social revolution. An official British memorandum of February 1919 stressed this shift: "The fundamental causes of labour unrest" were to be found in "the growing determination of Labour to challenge the whole existing structure of capitalist industry," and no longer only in "special and smaller grievances which come to the surface at any particular time."[21]

Workers rebuffed the core assumptions of capitalism. As the British report put it, they were "no longer prepared to acquiesce in a system in which their labour is bought and sold as a commodity in the labour market" (Cole 1920a, Appendix 1, 250), and once put to work they demanded to be treated "not as 'hands' or part of the factory equipment" but "as human beings with a right to use their abilities by hand and brain in the service not of the few but of the whole community" (ibid.).

Frank Hodges, a miners' union leader in Britain, described the movement as a secession from capitalism: "He (the worker) wants to know the social purpose of his work; in short, he wants to feel the joy that comes to a man whose whole personality is impressed on the object which he is in the process of creating, instead of being mere plastic clay in the hands of a system which turns his whole being into a marketable commodity" (Hodges 1920, 110–11).[22]

In Italy, the urge for popular self-governance spread like wildfire in the factories and in the countryside across the country. While industrial workers in northern Italy continued their call for control of the means of production, agricultural workers paralyzed production in a vast area of Piedmont and Lombardy (including Novara, Pavia, Vercelli, Voghera, Casale Monferrato, Mortara, Biella, and Alessandria) for a total of fifty days during 1920, holding constant citywide assemblies (see *L'Avanti*, April 2, 1920). These strikes erupted in March 1920 and involved more than 300,000 people. Their demands were at once economic (adoption of a global annual minimum wage, efficacious organization against unemployment) and, most importantly, political. Agricultural workers secured control of labor within the production process and official recognition of their employment bureaus (*Uffici di collocamento di classe*).[23]

Among the countless other revolutionary events in 1920, the peasant invasion in Medicina, in the Bolognese region, stands out. What began on March 22 was, by the evening of the second day, a display of peasants "reunited in a march, carrying blades, shovels, scythes, chanting the Internationale and the hymn of the workers" (Tasca 1920,

69–70), a remarkable scene of solidarity and organization. In a feature written months later to describe the events, the political leader Angelo Tasca commented that the peasants demonstrated "the most evident truth" of the working class: to take on "for itself the problem of production." Tasca detailed how the peasants of Medicina put into operation their own institutions of governance and organization, including an employment office that coordinated employment and a production cooperative that furnished machines and fertilizers. Spontaneous local "councils"—committees to discuss the technical issues of production— were common. The community organized production according to the "social necessities of nutrition," not the organizing principle of capital. Instead of harvesting industrial cannabis, they cultivated cereal, rice, and medicinal herbs. As a peasant told the reporter, "One has to produce first what is necessary to eat, then one can think of profit." The case of Medicina spearheaded a national subversion of capitalist priorities.

Overall, the "red years" of 1919–1920 saw the call for workers' control of land and industry reach its climax and become one of the most important political demands of the British and Italian postwar labor movements, taking center stage among the rank and file and even in the official policy of the main unions.[24]

What follows is an exploration of the varieties of workers' battles for the common objectives for a post-capitalist society: union campaigns, agricultural cooperatives, and building guilds.

The Miners' Struggle and the Sankey Committee

THE MINERS TAKE CHARGE

For the British mining community, World War I was a period of dramatic strengthening as an industry and dramatically increased class awareness as an employment sector. The wartime state control of coal brought a significant advance in the miners' position, including official recognition of the Miners Federation of Great Britain (MFGB). Successful national bargaining directly with the state gave basis to the miners' audacious postwar program. By the end of the war, the miners' union was powerful, nationally structured, and active in fostering solidarity among different sectors. It organized about one million men, making it by far the largest union in Great Britain. In 1919 roughly one in eight people nationwide either lived in, or came from, a mining community, where "class bitterness and class solidarity in mining villages was without parallel in the rest of British industry" (Morgan 1979, 65).

On January 31, 1919, with the industry still under de facto public management after the war, the MFGB presented its demands to the government for an increase of 30 percent in basic wages, a six-hour working day, nationalization, and joint control—and warned that unless these demands were met in full, the consequence would be a national coal strike.

Politically, circumstances favored the workers. After the war the country was experiencing a coal shortage: not only would a strike directly impede the provision of energy to households; it would also close down industries in the early stages of conversion to peacetime production and imperil the effort to recapture overseas markets (shipping vitally needed coal). Moreover, the stakes were extremely high. The political situation was unpredictable: with the industrial unrest prevailing throughout the country a miners' strike could potentially escalate into a political breakdown. For the Scottish Socialist John Maclean and other influential members of the MFGB, "a miners' strike over hours and wages might, in the context of mass mobilization, pull in millions of workers from other industries with potentially revolutionary results" (Ives 2016, 47). These were not completely unrealistic thoughts. In the early months of 1919, the forces of law and order were—in the British government's own estimation—unreliable. If upheaval occurred, the likelihood of containing it seemed low.

Cabinet evidence shows that most ministers were hostile to the miners' claims. But given the circumstances, "in much haste and alarm" (Morgan 1979, 62) the cabinet opted for a reconstructionist approach and suggested that miners' demands be investigated by an impartial government commission under the neutral chairmanship of Sir John Sankey, a judge of the high court. *The Times* detailed the tense setting from which this commission emerged, how it represented a "breathing space" that might allow the nation to avoid the perennial menace of a resurgence of strikes: "A week ago the atmosphere was highly charged, and there were all the signs of an approaching storm so devastating and so far-spreading that none of the people would escape its effects. To-day the air is clearer . . . [t]he danger of an industrial upheaval has not been removed; but . . . [t]he miners will have full scope for providing the justice and practicability of their claims at the inquiry of the Coal Industry Commission which opens to-day" ("Lull in Labour Strife," *The Times*, March 3, 1919, 11).

The miners' leaders accepted the offer, provided that the MFGB were allowed to nominate half the members of the commission (the other half representing the capitalist side).[25] They picked the three most charismatic leaders of the miners: Robert Smillie, president of the MFGB; Frank Hodges, general secretary of the MFGB; and Herbert Smith, vice president of the MFGB and president of the Yorkshire miners' federation. They also nominated three experts who embodied the reconstructionist spirit detailed in previous chapters: the economists Leo Chiozza Money and Sidney Webb, and the socialist historian Richard H. Tawney.

Although some historians' retrospective accounts (for example, Mowat 1955, 30–36; Kirby 1977, 37) have tended to view the episode of the Sankey Committee as an event that, by buying time, killed the revolutionary potential of the miners, it is certainly the case that the workers had produced a historical breakthrough. Their challenge to the pillars of capitalism entered the foyer of the capitalist fortress. The threat of direct action and its paralyzing effect sparked a political debate that shook the heart of the British establishment, intimately involving the parliament and the national press.

IN THE FOYER OF THE CAPITALIST FORTRESS

In their negotiations with the British government, the three miners' representatives, together with the three economic experts, all agreed on a basic point: free-market capitalism had to be denounced and overcome. Smillie and Hodges openly addressed it as "the old regime"

(Arnot 1919, Preface). Private initiative and private profit as the motives of production were put on trial, thoroughly examined, and publicly rebuked.[26] The fact that "the commission met in the King's Robing Room of the House of Lords made its deliberations all the more impressive" (Pelling 1987, 162).

The hearings, held under the watchful eye of national public opinion, overthrew the status of private property—and private industry—as an impenetrable domain.[27] Arthur H. Gleason, staff member of the American Bureau of Industrial Research, noted that "no such latitude of questioning has ever before been permitted in an official industrial investigation. Here you had a miner cross-examining a millionaire employer and driving him into a corner from which he did not escape" (Gleason 1920, 34).

In fact, the first session of the hearings was publicly recognized, even by the bourgeois press, as a triumph for the workers. The *Daily News* wrote: "no one who attends its proceedings can help coming away with the impression that it is the mine owners, not the miners, whose case is on trial" (cited in Gleason 1920, 48). And again, in *The Times*: "there will be no difference of opinion amongst dispassionate readers on one point, which is that of the three parties concerned the miners come out far the best. Their case was better presented, but it was also a better case than that of the Government or the mine owners" ("The Industrial Crisis," *The Times*, March 18, 1919, 11).[28]

The hearings were not simply a theater for the miners to demonstrate their leverage. Rather, the Sankey proceedings laid bare the profound failings of the prewar system of capitalist competition. Along with the dismal picture of the miners' working conditions,[29] a critique of the structural flaws of capitalism emerged. Economic inefficiency "is not to be ascribed to personal shortcomings" (Great Britain, Royal Commission on Coal Industry 1919b, 477); it instead sprang from the very functioning of market competition, which impeded rational central planning of the extraction and use of natural resources and instead systemically led individual capitalists to try to pressure labor to work more at inhumane wages and to save on infrastructure. In the case of Britain's largest industry, the effects of the invisible hand were not as optimal as Adam Smith had promised. Numerous depositions emphasized that far from being virtuous, competition for profit had not resulted in collective prosperity.[30] Rather, it had created a lack of coordination and excessive waste, combined with a structural disincentive to undertake the kind of long-term investment that was needed to increase the supply of coal and keep prices low.[31] Indeed, coal company owners could guarantee high profits through pressure on wages: "We have, in fact, as a nation, got the mine workers' labour too cheap for our economic health" (Great Britain, Royal Commission on Coal Industry 1919a, xviii).

This modest attack on the capitalist tradition—an attack that asserted a contradiction between private interests and public gains—reached economic experts at home and overseas. The 1919 article by H. D. Henderson published in the *Economic Journal* discussed the case of the Sankey Committee and concluded: "It is very doubtful whether any considerable section of the consuming public would be prepared, when it came to the point, to back their faith in private ownership at so high and so obvious a price" (Henderson 1920, 273).

The problem of competition producing inefficiency could potentially be solved by unification under private ownership. Another source of inefficiency did not admit of such an easy solution. The antagonistic relationship between capital and labor was inherent to the nature of private capitalism. The solution, as presented by Sankey, was to accept a new role for workers in the production process, one that satisfied a "higher ambition of taking their due share and interest in the direction of the industry" (Great Britain, Royal Commission on Coal Industry 1919b, vii).

NATIONALIZATION AND WORKER CONTROL

Clause IX of the Sankey Report announced seismic changes to come in British industry: "Even upon the evidence already given, the present system of ownership and working in the coal industry stands condemned, and some other system must be substituted for it, either nationalization or a method of unification by national purchase and/or by joint control" (Great Britain, Royal Commission on Coal Industry 1919a, viii).

Fearing a national miners' strike, or worse, a strike of the triple alliance (the three main unions of miners, railway men, and transport workers), on March 20, 1919, the cabinet accepted Sankey's report with its groundbreaking Clause IX. *The Times* voiced the extreme nature of the events with the headlines in capital letters: "COAL REPORT. BIG CONCESSIONS TO MINERS. EFFECTIVE VOICE IN DIRECTION. PRESENT SYSTEM CONDEMNED" ("Coal Report," *The Times*, March 21, 1919, 11). The article specified that "[t]he miners are in fact offered more than nationalization, as that term is usually interpreted. The owners are to go, as owners, and the only question is what is the best form for the new system, which will give miners a direct say in the management" ("To Strike or Not to Strike," *The Times*, March 21, 1919, 11).

A second stage of the commission's hearings ensued, this time dealing directly with nationalization and workers' control. Union leaders Smillie, Hodges, and Straker (the secretary of the Northumberland Miners), as well as Cole, who was asked to give a deposition, argued for a binding relation between workers' control and nationalization (in the form of abolition of royalties and state ownership of coal seams): "Just as national ownership is inadequate without workers' control, so workers' control is inadequate without national ownership" (Cole, in Arnot 1919, 33). Indeed, nationalization in itself did not secure the abolition of the wage system, under which "the worker sells his labour to an employer in return for a wage, and by this sale is supposed to forgo all right over the manner in which his labour is used" (ibid.). The bold demand was for economic democracy: joint control, shared between miners and the state.

Workers' control over the workplace was an emotional issue among miners' rank-and-file movements even before the war.[32] These movements grew stronger during the war, leading to considerable left-wing pressure and influence in the coal fields and even on the policy of the MFGB. What was remarkable in 1919 was how the core of this vision, stripped of its explicit revolutionary message, had found circulation within the establishment. It proposed a radically different image of industrial society through governmental reform—and it had an audience. The appeal of the argument put forward by the commissioners rested upon its reconstructionist tone, which turned workers' control into an issue of national rather than class interest.[33]

Sankey's final report was accepted by the six workers' representatives (thereby becoming virtually a majority report). It combined with the Bill of the Miners' Federation[34] to emerge as concrete blueprints for the democratic management of the coal industry. The two reports envisaged the avoidance of hierarchical bureaucratic administration and the effective participation of workers in production through councils—electoral bodies with substantial worker representation.[35] A three-tier scheme was formalized: Pit Councils, District Councils, and the National Mining Council. While the latter had the chief coordinating role, the other local councils held a large degree of productive and financial autonomy.[36]

THE RISE AND DEFEAT OF THE COAL MINERS

The reports of the Sankey Commission were released in June 1919, to wide attention in the national and international press.[37] In his article Henderson echoed the potential of these epochal events: "There is no real guidance to be obtained from the experience of past or contemporary institutions" (Henderson 1919, 269); thus, the new political experiment offered "an objective and rallying-point to those who are seeking to transform the whole structure of society" (ibid., 276).

According to Vernon Hartshorn, a leader among Welsh miners who had given witness during the Sankey proceedings, the miners had unearthed a constitutional mechanism by which structural change could take place in Great Britain. Commenting on the proposals of the second report, Hartshorn wrote: "They go to the very roots of the capitalist system. The recommendations comply with all the forms of constitutional procedure, though they foreshadow change which is truly revolutionary" (*South Wales News*, June 30, 1919, reprinted in Ives 2016, 208).

Indeed, workers knew that coal's "foremost position in the industrial hierarchy" made it a vanguard case to accomplish a full-blown system of workers' control (Hodges 1920, 114). The *Daily Herald* frequently re-iterated the point: "the whole labour movement looks at the miners to hew out of the capitalist system a platform from which it can make a great leap forward" (*Daily Herald*, March 22, 1919).

The rising threat to capitalism was recognized also by the coal mine owners, who repeatedly warned from the witness box that as they went, so went Britain: "nationalization of mines must be followed by nation-alization of all industries . . . retracting our steps [across industries] would end in national disaster" (Great Britain, Royal Commission on Coal Industry 1919b, 1054). In a hustle, the federation of the coal own-ers, MAGB (Miners Association of Great Britain), together with the national association of the chamber of commerce, coordinated a wide-spread anti-nationalization campaign to win a battle that, if lost, would mean "England will change hands" (Ives 2016, 226). Indeed, the battle had to be *fought*: the controversy over the nationalization of the mines dominated British politics throughout the summer of 1919.

However, in August, after months of procrastination and political uncertainty, the government officially rejected Sankey's final majority report (which had won the support of seven out of thirteen commis-sioners). Pressures from economic experts at the Treasury to abandon state control of industry in order to safeguard public finances had a de-cisive weight in the rejection. Starting in July, the government sought to exploit the fear of poor fiscal balances "to paint the miners' demands as excessive and damaging" (Ives 2016, 232) to the national coffers. These rationales were the early antecedents of formal austerity; the refrains were picking up steam.

By that time, workers found little hope in fighting back. In March 1920 the end of the economic boom sounded a death knell for the min-ers' political power. Indeed, as Cole recalls, priorities changed: "Trade Unions were more concerned with looking to their own defenses, in-dustry by industry, in face of the threatened depression than with sup-porting the miners or any other section in essentially socialistic de-mands" (Cole 1958, 419).

This economic depression was not a "natural disaster," but rather the outcome of a well-thought-out policy of the Treasury and the Bank of

England that operated to drastically deflate the economy by increasing the interest rate and curtailing credit. Monetary austerity inflicted heavy damage on British trade, especially coal exports: sterling rose against other currencies, making British goods more expensive than those of other countries in world markets. Bad business meant a surge in unemployment, which crushed unions and especially their power to press for social change.[38]

Such an austerity policy might appear economically irrational in the sense that it damaged the economy. But it was very rational in that it guaranteed the survival of capitalism and its relations of production. G. D. H. Cole put his finger on the essence of the austerity counteroffensive, which will be explored in the coming pages: "The big working-class offensive had been successfully stalled off; and British capitalism, though threatened with economic adversity, felt itself once more safely in the saddle and well able to cope both industrially and politically with any attempt that might still be made from the Labour side to unseat it" (Cole 1958, 419). In a nutshell, the economic downturn fortified capitalism. Not only were the pillars of private property and wage relations reaffirmed—austerity also guaranteed wage repression and a resurgence of private profit.

Indeed, with the industry sliding into permanent depression in the spring of 1921, miners lost most of the material gains they had obtained during the war, along with the increase in wages once guaranteed by the Sankey outcome. The miners' strike that followed began on April 1, 1921, nominally to fight for a national wage; it represented the last heroic effort to counter declining living conditions. The strike went down in defeat, when on April 15 the leaders of the railway and transport unions decided to back away and left the miners on their own. This episode is famously known as Black Friday: the moment the British labor movement was forced onto the defensive. Later that year coal returned to inter-district competition for business, and with it the full rigors of the private system. By 1922 the miners who were still at work were earning about half of what they earned in 1919; in just two years they saw a nominal weekly wage drop of 46 percent (Scholliers and Zamagni 1995, table A.23, 261).

At that juncture, the retreat of the government from coal production meant that wage repression was no longer a matter of "political strug-gle" that involved the state as the employer. Class struggle was once more confined to the realm of economics, where the impersonal laws of supply and demand dominated. As market dependence increased, workers' agency decreased.

To conclude, the miners' movement for workers' control opted for an alliance with the state, but found in the state its ultimate defeat. As we shall explore, the Treasury and the Bank of England were capable of prompt reaction: they unleashed monetary austerity at the height of these events. At that point institutional change became impossible, caught as it was in the clasp of broader change in the name of auster-ity: the new priorities were cutting labor costs and cutting government expenses at whatever price.

Cooperatives and Guilds

Miners weren't the only workers who sought to build on the industrial reforms of World War I. Two other groups, the Italian cooperatives and the British building guilds, embodied the same aspirations of the working class. Although they shared the same goal with the miners—a system based on production for use instead of profit—cooperatives and guilds did not directly act against private capitalists. Rather, they exper-imented with a different order of society *within* the capitalist system, alongside private capitalists and with the aid of the state.

ITALIAN CO-OPS

In Castenaso, a small town of 6,000 in the Bolognese countryside, the Italian government had requisitioned the town's factory for tomato preserves to produce the iron and steel that went into ships and rail-ways during the war. Upon demobilization, the factory was sold to a group of industrialists, with one of the terms of sale specifying that the buyer would "enact the experiment of collaboration between capital and labour,"[39] otherwise ownership would go back to the state. The sale proceeded, but the terms were quickly breached; following the ensuing long workers' strike and much negotiation, the government eventually secured the termination of the industrialists' contract. In March 1920 a consortium of metallurgical workers bought the factory, granting use of it to a new type of organization embodying the spirit of a workers' cooperative.

The co-op's 300 worker-members were organized in a committee structure operating under an administrative board composed of elected co-op members. The organization's constitution included specifications for how surpluses would be reinvested, namely in the reserve fund (50 percent), social insurance and instruction (20 percent), and dividends among workers in proportion to their actual exercised labor (30 percent). A month into their experience of free management, the Castenaso co-op members wrote a manifesto for other Italian workers: "We wish and hope the story of the Castenaso workshops can serve as an example to all Italian workers—still oppressed and exploited by capitalist gluttony [*ingordigia*]—so that they can once and for all redeem themselves from the servitude of the boss to set out courageously towards a Communist Society!"[40]

Castenaso was one co-op among many. The cooperative movement exploded during the Italian "red biennium" (1919–1920). It was "a form of reaction against the abuses of capitalism" (Buffetti 1921, 360) that offered an overcoming of private capital accumulation and traditional wage relations. Workers were members of the cooperative; thus they owned their means of production and shared in their surplus.[41]

A 1921 cooperative handbook described the nature of this alternative: "Industrial-commercial business are managed by *capitalists* who aim for the greatest profit of capital invested"; on the other hand, "cooperatives are managed by people who have in production a central aim that is different from that of the capitalist—that is, workers who want to benefit the most from their labor power. . . . The net profit that in an ordinary enterprise increases the benefit of capital, in a cooperative enterprise increases the benefit of cooperators" (Buffetti 1921, 35).

These institutions flourished thanks to state support. Important in this respect is the (already mentioned) decree of September 2, 1919 (Royal Decree Law 1633, September 2, 1919, in GU 219 [September 13,

1919], 7862), which authorized prefects to requisition land and give it to peasant cooperatives for four years, or permanently. Also central for a co-op's livelihood were public works contracts (road building, schools, etc.—see Ufficio Municipale del Lavoro 1920, 7–8).

Most cooperatives, especially industrial cooperatives, were often short of their own capital, and thus relied on another outgrowth of the co-ops' relationship with the government: low-interest credit from an extended network of cooperative banks. La Banca del Lavoro e della Cooperazione, with branches in key Italian cities (Milan, Turin, Rome, Naples, Salerno, Cremona, Magenta, etc.), and L'Istituto Nazionale per il Credito e la Cooperazione in Rome were prominent facilitators. The latter was endowed with public grants to give credit to cooperatives.

In the Bergamo province in northern Italy, 8 out of the 10 production cooperatives that existed as of 1921 had been founded in the red years of 1919–1920. Likewise, in the larger region of Lombardy, 41 percent of the 87 cooperatives were born during the same period.[42] Thousands of workers, both men and women (since married women could associate completely independently from their husbands), in the most diverse sectors were co-op members: builders, masons, woodworkers, glassworkers, agricultural workers, carpenters, tailors, miners, etcetera.

By 1920, when the CGdL led some 800 of these cooperatives, there was seething unease among the country's economic establishment. Even in their gradualism, the extent and political influence of these noncapitalist organizations was a menace to the status quo. Economists like Maffeo Pantaleoni branded them "Bolshevik associations" [associazioni bolsceviche] or "red cooperatives" [cooperative rosse], organizations that were "destroying the bourgeoisie who had created all the existing enterprises" (Pantaleoni 1922, viii).

Indeed, the statutes of the cooperatives were starkly democratic. The template was the same as in Castenaso. Cooperative members could only be workers; its deliberative body was the general assembly (the ordinary meetings occurred three times a year), in which the members had the right to vote on the annual budget and the destination of the net revenue. During the assembly, co-op members elected the management board from among their number.[43]

BRITISH GUILDS

Like the Italian cooperatives, the British guilds were groups that collectivized their means of production and were organized so that production rested democratically with the workers, emphasizing local managerial and financial autonomy.[44]

However, guilds in Britain went a step further since they got rid
of not only the pillars of private property and wage relations, but also
profit as the driver of production altogether. Like the miners, the guilds
intended to enable a "new industrial system" based on a new motive,
"the motive of public service under free conditions" (Cole 1921b, 17),
deemed far superior to that of private profit. Guild Socialist leaders,
including Cole, Frank Hodges, and S. G. Hobson, envisaged a starting
point for the full-blown realization of a guild socialist society based on
a democratic economy and a new industrial system.

In Britain, furnishing guilds and tailoring guilds were formed in
Manchester, London, and other cities; there were also guilds of agricultural workers (at Welwyn, in Hertfordshire, an agricultural guild had
begun operations on a 500-acre tract of land), dock laborers, post office
workers, office clerks, musical instrument makers, and engineers; the
manufacture of packing-cases and horse-drawn vehicles too was carried out by workers organized into guilds. The most successful among
these was certainly the building guilds movement. The University of
Chicago business professor Garfield V. Cox, who detailed the experiment in the *Journal of Political Economy* in 1921, pointed out two favorable conditions that bolstered the builders.

The first had to do with the nature of the industry itself. Building
was an industry that required little fixed infrastructure (e.g., no factory or expensive machines), "so that the problem of the ownership
of the instruments of production is relatively unimportant" (Cox 1921,
788). For this reason there was not, as had been the case with the miners, a binding need for a direct political struggle over systematized
nationalization. Second, guilds were good at picking their spots: "the
guilds compete in a field in which the capitalist system, with its motive

of profit-making, has proved itself exceptionally incompetent to fill a great and widespread public need" (ibid.).

As we know from chapter 2, after the war Britain faced an acute shortage of housing; combined with strong popular pressure for change, this induced the government to adopt the ambitious Housing Acts. These initiatives divided England into eleven districts, with each local authority held responsible for investigating the housing needs of the community, raising the money to meet those needs, and accepting contracts (approved by the Ministry of Health). The government would offer subsidies.

In the throes of this expansionary policy, building guilds were able to bid on housing contracts. In September 1920, the Ministry of Health approved contracts with the Manchester and London guilds for a total of more than 800 working-class houses. By November, more than eighty local guild committees of building-trade workers had organized for work. By December, "contracts involving the erection of more than a thousand houses had been accepted and were waiting the approval of the Ministry of Health" (Cox 1921, 780).

The guild system was grounded in the spirit and principles of democracy inasmuch as it rejected the motives of capitalism: individual members were fueled by a "creative and cooperative spirit" and a belief that "if men are given good cause to work well, and a sense of freedom and service in their work, the results will be vastly different from those secured by ordinary capitalist methods" (Cole 1921a, 291). In practice, the guilds eliminated structural incentives to competition among workers, rejecting individual payment by result and differential treatment based on efficiency in favor of "a communal basis of remuneration" (Joslyn 1922, 116). Thus, wage contracts—which were based on the commodification of labor—were replaced by a system of remuneration that recognized the social value of labor "which shall more adequately meet the needs of the worker as a human being" (ibid., 97). The so-called "provisions for continuous pay" (ibid.) were the core of the building guild policies, providing for full support of the worker during bad weather, sickness, accidents, and holidays.

Although each worker had a share of one penny in the guild, they were paid no dividends. The shares were merely symbolic, as the guild had no intention of accumulating surplus value: "'profit' and 'loss' are both ideas which have no say in the Guild system" (Cole 1921a, 291). The guilds operated on a principle of cost-price service that was strictly nonprofit. Accordingly, the state and local authorities—in entering into contracts with guilds—paid the cost of material and labor at standard rates, with an additional £40 per house that would ensure the guild's ability to maintain continuous pay for its workers. If the costs turned out to be less than the estimated amount, nothing was pocketed; overages were returned to the local authorities.

The experiment of British building guilds had attracted widespread attention not only from British militants but also from foreign economic observers, to the point that the most prestigious economics journals expressed surprise at its positive results and were earnestly considering its potential as an alternative for organizing production.

For example, at the time of the guilds' first announcement of the policy of continuous pay, predictions were largely pessimistic: economists thought that malingering would be rampant, and that workers would endeavor "to make their job a convalescent home" (Joslyn 1922, 109). But statistics that were widely published and appeared in, among other places, the *Quarterly Journal of Economics* and the *Monthly Labour Review*, silenced the doubters. The days lost by the building guild workers for sickness and accident turned out to be fewer than those lost in private business, both in Britain and in other countries.[45] An analysis of comparative labor efficiency showed that even according to orthodox economic criteria, guilds performed far better than private builders, allowing the former to underbid private contractors and save local authorities money. Guilds could build houses not only of better quality, but at lower costs—and not just for public authorities, but for private clients as well. In the words of the article in the *Quarterly Journal*: "the evidence points unmistakably to the conclusion that the Guild organization of industry, with its policies of workers' control and continuous pay, has demonstrated itself superior, in respect both of quality and economy of workmanship, to private enterprise taken at its mean level" (Joslyn 1922, 127).

However, the peaceful approach of the guild socialists that sought to achieve revolution through gradual change meant that in practice guilds would have to operate and survive, at least initially, within a monetary capitalist economy. Producing in a capitalist economy meant that the building guilds had to purchase their plants, equipment, and raw materials in an inherently volatile market. As guild socialists themselves realized, "it is not easy to isolate a particular industry or a part of a particular industry and to make of it an oasis of Guild organization in the midst of a capitalistic system" (Cole 1921b, 18).

Within an economic boom and with the benefit of state support, the building guilds thrived for eighteen months. But the clouds of austerity loomed on the horizon. By July 1921, amid a rollout of monetary austerity, an economic downturn, and a mounting "economy campaign," the government decided to withdraw all state aid from local authorities, leaving them stripped of the ability to finance housing projects, even though less than one-fifth of the houses urgently required had been built.[46]

In 1922, the Geddes Axe[47]—arguably austerity's most malignant policy, detailed in chapter 6—halted the expansionary housing program, effectively beheading the building guilds and beginning their decline and eventual disappearance over the years that followed. All other guilds followed the same path, so that by 1924 there was no longer a separate and organized guild socialist movement (Ostergaard 1997, 77).

Cole commented on the encroachment of austerity:

The Building Guildsmen, who are as much interested in the provision of good houses as in the development of the new form of democratic industrial service for which they stand, have entered a vigorous protest against the British Government's breach of all pledges about "houses for heroes" which it gave lavishly during the period when it was still the fashion to speak of "reconstruction." Nowadays, the word has vanished from the language, save as an archaic survival, and the word "economy" has taken its place as the governing maxim of political wisdom. (Cole 1921a, 290)

Conclusion

Following the economic interventions of their governments during World War I, the working classes of Britain and Italy were uninterested in a smooth reintroduction of capitalism. By 1919 the old system was in full-blown crisis, and its component parts—workers, union leaders, and economic experts—were all announcing the end of the old order. Post-capitalism, whatever its form, was on its way.

What was the basis for this conviction, which was mirrored by a sense of apocalyptic panic among the bourgeois establishment? Capitalism was strongly contested at its very core.

In these pages we have shown how political imagination toward the abolition of private property and wage relations moved from abstraction to reality. In the first place, the soaring "strikomania" of the British and Italian workers was *political*: it demanded new relations of production. These demands took the form of the struggle for workers' control that peaked in 1919–1920 with the objective of self-government to secure the emancipation of the majority.

Certainly, the direct action of politicized workers was proving to be a far more serious enemy to capitalism than the reconstructionist project that the reader encountered in chapter 2. Indeed, the miners, the building guilds, and the cooperatives directly attacked production for profit, wage relations, and private ownership of the means of production. However, the struggles we have encountered here share with the reconstructionists a faith in state aid to defeat the old order through constitutional means. To complete the sketch of capitalism in crisis we must still address its gravest enemy.

Chapter 4 explores the movement for industrial councils that emerged in the Clydeside region of Britain and reached its peak in Turin, Italy. The efforts of these rank-and-file workers took on a clear-cut revolutionary form in opposition to both capital accumulation and the state—and pushed capitalism to the brink. In this space, a class of experts found their most useful tool: a new rationale for austerity, one that became the narrative of the threatened and powerful.

CHAPTER 4

The New Order

Institutions and Thought after the War

> We say that the present period is revolutionary because the working class is
> beginning to exert all its strength and will to establish its own State. That is
> why we say that the birth of the factory councils is a major historical event—
> the beginning of a new era in the history of humankind. . . .
>
> Antonio Gramsci, "The Factory Council" [Il consiglio di fabbrica] (1920d, 25)

Among the metalworker rank and file in Britain and in Italy after
World War I, self-government in the form of factory committees was
the basis for an alternative economic system—"a new order in the relations of production and distribution."[1] The system was rooted in the
elimination of private ownership of the means of production and wage
relations—the two central pillars of capital accumulation. The endgame
was a classless society in which "the proletariat dissolves as a class and
becomes humanity itself."[2]

These metalworkers shared the same objective as the miners, builders, and farmworkers: building a different society that did not content
itself with the formality of political democracy but instead grounded
itself in economic democracy. In this sense the workers regarded the
divide between the economic and the political as impossible; they
battled for "the emancipation of the Wage-Slave" (Walsh 1920, 8)
through collective action and participation in production. In short,

there could be no political emancipation without economic emancipation. In the words of the British shop steward leader J. T. Murphy, "Real democratic practice demands that every member of an organization shall participate actively in the conduct of the business of the society" (Murphy 1917, 4).[3] Hence, echoed Tom Walsh, "a new spirit is spreading . . . this spirit is not for a paltry increase of wage but for the absolute abolition of the present system of robbery, the sweeping away of Capitalism, and the Establishment of a People's Commonwealth!" (Walsh 1920, 4, capital letters in original text).

The strategies, however, differed. Whereas the miners with the Sankey Committee and the farmers and builders with their cooperatives or guilds attempted an alliance with the state to overcome the pillars of capitalism, the British and Italian councils declared war on the entire capitalist system—defining themselves in opposition to both the state and the private capitalists. Indeed, they abhorred the statism of the more docile reconstructionists, and they refuted the reconstructionist ideal of a transition from war collectivism to a socialist state, including the notion that it would serve as the path to workers' emancipation. State ownership was understood as "the final word in capitalist domination" and "pregnant with sinister dangers for the workers, who would become state serfs" (*The Socialist*, September 1916, from Hinton 1973, 47).

This radical movement was mostly led by left-wing socialists (later members of the Communist Party) who rejected any form of joint control[4] (among the workers, capitalists, and the state) and embraced the drive for total proletarian power under the strong influence of the Russian revolution. They stood for direct action, which in the Italian case meant the actual seizure of the private means of production during the hot summer of 1920, when the workers ran the factories themselves for almost a month. Starting in September, some half-million workers occupied factories throughout Italy.[5] Workers took control of the production process: not only in the industrial north, but in Veneto, Emilia, Toscana, Marche, and Umbria, all the way to Rome, Naples, and Palermo. As the historian Paolo Spriano emphasized: "wherever there was a factory, a dockyard, a steelworks, a forge, a foundry in which *metalos* worked, there was an occupation. The universal character of the phenomenon is remarkable" (Spriano 1975, 60).

The legendary Italian factory occupation of 1920, discussed in detail here, was the realization of the incessant practical and theoretical work of the *Ordinovisti*, a militant group that revolved around the weekly paper *L'Ordine nuovo* (The New Order), centered in Turin—the reddest of Italian cities—and largely inspired by the struggles of the British shop steward committees.

The movement led by factory committees constituted Italy's most explicit challenge to capitalism. By debunking bourgeois institutions, factory workers also debunked kernels of the bourgeois worldview: the belief that capitalist institutions are a fixed necessity; the belief that workers are secondary inputs in the production process; the prevalence of abstract theory over practice; and the strict division between the economic domain and the political. As the following pages will explore, the committees were a break from both the hierarchical relationships of production and the hierarchical understanding of the world. This pivot was the gravest enemy to the system, and an enemy that our economic experts with their austerity doctrine were determined to defeat. Indeed, these events are explored as detonators of the revolutionary fear that prompted the emerging austerity counteroffensive.

The War and the Seeds of the Factory Committees

During the Great War, independent (often rebellious) worker organizations surged in Britain and Italy. Their rise can be attributed to a form of combined antagonism: toward the state, toward the official trade unions, and ultimately toward war.

As chapter 1 detailed, the wartime economic interventions of the British and Italian states to guarantee a disciplined and mobile labor force removed all notions of "naturalness" on the hierarchical relations of production. In doing so, they also revealed the unbreakable coalition between state and capital: "the capitalist class [in the UK] is more than pleased with the State subjugation of Labour. . . . Capital needs State ownership" (*The Socialist*, September 1916, from Hinton 1973, 47). The Italian leaders echoed the same thoughts: wartime events only confirmed the true face of the bourgeois state as the "supreme guarantor" [*garante supremo*] of exploitation (Togliatti 1920, 249–50).

Meanwhile, unions demonstrated their complicity in these power structures and were no longer seen as reliable. They had surrendered the right to strike, postponed their demands for higher wages, and accepted restrictions on the mobility of labor. The official 1917 British *Enquiry on Industrial Unrest* documented the widespread rejection of organized labor's efficacy. The belief among workers was that "the executive officers of their unions are now powerless to assist them in their present difficulties . . . that the Government when dealing with such officials, ha[s] not been dealing with the general body of workers, of whose real opinions, the executive or London officials of the unions are now in no way representative."[6] Even Prime Minister Lloyd George's trusted advisor, Tom Jones, had to admit that "much of the present difficulty springs from the mutiny of the rank and file against the old established leaders" (Cronin 1984, 21).

The same British governmental enquiry detailed how animosity from below resulted in the formation of "a vigorous defensive organisation for the protection of the workmen inside their own separate workshops, known as the 'Shop Committee'[7] or 'Rank-and-File' movement, with shop stewards elected from the workers in every shop."[8] Against the orders of official leadership, the shop committee movement practiced two interconnected forms of direct action: strikes and workers' control.

Strikes were effective because they stimulated the construction of instruments of direct democracy: workers' committees. Workers' committees placed "the control of the product in the hands of the workers themselves" (Gallacher and Campbell 1972, 31) and allowed for the coordination of strikes, boosting the workers' power to develop more committees. Hence, workers' industrial organization was the main organ of industrial control—and potentially, of political emancipation.

Strikes and workers' committees marked the birth of a revolutionary organization, one that was painstakingly refined during the war and postwar years.[9]

In Britain this development began in Clydeside, a dense area of munitions industries in Scotland that was at the forefront of the opposition to the government's authoritarian manpower policies. In February 1915, during an unofficial strike for higher wages and shorter hours, metal workers collectively organized so as to impede the divide-and-conquer strategies of the employers, who tried to negotiate separately with different categories of workers. The first strike committees developed into a more permanent body, the Clyde worker committee, that represented all grades of workers regardless of their skill. The strikes of May 1917 were the largest of the war, involving 200,000 metalworkers for more than three weeks. W. C. Anderson, MP for Sheffield Attercliffe, reported to parliament that the unrest had insurgent connotations. 70,000 people marched through the streets of Glasgow "with bands and banners, every one of the members of the procession wearing the revolutionary colours" (see HC Deb 93, 5s, 14 May 1917, cc 1395–96; reprinted in Coates and Topham 1968, 115).

By the end of the war the movement had become a nationwide phenomenon. As the historian Branko Pribićević remarked, "[n]ever before or since has an unofficial rank-and-file movement exercised such power and influence in this country [Britain]" (Pribićević 1959, 83). This was no minor challenge to the capitalist system, given the workers' explicit political ambitions. *The Socialist* of January 1919 announced: "the striking masses have spontaneously created the workers' committees, the basis of the workers' state . . . these committees representing every department in every mine, mill, railway, or plant, contain the elements of an organization which can transform capitalism into a Soviet Republic. . . . All Power to the workers' committees" (*The Socialist*, January 30, 1919, reprinted in Hinton 1973, 302). That same year, the Italian worker Mario Montagna expressed similar optimism for his own country: "we believe that the construction of the workshop councils (*consigli di officina*) represents the first concrete affirmation of the communist revolution in Italy and that these councils of peasants and workers are the basis for the whole future system" (Montagna 1919, 202–3).

The young Italian political leader Antonio Gramsci[10] had been closely monitoring the British shop stewards during their war struggles, with a special interest in their autonomy, militancy, and conflictual relationship with the traditional trade unions. Excused from war deployment due to bad health, Gramsci undertook a crucial political apprenticeship as head of the local section of the Socialist Party. For Gramsci this proved to be a formative period; his work thereafter reflected a revolutionary spirit synonymous with the Turin proletariat.

Labor's momentum in Italy rose a few months after the Clydeside struggles, beginning with the Turin upheavals of August 1917. Turin, a northern industrial city where anti-war and anti-capitalist sentiments had escalated during the war, became the epicenter of the rank-and-file offensive.[11] For five days, thousands of workers, including a massive female contingent, protested the widespread economic hardship by walking out of their factories, staging a general strike, looting shops, occupying entire quarters of the city, and building trenches and barricades against the troops and the police. The episode, led by the factory committees of the metalworkers, took the "character of armed revolutionary struggle, on a large scale."[12]

The dual strategy of strike action and workers' committee organizations—the same two-pronged approach pioneered by the British comrades—was refined in Italy during the postwar years. As Gramsci put it, "[t]he activity of the councils and of the internal commissions showed itself more clearly during the strikes." In fact, the councils' "technical organization" and their capacity for action was so well developed that strikes lost "their impulsive, chancy nature" and it was possible "to obtain in five minutes the suspension of work by sixteen thousand workers in forty-two sections of Fiat" (Gramsci 1921).

Indeed, by 1919 the factory workers' committees had vastly extended their level of inclusivity, competence, and influence so as to develop into a qualitatively different form of themselves.[13] They were now being addressed as councils. The Italian workers' representatives could now be elected from among all the rank and file; they did not have to be union members to move into leadership. Most importantly, the functions of workers' councils transcended economics to become political. A group of workers based at the Fiat Centro factory well summarized their tasks: there were immediate "economic" ones—including "the defense of the interest of the working class against their bosses, to promote the associative spirit between all those who endure exploitation"—and more importantly, the long-term political objective "to prepare for a new society."[14]

It was the Turin metallurgical workshop Brevetti-Fiat—the largest in Italy—that first affirmed the formal recognition by their employer of a council of factory commissars in September 1919. The episode, Gramsci recalled, "filled the souls of our worker comrades with enthusiasm and active fervor" ("Chronicles of the New Order" [Cronache dell'Ordine Nuovo], L'Ordine nuovo 1, no. 18 [September 13, 1919]: 135) and was quickly replicated throughout the city, producing over 50,000 commissars and becoming a truly mass phenomenon.[15] The tide of the council movement reached beyond the pioneering metallurgical industry, into wood, chemical, and shoe factories. Gramsci quoted a worker from the Brevetti factory who enthused about how, with their new institutions of self-government, workers had begun "the march 'within' the Revolution and no longer 'towards' the revolution" to reach "the greatest end; the liberation of labor from the slavery of capital."[16]

L'Ordine nuovo and the Exchange of Ideas

Also in 1919, A. Hamon, a British correspondent for the Italian paper L'Ordine nuovo, wrote of the developments in Britain: "The masses are pushing for radical changes and the councils are meeting these demands." He detailed the diffusion of the British movement beyond the metallurgical industries, concluding his article with an optimistic note: "this organization has now reached a level of development that allows us to foresee that it will extend to all the British proletariat" (Hamon 1919, 145).[17]

The relevance of British labor developments to Italian audiences was neither passing nor accidental. Palmiro Togliatti, one of the founders of L'Ordine nuovo, explained the necessity of international correspondence: "if we bring and continue to bring foreign examples, this helps to demonstrate that the class-war follows everywhere a similar rhythm and the same problems are posed in all countries . . . as we speak of what the British do, the British comrades, as we have the proof, are interested in our doings" (Togliatti 1919b, 190).

If the most impressive of the Italian "doings" was the articulate leadership of the council movement, then this "collective and absolutely new experiment" was catalyzed by the deep-seated commitment of the militants in the orbit of *L'Ordine nuovo* ("The New Order"). The weekly paper, founded and led by four young Marxists—Gramsci (28 years of age), secretary of the editorial staff and director; Palmiro Togliatti (24 years of age); Angelo Tasca (28 years of age); and Umberto Terracini (24 years of age)—began as an independent cultural-political experiment in May 1919: "a lively and fecund exercise (training ground) of discussion on the fundamental motives of a communist society and its practical organization."[18]

The journal was a crucible of thoughts that spanned from workers to socialist leaders and intellectuals. It documented and discussed the revolutionary movements and theories that were sweeping across Europe. It was the main sounding board of the program of the Third International and its leaders, presenting articles from the likes of the Russians Vladimir Lenin, Nikolai Bukharin, Grigory Zinoviev, and Leon Trotsky; the Hungarians Béla Kun and György Lukács; the Polish Rosa Luxemburg, active in Berlin; and Sylvia Pankhurst of England—all of whom widely reported on the British shop steward movement.[19]

The unique contribution of the community's *Ordinovista* movement was a formidable methodological breakthrough, or better, a new approach to knowledge that embodied the most groundbreaking consequences of the process of the politicization of economics. This methodological innovation grounded the movement's revolutionary charge and was most devastating to the capitalist order. Indeed, the "new order" of human liberation envisaged an emancipatory approach to knowledge.

The *Ordinovisti* stood fast on the idea that any approach to knowledge was inherently, deeply political, since the lens through which one looks at the world may foreclose or open spaces for imagination and thus establish if and what alternatives—both conceptual and practical—are viable. While the predominant lens to interpret the world foreclosed imagination and nurtured acceptance of the capitalist order, the emancipatory lens opened up possibilities to envisage a different society. This was political.

There were four main features—still timely today—that define the methodological breakthrough of the *Ordinovisti*, especially Gramsci and Togliatti. Their emancipatory approach rejected all forms of orthodoxies—both liberal and socialist—and especially negated the epistemic stances of traditional economic science. To these writers, all forms of capitalist ideologies—even those embodied in reformism—fall. What follows are their four key and intertwined principles.

THE FOUNDATIONS FOR AN EMANCIPATORY FORM OF KNOWLEDGE

Against the Naturalization of the Capitalist Order

> Economics is not a science of economic reality "as it is" but is a science of reality as "men want to build it." . . . Economics is not a science if it is not a practice, a will, a force that realizes itself.
>
> Antonio Gramsci, "Socialism and Economics" (1920e, 265)

Togliatti and his comrades labeled the discipline of economics "the dismal science of economic facts"[20] because, dating back to the likes of Ricardo and Malthus, it affirmed fixed "economic necessities"—natural economic laws that are separate from us and are to be passively accepted. In this telling, capitalism is inevitable and human agency is not guaranteed. And by internalizing the notion of the inevitability of our socioeconomic structure, we come to feel powerless to bring about any historical initiative. This sense of powerlessness reinforces the idea that our capitalist society is fixed and functions independent of us.

This far-reaching ideological trap also transcends political affiliation. In *L'Ordine nuovo*, Gramsci observed: "The socialists have accepted, often supinely, the historical reality that is a product of the capitalist initiative. They have fallen into the mistaken way of thinking that also affects Liberal economists: a belief in the perpetuity of the institutions of the democratic State, in their fundamental perfection. In their view, the form of democratic institutions can be corrected, touched up here and there, but, fundamentally, it must be respected" (Gramsci 1919d, 64).

The *Ordinovisti* challenged this "narrow vainglorious psychology" [*psicologia angustamente vanitosa*] (ibid.) in the hopes of uprooting capitalist omniscience. No institution, they argued—and especially no economic institution—is *natural*; rather, such institutions are the product of specific *historical* social relations of production. As Gramsci put it: "No institution is definite or absolute. History is a perpetual becoming" (Gramsci 1919e, 117).

In the view of Gramsci and his cohort, economic conventions such as private property were not *fixed* and *indisputable* givens, but rather the embodiment of *collective actions* that constitute a historically specific economic system—i.e., capitalism. In its simplicity this intuition actually carries radical political significance: it allows us to realize that strong and conscious class struggle may completely overthrow the current order and reinvent a new social world.

Togliatti wrote that workers "put a limit to the absolute freedom of the boss"; they subverted "the 'natural' conditions of the market"; and thus, their labor power ceased "to be a commodity that is subject to the iron 'laws' of supply and demand." In other words, "men have rebelled against economics: [now] their conscience and wills count more than the 'scientific laws' of economics" (Togliatti 1919a, 72).

Workers' councils after World War I impeded the "natural" price-setting of labor as well as the "natural" laying-off of workers by employers. These were only the first steps toward a radical reconfiguration of economic relations whereby the workers could gain full sovereignty of their production process—elevating their status from wage workers to self-governing producers.

In the local nomenclature, the revolutionary process was an "act of liberation" [*l'atto di liberazione*][21] that substantiated the passage from "oppression" [*oppressione*] to "freedom" [*liberazione*]. Indeed, this freedom was in the first place a freedom from *market dependence*, the most basic form of economic coercion that to this day dictates our lives:

under capitalism the majority of us have no other option than to sell our labor power on the market in exchange for a wage in order to get money to buy what we need to make a living.

These thoughts lead immediately to the second crucial methodological breakthrough: the recognition of the central economic and political agency of the working classes, who finally realize that they are the agents of history; it is the workers themselves who are "revolutionary in a positive sense" [*rivoluzionari in modo positivo*] (Togliatti 1919c, 196).

For Workers' Agency

> Make, work, find yourself—we say to the workers. The things written in the journal, re-think them through, see them with your own eyes . . . only that which is conquered by oneself has value and this is true especially for the social battles and for intellectual life.
>
> "Chronicles of the New Order" [Cronache dell' ordine nuovo], *L'Ordine nuovo* 1, no. 10 (July 19, 1919): 71

As workers came into a new status as protagonists of a political process advancing toward a new economic system, bourgeois economists categorically denied this agency (and continue to do so today). Indeed, mainstream economists portray workers as substitutable cogs in the economic machine—in essence, inputs in the production machine. Workers' only constructive action is their choice of moving from one wage job to another.

Once again, after World War I the *Ordinovisti* shook these *bien pensants* in their primary assumptions: "those who speak of fallacious illusions necessarily imply that the working class always has to bend its neck in front of the capitalists, [they] imply . . . that the working class has to persuade itself of being incapable of having its own conception to counterpose to that of the bourgeois, of having ideas, sentiments, aspirations, and interests that are contradictory to the ideas, sentiments, aspirations, and interests of the bourgeois class" (Gramsci 1920f, 2). On the contrary, workers *were* the revolutionaries whereby "being revolutionary means working effectively toward transforming the whole productive order" (Togliatti 1919a, 72).

For workers in capitalist settings, a sense of being superfluous—or being perfectly exchangeable with one another, and thus feeling powerless against the forces of capitalist competition—might sound familiar. Even today the orthodox models of economics support this perception of powerlessness. The assumption is that the employer and employee engage in individual contracts—where the latter is thus interchangeable with another equally skilled employee.[22] By limiting the liberty of individuals, capitalism suffocates the collective.

By contrast, the *Ordinovista* movement stressed that the employees' power came not as individuals but as a group. It is only as a member of a class, as a *producer*, that the worker can perceive the absolute indispensability and centrality of labor in the production process and in the construction of a post-capitalist society—a society where the majority is freed from wage labor and elevated to the position of self-governing producers. The inclusive organization of the factory councils—which superseded all labor divisions of traditional trade unions and united skilled and unskilled workers—concretized this principle of collective agency. As Togliatti put it, "the title required for entering the new system, that is the embryonal form of a new society, is only one: be a worker, a cell of the productive organism" (Togliatti 1919c, 196).[23] This is why the factory councils were primarily and directly "an emanation, an expression of the will of the workers" (Togliatti 1919b, 190).

A third (and arguably the most jarring) principle accompanied these declarations of proletarian agency: its assertion repudiated intellectualism and the technocratic approach to knowledge that is typical of bourgeois economists.[24]

Praxis

> The concrete task of building the future cannot be undertaken without a collective, collaborative effort of explanation, persuasion, and mutual education.
>
> Antonio Gramsci, with Palmiro Togliatti, "Workers' Democracy" [Democrazia operaia] (1919, 47)

Of course, ideas and concepts cannot be imposed from above; humans rarely act out blueprints. The *Ordinovisti* reconcile the dichotomy between theory and practice with the concept of *praxis*—the idea that theory and practice reciprocally inform and strengthen each other and can reinforce the transformative dynamics already underway. *Action is thought, and thought is action.*

Nothing could better embody this epistemic turning point than the praxis of the *Ordinovista* movement: study groups, assemblies, collaborative discussion, and "mutual education" among workers and intellectuals were the order of the day. In Gramsci's words, "the articles of *L'Ordine nuovo* were almost like a 'recording' of real events, seen as moments in a process of inner liberation and self-expression on the part of the working class."[25] The journal never endorsed "a cold application of an intellectual scheme" [*fredde architetture intellettuali*]; rather, it "satisfied a need, it favored the concretization of an inspiration that was latent in the workers." Gramsci continued, "we understood each other so easily for this reason, so certainly we could pass from discussion to action."[26]

L'Ordine nuovo was a collective effort composed of public intellectuals, rank and file, white-collar workers, and university students, all of whom supplemented their day-to-day practices with concepts that could better clarify and invigorate their mission. Forming knowledge was itself a political act. In the words of the journal, "[a]n economic and political problem is not concrete in itself, but rather because it is thought and rethought concretely by those who have the duty to transform it into historical reality."[27]

L'Ordine nuovo movement was a full-blown experimental trial of Marx's *Second Thesis on Feuerbach*: "Philosophers have only interpreted the world; now it is the time to change it."[28] Thus the practical experience of organizing within factory councils was understood as the people's "new school":[29] "The rallies [*comizi*], the discussion for the preparation of the councils, have benefited the education of the working classes much more than the ten years of studies of the pamphlets and articles written by the possessors of 'the devil in the lamppost'" [*diavolo nell'ampolla*].[30]

The factory councils were the living expression of praxis; their regulations guaranteed a melding of theory and practice that was in concept essential for self-government. Part of this was the formation of a school for the workers, which manifested in November 1919 in Turin with a school open to all and focused on the theories and histories of capitalism and socialism.[31] Moreover, within the factories themselves, executive committees were dedicated "to assur[ing] the free circulation of newspapers within the workshop during the hours of break from work" and "publish[ing] a fortnightly factory bulletin with the objective of collecting statistics apt to deepen workers' knowledge of factory life, explain the work done by the EC and the factory council, collect from the newspapers news regarding the factory, etcetera."[32] At Fiat Centro, the executive factory committee negotiated with administration to organize a workshop library "rich in books on industry, on history, and on political economy" ("The Opinion of the Executive Committee on the Workshop Councils," [*Il parere del C. E. sui consigli d'officina*], *L'Ordine nuovo* 1, no. 42 [March 27, 1920]: 335).

These projects, revolutionary in their motives, constituted a further escalation against the most fatal of bourgeois ideologies—one which economists were the first to uphold in their theories: the separation between politics and economics.

Against the Political and Economic Divide

> The communist revolution puts into practice the autonomy of the producer in the economic and the political field . . . for political action to be successful it needs to coincide with the economic action.
>
> "The Instrument of Labor" [Lo strumento di lavoro] (*L'Ordine nuovo* 1, no. 37 [February 14, 1920]: 289)

The Italian philosopher and academic Zino Zini gave the inaugural lecture of the newly founded Turin school of socialist culture, a speech titled "From Citizen to Producer" [*Da cittadino a produttore*], in February 1920. He argued that the citizen, as typically understood in bourgeois democracy, is an abstract individual, one who is "[s]overeign in theory, [when] in fact he is only such on the day of elections, all the rest of his time he is nothing but a subordinate to laws and rules drafted outside of his contribution."[33] An individual's political servitude is founded upon economic servitude [*servitu' economica*]. The inequality of economic conditions (or better, the inequality of the positions within the relations of production) impedes any genuinely democratic relations among free and equal human beings. On the other hand, Zini wrote, the post-capitalist society will give rise to "a new man" [*un uomo nuovo*]—the "conscious producer" [*produttore cosciente*]—who exercises at once economic and political freedom. It will be "the new society of free and equal producers" [*la nuova società di produttori liberi ed eguali*] (Zini 1920 301–2).

Zini critiqued the abstract, indirect concept of political freedom: in short, he said that political freedom is impossible in the presence of "economic unfreedom," the state of market dependence in which the majority of people are forced to sell their labor power in order to survive. The theories from bourgeois economists often concealed such forms of economic coercion, but these were nonetheless felt by workers: "Today all men, if they want to live, if they don't want to die of hunger and of cold, are obliged . . . to position themselves in the capitalist hierarchy . . . the number of those who no longer feel able to adapt to the existing social form becomes ever larger" (Togliatti 1920, 249).

The factory council, as "an absolutely original institution" of the proletariat, was a strategic vehicle for toppling the pillars of capital accumulation. It was also a venue in which workers could concretely experience political-economic unity: "born from labor, [the council] adheres to the process of industrial production . . . within it economics and politics merge, in it the exercise of sovereignty is all one with the act of production . . . in it the proletarian democracy is realized" (Gramsci 1919b, 117). Indeed, within the councils, the organization of the production process was deeply political. Thus, in their proceedings, councils put into practice the core of an alternative society, one in which "the mendacious bourgeois democracy" [*menzognera democrazia borghese*] and its expression in "parliamentarism" was suppressed in favor of an anti-authoritarian "self-government of the people" embodied in the "proletarian state"—an institution that would no longer be alienated from the people but rather be part and parcel of their daily activities.[34]

In Togliatti's telling, the new social order "traces politics back to the economic, that is, to the collective productive activity of each man, and in doing so, traces back sovereignty to its true and prime source, to individual consciousness" (ibid., 71). Self-government, not to mention the reunification of the political and the economic realms of life and thought, was no small task.[35]

The spirit of the movement also placed imperatives and pressures on how the workers' councils were structured, and in particular a focus on ensuring that the organizations were both horizontal and fully representative—a structure that assured direct accountability from the base. Debates flourished on the pages of *L'Ordine nuovo*, in assemblies, and in other proletarian venues.[36] (These mirrored preoccupations in Britain, where between 1917 and 1921 the main leaders of the shop-steward movement produced more than seven alternative democratic schemes,[37] often discussed in their main newspapers—*Solidarity* and *The Worker*.)

In Italy, the turnover of factory commissars every six months—and their "obligation to announce frequent referenda in their departments on social and technical questions and hold frequent assemblies"[38]—institutionalized the urge to keep the decision-making power with the workers themselves. Moreover, in both countries, the council organizers sought to guarantee horizontal representation outside the single workshop through a form of federalism: "central bodies would emerge in every department, for every factory, for every city, for every region up to the supreme national council [of the worker and peasant delegates]."[39] The British workers' organizations consisted of four main levels: workshop committees, plant committees, local workers committees, and the national organization.[40] Meanwhile the Italian councils strived for a stable national network, including an alliance between the city and the countryside—a central element for revolution, as the Russian experience had laid bare. The council aspired to channel the spontaneous fervor for land occupation (discussed in the previous chapter) into structured institutions.[41]

In sum, there were four intellectual threads that informed and motivated the factory councils' subversion of the bourgeois approach to knowledge in interwar Italy and Britain: the denaturalization of capitalism; the centrality of workers' agency; praxis; and the unity of economics and politics. This methodological breakthrough was a powerful element of the period's crisis of capitalism; indeed, it represented a counter-hegemonic alternative to conceiving the social world. No longer did knowledge trickle down from above to bolster passive consent for the current system. Now knowledge empowered action from below. That the four methodological attributes found a concrete institutional realization in the factory councils amplified the threat to the capitalist social order.

The tides of change were lashing at the shores of capitalism, at once in the form of a methodological revolution and a political revolution. Workers' organizations expressed this twofold approach, embodying the alternative foundations for new social relations of production. These new institutions would upend, however fleetingly, the very concept of wage-work and private capital. The move to seize the means of production exacerbated the fears of the old order. To this day it represents a unique episode in the history of Western capitalism.

The Factory Occupation

> Today, with the workers' occupation. . . . Every factory has become an illegal state, a proletarian republic living from day to day, awaiting the outcome of events . . . the political capacity, the initiative, the revolutionary creativity of the working class are now being put to the test.
>
> Gramsci, "Red Sunday" (*L'Avanti*, Piedmont Edition September 5, 1920)

By the fall of 1919 the popularity of the movement among the Italian rank and file and the labor leaders was at its peak: "The propaganda for the factory councils was greeted with enthusiasm by the masses," Gramsci reported. "In the course of half a year, factory councils were established in all the engineering factories and workshops, communists won a majority in the engineering union; the principle of the factory council and of control of production was approved and accepted by the majority of Congress [FIOM] and by the major part of the unions belonging to the Camera del Lavoro."[42]

As the political ferment of the council's movement grew, so too did the concerns of industrialists, who were quick to launch a frontal attack against the councils. In March 1920, the industrialists Gino Olivetti, president of the Italian Employers' Federation, *Confindustria* (The

General Confederation of Italian Industry), and Giovanni Agnelli, the owner of Fiat, met with the Turin prefect, announcing their intention of initiating a lockout. As Olivetti stated, "two powers could not coexist" in the workshop, especially when one of them "was a cell [*cellula*] of communist society."[43]

The struggle between the metallurgical industrialists and the workers erupted a month later, in April 1920, when industrialists attempted to curtail the rights of the workers' councils. The metallurgical workers responded with a strike that lasted a month, with more than 200,000 rank-and-file workers confronting the armed forces. In the last ten days it grew into a general strike that spread throughout the Piedmont region and beyond, mobilizing around half a million industrial and agricultural workers. On April 18, the Milan edition of *L'Avanti* reported, "the fire of Turin, first extended to the province of Alessandria, includes all of our province . . . we can say that almost all northern Italy is on its feet against the right and the arrogance of the bosses" (*L'Avanti*, Sunday, April 18, 1920, 2).

What was at stake was the existence and the legitimacy of the factory councils, the future of workers' control of production, and in general, capitalism. After much bloodshed, the strike ended with an agreement that recognized internal commissions—but also grossly limited the powers of the commissars. The unyielding reaction from the Turin workers was expressed in the last bulletin of the strike committee: "the battle is over, the war continues" (Spriano 1971, 100). *L'Avanti* commented, "the Torinese proletariat has been locally defeated, but it has won nationally as its battle has become that of the national proletariat. The Italian revolution finally has a concrete plan, a real objective to achieve: the control of production and exchange."[44] Indeed, this was only the beginning of the struggle.[45]

In the summer that followed, amid a bitter four-month-long negotiation of a labor contract between FIOM and the metallurgical industrialists, the metalworkers' union called for "a white strike"—a slowdown of work to the bare minimum levels, an obstructionist gesture in the eyes of the factory owners.[46] The industrialists were quick to respond with lockouts, beginning first in the Romeo factory of Milan. The Milan chapter of FIOM countered with the launch of a factory-occupation movement that spread like wildfire. On August 31, 1920, workers took over 280 factories in Milan, and within two days the movement extended in a capillary fashion across the entire peninsula. About half a million workers in at least sixty cities took over factories, blast furnaces, mines, shipyards, railways, dockyards, and non-metallurgical plants. By the second half of September, shoe, rubber, chemical, and textile factories had also joined (see Ministero dell'Economia Nazionale 1924, 174–97). Gramsci wrote in *L'Avanti*, "[t]he social hierarchies are broken, historic values overthrown. The *executive* classes, the *instrumental* classes, have become *directive* classes" (*L'Avanti*, Piedmont edition [September 1920]; reprinted in Spriano 1975, 66).

In Turin, Milan, and Genoa, the occupation grew into a mass popular movement. It by turns captured, riveted, and alarmed the Italian public. It bubbled with novelty. Neither FIOM nor the industrialists had in any way intended or accounted for their industrial confrontation to spiral into an unexpected revolutionary experiment: the enthusiasm of the rank and file was about to produce something unimaginable.

Il corriere della sera, a mainstream Italian newspaper, vividly captured the improvised and vibrant beginnings of the Milanese occupation: "the factories yesterday evening presented a singular spectacle. One reached them through crowds of women and children, coming and going with dinners for strikers, voluntary prisoners of the factories . . . entrances were strictly guarded by groups of workers. Not the ghost of an official or a police officer in sight. The strikers were complete masters of the field. Whoever passed, in car or cab, was subjected to control as if he were crossing the frontier, control exercised by vigilance squads of workers and their enthusiastic companions" (*Il corriere della sera* [August 31, 1920]; reprinted in Spriano 1975, 54).

Occupations proceeded in a relatively peaceful manner. The workers' anthem was sung, and red flags were erected to the factory fences and chimneys. Battista Santhià, a worker on strike in Turin, described the experience: "In those days it really seemed like the future of the working class was in our hands. The master was overthrown from the factory which was directly managed by the workers."[47]

In one photograph in the *Socialist Almanac* of 1921, workers sit at a table in a canteen. The photo is captioned "Communist kitchen during the occupation" (Spriano 1975, 21). In other photos, occupiers are armed with clubs and rifles, giving the clenched-fist salute. The most symbolic: a group of workers of the factory council sit at the desk of Agnelli, the owner of the greatest automobile factory in Italy. The hundreds of thousands that worked, slept, and kept watch in the factories were living the revolution in progress.

Factory councils took on the direct control of production in its entirety; they had no other choice after higher-ranking technicians and engineers left their posts on industrialists' orders. The *Ordinovisti* actively participated in the occupations, broadcasting the work of the councils in the improvised coordination of production, exchange, sale of products, and the assistance and defense of the factories. In Turin, by the second week of occupation, most of the working classes across all industries were involved. Not only the small, medium, and large metal firms (cars, coaches, foundries, service factories, railway material, marine engines, machine tools, typewriters, etc.), but also rubber firms, footwear plants, textiles, and silk industries were occupied, extending from the city to the province. In Milan too, the novelty of the second week of occupation spread to the non-metallurgical establishments, especially the chemical industries, which controlled the supply of raw materials (see *L'Avanti*, September 11, 1920).

Production continued at its normal pace (still under obstructionist orders from the unions), even with financial and technical restraints, with workers without wages,[48] and with difficulties in securing supplies of materials. Here the workers' cause was aided by the solidarity of the railwaymen, who regularly supplied truckloads of raw materials and fuel to the occupied plants. The council likewise organized exchanges of raw materials among different factories (*L'Avanti*, September 10, 1920).

The struggle was meant as a demonstration—and glorification—of industrial production in the absence of hierarchies and in the hands of the workers' councils. In the words of Antonio Oberti, a worker at the Ansaldo Factory in Turin, "we had to demonstrate to industrialists that also without them, and notwithstanding all the difficulties, we could produce the same and at maximum capacity."[49] Another worker, Piera Stangalini, an apprentice in the Rotondi factory in the city of Novara, recalled, "[o]ne worked with alacrity since we were all euphoric for being there and it was a great party because on the flagpole of the factory we hoisted the red flag and that was all euphoric because I saw that red flag flapping and I was thrilled. I was happy."[50]

The conciliatory sentiments of the establishment that followed reveal the power gained by the workers. First, the head of the government, Giovanni Giolitti, categorically refused to intervene due to the inordinate martial effort that the task would entail. Giolitti told parliament, "How could I stop the occupation? It is a question of 600 factories in the metallurgical industries. To prevent the occupation, I would have had to put a garrison in each of them, a hundred men in the small, several thousand in the large. To occupy the factories I would have had to use all the forces at my disposal! And who would exercise surveillance over the 500,000 workers outside the factory? Who would guard the security of the country?" (Acts of Parliament, session of September 26, 1920, ACS, Legislaturua 22, 1st session, 1711–12). The heads of the *Banca Commerciale* likewise assured FIOM of their benevolent neutrality, while requesting assurances in case the movement should have a revolutionary outcome. Benito Mussolini himself—the leader of the newly founded Fascist movement—took political precautions by declaring sympathy for the occupations (Tasca 1965, 127).

The revolutionary tension reached its peak on September 6 and 7, when the movement expanded beyond factories to include land occupations in the agricultural southern provinces.[51] Although there was no explicit coordination, the Socialist Party launched a concurrent manifesto aimed at peasants and soldiers across all editions of *L'Avanti*: "If tomorrow the hour of decisive struggle strikes, you, too, must rally in the battle against all the bosses, all the exploiters! Take over the communes, the lands, disarm the *carabinieri*, form your battalions in unity with the workers, march on the great cities, take your stand with people in arms against the hireling thugs of the bourgeoisie! For who knows, the day of justice and liberty is perhaps in hand" (*L'Avanti*, September 6, 1920; in Spriano 1975, 75).

In the northern city of Brescia, one inspector warned state officials that arms and bombs were being manufactured in the occupied factories (telegram, September 8, 1920, in Spriano 1975, 78). The minister of interior, Enrico Corradini, likewise reported to Giolitti: "It seems the occupiers have machine-guns. They claim to have armed a tank, [which was originally] built at Fiat for the state. If this kind of thing goes on, the crisis will become extremely grave" (ACS, Ministero degli Interni 1920, in Spriano 1975, 76). The prefect of nearby Milan, Lusignoli, made plain to Corradini that armed forces could only defend a fifth of the city in the event of escalation; Lusignoli asked the central government to send a squadron of royal guards, troops, and *carabinieri* (ACS Ministero degli Interni, Ufficion Cifra, n. 16, 325, 1920, in Spriano 1975, 179). Here it became increasingly clear to the workers that their permanent self-installment as self-governing producers rather than wage earners constituted an attack "against the real centers of the capitalist system, i.e., the means of communication, the banks, the armed forces, the state."[52] Ultimately, however, difficulties in achieving national coordination and a common direction paralyzed this moment of insurrection.

The workers' brief, heady experiment with free production eventually came to an end with an agreement between the newly founded union of industrialists (called Confindustria), FIOM, and CGdL.[53] The industrialists had capitulated, under heavy pressure from the government:[54] the owners signed a contract that a month prior they had refused to even discuss. They had to accept unions' control of industry, which they previously strongly opposed, as well as significant wage improvements, paid holidays, and compensation for workers who were dismissed.

On September 19, 1920, the government summoned the parties to Rome and mediated the final phase of negotiations. Prime Minister Giolitti, who had fully supported the CGdL's proposal for worker control, asserted that the historic moment demanded a radical transformation in the relation between capital and labor. It was no longer tolerable that in industry "one man should command, and thousands obey. We must give the workers," said Giolitti, "the right to know, to learn, to raise themselves, the right to share in the running of the firm, to assume some of the responsibility" (reprinted in Spriano 1975, 103).

The journalist Mario Missiroli described the fearful reaction in the assembly of industrialists in Milan upon hearing the announcement: "it was a thunderbolt. The assembly was struck by a kind of panic and dissolved, to reconvene some hours later in indescribable tumult, a confusion of words and ideas."[55] Several years later, union leader Bruno Buozzi commented that "the victory of the metalworkers had no parallel in the whole history of the international workers' movement" (Buozzi 1935, 82).[56]

Impressions and Reactions

Labor's victory was far from satisfying relative to the revolutionary expectations of many rank-and-file workers. The PSI and FIOM had recoiled from leading a general insurrection for the final seizure of power, amplifying their conflict with the *Ordinovisti*, who accused them of hesitation and ultimately sabotage of the popular revolutionary momentum.

While historians today read this moment as marking a crucial endpoint for the postwar revolutionary wave,[57] a more historically accurate reconstruction requires that we not lose sight of the spirit of the time. Indeed, it was part of a larger process toward drastic social change. This understanding was not limited to socialist circles. In September, once the agreement was signed, the director of *Il corriere della sera*, Senator Luigi Albertini, explicitly told then deputy of the Democratic Liberal Party Giovanni Amendola in a phone conversation that "the only thing left is to resign and give power to CGdL."[58] Albertini even visited the reformist-socialist leader Filippo Turati and told him that the time had come for the socialists to govern. Once back at his desk at Fiat, Agnelli himself formally proposed to transform his whole company into a cooperative. In an interview with *La gazzetta del popolo* he explained: "under the present system, relations between managers and workers are simply impossible. The masses today no longer have a mind to work. They are moved only by political notions. Their recent gains are nothing to them. . . . How can one build anything with the help of 25,000 enemies?"[59] A few years later, Gaetano Salvemini would remark that "[t]he bankers, the big industrialists, the big landowners, were waiting for the socialist revolution like a ram waits to be led to the slaughterhouse."[60]

From that autumn into 1921, the members of the socialist party (from the maximalists to the reformists) and the *Ordinovisti* all fundamentally understood the occupation of the factories as a dress rehearsal for revolution. *L'Avanti* of September 21, 1920, announced that "the conquest of the control of industry and the victory of the metallurgical workers cannot slow down the battle against the employers [*padronato*]." The article continued, "this agreement is not the whole way, it is but a step. The agreement does not end the class struggle . . . this first proud blow to private property calls inevitably for more. If the workers will know how to battle skilfully they will win forever."[61] The Milanese rank and file interviewed for the article shared the same revolutionary spirit.

L'Ordine nuovo was treated to the same sort of appreciation,[62] including from Cesare Seassaro, a socialist publicist and frequent contributor to the journal. He proclaimed, "[t]hese memorable days that will be written in flaming letters in the memory of the proletariat and human civilization, have been the *great maneuvers* of the proletariat army" (Seassaro 1920, 133–34). To him, the revolutionary vanguard had to cherish these past events proudly to succeed in "the future final and definitive invasion of the feuds of bourgeois tyranny." The main lessons to take from the episode were the intensification of armament and the urgent creation of a truly communist party to channel and guide the revolution for the conquest of political power. "Revolution won't be avoided," the article concluded. "Don't rejoice, pot-bellied bourgeois, since revolution is fatal."[63]

The Seeds of Counterrevolution

> The present phase in the class struggle in Italy is the phase that precedes either the conquest of political power on the part of the revolutionary proletariat and the transition to new modes of production that will allow a recovery in productivity; or a tremendous reaction on the part of the propertied class and the governing caste.
>
> Antonio Gramsci, "Toward a Renewal of the Socialist Party" (1920g, 3)

The industrialists had undergone a transformative psychological shock, and they emerged belligerent. They accused Giolitti's government of "complete absenteeism and connivance with the violators of the law." They further lamented that not one soldier or police officer was sent to defend "property" and "personal liberty" (Letter of the Turin industrialists to Giolitti, September 10, 1920, in Tasca 1965, 141).

The neutralist behavior of the government was not the only factor that incensed industrialists and agrarian capitalists. They viewed the events' concluding agreement in apocalyptic terms. There was also the presence in parliament of a socialist minister of labour, Arturo Labriola, who in interviews and statements spoke openly of a phase of transition from a capitalist to a socialist economy. Moreover, as we have seen in chapter 3, those years marked an assault on capital through reforms, including measures against speculation, the taxation of excess war profits, the extraordinary tax on property, the compulsory registration of shares in the owners' names, steeper death duties, the legalization of land occupation, and much more.

In March 1920 the *Confindustria* had situated itself as a national organization, complete with its own general political line and tactics. Industrialists could now think of themselves as a national political power—an "industrialist class" (*Il corriere della sera*, March 9, 1920) with a centralized membership. Seventy-two associations were federated, with 11,000 members. All large industries, and three-quarters of the medium- and small-scale industries, adhered to this association. That August the agriculturalists had done the same: they founded *La Confederazione Generale dell'Agricoltura*, which united large and small agricultural property and industry. It was a new "political body of battle and resistance to coordinate all the forces of property and agriculture industry" (Bachi 1921, 302).[64]

Alongside these developments, Gramsci's analysis could not have been more timely: "industrialists are divided among themselves because of profit, because of economic and political competition, but in front of the proletarian class they are an iron block" Gramsci 1920f, 2). Both Lenin and Gramsci foresaw the unleashing of a bourgeois reaction of a new type, one that went beyond the traditional liberal-democratic framework—it was the coming of a violent civil war. The impulse of revenge (an impulse the government failed to address) was to be satisfied with Fascist violence. Fires would soon burn down many worker organizations' headquarters. *Camere del lavoro* (chambers of labor), *le case del popolo* (citizen centers), cooperatives, and newspaper offices were reduced to ash. Armed attacks would kill thousands, from socialist majors to rank-and-file workers, until the ultimate advent of the Fascist government in October 1922.[65]

Tasca eloquently captured the counterrevolutionary spirit: "They [the industrialists] received the jolt [*scossa*] of [one who,] having bordered death and now returning to life, feels like a new man" (Tasca 1965, 129–30). He added, "the blood that they will have spilled will appear to them as a ritual of an expiatory ceremony, necessary for the purification of the violated temple of private property" (ibid., 143).

Conclusion

This chapter has delved into the shattering of capitalism after World War I as embodied by the rise of the factory committee movement in Britain and Italy. The threat to the old order emerged from the war struggles of the metalworkers against capital and the state. The threat exploded in Italy in 1919–1920, where it reached a dimension second only to Soviet Russia and Soviet Hungary. Under the leadership of the *Ordinovisti*, for two whole years the Italian rank and file practiced and advanced a concrete alternative to capitalism that found a testing ground during the factory occupation of 1920. At that point it was no longer a matter of whimsy to declare that workers had begun "the march 'within' the revolution and no longer towards the revolution" to reach the greatest end: "the liberation of labor from the slavery of capital" ("Chronicles of the New Order" [*Cronache dell'Ordine Nuovo*], *L'Ordine nuovo* 1, no. 18 [September 13, 1919]:135).

The *Ordinovista* movement proposed a twofold break from the capitalist order, one that was at once institutional and methodological. Rather than being a means to strengthen peoples' passive consent to the capitalist order, knowledge became critical and empowering. Its emancipatory potential rested on the four main foundations explored above: the abolition of the fetish of "economic necessity"; the centrality of workers' agency (theoretical, economic, and political); the connection between theory and practice; and the connection between the political and economic domains. These foundations broke away from any top-down and technocratic conception of knowledge—a conception of knowledge that the austerity experts would indefatigably strive to reestablish.

The factory councils embodied such a methodological revolution. Councils united workers of all ranks as thinkers and producers—to control production, to end private ownership of the means of production and wage relations, and to bridge the divide between economics and politics in order to give true force to economic democracy.

The nationwide occupation of factories coordinated by the councils ignited the establishment's greatest fears, and cemented the antisocialist bloc across liberals, nationalists, and conservatives alike. These factions would soon merge in the armed offensive of Fascism and a widespread austerity agenda that proved itself in its full anti-labor force.

Mussolini's Fascist regime represented more than stick and castor oil—it was an "austere" fascism. The *Duce* surrounded himself with economic experts who firmly re-imposed—both through theory and policy making—the divide between the economic and the political that the workers had breached. As we will see in the second part of this book, austerity's birth as the new champion of capitalism operated to foreclose any alternative to it. Indeed, in a crisis of this proportion, either the organizations of people can move beyond capitalist relations, or the ruling class will reimpose its rule. Austerity served the latter end.[66]

Part II

THE MEANING
OF AUSTERITY

The crisis of capitalism that followed the Great War was, for some people of means, an acute and terrifying development.

Once workers stormed the stage of history with ideas for an alternative society, the defense of capitalism took on novel and more powerful forms. Guardians of capitalism went back to the drawing board to refurbish the old order, and their manufacture of austerity became their main weapon. Austerity consisted of a twofold process, at once material and ideological. Or better, it consisted of a twofold strategy—coercion and consensus.

The coercion of workers was clear in the motto of austerity that was formulated at two pivotal international financial conferences, in Brussels (1920) and in Genoa (1922): "work more, consume less." The capitalist states and their economic experts secured capital accumulation through policies that imposed the "proper" (i.e., class-appropriate) behavior on the majority of their citizens. The three forms of austerity policies—fiscal, monetary, and industrial—worked in unison to disarm the working classes and exert downward pressure on wages.

The operation of this austerity trinity and its material unfolding as a strategy for economic coercion is illustrated in the box below. This illustration stresses the mechanisms through which fiscal, monetary, and industrial austerity mutually reinforce one another. These general concepts will be studied concretely in the chapters in this part; however, this analysis may help readers with the overall mechanics of coercion under austerity.

FISCAL AUSTERITY → MONETARY AUSTERITY

Fiscal austerity takes the form of budget cuts, especially welfare cuts, and regressive taxation (i.e., tax policy that takes a greater proportion of money from people who have less of it). Both reforms allow the transfer of resources from the majority of citizens to the minority—the saving-investing classes—so as to secure property relations and greater capital formation. Meanwhile, budget cuts also curtail inflation through two main mechanisms. First, the reduction and consolidation of public debt diminishes the liquidity in the economy, since debt-holders can no longer use maturing bonds as means of payment. Second, budget cuts reduce aggregate demand: the general public has less disposable income, and the state itself is investing less. Less demand for goods and capital means that internal prices are kept down. Moreover, such stifling of aggregate demand also increases the foreign value of the currency by discouraging imports and thereby improving the balance of trade (i.e., ensuring that exports exceed imports). Indeed, the foreign value of a currency is favorable if the balance of trade of a country is favorable.

MONETARY AUSTERITY → FISCAL AUSTERITY

Monetary austerity (or monetary deflation, described above) entails a curtailment of credit in the economy, and it primarily coincides with a rise in interest rates. This so-called "dear money" policy, in which money is harder to come by, increases the cost to the government of borrowing money, and thus limits its expansionary projects. In twentieth-century history, the limit to state expenditure becomes more entrenched once the gold standard is reestablished (for Britain this occurred in 1925): in order to maintain gold parity, the avoidance of capital flight takes precedence; hence, fiscal policy has to prioritize retaining capital in its economy. It does so by minimizing government expenditure and creating a capital-friendly environment via lower taxation on capital.

INDUSTRIAL AUSTERITY → MONETARY AUSTERITY

Industrial austerity refers to an imposition of industrial peace, i.e., non-contested, hierarchical relations of production. Such "peace" is of course the basis of capital accumulation, as it secures property rights, wage relations, and monetary stability in the long run. Industrial austerity also guarantees expedient monetary deflation—which makes assets on hand more valuable. In fact, successful revaluation (i.e., an increase of the value of money) crucially requires downward price adjustments, particularly labor prices (i.e., lower wages), in order to cut the costs of production. This is because lower production costs keep commodity prices low, thus boosting international competitiveness at a moment when a country is seeking to improve its exchange rates through greater exports. Thus, lower production costs are ever more essential to compensate for a loss of competitiveness once the currency is revalued so as to not lose foreign market share. If the state has enough coercive powers, as the Italian Fascist state did, it can intervene directly to curtail nominal wages through legal action, thus securing immediate downward price adjustments and ensuring the competitiveness needed to achieve the gold standard. Of course, even in less authoritarian societies, such as Britain, restrictive labor laws may limit the legitimacy of industrial manipulations, for example through a criminalization of solidarity strikes. Industrial peace and wage repression are also important to attract capital and avoid its flight, another prerogative for gold convertibility. Low wages also decrease consumption demand, which in turn decreases imports and thus has a positive effect on the exchange rate that favors revaluation.

MONETARY AUSTERITY → INDUSTRIAL AUSTERITY

Dear money policy means that the economy will slow down because borrowing becomes costlier and investors are disincentivized. Once deflation kicks in and prices decline, pessimistic expectations regarding future profits reduce investments further. Less investment means less employment. Higher unemployment not only reduces workers' wages, it also ensures "industrial peace" by killing the political leverage and militancy of labor.

INDUSTRIAL AUSTERITY → FISCAL AUSTERITY

A weak and docile working class is one whose pressuring action for social measures, progressive taxation, and other redistributive policies is subordinated to the austere priorities of shifting resources, which favor the saver-investor classes. Unions forgo radical proposals and practices that challenge private property and are willing to engage in collaboration toward increasing the efficiency of production in the name of a national cause.

FISCAL AUSTERITY → INDUSTRIAL AUSTERITY

Budget cuts mean curtailment of public works and of public employment more generally, leading to an enlargement of the reserve army of labor (the pool of people wanting to work), which jeopardizes unions' bargaining power, depresses wages, and increases competition between workers.

The circular blueprint we have just detailed makes an important point in the story and history of austerity. Upon closer inspection, governments' austere fixations on balancing budgets and curbing inflation serve the main goal of making sure *capital* (as a social relation) is indisputable, and that its pillars of wage relations and private property remain strong. For example, the main achievement of fiscal and monetary austerity was identical to that of industrial austerity: the subjugation of the working class to the impersonal laws of the market. Indeed, all three forms of austerity served to recreate the divide between economics and politics that war collectivism had temporarily suspended. Once the state stepped down as an economic actor (and as an employer), wage relations would again be subjected to impersonal market pressures. Austerity ensured and facilitated this retreat to the norm.

Here emerges a core argument of this book: the main objective of austerity was the *depoliticization of the economic*—or, the reinstallation of a divide between politics and the economy—after the wartime political landscape had dissolved it. In practice, the reinstallation of this divide took three forms.

Depoliticization refers to the state's backing off of economic pursuits, which in turn allowed for (1) relations of production (owners versus labor) to revert to the command of impersonal market forces—while also suffocating any political contestation of such wage relations, or of private property. There was more to depoliticization, however. The following pages will show that depoliticization also meant (2) exempting economic decisions from democratic scrutiny, especially by establishing and protecting "independent" economic institutions; and (3) promoting a concept of economic theory as "objective" and "neutral" and thereby transcending class relations—the sort of omniscience that was the foundation for one of austerity's ends: building consensus.

These three conventions were mutually supportive. Cultivating a notion of economic objectivity (3), for example, first required the rehabilitation of the rule of the impersonal laws of the market (1). This, particularly in a moment of high contestation, could only be achieved through their unchecked governance (2).

Hence, austerity found its primary ally in technocracy—a belief in the power of economists as guardians of an indisputable science. Chapter 5 explores the consolidation of this powerful austerity-technocracy partnership. It introduces the reader to two international financial conferences, at Brussels (1920) and Genoa (1922), that contemporary scholars have largely disregarded. But the reality is that these two events were pivotal in securing the longevity of capitalism as a socio-economic system.

As detailed in chapter 6 and chapter 7, economic experts—in their high position within the state apparatus—constructed consensus through economic models that excluded *capital* (as a social relation of production) as a variable; instead it became a given. By embedding hierarchical social relations within their equation, these neoclassical models also replace the concept of exploitation as the basis of profit with an idea of "market freedom"; labor is no longer the central motor of the economic machine, it is a choice or calling. Meanwhile it is the *entrepreneur*'s capacity to save and invest that drives the economy (note the vernacular switch from "capitalist" to "entrepreneur," which connotes a sense of individual achievement). Indeed, these models do not envisage class conflicts between the capitalists and the workers, but rather postulate a society of individuals who can all *potentially* save (and invest) their money (that is, if they act virtuously) and whose interests harmonize with those of the other members of society. In this way, technocrats counteracted any critique regarding vertical relations of production and justified capitalism as a system that benefits society as a whole. The austerity economists conflated *the good of the whole* with the good of the capitalist class. They postulated the national interest as congruent with the interest of private capitalism. These beliefs imbue austerity today, as then.

Austerity—both in its material form as a coercive policy and in its theoretical form as a consensus-building set of theories—repudiated the workers' revolutionary wartime and postwar gains, especially those of the *Ordinovista* movement. The group's practical and theoretical alternatives were the gravest enemy to the capitalist system, an enemy that originators of the austerity doctrine were determined to defeat. In fact, and as we shall further explore in the second half of the book, austerity smashes the *Ordinovista* methodological/institutional foundations. Austerity a) re-naturalizes the capitalist pillars of private property and wage relations; b) denies the political and economic agency of workers; c) vindicates the priority of top-down economic science; and d) reasserts the divide between the economic and the political.

This austere view of the social world is also reflected in its liberal thought leaders' support of the Italian Fascist regime. Indeed, as chapter 8 investigates, the international liberal establishment was convinced that Mussolini's dictatorship was the only solution to force the austerity pill upon the "turbulent" Italian people. Fascist political methods to achieve economic success, however gruesome, could be largely tolerated thanks to their accompanying conviction that the economic and the political were two separate domains. Chapter 8 details how liberal technocrats played no minor role in consolidating Mussolini's rule.

Chapter 9 presents empirical evidence on the motives and political endgame of those who conceived austerity as policy. What was presented then and now—the rehabilitation of capital accumulation as a means to save the hungry masses—has time and again delivered on its true purpose: to facilitate permanent and structural extraction of resources from the many to the few.

Finally, chapter 10 looks at the one hundred years that follow the events narrated in this book to trace how austerity's workings have continued to shape our society and have constantly protected capitalism from potential democratic threats.

CHAPTER 5

International Technocrats and the Making of Austerity

The resolutions come to by the commission, which this conference is asked to adopt, constitute a financial code no less important to the world today than was the civil code of Justinian. The institutes of Justinian have been the basis for the jurisprudence of not merely a large part of Europe, but of the world itself. Here at Genoa there have been assembled experts in finance and economics, each known in his own country as the leading authority upon the subjects with which we are dealing, and their combined wisdom . . . has resulted in agreement upon a series of resolutions which will be a guide, and I hope a code, to be followed and observed in the same way as the laws due to the learning of Justinian.

President of the Genoa Commission on Finance, Laming Worthington-Evans, the British Secretary of State for War (in Medlicott et al., eds. 1974, vol. 19, 705–6)

In the moment of capitalism's gravest crisis, when the working classes had stormed the stage of history, another set of actors entered from stage right to take back command. Among them were "experts in finance and economics" who were brought together for the first international financial conferences—in Brussels (1920) and then again in Genoa (1922)—and achieved unprecedented sway. Sir Worthington-Evans, a British Conservative minister, in chairing the plenary of the Genoa finance commission, had no doubts that the combined wisdom of these leading authorities would serve as the foundation for a new "financial code." This code amounted to the core principles of modern-day austerity: "economy" (in the sense of cutting both state expenditures and the expenditures of the working classes) and "hard work" (again enforced on the working classes). That Worthington-Evans would set these principles in terms as grandiose as the Justinian code of AD 529 speaks to the power and scope of what they set out to do: just as the Justinian code established the legal backbone of Europe, the austerity code would shape our society, as in fact it has till this day. In this, the assembled group was successful.

This chapter considers the code's originating moments, at a pair of high-profile and highly academic conferences which conceived and articulated an international blueprint for austerity. The purpose was to defend capitalism from its "enemies"; the logic was to blame said enemies for national economic troubles and to enforce upon these populations the sacrifice of hard work and low consumption. The circular nature of austerity, in policy terms, guaranteed this form of coercion: fiscal, monetary, and industrial policies operated harmoniously to re-establish the economic-political divide, to re-naturalize wage relations and private property, and finally to usurp peoples' agency. These outcomes ran in direct opposition to the foundations for an alternative society set forth by the Italian *Ordinovista* movement that we studied in chapter 4, and even in direct opposition to the British guilds of chapter 3 as well as the reconstructionist movement in chapter 2.

Rescuing the structures of capital accumulation meant quashing all popular expectations for social emancipation following the sacrifice they underwent during the war. The prize of postwar reconstruction was no longer democratic control of industry, nor "a home fit for heroes"; it was, in the words of the merchant banker R. H. Brand of Lazard Brothers, London, the "hard truth" of "labour and suffering" (League of Nations, Brussels International Finance Conference 1920, Verbatim Record, vol. 2, 20; documents from the Brussels conference will hereafter be cited as Brussels 1920 followed by volume and page numbers). These ideas resonated with his expert colleagues at the conferences. Lord Robert Chalmers, the former permanent secretary at the British Treasury, noted that to regain "equilibrium," the "painful" solution was to *"work hard, live hard, and save hard"* (Brussels 1920, Verbatim Record, vol. 2, 26–27, italics added).

Such a frontal attack on labor—one that would slash social resources and wages and especially kill visions of an alternative society—required a sturdy justification. The authority of the experts provided a channel to build consensus for a truth that, even if *hard* and *painful*, was "universal" and "objective," and thus had to be swallowed. For these technocrats, austerity's rationality was synonymous with rationality itself, because they held that the capitalist order was the only order possible.

Reassessing Brussels and Genoa

In February 1920, the Council of the League of Nations met in London to summon the "world's first International Financial Conference," to be held in Brussels from September 24 to October 4, 1920. Thirty-nine nations were called to the table, representing three-quarters of the world's population. The conference had the primary objective of "studying the financial crisis and looking for the means of remedying and of mitigating the dangerous consequences arising from it" (Brussels 1920, Report of the International Financial Conference, vol. 1, 3).

Less than two years later, at a moment when inflation in Britain had been dramatically replaced by deflation and a troubling economic slump, the Supreme Council of the Allies announced the Genoa economic-financial conference (April 10–May 19, 1922).[1] The aim, yet again, was to tackle the economic crisis and to reestablish normal economic conditions in a spirit of cooperation among nations toward the "pacification of Europe and its reconstruction."[2]

Scholars have largely ignored the Brussels conference, while noting the one in Genoa primarily for its diplomatic impact.[3] The few economic historians who have studied the conferences speak of a fiasco. For example, in his famous *Golden Fetters*, Barry Eichengreen talks about their "failure to provide a framework for systematic international cooperation" (Eichengreen 1992, 153), mainly due to a congenital limitation: the unresolved issues of war debts and reparations were

expressly excluded from the agenda of the conferences, thereby eliminating the chance that the meetings would have any great or lasting relevance. Eichengreen's observations echoed those of earlier economists
like John Maynard Keynes, Gustav Cassel, and Francesco Saverio Nitti,
who collaborated on a 1922 special issue of the *Manchester Guardian
Commercial* regarding the events at Genoa.[4] These voices agreed that
the mutual assistance cited by Eichengreen as missing was a mirage to
begin with. In the words of the *Economist*, no "plan has been evolved
under which the Governments of relatively prosperous states shall
help out their weaker neighbours" ("Brussels," *Economist*, October 16,
1920, 579).

This common assessment of the meetings as having accomplished
nothing changes drastically if one adopts a different lens—one that
acknowledges the centrality of class struggle to the moment in which
the participants were gathered. With this new perspective the conferences acquire a central and foundational role, which has until now been
disregarded. They were in fact the pioneers of the modern version of
austerity, embodied, as we shall see, in the essential motto: "economy"
and "hard work."

The conferences succeeded in establishing an agenda to solidify the
faltering pillars of capitalism. While the capitalist powers may have
failed in their *horizontal* relationship—establishing a system of power
with one another—they most certainly achieved success in their *vertical* relationship—to labor, that is, in subjugating it.

Stanford economics professor Joseph S. Davis commended Brussels
as a "conference of specialists in financial disease." Their assembly "for
diagnosis of the acute illness of the nations" was a victory, Davis argued, in that the attendees reached "unanimous agreement upon the
main points of a diagnosis and upon the mode of treatment appropriate
to the present stages of the disease" (Davis 1920, 350). Davis's claim of a
unanimous agreement was centered less on international cooperation
than on austerity. Or better, international cooperation found useful expression in austerity, with the latter silencing the powerful enemies of
capital accumulation and foreclosing any noncapitalist alternatives of
postwar reconstruction, including projects for economic democracy.

The same *Economist* article that had stressed the conference's failure to achieve a plan of mutual assistance highlighted the importance of the Brussels conference in setting an international austerity agenda. The article bemoaned "the tendency to minimise the importance of the [conference] resolutions" ("Brussels," *Economist*, [October 16, 1920]: 579) and congratulated the delegates for "securing, *against many powerful advocates*, the acceptance by the conference of the policy of deflation, of course gradual, as opposed to that of devaluation, and also that of dear money as opposed to the prevailing continental doctrine of low rates" (ibid., my italics). The magazine added that the attendees' consensus on monetary austerity went hand in hand with an agreement on the inevitability of fiscal austerity: "The representatives of the weaker states have gone back strengthened in the conviction that sound finance is not only the right policy, but the only possible policy for their countries if they are to secure foreign confidence and assistance" (ibid., 580). Accepting this necessity for austerity provided "the basis of any economic recovery of Europe" (ibid., 579). In 1922, the Genoa financial conference reaffirmed the unanimity on austerity principles.

In sum, the two conferences reunited the European establishment under the flag of technocracy[5] to construct and implement austerity. Technocrats were rising as the new protectors of capitalism—and their sermon was heard loud and clear across the continent.

Technocrats Take Charge

Economic observers expressed a real excitement for the high scientific quality of the Brussels conference. The technical footprint of the conference, or at least the prevalence of the "economic" over the "political," was discernible in a number of ways. In the first place, the social composition of the national delegations was mainly without explicit political affiliation and was noticeably purged of working-class voices. Of the delegates of each country, wrote the economics professor H. A. Siepmann, "very few of the representatives were either politicians or diplomats, but fewer still were representatives of Labour" (Siepmann 1920, 443). Countries were not expected to include representatives of labor in their delegation. Rather, as Davis noted, "[t]he representatives were in the main leading bankers and treasury officials, who 'attended as experts and not as spokesmen of [existing] official policy'" (Davis 1920, 349).

Secondly, technical documentation was unprecedentedly abundant. The secretariat of the League of Nations requested prior to the meeting that states and their banks submit information on currency, public finance, international trade, retail prices, and coal production, thereby collecting a considerable amount of economic statistics. Siepmann highlighted that "[n]o Conference was ever so well provided with documents as this one" (Siepmann 1920, 441).[6] He reported them to have "an aggregate thickness of four inches" (ibid., 436). Davis praised the "great advance in the utilization of statistics by an international conference" and the sophisticated efforts to standardize national statistics (on budgets, for example) for international and comparative use.[7]

Thirdly, and most importantly, it was specifically economics professors who drafted the most influential body of memoranda. Here the (self-adulating) biases of the conference's advisory committee[8] were on display: they defended the decision to invite only the "leading economists of international repute" on the basis that, unlike the different delegations from other fields, they would not represent "the individual national point of view" but rather "the world point of view" (Report of the Advisory Committee, Brussels 1920, 9).

The systematic use of academic expertise and its full-blown justification as being "above bias" was impressive. Thus, five prominent economists, professors all, took the stage: Maffeo Pantaleoni (Italy), Charles Gide (France), Gijsbert Weijer Jan Bruins (Holland), Arthur Cecile Pigou (Great Britain), and Gustav Cassel (Sweden). They submitted individual papers to instruct conference participants. Subsequently, the five acceded to a request and met and prepared a joint statement that set the stage for the austerity agenda of the conference.[9] The final official resolutions of Brussels fully incorporated the experts' "scientific" advice.

Similarly, the financial commission of the Genoa conference two years later heeded the advice of economic scholars, financiers, businessmen, and bankers.[10] Treasury official Sir Basil Blackett, who will be a pivotal actor in this story, headed a committee of experts that included other highly regarded figures: R. H. Brand, the Swedish economist Gustav Cassel, the Dutch central banker Gerard Vissering, the German central banker Rudolf Hevenstein, and Henry Strakosch, the future chairman of the *Economist*. These experts had already met in London a few months prior to package an austerity plan. On that occasion, it was the British Treasury's in-house economist, Ralph Hawtrey, another protagonist from whom we will hear more in chapter 6, who took the lead to prescribe drastic austerity as a "natural" antidote against capitalist crisis. The official resolutions of the Genoa conference fully transcribed Hawtrey's austerity therapy, and they were accepted with almost no debate.

The proceedings of these two conferences embodied the first fundamental feature of technocracy, or rule via economic expertise: economists acquire unprecedented influence in advising and implementing economic policies. This type of social authority holds to the extent that the second fundamental feature of technocracy also holds: economists have achieved a "classless" and "neutral" status. They are recognized as spokespersons of universal and value-free truths about the economy, viewed as an ahistorical object. Austerity embodies the enforcement of these "truths," and as such is inherently technocratic.

Davis's characterization of the Brussels conference as benefiting from the technocratic attendees and their data-driven arguments shows the bourgeois urge to concretely reconfigure society: "Its prestige was considerable; the unanimity of its conclusions is impressive; its views are probably in the main those of financial leaders in most countries. There is therefore reason to believe that influential pressure will be brought to bear upon the various European governments to heed the recommendations and put them into operation" (Davis 1920, 359).

In the following sections, we will explore those very recommendations to see how these technocrats planned to turn austerity's principles of "economy" and "hard work" into reality.

On the Nature and Purpose of Austerity

> Without paying your way as a nation, without getting that equilibrium and stability which is at the basis of confidence, there can be no hope whatsoever. To that we have to devote all our energies. How are we to do it? I think the answer is a very painful one and yet a very simple one. It is this: that we must all work hard, live hard and save hard.
>
> Lord Chalmers (Brussels 1920, vol. 2, 26–27)

The austerity agenda that was shared among the Brussels meeting's "specialists in financial disease" (Davis 1920) consisted of both a "diagnosis" and "a mode of treatment." The diagnosis was harsh and evoked a sense of dramatic emergency: the world economy was in severe crisis and "the severity of the malady" varied immensely "in proportion to the degree in which each nation has been immersed in the maelstrom of the war" (Brussels 1920, vol. 1, 4).

The first ten days of the Brussels conference were devoted to hearing the financial statements of the participating countries:

> The examination of these statements brings out the extreme gravity of the general situation of public finance throughout the world, and particularly in Europe. . . . *Public opinion is largely responsible for this situation.* . . . Nearly every Government is being pressed to incur fresh expenditure; largely on palliatives which aggravate the very evils against which they are directed. The first step is to bring public opinion in every country to realise the essential facts of the situation and particularly the need for re-establishing public finances on a sound basis as a preliminary to the execution of those social reforms which the world demands. (Resolutions proposed by the Commission on Public Finance, Brussels 1920, vol. 1, 13, my italics)

After the presentation of empirical evidence of the financial predicament,[11] the conferences did not portray the causes of such evil as, say, structural economic contradictions or the decision to wage a big, expensive war; rather, they laid the blame at the feet of the nations' citizens. Citizens were guilty of a desire to live above their means and of pressuring governments to satisfy these "excessive" desires not just through social measures, but through the subversion of the pillars of capitalism. This, as the financier R. H. Brand put it, was a historical paradox:

> It is a paradox of the situation that, urgent as is this limitation of expenditure on financial and economic grounds, *the whole force of public opinion still seems to be exerted in the opposite direction.* The war has led to an almost universal demand for the extension of Government functions. Everyone has grown accustomed to State assistance and State activity. Socialism and nationalism are the order of the day. The manual workers . . . were encouraged to expect, and do expect, *some new way of life*, some great betterment of their lot. These changes, they believe can be achieved if the system of private industry is replaced by a sort of Government or common ownership. They do not realize the *hard truth* that . . . a better life can, owing to the losses of the war, be now reached *only through labour* and *suffering.* (Verbatim Record, Brussels 1920, vol. 2, 20, my italics)

In the midst of this deeply troubling moment in which societies' masses sought more for themselves, the "hard truth" lay in their "mode of treatment": citizens' behavior had to be shaped and controlled according to the principles of economic science that would rehabilitate the conditions of capital accumulation. Individuals had to work harder, consume less, expect less from the government as a social actor, and renounce any form of labor action that would impede the flow of production. Lord Chalmers had stated it succinctly: "work hard, live hard, save hard."

Gerard Vissering of the Netherlands Central Bank, vice chairman of the Commission of Currency and Exchange, well summed up the austerity treatment: to assure economic recovery, "labour efficiency will have to be increased, in the first place by avoiding strikes, but further also by a more intensive supply of labour-service." Moderation, too, could serve to complement workers' discipline. Economic recovery required "reducing the home-consumption to the strictly necessary and avoiding the superfluous, e.g., excessive consumption of butter, sugar, etc." (Verbatim Record, Brussels 1920, vol. 2, 61).

Hard work and economy—as in budget cuts and individual abstinence—were the guiding principles that formed the essence of austerity as a response to crisis. In themselves these were not much of a novelty; they had been an integral part of the conceptual toolbox of the renowned classical economists Adam Smith, David Ricardo, and Thomas Robert Malthus for at least a century. What was new in the early twentieth century was that the general public had seen the fault in such narratives.

After World War I the general public was not going to accept austere economic "remedies," and the technocrats in Brussels and Genoa understood as much. Indeed, the economic experts intuited the widespread challenge to traditional orthodox finances, especially among the working people who were being seduced by "bolshevism." The *Economist* spoke of the "revival of Marxism";[12] in his memo Gijsbert Weijer Jan Bruins referred to "what may be called a certain postwar mentality [*ce qu'on pourrait appeler une certain mentalité d'après-guerre*]"[13] the diffusion of which was "common knowledge," while Pantaleoni denounced how "public opinion is largely favourable to Socialism and Paternalism" (Brussels 1920, vol. 5, 103). The inescapable confrontation of technocrats with these realities of crisis deeply molded the nature of modern austerity, which accordingly embodied two clear-headed strategies—consensus and coercion.

The first strategy, consensus, entailed a conscious attempt to "intensely awaken" (Pantaleoni in Brussels 1920, vol. 4, 107) the general public to the scientific and necessary reforms toward economic stabilization. The sense of alarm had to be spread, the right economic priorities had to be understood. Such an impulse to "enlighten" is explicit in many resolutions of the two conferences. For example, "[i]n order to enlist public interest it is essential to give the greatest publicity possible to the situation of the public finances of each State" (Resolution IX, Commission on Public Finance, Brussels 1920, vol. 1, 15). And again, "*All superfluous expenditure should be avoided.* To attain this end the enlightenment of public opinion is the most powerful lever" (Resolution VII, Commission on Currency and Exchange, Brussels 1920, vol. 1, 19, italics in original). Countries were urged to regularly collect budgetary information and any other suggestion that could be useful "for the financial education of the public opinion of the world" (Resolution IX, Commission on Public Finance, Brussels 1920, vol. 1, 15).[14]

In the same vein, the League of Nations had addressed the necessity of "keeping expenditure within income," balancing expenditure out of revenue: "This principle must be clearly brought home to the peoples of all countries; for it will be impossible otherwise to arouse them from a dream of false hopes and illusions to the recognition of hard facts" (*Three months of the League of Nations*, vol. 3, 1920, 77).

The second strategy, coercion, emerged out of the apprehension that consensus might not be achieved or might not be sufficient. Democracy, if necessary, would have to be bent in the pursuit of economic soundness, and this process would be imposed. Pantaleoni—an architect of austerity and later an adviser of Mussolini's dictatorship—pointed out "where Socialism is strong, where democracy is strong, public finance will go the wrong way" (Brussels 1920, vol. 4, 109). Economic experts seemingly did not trust the restless public to make the "correct" decisions regarding its own well-being. As we will see, austerity carried within it the principle of exempting economic policy decisions from democratic procedures, either through technocratic institutions or, as in the case of Italy, through a Fascist government. Austere economists demonstrate the same anti-democratic intuitions to this day.[15]

Coercion resided not only in how economic policies were passed, but in how these policies worked. Technocrats devised monetary, fiscal, and industrial policies that imposed hard work and economy on a population in need of discipline. After all, as the official proceedings of the Brussels resolution pointed out, "[t]he country which accepts the policy of budget deficits is treading the slippery path which leads to general ruin; to escape from that path no sacrifice is too great" (Resolution II, Commission on Public Finance, Brussels 1920, vol. 1, 13).

What follows is an examination of these recommendations as they were presented in the Brussels resolutions of the Commission on Public Finance and the Commission on Currency and Exchange; the

Commission on Finance at Genoa forcefully restated them, citing the resolutions adopted by the prior conference "as basis for its own work" (Medlicott et al., eds. 1974, vol. 19, 704). At both meetings, the participating nation-states unanimously endorsed these austerity principles.

FISCAL AUSTERITY

> Nations, like individuals, must earn their living and must pay their way.
>
> Lord Chalmers (Verbatim Record, Brussels 1920, vol. 2, 25)

The joint statement from the experts at Brussels left no doubt about the European states' new economic legislative priorities: "The equilibrium of State budgets must be restored" and "[f]loating debt should as soon as practicable be funded" (Monetary Problems, Joint Statement of Economic Experts, Brussels 1920, vol. 5, 2–3). The Genoa conference repeated the refrain: "The most important reform of all must therefore be the balancing of the annual expenditure of the State without the creation of fresh credits unrepresented by new assets" (Genoa Conference 1922, Report of the Second Commission [Finance], Resolution VII, in Gordon and Montpetit 1922, 68–69).[16]

This obsession with balancing the budget had the clear motive of securing the conditions for capital accumulation. Indeed, Resolution II was adamant that "[p]ublic attention should be especially drawn" to the priority of increased production. Note that this production was to be private: "the continual excess of Government expenditure over revenue represented by budget deficits is one of the most serious obstacles to such increase of production" (Commission on Public Finance, Resolution II, Brussels 1920, vol. 1, 13).

The most urgent social and financial reform "on which all others depend" was a broad budget cut, both in ordinary and extraordinary public expenditure (Resolution III, ibid., 14). Resolution IV of the Brussels conference emphasized that the first cut should be in armaments and war expenditures. The following resolution pressed further: "The Conference considers that every Government should abandon at the earliest practicable date all uneconomical and artificial measures which *conceal from the people the true economic situation*" (Resolution V, ibid., 14). Such measures included welfare and social expenses, price controls over primary goods such as "bread and other foodstuff," unemployment benefits, and low transportation service fares and postal rates. The resolutions condemned the existence of these policies as "wasteful" and "extravagant" public expenditures and interferences with markets.

Indeed, fiscal austerity operated through two parallel logics. The first was predominantly interested in safeguarding private ownership of the means of production. During his discussion on public finance, the Belgian prime minister and finance minister Léon Delacroix spoke explicitly: "we must economise . . . we must avoid the adoption of social measures which might tend to thwart industry, and also the adoption of such measures of nationalization and socialisation which might substitute Government action to private enterprise" (Verbatim Record, Brussels 1920, vol. 2, 22). The second logic sought to ensure that resources would be shifted to the classes of society that could save and invest. Indeed, in this framework savings were the sole driver of capital accumulation and all savings would be automatically channeled into investment—an assumption that the Keynesian framework of the 1930s would later largely challenge.

By debunking the immediate connection between savings and investments, Keynes's *General Theory* of 1936 (Keynes 1964) rehabilitated public investment as a prerequisite for stable capital accumulation, not as a hindrance to it. In the Keynesian framework, when the economy is not at full employment, budget deficits actually boost private production given that an increase in aggregate demand has a positive influence on entrepreneurs' profit expectations. In a nutshell, public investments incentivize entrepreneurs to invest.[17] However, before this, during the critical red years after World War I, our austere economic experts— including, notably, Keynes himself—had a graver concern: the defense of *capital* as a social relation. Indeed, the existential prerequisite for *any* investment was its security.

Cuts in welfare expenditures and social services increased the pool of surplus, which could be used for private investment or paying back government debt, which would in turn reward creditors (i.e., the virtuous savers in society). It follows that a state that utilized fiscal austerity to reach budgetary equilibrium demonstrated its financial stability and creditworthiness, and thus fostered savers' confidence in its capacity to uphold favorable conditions for capital accumulation. In the words of Lord Chalmers: "without paying your way as a Nation, without getting that equilibrium and stability which is at the basis of confidence, there can be no hope whatsoever" (Verbatim Record, Brussels 1920, vol. 2, 26).

The same logic of regressive redistribution from the bottom to the top in order to promote capital accumulation also applied to the revenue side. Increases in universal taxation contributed to a transfer of wealth from the many to the few, under the guise of benefit for all. Resolution VI of Brussels read, "fresh taxation must be imposed to meet the deficit, and this process must be *ruthlessly* continued" (Resolution VI, Commission on Public Finance, Brussels 1920, vol. 1, 14). Of course, there was a central caveat: taxation which "might be a burden on private industry" (Delacroix, Belgian representative, Brussels 1920, vol. 2, 22) was to be avoided. Most delegates at Brussels were skeptical of a capital levy that would entail "leakage of capital" (Verbatim Record, Brussels 1920, vol. 2, 34) to other countries, hampering capital accumulation. The intent was thus to hit the "general masses." Like others, the Swedish banker Oscar Rydbeck sang the praises of consumption taxation (the quintessence of regressive taxation) as "a method of taxing which directly promotes savings [of the popular masses]," since "everyone who wants to buy an article on which he has to pay a certain tax has to consider whether he can afford it or not, whether he can save the expense or not" (Verbatim Record, Brussels 1920, vol. 2, 33).

The larger point was clear: a re-education of the general population, which would learn the "virtue" of thrift. The Swedish banker Rydbeck was adamant that his people had to cut back on their daily purchases: "When speaking of saving, we must not forget that if saving is not effected by the general masses of the people, who at the present time have come into possession of more money than they were accustomed to, very little good will be done. In order to induce the broad masses to save, indirect taxation must be introduced [*pour forcer les masses populaires à faire des économies, if faut recourir à la taxation indirecte*]" (ibid., 33).

Technocrats were well aware that, in a historical moment in which the masses appeared hostile toward the old order of things, inducing them to save was easier said than done. Alberto Beneduce, an Italian professor of economic statistics and CEO of the National Institution of Insurance (INA)—who would go on to have a lasting career as parliamentarian, senator, and economic adviser of Mussolini's regime—had no doubt: it was necessary to "act upon public opinion, on the psychological state of the masses, so that they would no more *impede* but help to re-establish the budget of the State" (Verbatim Record, Brussels 1920, 75, my italics). Beneduce gave voice to these preoccupations during the plenary discussion of September 20, 1920. The date is significant: on that day in his own country an unprecedented class struggle was at its peak. The factory occupation had been going on for almost a month. The "psychological state of the masses" seemed rather projected toward a post-capitalist society where private ownership and wage relations were to be abolished.[18]

How could austerity proceed in such a turbulent time? Here again, experts induced consensus through the persuasive powers of an "objective" economic science. Experts justified the necessity of fiscal austerity by suggesting that social reforms were only "concealing from the people the *true* economic situation" (Resolution V on Public Finance, Brussels 1920, vol. 1, 14). Once again, we notice the "neutral" standpoint taken by these experts whose purported role was to "inform" the people—incapable of understanding on their own—of the "true" road to economic redemption.

Where consensus failed, coercion was the substitute. Indeed, even in cases where public opinion opposed these economic "truths," the beauty of budget cuts was such that, once set in motion, they secured compliance anyway; the elimination of welfare programs *imposed* thrift on the majority. Moreover, fiscal austerity meant that workers were left to compete in the free market with no social safety net.

Thus, the survival instinct would kick in, killing strikes, bottling demands for higher wages, and penalizing all manner of insubordinate behavior.

In fact, the state—in its role as eliminator of expenditures—was a fundamental precondition to reconstruct the material (and ideological) conditions necessary for the divide between the economic and the political domains to regain its hold. Clearly the very withdrawal of the state from the realm of economic interventions was a drastic and hefty political decision, but it was nonetheless justified as apolitical and economically necessary—a process guided by technical reason, thus fundamentally uncontroversial.

To conclude, we have seen how fiscal austerity in the form of budget cuts—especially welfare cuts—and regressive taxation enabled the transfer of resources from the majority of citizens to the saving-investing classes so as to secure property relations and greater capital formation. Fiscal austerity also served another fundamental purpose: to restore monetary stability and to secure the rule of technocratic institutions.

MONETARY AUSTERITY

Inflation and Dear Money

> The essential requisite for the economic reconstruction of Europe is the achievement by each country of stability in the value of its currency.
>
> Genoa Conference 1922, Resolution 1 of the Second Commission
> (Finance) (in Gordon and Montpetit 1922, 68)

A stable means of monetary exchange is a precondition for efficient market transactions and investment. The experts at the Brussels and Genoa conferences argued that "[i]t is not sufficient for trade and industry merely to have capital. They require stable prices, stable exchanges, stability of the internal and external financial mechanism" (R. H. Brand, Verbatim Record, Brussels 1920, vol. 2, 17). The currency commissions of the two conferences set out to defeat inflation: "It is essential that the inflation of credit and currency should be stopped everywhere at the earliest possible moment" (Monetary Problems: joint statement of economic experts, Brussels 1920, vol. 5, 2).

Economic experts at the two conferences defined inflation as an "artificial and unrestrained expansion of the currency" that had the effect of reducing the currency's purchasing power per unit. Inflation "debased the currency," and its degeneration could be monstrous: to buy the same goods at higher prices, one needed additional currency, which was procured by further "inflation," thereby creating a "vicious spiral" of "constantly rising prices and wages, and constantly increasing inflation" (Recommendations of the Conference, Brussels 1920, vol. 1, 9).

Inflation was diagnosed as a pernicious outcome of war collectivism: i.e., of state interference with the "natural" laws of supply and demand. The wartime politicization of the economic domain was characterized as the main catalyst for inflation, especially its consequent rise in wages and production costs, all of which hindered capital accumulation. "It is generally recognized that continued inflation, which is primarily due to excessive Government expenditure, has a serious effect on production," noted R. H. Brand (Verbatim Record, Brussels 1920, vol. 2, 17). It followed that fiscal austerity was a primary remedy for inflation, since—in the framing of the conference experts—budget deficits forced governments to finance their expenditures by issuing either more paper currency or fresh credit, thereby increasing the amount of legal tender in circulation.[19]

The Genoa proceedings relied heavily on one of Hawtrey's insights: that budget cuts were indispensable to check the consumption not only of the state but also of the general public. In effect, Hawtrey's principle reduced the disposable income of the working classes. This amounted to a check on public demand, which lowered and stabilized internal prices while also securing external monetary stability, since a reduction in both government and private outlay discouraged imports and thus improved the balance of payments.[20]

To defeat inflation and to fully rein in the purchasing power of workers, fiscal austerity was to be supplemented by monetary austerity. The latter meant a direct and deliberate credit contraction through an increase in interest rates, which would deflate prices and in turn boost confidence in the value of the currency. This was the core of the so-called policy of "dear money" (Resolution VII, Commission on Currency and Exchange, Brussels 1920, vol. 1, 19). Vissering declared: "the purchasing power of money [can], by way of remedy, be forced up somewhat by making money scarce" (Verbatim Record, Brussels 1920, vol. 2, 45).

Like fiscal austerity, monetary austerity fundamentally worked to shape the behavior of economic agents in a way that was favorable to capital accumulation. If depreciation "leads to a spirit of reckless extravagance and a determination to spend at once what in any case is likely to be lost" (R. H. Brand, Verbatim Record, Brussels 1920, vol. 2, 18), then revaluation incentivized savings—the most virtuous economic behavior—on the part of those who have the means to save. The former governor of the Bank of England, Brien Cokayne, under his new title as first Baron Cullen of Ashbourne, sat as a member of the Commission on Currency and Exchange. He was adamant that "the last rise in money rates in Great Britain appears to have acted, as it naturally should, as a considerable stimulus to thrift. Bankers now receive numerous enquiries as to the terms on which they will accept deposits now that rates are so high" (Verbatim Record, Brussels 1920, vol. 2, 71).

The experts were aware that, along with fiscal austerity, the addition of a "dear money policy" would be extremely unpopular. Monetary austerity had the same purpose of promoting savers at the cost of the rest of society, especially the working classes. The deflation that ensued would mean that public borrowing for social expenditures would become costlier and that, more destructively, wages would be curtailed. Dear money, after all, produced a rise in unemployment that mitigated labor's bargaining power and its capacity to resist wage cuts. Accordingly, credit contraction produced unemployment, which slowed down the domestic economy and made countries less competitive abroad (due to monetary revaluation), which further exacerbated the economic downturn. As Henry Strakosch of the South African delegation put it, dear money equaled "hard times and unemployment" (Verbatim Record, Brussels 1920, vol. 2, 78).

The negative, inequitable repercussions of deflation were both known and heavily criticized, especially in Britain, where the public had already begun gnashing its teeth. The British *New Statesman* magazine regularly denounced its effects, in particular how in the midst of deflation "the only people who benefit are rentiers and creditors, whose money incomes grow steadily more valuable as prices fall."[21]

Achieving Political Immunity and Reconfiguring the Relations of Production

The experts who convened in Brussels and Genoa faced a practical problem: how do you design policies (i.e., ensure their unfettered function and entrenchment) that run so counter to public interest and sentiment? The solution was immediately coercive. Experts pressed to use technocratic power—as justified by the purity of science—to enforce the depoliticization of economic institutions and decisions. For the Baron Cullen of Ashbourne, the path forward depended on "placing the issue of paper currency outside the direct control of the State" (Verbatim Record, Brussels 1920, vol. 2, 71). Vissering elaborated: "A national or municipal government might possibly be powerless against such pressure on the part of the employees, because the latter can make their political influence felt on the national government." On the other hand, "[a]n independent banking institution need not however allow itself to be led by the nose by any power whatsoever exercised by the employees" (ibid., 57).

These political strategies of depoliticization were embodied in the official resolutions of the two conferences. They asserted the necessity for banks, in particular central banks, to be independent technocratic bodies—"freed from political pressures"—in order to guarantee that they *should be conducted solely on the lines of prudent finance*" (Resolution III, Commission on Currency and Exchange, Brussels 1920, vol. 1, 18, italics in original; and Resolution II of the Report of the Second Commission [Finance], Genoa, in Gordon and Montpetit 1922, 68). With this intention, "in countries where there is no central bank of issue, one should be established" (Resolution II, Genoa, in Gordon and

Montpetit 1922, 68). Moreover, at Genoa it was made explicit that central banks would enjoy absolute discretionary powers, since "the discretion of the central banks" should not be "fettered by any definite rules" (Resolution XI, Report of the Second Commission [Finance], in Gordon and Montpetit 1922, 70).

In other words, the power of monetary management that the war had dislodged from technocratic hold could not rest in the hands of the representatives of the people, who would likely be more sensitive to social concerns; rather, it would rest in the hands of technocrats who had as their priority the rehabilitation of the purity of capital accumulation, a priority unfettered by any other preoccupation.[22]

In this light, the fixation with reasserting the gold standard, which was loudly announced at Genoa,[23] was primarily explainable as a political buffer to protect the primacy of economic conventions over "the community in its collective capacity" (Resolution IV of the Commission on Currency and Exchange, Brussels 1920, vol. 1, 18). Of course, a return to gold was deemed necessary for international monetary stability.[24] But more important still, the gold standard would force governments to accept the necessity and inevitability of both monetary and fiscal austerity.

In the first place, going back to and maintaining the gold standard ensured a constant justification of the deflationary choices of central banks. Indeed, even once the gold standard was achieved, the central banks could operate with the exclusive intention of maintaining gold parity.[25] Monetary austerity—in the form of increasing the rate of interest—was the main tool used to avoid gold flights.[26] A gold standard regime was also, by definition, a fiscal austerity regime in which public expenditure was to be kept at a bare minimum. Reforms would no longer be a matter of political dispute, but of economic necessity: to avoid gold flight, domestic consumption and imports had to be minimized.[27] Thus, the gold standard was an object of fixation for experts. It enforced austerity, and with it, proper capitalist class relations.

At least notionally, these same economists regarded fears of violent deflation and the economic downturn that could result as the price to pay to go back to gold.[28] These risks were insufficient to forgo such a "painful treatment" (Baron Cullen, Verbatim Record, Brussels 1920, vol. 2, 70); the goal was too important. Tellingly, experts' awareness of deflation's likely burdens on the community—concretely manifested in the 1921 British deflationary crisis—did not dissuade them from recommending deflation at Genoa. To them the suffering that came with returning to the gold standard was justified as a matter of "general interest" (Genoa Conference, Resolution 6, in Gordon and Montpetit 1922, 68).

In sum, monetary austerity and fiscal austerity were two sides of the same coin that worked in a reciprocal fashion. British Treasury official Sir Otto Niemeyer summarized this clearly when he advised the Brazilian government, in his capacity as executive director of the Bank of England: "The two factors, budget equilibrium and stable money, must march together; and neither one can be maintained without the other" (Niemeyer 1931, 4). Indeed, we have seen how budgetary orthodoxy was a prerequisite for the revaluation of currency. At the same time, deflationary monetary policy—in the form of rising interest rates and the curtailment of money supply—increased the cost for the government to borrow, thus limiting its expansionary projects. Resolution VII of the Brussels Commission on Currency and Exchange was explicit: "If the wise control of credit brings dear money, this result will in itself help to promote economy" (Resolution VII, Commission on Currency and Exchange, Brussels 1920, vol. 1, 19).

Not only did the two mutually reinforce one another, they also stood for the same purpose. Fiscal and monetary austerity favored wealthy savers while the rest of society was forced to consume less via diminution of government resources, payment of taxes, and lower wages. The dual operation of fiscal and monetary austerity put the burden of capital accumulation on the working classes to ultimately reestablish the divide between the economic and the political and protect private property and wage relations. Most importantly, these policies robbed the people of all economic agency, and silenced their demands for higher wages and social redistribution, not to mention their demands for nationalization and alternative relations of production.

If one digs deeper, it is easy to see how, disguised as a monetary phenomenon, the vilification of inflation was aimed at shoring up the capitalist social relations of production, especially through notions of decreased consumption and increased production. This was explicitly stated in the resolution of the Brussels Commission on Currency and Exchange reproduced below. Indeed the second austerity motto, centered on "hard work," was an indispensable condition for the final rescue of capital accumulation. It is the topic of the next section.

INDUSTRIAL AUSTERITY

> The complementary steps for arresting the increase of inflation by increasing the wealth on which the currency is based, may be summed up in the words: increased production and decreased consumption. The most intensive production possible is required in order to make good the waste of war and arrest inflation and thus to reduce the cost of living; yet we are witnessing in many countries production below the normal, together with those frequent strikes which aggravate instead of helping to cure the present shortage and dearness of commodities. . . . Yet in our opinion the production of wealth is in many countries suffering from a cause which it is more directly in the power of Governments to remove, viz., the *control in various forms* which was often imposed by them as a war measure and has not yet been completely relaxed. In some cases business has even been taken by Governments out of the hands of the private trader, whose enterprise and experience are a far more potent instrument for the recuperation of the country. Another urgent need is the freest possible international exchange of commodities.
>
> Resolution V, Commission on Currency and Exchange (Brussels 1920, vol. 1, 19)

So far, we have emphasized that the primary goal of austerity, as formulated by the experts of the two international conferences, was the resumption of capital accumulation. To this end, both fiscal and monetary policies diminished the consumption of the many and increased the saving and investment of the few, while also reestablishing the divide between the economic and the political sectors that would reset capitalism's pillars.

These efforts would be moot if the production process was hampered; "the principal need of Europe is a resumption of work and production" (Monetary Problems, Joint statement of economic experts,

Brussels 1920, vol. 5, 2).[29] But it wasn't *just* an increase in production that the experts were aiming at; they sought production under reinstated capitalist relations of exploitation, which in no other moment of history had been so gravely challenged. And as Resolution V, quoted above, illustrates, in order to secure the stability of money, the fundamental pillars of wage relations and private property also needed to be reinforced.

Resolution V explicitly states that capitalist production required the elimination of any aspirations of the working people for alternative organizations of production. Such aspirations could be thwarted through two measures: privatization and the control of labor. The two would ultimately guard against the fundamental culprits of economic crisis—the wrong actions of governments and of individuals (or better, of employees). Vissering, praised for his "high scientific and practical competence" (Verbatim Record, Brussels 1920, vol. 2, 83), asserted that "depreciation of money is not a cause in itself," but "is only the effect of other causes, and that these other causes are to be found in the acts of national and municipal governments on the one hand, and in the acts of individuals, more particularly employees, on the other." He concluded that "[o]nly when both governments and citizens arrive at more reasonable actions can other measures be properly applied with a view to attaining better conditions in the monetary system" (ibid., 51).

Notwithstanding the *prima facie* interpretation of inflation as a monetary phenomenon, economists made clear that, beneath it, the solution was about subordination of the citizens to capitalism. These thoughts were coherent with a deep-seated fear about the political consequences of inflation. Keynes, the economist who at that time advocated for harsh dear money,[30] used words that are by now famous: "a continuance of inflationism and high prices will not only depress the exchanges but by their effect on prices will strike at the whole basis of contract, of security, and of the capitalist system generally."[31] In a similar vein, the Italian economist Luigi Einaudi wrote: "what appeared to profoundly shake the entire society and prepare a social revolution . . . was called with a technical word monetary inflation" (Einaudi 1933, 337).

Privatization and the Crowding-Out Argument

The policy change advocated for by austerity economists was one that "diminish[ed] the sphere of government" (Verbatim Record, Brussels 1920, vol. 2, 20). Such "sound policy" would "allow the natural economic laws to have full possibly of acting in all their intensity" (Beneduce, ibid., 73), thus leading to "sound finances" (ibid., 142) and especially to a boost in the efficiency of production.

To sell their recipes, the austerity advocates leaned heavily on a "crowding out" argument—a battle horse of the British Treasury—that the British delegates shared during the conference discussions: "Since there is not enough capital to go round, which is to have it—governments or private industry? . . . The more capital is absorbed by Governments, the less is available for private industry. . . . Which is likely to use capital more productively, Governments or private industry? The answer is in favor of private industry" (ibid., 17).[32]

A memorandum from the Italian professor Pantaleoni bolstered this view by violently attacking "state socialism."[33] Governments had to stop their interference and stick more closely "to their proper business, which is to furnish the general conditions for unfettered private activity" (Brussels 1920, vol. 5, 103).

It is useful to pause here and contrast these perspectives with those depicted in the first chapters of this book. The lessons of World War I were so compelling that they pushed many bureaucrats, social and economic experts, and of course workers to break away from the dogmas of laissez-faire capitalism and promote the productive superiority of state control and forms of central planning. "A wholly new school of thought" was "laying hold of people,"[34] as Viscount Haldane had commented. In his 1920 book *The Triumph of Nationalization*, the economist Leo Chiozza Money exposed the irrationality of "doctrinaire individualism," while his colleagues on the Sankey committee put private property on public trial on the grounds that it was "wasteful" and "antisocial."

By putting the capitalist resolutions of the conferences into this context, it is clear that the technocrats in attendance were not expressing objective truths, as they purported, but were instead defending private property to the hilt. Indeed, the return of private enterprise's primacy had stakes that were much higher than the mere objective of productive efficiency: the return of privatization was about the depoliticization of the economy, which would bring the aspirations of the working classes away from alternative social organizations and back into the boundaries of capitalist production. In other words, if the production for profit were to prevail over production for use, privatization had to be made safe.

Disciplining Labor and Cutting Wages

Privatization was meaningless if not accompanied by the "cooperative" behavior of those who were expected to labor within the capital order. As such, the unprecedented industrial mobilization of the interwar period would have sent a chill down experts' spines: instead of working hard for increased production, a great number of workers were doing the exact opposite. Vissering voiced concern: "They demand shorter working hours, without correspondingly improving their work which would permit of intenser production," and in order to enforce these demands "they moreover frequently strike, which means a fresh drop in production" (Verbatim Record, Brussels 1920, vol. 2, 50). He further suggested that the hours of lost labor "represent a value of hundreds of millions, if not milliards, in money" (ibid.). Critiques of labor disputes went together with chastising the generalized work ethic: "And even where they do work, many of them exhibit a kind of work-shyness so that their efficiency is thereby again reduced. This in turn again leads to decreased production and increased cost of goods" (ibid.).

Maffeo Pantaleoni used even harsher terms, denouncing workers as violent, dishonest, and blackmailers of government. The shortening hours of work reflected the leisurely, "pipe-in-mouth way" in which work was done (Brussels 1920, vol. 5, 106). Here Pantaleoni expressed no doubts: "wages are much higher than their marginal productivity of labour," and the culprits were the "laws and government actions" that acted "first under the stress of war, then under the stress of Socialism and Bolshevism" (ibid.).

If one could not convince the majority to work hard (while consuming less), the experts knew that the depoliticization of the economy would get them to submit. Indeed, the agenda was to remove "controls in various forms," including laws that protected labor. The reestablishment of an unfettered labor market, especially in times of deflation, warranted a natural disciplining of the labor force through a threat of ending up in the ranks of the reserve army of labor if they refused to accept lower wages. As we shall see in chapter 7, the assembly of Italian academics went so far as to justify explicitly repressive labor laws under a Fascist regime in order to guarantee the ultimate austerity objective of hard work.

Conclusion

Viewed through a lens of capitalist crisis, the financial conferences of Brussels and Genoa are neither irrelevant nor unsuccessful, as some have characterized them. They actually represent a landmark moment within the history of capitalism: the emergence of austerity in its modern form, as a global technocratic project.

Austerity as it is known today was an offspring of crisis—not merely economic crisis, but crisis of capitalism as a socioeconomic system. The preceding chapters have shown that after the war, for the first time, the challenge to the pillars of capitalist accumulation became a mass phenomenon. The working classes acquired a sense of entitlement and participated as protagonists in the political scene. In the minds of the people, private ownership in the means of production and wage relations were no longer natural, indisputable givens.

In that moment, unlike ever before, capital required protection. This is what the experts at the conferences set themselves to do: their ultimate objective was to secure the reproduction of the capitalist system.

The conferences diagnosed the cause of the crisis as the individuals who were contesting the system and were responsible for its breakdown. These individuals demonstrated excessive consumption combined with an unwillingness to work productively at low wages. Inflation and budget deficits, the two great evils of the time, were nothing more than symptoms of a much deeper "flaw": individual behavior.

Hence, the experts forged the drastic cure of austerity: a doctrine of economy and hard work, ostensibly for the good of nations (or at least their economies). As framed, austerity was about individual sacrifice on the part of "patriotic" citizens who had to practice frugality in lifestyle and discipline in labor. Half a century later, in 1979, the powerful Chair of the American Federal Reserve, Paul Volcker, used the same mantra to tackle another great crisis: "the American standard of living must decline" (Rattner 1979), he announced, while supporting the government's firm resolve to break strikes and delivering on a shocking dosage of dear money.

The closing resolution of the Brussels commission on public finance encapsulates the repressive nature of the austerity project that still resonates today:

> The Conference is of opinion that the strict application of the principles outlined above is the necessary condition for the re-establishment of public finances on a sound basis. A country which does not contrive as soon as possible to attain the execution of these principles is doomed beyond hope of recovery. To enable Governments, however, to give effect to these principles, all classes of the community must contribute their share. . . . Above all, to fill up the gap between the supply of, and the demand for, commodities, *it is the duty of every patriotic citizen* to practi[c]e the strictest possible economy and so to contribute his maximum effort to the common weal. Such private action is the indispensable basis for the fiscal measures required to restore public finances. (Resolution X, Commission on Public Finance, Brussels 1920, vol. 1, 15–16, my italics)

In such a turbulent moment, the application of the austerity principles required an emphatic justification. One of the most novel aspects of modern austerity was that, as an antidote to capitalist crisis, it could no longer dismiss or disregard the actors that were deemed responsible for that very crisis. Experts had to deal with public opinion, either through consensus or through coercion—or, most practically, through both. This constituted the dual strategy of austerity.

Austerity sought consensus through the sponsorship and intellectual authority of technocracy, which operated as both its epistemic grounding and its political force. As preachers of "pure economic science," experts imparted their teachings to all citizens. They set out to educate the general public about the truthfulness of the prescriptions upon which their economic behavior should be shaped. Once disarmed of any agency to advance economic alternatives, the people had no choice but to either comply or be forced to comply with the economic necessity. And once the economic/political divide was reestablished, the coercive market forces would naturally work to discipline disarmed workers.

Austerity proved to be more than just wishful thinking on the part of the experts at the international conferences of Brussels and Genoa. Chapters 6 and 7 will investigate how these experts successfully implemented the international code of austerity. We will begin by looking at Britain, a country that pioneered austerity starting in 1920, then explore how, starting in 1922, Mussolini's Italy painstakingly followed in those footsteps. That these dates are so close to the two international conferences (Brussels and Genoa) is telling of the rapid ascent of austerity across Europe.[35]

CHAPTER 6

Austerity, a British Story

> Increased production, cessation of Government borrowings, and decreased
> expenditure both by the Government and by each individual member of the
> nation are the first essentials to recovery.
>
> HMSO, *Final Report of the Committee on Currency and Foreign Exchange*
> (1919c, 3)

Even before the principles of austerity were codified in Brussels and
Genoa beginning in 1920, its component policies were already spreading. This was particularly the case in Britain, which at the time was
the most advanced capitalist country in Europe. Faced with rising
labor mobilization and rising prices, the country adopted two public
axioms—produce more, consume less—that served to smother any
rays of hope for a reconstructionist program, to say nothing of a non-
capitalist future.

As a governmental matter, this campaign began with the 1918 con-
vening of the Committee on Currency and Foreign Exchange (or Cunliffe Committee, named after the lord who chaired it), which gathered
experts from the Treasury, academia, and the Bank of England[1] to discuss ways to combat the "uncertainty of the monetary situation"[2] in the
reconstruction period and formulate an agenda that became an intellectual predecessor to the Brussels and Genoa outputs that followed.
This chapter's opening epigraph speaks to the committee's perception

of a soaring capitalist crisis, along with the now familiar imperatives ("increase production" and "decrease expenditure").

Notable in this early iteration of British austerity was its demand for extreme sacrifice; even personal consumption of the most basic of commodities like bread was secondary "to the interests of economy."[3] Chancellor Austen Chamberlain's thoughts on the bread subsidy reveal where the priorities of austerity stood: "There is £45,000,000 for the bread subsidy. Nothing would give me greater satisfaction than to deal with that . . . the sooner we get rid of these subsidies the better. I agree that they conduce to conceal the real facts of the situation from the country and that they put a most onerous burden upon the State and on the national finances . . . the sooner they are got rid of the better."[4]

Beginning in spring 1920, harsh monetary deflation took a toll on British employment. Fiscal and industrial austerity quickly followed, with unprecedented cuts, regressive taxation, privatization, and repressive measures to control workers' direct action.

By 1922 money wages in industry were a third of their 1920 levels.[5] By 1926 the austere British state denounced labor militancy, buried welfare resources, and restored the gold standard, with the pound back at its prewar parity.[6] Now just a few years removed from the war, the sentiments of collectivism and its purported "wholly new school of thought" had been relegated to the archives of history.

It was a handful of Treasury officials who played a crucial role in orchestrating this turn of events—a turn that had been unimaginable in the immediate aftermath of the Great War. In their role as controllers of finance during the turbulent postwar years, Basil Blackett and Otto Niemeyer had the largest sway over the chancellor of the exchequer, the head of the Treasury. They did not have to worry about political reelection, and their names were not under the public eye; thus these experts could act behind the scenes to shape and rationalize austerity.

Still, the job was no piece of cake: the political circumstances could not have been more unfavorable. As we know from earlier chapters, the war duress had politicized citizens. For the majority, economic sacrifice was a relic of the war; the country, it was largely thought, had "entered an entirely new epoch" of social redistribution and economic collectivism (Dawson 1917, 7). In this uneasy context austerity had to thump its way forward under the guise of its proclaimed sound economic theory. Ralph Hawtrey—the in-house Treasury economist and a pioneer in macroeconomic theory—provided just such a theoretical grounding.

Hawtrey modeled the economy as a great credit machine, and he understood inflation, i.e., the expansion of credit, as an insidious threat to the economy. As he vividly put it, "[i]nflation is a deadly blight; once it has gained a hold, it will poison the whole economic system, and can only be eliminated, if at all, at the cost of exhausting efforts" (Hawtrey 1923, 230). To Hawtrey, credit stabilization required constant monetary management; it was not going to stabilize on its own. The key to such management was to control—or better, to subjugate—the consumer.

It is easy to overlook—as the canonical literature does—the classist nature of a seemingly apolitical over-consumptionist model. Indeed, part of the construction of consensus and coercion around austerity rested in expelling class awareness from economic theory, even while terrorizing certain classes. Looking closer, these economic theories re-introduce class differences through the back door when they understand that not all consumers are equally virtuous. For the experts it was the unproductive consumer, i.e., the worker, who required control, while the productive consumer, i.e., the creditor/investor, required reward. The austerity policies that the experts envisioned were thus an essential instrument of forced redistribution in favor of the savers-investors and against the low-income, low-saving working class. This was the recipe for stabilizing money, increasing private capital, and normalizing wage relations.

Austerity was most certainly a political project, but its assumptions weren't necessarily wrong. Indeed, it laid bare an undeniable truth: for capitalism to function, workers had to be disciplined into accepting the two pillars of capital accumulation—the primacy of private property and wage relations.

These core principles of austerity double as the assumptions underlying today's mainstream economic theory, especially its tendency to serve political ends. This can be seen extensively in Hawtreyan theory, which experimented with many of the social abstractions that are typical of today's standard economic theory. In the preface of his most influential work, *Currency and Credit*, Hawtrey expressed grave concerns regarding the epochal changes he was witnessing. Prewar institutions were largely understood as "things of the past" (Hawtrey 1919a, Preface, vi). To him, "[t]here never was a time at which the currency systems of the world were so exposed to danger as they are likely to be in the immediate future" (ibid., 363). Apart from his clear distress over a deviation from the "normal" that was codified in his theories, Hawtrey's embeddedness in class struggle is revealed by his silent class bias and his clear-cut technocratic (anti-democratic) resolution to the crisis. Such an agenda, best embodied by his prescription of independent central banks (i.e., exempt from democratic pressures), soon became the common ploy of the British establishment.

The austerity experts' overarching goal was to bulwark economic relations from the influences of politics and state intervention; in doing so they both exempted economic policies from democratic decision-making and cast economic theory as *apolitical*. Of course, to conceive economic theory as apolitical required an unfettered market that was influenced only by its objective laws—a feat that, in a moment of public fervor, could only be achieved by shielding economic decisions from the general public. Indeed, the nature of depoliticization and the close interconnection of its three main features (i.e., removing the state from economic relations; removing economic policies from democratic decision-making; and understanding economic theory as *apolitical*) highlight how austerity—even in a parliamentary democracy like Britain—was essentially anti-democratic in nature. If we combine this characteristic of austerity with its main prescription—subduing the working classes into producing more and consuming less—we can easily say that austerity was (and still is) an outright repressive project.

Such repression required a team. What follows is an introduction to the characters and levers who facilitated it, stitching together austerity policies (in their threefold form of fiscal, industrial, and monetary) and the economic theory that molded and rationalized them. The telling of this story is based on a study of both Treasury policy memoranda (most of which had been unmined in the economic or historical literature) and Hawtrey's published and theoretical contributions from the period. These sources tell a story that to date has not been told: how a tight connection between the theories of monetary management and the urge to shape individual behavior was conceived and built to last. To achieve these ends, a campaign for an independent central bank (another story that has escaped scholarly attention but is in fact indispensable to understanding the nature of austerity to this day) was essential.

Technocrats at the Helm of Power

After World War I, the British Treasury had risen in stature[7] and came to be considered the central department of British government. Its powers as a department were embodied by the outsized personal sway of two civil servants, Sir Basil P. Blackett and Sir Otto Niemeyer. These two experts were the principal direct advisors to the chancellor of the exchequer[8] on all financial matters, including taxation, debt management, and domestic and international monetary policy. Their department of finance prepared the annual budget and often wrote the budget speeches for the chancellor himself.[9] Blackett vividly described his almost ubiquitous role: "the day-to-day work of the . . . Department . . . involves the assumption of responsibilities by the Controller of Finance which, when he makes the mistake of turning [his] mind to consider their magnitude, are really staggering" (August 17, 1921, T 199/3, fol. 133349).

All relations between the Treasury, the Bank of England, and the money market were in the controller's hands. Blackett and Niemeyer were both in direct and personal contact with the Bank's powerful governor, Montagu Norman (who held the office from 1920 to 1944), and Niemeyer was even Norman's close friend (Sayers 1976). After the war, the Bank of England and the Treasury shared monetary authority. With the large amount of Treasury bills in circulation until the spring of 1921, the Bank of England was dependent on the Treasury in order to raise the Bank rate (see Howson 1975, 10).

These "neutral" economic experts came from the high echelons

of society. Hailing from upper-middle-class families, they were educated in the prestigious halls of Oxford, where they were taught about
society—though notably not economics—through a lens of "national
interest."[10] Placing first in the civil service examinations (in 1904 and
1906, respectively), the two immediately secured posts at the Treasury
and began long careers. Blackett became controller of finance in 1920;
Niemeyer, his deputy, succeeded him in 1922 and held the post for the
ensuing five years.

The controllers' was a technocratic form of power. Their profound
clout and decision-making leeway over policy making came with their
position as permanent senior officials, insulated from the pressures
that come with universal suffrage and political competition. Until 1925,
Blackett and Niemeyer were more influential than the chancellor himself, who was usually in office for a very short period and was generally
not a financial expert (Peden 2000, 136–37). This remained true even
with a heavyweight like Churchill in office. A 1927 note by the governor
of the Bank of France, Emile Moreau, referred to the opinion of the
French ambassador in London: "He points out that Winston Churchill,
who detests [French Prime Minister] Poincaré, isn't really in control of
the Treasury. The man who does in fact control it is Sir Otto Niemeyer,
the intimate friend of M. Norman" (Boyle 1968, 229).[11]

The influence of the two experts extended later in their careers to
the Bank of England. Both Niemeyer and Blackett were recruited by
Governor Norman to high posts; Blackett was a director at the Bank
from 1929 until his death in 1935; Niemeyer was first executive director
and advisor to the governor (1927–1938), and then, for a long tenure, a
director of the Bank (1938–1952).

Most importantly, their political impact extended well beyond
national borders: the two technocrats devised austerity reforms that
spread to many other countries. Both were members of the financial
committee of the League of Nations and worked to implement the postwar financial reconstruction plans for Austria, Bulgaria, and Greece.[12]
The schemes made international loans conditional upon efforts to
balance the budget, to stabilize the currency, and especially to create

private central banks, independent of government—all central tenets of austerity.

Blackett pressed his hand particularly on the global East. As finance member of the Viceroy Executive Council in India (1922–1928), he pushed his austerity mandate by getting the colony to fund its floating debt, balance its budget, cut expenditures (especially in the railway system), stabilize the exchange rate, establish an independent central bank, and attain gold parity. Niemeyer advocated the same types of measures in his missions as a financial expert in Australia (1930), Brazil (1931), and Argentina (1933).[13]

Certainly, the two experts were no outliers relative to the history of the British Treasury: since the Victorian era, budgetary orthodoxy and monetary rigor had represented the uncontested doctrine of the department.[14] Yet, given the unprecedented climate following World War I, Blackett's and Niemeyer's influence during this period lends them special relevance to the evolution of modern-day austerity. The two defended capitalism in its purest laissez-faire form in a moment when it was widely challenged, both by the working classes (as studied in chapters 3–4) and by members of the British establishment (chapters 1–2). Austerity was crystallized out of this very challenge. Ironically, it became clear that to defend the "natural doings" of laissez-faire capitalism, direct coercive action was required.

The Challenges to Austerity from Within

The opposition to economic orthodoxy that exploded after the war would have been enough to keep the Treasury controllers up at night. Opposition to Britain's traditional economic and monetary views had seized government officials and civil servants, who with the war had been introduced to the seemingly limitless fiscal potential of the state apparatus. The orthodox "Treasury View,"[15] according to which there were natural limits to capital creation and government borrowing, no longer had a leg to stand on. The point was made over and over again that the reconstruction necessities and social projects required cheap loans. The formal suspension of the gold standard in March 1919 spoke for the newfound priority of avoiding unemployment. As even the establishment's newspaper had put it, the moment marked a palpable "defeat of the dear-money party," which was labeled "ineffective" and "expensive" ("City Notes," *The Times*, March 31, 1919, 21).

Published expressions of economic rebellion were collected in the confidential files of the controllers of finance, testifying to their seeming willingness to observe their enemies before running them down. Even when the bite of austerity began to sting, the opposition did not immediately wilt; these Treasury files kept meticulous track of it. Figures 6.1 and 6.2 give a sense of the continuity of the disgruntlement throughout the first part of the 1920s.

In May 1920, harsh words appeared in *The Times*. The paper published a reader's letter that expressed one of the guiding intuitions of this book: "Is the reduction of purchasing power a practicable proposition at this time? Is it consistent with the hopes which have been held out of the betterment in the conditions of the working class?" ("High Prices," *The Times*, May 18, 1920, 10).

In October 1923, *The Times* reported criticisms from Mr. McKenna, chairman of the London Joint Stock and Midland Bank and former

6.1. Clipping of a reader's letter titled "High Prices" (*The Times*, May 18, 1920, 10)

CITY OFFICE: 15, COPTHALL-AVENUE, E.C.2.
TELEPHONE:. LONDON-WALL 7767.

CITY NOTES.

BETTER MARKETS.

MR. MCKENNA'S SPEECH.

"Forced" Credit Restriction?

Some people, we imagine, in perusing the full speech, may stumble over the last portion of it. Mr. McKenna said that a forced restriction of purchasing power could not fail to depress trade and cause unemployment.

6.2. "City Notes" (*The Times*, October 25, 1923, 18).

chancellor of the exchequer (1915–1916), who in an address before the Belfast Chamber of Commerce condemned the consequences of the Treasury's deflationary policy that brought down prices by "forced restriction of purchasing power . . . [that] could not fail to depress trade and cause unemployment" ("City Notes," *The Times*, October 25, 1923, 18; also see in T 176/5, fol. 150). Hence, a double sacrifice for the general public: no consumption and no jobs.

In June 1924, the Advisory Committee of Finance and Commerce of the Trades Union Congress and the Labour Party released a memorandum declaring their "grave objections" to further deflation in order to secure the gold standard: it would condemn people to unemployment. They admonished: "an insistence on a rise in the Bank Rate at the present time, whatever may be said for it in the long run, looks very much

Private and Confidential.　　　June, 1924.　　　No. 34.

GENERAL COUNCIL　　　　　EXECUTIVE COMMITTEE
TRADES UNION CONGRESS.　　　　LABOUR PARTY.
　　　------------　　　　　　　-------------

JOINT RESEARCH AND INFORMATION DEPARTMENT.

ADVISORY COMMITTEE ON FINANCE AND COMMERCE.

M E M O R A N D U M

on

THE PROPOSED RAISING OF THE BANK RATE IN THE NEAR
FUTURE.

By J. E. Norton.

The prevailing low rate of the dollar exchange and the
desire to take some definite step towards the restoration of the
gold standard have led to a wide-spread expectation, and, in
certain influential quarters, to definite propaganda in favour
of an immediate raising of the Bank Rate to 5%. Any such step
at the present moment, would appear to be open to grave objections

Whatever may be said in favour of submitting to some
measure of deflation in order to secure the advantages of a
gold standard, a moment when the trade revival is hesitating,
when prices in America are falling and when we are entering
on the period of the normal seasonal downward fluctuation in
exchange rates, seems a particularly inopportune one for
putting such a policy into practice. An insistence on a rise
in the Bank Rate at the present time, whatever may be said
for it in the long run, looks very much like a sacrifice of
the immediate interests of the general community to the
immediate interests of the bankers. It seems urgent that any
pressure which can be brought to bear to prevent such a rise,
should be exercised.

6.3. Advisory Committee of Finance and Commerce of the Trade Union Congress, memorandum on the proposed raising of the bank rate in the near future, June 1924 (T 176/5, part 2, fols. 2–4).

like a *sacrifice of the immediate interests of the general community* to the immediate interests of the bankers."[16] As figure 6.3 shows, Niemeyer heavily underlined and annotated the memorandum. The document, like many others, attests to the general awareness of the primary political issue at stake: austerity policies had at their basis the sacrifice of the vast majority of British citizens.

How were the experts capable of contending with such an onslaught stemming from the very heart of the establishment? The answer lay in an appeal to high economic theory. Indeed, the entwinement of economic theory and austerity policies—so crucial in a moment of high contestation—is the defining characteristic of austerity as we know it today, where consensus complements coercion.

The Defense of Austerity: Economic Theory to the Rescue

In the face of unrelenting opposition, Niemeyer and Blackett needed solid intellectual grounds to urge the chancellor of the exchequer to move for dear money and drastic cuts in public expenditures. In examining the controllers' confidential Treasury files—virtually the only direct source of information we have about their economic beliefs—one is struck by the ubiquity and influence of the economist Ralph G. Hawtrey,[17] the primary source of economic knowledge for Blackett and especially for Niemeyer. In fact, there is ample evidence that Hawtreyan economics refined and strengthened[18] the economic stance of the senior Treasury officials, so as to enable the emergence of a full-blown austerity doctrine.

Hawtrey was born into a well-to-do family in Slough, a town twenty miles west of central London. He followed the *cursus honorum* of the British elite: he graduated from Eton, the number one private school, and after reading mathematics at Trinity College, Cambridge, undertook a career as a civil servant. In 1919, he was appointed Director of Financial Enquiries and was finally "sufficiently high placed in the Treasury to be part of the inner process of policymaking" (Black 1977, 378).[19] Hawtrey's role was that of the first "in-house economist," whose duty was to comment and offer advice on every aspect of economic policy,[20] a position he kept until his retirement in 1947, when he accepted a professorship at the Royal Institute of International Affairs. During his tenure at the Treasury, Hawtrey was the sole official to be an economic scholar of international standing; the crowning of his academic career came in 1959 with an honorary fellowship at Trinity College, Cambridge.[21] Hawtrey established his name as a prominent monetary economist with his 1913 *Good and Bad Trade*—a book that articulated the monetary business cycle. His repute increased in 1919 with *Currency and Credit*.

Keynes, who was hugely influenced by his colleague and friend Hawtrey, hailed *Currency and Credit* as "one of the most original and profound treatises on the theory of money which has appeared for many years" (Keynes 1920, in Peden 1996). The text first developed insights that are today understood as Keynesian, including the centrality of consumer income and consumer outlay in influencing the monetary business cycle, and its necessary implication: the essence of monetary management is much more than simply manipulating the quantity of money in circulation, as the traditional quantity theory of money purports.[22] It lies more deeply in manipulating the behavior of real economic agents in terms of their incomes and expenditures.

Currency and Credit was widely used as a textbook in the 1920s. It became a standard text for the Cambridge Tripos in economics as well as overseas, including in the Harvard economics department, where Hawtrey taught as a visiting professor in 1928–1929. David Laidler has documented how during the interwar years Hawtrey's influence even reached the Chicago School of Economics (Laidler 1993).

Hawtrey had some shining moments, especially at the 1922 Genoa Financial Conference, where his voice dominated all others. Years later the expert recalled the "regular meetings with the delegates and other officials every evening after the day's proceedings."[23] Hawtrey had already presented his draft prescriptions (approved by Blackett and Norman) at the preliminary meetings of experts in London; the Genoa austerity financial code incorporated these. Another high moment came when he personally advised Chancellor Churchill to make the controversial decision to declare the return to the gold standard (Peden 2004b, 33–39).[24] More than these specific episodes, however, Hawtrey's real impact was an indelible imprint on the most powerful minds of the Treasury.[25]

Blackett and Niemeyer regularly wrote notes to Hawtrey asking for advice on economic matters, from the most technical and statistical questions to specific policy suggestions.[26] Hawtrey's prolific responses in the form of memoranda were thoroughly underlined, studied, exchanged, and discussed. His advice on monetary and fiscal principles even spread outside the Treasury, including to the other main technocratic institution in Britain—the Court of the Bank of England.

Hawtrey had frequent personal exchanges with the Bank's governor, Montagu Norman, especially during the hot years of 1919–1924. Norman often asked Hawtrey for advice regarding the monetary policy that should be implemented, and the two were often in fundamental agreement. In 1920 Norman showed a spirit both keen and questioning in his response to Hawtrey's memo endorsing the decision to raise the Bank's interest rate all the way to 7 percent: "I am of course much in agreement with respect to the memorandum you have kindly sent me. . . . I would like you to consider this note—might not we, of the dear money school, be taxed with bad faith if the rate were put up now?"[27]

Norman's appreciation for Hawtrey's economic work was spread to the whole Court, which throughout the 1920s was educated in Hawtreyan economics. "Dear Mr. Hawtrey," Norman wrote in 1923, "it was very good of you to send me a copy of your new volume of Essays. Your papers are always read here with great interest and although we have studied one or two of the present series before, we shall not value the book any less on that account. Yours very Truly" (February 6, 1923, GBR/0014/HTRY 10/11, Churchill Archives Centre). Occasions for intellectual suasion among the members of the British governing elite were frequent. Bankers, Treasury officials, and economists were often seen mingling. For example, the Tuesday Club—a small dining club started by the stockbroker Oswald Toynbee Falk in 1917—convened financiers, financial journalists, academic economists, and Treasury officials to discuss economic questions and the post-financial problems

(Skidelsky 2003, 203).[28] Regular members included Blackett, Niemeyer, and Norman, as well as Keynes, who was a founding member.

In sum, Hawtreyan economics spread far and wide, becoming embedded in the worldview of the most commanding minds of the leading technocratic institutions that implemented austerity after World War I. In a moment when budget cuts and dear money policies had lost their veneer as "natural" policies and faced harsh public backlash, they required economic theory to justify them. Their grounding in economic theory came through the personalities at the levers of power. This was the true novelty of austerity—a project that was at once theory- and policy-making, at once an ideological, material, and personal process.

Tackling Inflation

Currency and Credit was written as a general model of the world economy, but it also reflected Hawtrey's preoccupations with the economic struggles at hand. Indeed, his analysis was driven by one main fixation: the inherent tendency for a market economy to spiral into inflation.

Inflation, Hawtrey believed, was the vicious expression of the "unruly nature" of credit. Credit was the basis of the market economy. Hawtrey modeled the market economy like a great credit machine, by which any sort of economic relation could be understood as an exchange of debt and credit between buyers and sellers.[29] In this framework, relations of exchange between consumers and producers overshadowed class relations within the production process.

Despite its technical jargon, the message of the Hawtreyan model was actually quite simple: inflation was the main threat to the market economy, and the causes of inflation fundamentally rested in exaggerated spending on the part of the general population—especially its lower ranks. Indeed, the "unruly" nature of credit and its tendency to expand excessively was fundamentally based on the *unruly* behavior of the majority of citizens who undertook "unproductive" consumption. The problem was not the expansion of credit *in itself*, but rather the resulting increase in *consumption* that would propel a further increase in credit. In Hawtrey's words, "[t]he credit created for the purposes

AUSTERITY, A BRITISH STORY

of production becomes purchasing power in the hands of the people engaged in production; the greater the amount of credit created, the greater will be the amount of purchasing power" (Hawtrey 1919a, 13).

Hawtrey pointed his finger at the impact credit expansion had on "effective demand"[30]—a crucial macroeconomic concept which he introduced in 1913, and which Keynes would further develop in his *General Theory*. Credit expansion increased effective demand, defined as the "quantity of purchasing power in the hands of the public" (Hawtrey 1919a, 350).[31]

To Hawtrey, such an over-consumptionist spiral was ever more dangerous because it was not capable of self-correction. In an economic upswing, increased incomes mean greater purchases by the general consumers (i.e., workers) that "will be quickly reflected in further orders to replenish the stocks of commodities" from the merchant (or dealer), setting the credit machine into hyperactivity.[32] After a certain point, society reaches its productive limits and prices begin to rise (i.e., supply fails to increase), further aggravating the credit machine and depreciating the value of money even more.[33] This spiral has a self-sustaining effect: peoples' increased demand supports their own employment, since their purchases deplete the stock of goods; merchants thus place more orders, inducing producers to increase production by hiring more workers.[34] In this sense, employment and higher wages are seen not as an achievement of economic progress but as a threat to the standard of value.

The war and immediate postwar climate made these dynamics even more pronounced: "Prices will be high because the depleted stocks of goods will be exposed to a large effective demand, the quantity of purchasing power in the hands of the public having been swollen under war conditions and the consumers' income being maintained at a high level corresponding to the activity of production" (Hawtrey 1919a, 350).

The "vicious expansion" of credit, Hawtrey argued, not only debauched the internal standard of value; it also debauched the external one. Hawtrey could not be more explicit: "It must be remembered that the *direct* cause of adverse exchanges is too much buying . . . the buying of the dealers tends to follow the buying of the consumers" (ibid.,

352, italics in original). In Hawtrey's model the increase in consumers' outlay—their capacity to spend—produces an adverse movement of the foreign exchanges, since it attracts additional imports and diverts some possible exports to the home market.[35]

In his advice to Chancellor Chamberlain, Blackett adopted a Hawtreyan take on the gravity of Britain's postwar inflation. The rise in prices was just the most visible indication of the rise in the "purchasing power of the community" ("Dear Money," February 12, 1920, T 176/5, part 2, fol. 50) that spiked with the government's expansionary war and postwar policies. Blackett argued that the government exacerbated this spiral by artificially increasing the amount of money in the hands of the people. More precisely, the controller made explicit that it was the increase in the purchasing power of a *specific* part of the population that was responsible for such a dramatic price spike: "redistribution of the purchasing power among the various classes of the community has been altered in favour of those whose purchases were most severely restricted by the narrowness of their purses" (ibid., T 176/5, part 2, fol. 48).

Blackett derived the class consequences that were concealed by the neutral syntax of the Hawtreyan model: the cause of the crisis rested in workers' wasteful behavior. Whereas before the war they were limited by economic constraints, once their wages had risen workers were fundamentally reluctant to save.

During his efforts for the War Savings Committee, Blackett had denounced how "[t]his war is bringing, in all the belligerent countries, large sums into the pockets of the wage earners" (ibid., 77). For once, Blackett said, there was "some surplus over bare necessities" that could be saved; however, "[t]here was unfortunately a terrible amount of useless and wasteful extravagance," and "[t]he cheap jewelry trade was booming." These classist attacks were indeed not far from Hawtrey's own understanding, at least once one pierces the veil of his economic abstractions.

Currency and Credit articulated two types of consumers: "Where there is an accession of income, the thrifty man will tend to invest his windfall, the unthrifty to spend it" (Hawtrey 1919a, 42). It was the "thrifty" and "prudent" man whose actions prevented inflationary spirals; he saved rather than spent. Hawtrey, Blackett, and Niemeyer shared an assumption that was well grounded in the economic orthodoxy of the time: savings automatically implied investment, thus restoring "the nation's equipment of fixed capital and of its stocks of commodities" (Hawtrey 1919a, 348).[36] Reconstruction required a plentiful supply of capital, and "there is no way that capital can be made available except through saving" (Blackett 1918a, 20–21).[37]

Such a moral and individualist framework portrayed all agents in society as *deciding* whether to be profligate or thrifty consumers. However, in his sparse references to workers (as contrasted with his predominant focus on consumers), Hawtrey himself could not help but tacitly consider the structurally different material conditions that ultimately boxed the worker as the "unthrifty" type. For Hawtrey, wage earners acted in a unidimensional way, that is, spending their wage "in the course of the week on their day-to-day expenses" (Hawtrey 1919a, 20). Capturing a concrete reality at the time, Hawtrey did not expect workers to possess bank accounts (except for the rare thrifty types,[38] he specified), with cash representing the entirety of the general population's liquid resources. In this sense the greater part of wages "comes back to retailers in return for goods purchased" (ibid., 22).

It followed that the only consumers who had the capacity to be virtuous and save were really the bourgeois. To be virtuous, the rest could only fall in line and abstain through a curtailment of income. Thus the presence within society of two categories of agents: those who could undertake savings in the positive sense (by investing), and the majority that should be led to undertake it in the negative sense (by abstaining).[39] Still today, mainstream economists provide these distinctions by talking about the differences in the propensities to save (or to consume), and if we look closely, these propensities are tacitly associated with class differences. The implication is that lower incomes are due to the unthrifty habits of individuals, as opposed to the subordinate positions of workers under capitalist social relations of production.

Blackett and Niemeyer denounced the postwar society as a distortion of the virtuous script of capital accumulation, a product of how individuals found themselves in uniquely inverted conditions. Indeed, the traditional distribution of purchasing power among classes had been altered in favor of organized labor. While inflation could erode real wages, trade unions were able to preserve workers' purchasing power by demanding higher money wages—even by going on strike if necessary. Workers thus attained new income and had the tendency to spend it all, on either domestic commodities or foreign commodities. On the other hand, sections of the middle and upper classes—whose income came from savings or deriving rents—had experienced a reduction of their real income and were unable to keep pace with prices.[40] These circumstances were the nemesis of monetary stability and capital accumulation.

From a classist diagnosis came a classist solution. Hawtrey himself put it bluntly: "The inflation of credit, by financing the war with less than the due amount of *sacrifice* on the part of the people, actually attracts superfluous imports; the problem is then not so much to finance the imports, as to avoid attracting them. The solution is to be found not in borrowing more money abroad, but in *encouraging or enforcing abstinence at home*" (Hawtrey 1919a, 230, my italics).

The focus on abstinence reveals the individualistic approach of the experts to tackling social problems. In a manner similar to the resolutions of the Brussels and Genoa conferences, they saw economic difficulties as the result of improper individual behavior, which in turn had to be fixed through sacrifice in the name of economic recovery. The reader might be familiar with this rhetoric, as it pervades much of public discourse even today.

Teaching Abstinence

Educating the general public to be thrifty was imperative—and, of course, tricky. The campaign for abstinence had already started during World War I, and Blackett and Niemeyer were prominent members of the War Savings Movement in Great Britain that "enforced the lesson of patriotic abstention from self-indulgence" (Blackett 1918a, 30). The movement preached "patriotic self denial" (Blackett 1918b, 210), with the immediate rationale of financing the state's war effort through the purchase of Treasury bonds.

Blackett took the mission to heart, and between 1916 and 1917 he traveled across Britain and the United States to zealously lecture audiences on how to "deny themselves comforts and luxuries" (Blackett 1918a, 16). In a public speech in New York City he spelled out the spirit of sacrifice that would become the basis of austerity: "Produce more, consume less, waste nothing . . . it does not matter whether or what you are paid for your services: spend your money and yourself in the service of your country" (ibid., 70).

This prescription was not to be interpreted as grim and exceptional, he clarified, but rather as a condition for economic progress to be developed into a universal norm. Blackett admonished the crowd, "[w]ere we not all tired of the ostentatious extravagances of the pre-war period? Has not the war taught us that our sense of values had gone wrong?" (ibid., 20). Learning the custom of thrift, he told the New York teachers, had to begin at a very early age: "By not buying candy, or by not going to the movies, they [children] could increase the amount standing to their credit in the school War Savings Association" (ibid., 73–74).

The wealthy classes had an important role to play as models of virtue: "What the well-to-do can do is by the force of their personal example acting upon and influencing public opinion to show the way to the workers. . . . It is amazing what a difference personal example among the well-to-do, and particularly in the case of women, makes on the effectiveness of the War Savings campaign among the workers" (ibid., 18).

Niemeyer shared these beliefs. A decade later, he exported the British model to Brazil by advising its government "to encourage the formation of a voluntary committee of suitable persons for the organization and propaganda of thrift throughout the country" (Niemeyer 1931, 22).

Britain's experts were, however, under no illusion: after the war, the degree to which the system was being contested meant that workers were no longer inclined to abide by the behavioral dictates of the ruling classes. Chamberlain's financial statement of April 1919 expressed the perceived change of people's attitude:

We all know what has happened since the signature of the Armistice. There has been a détente in men's minds. . . . People who during the War strove their utmost to save and to place their savings at the disposal of the Government are less willing to make those sacrifices now . . . both the House and the people are in a different mood to-day, and I am called upon . . . to provide the means for creating within a few months or a few years a new heaven and a new earth. (Austen Chamberlain, Financial Statement 1919, HC Deb 30 April 1919, vol. 115, cc 175–76)

Against this "relaxation" of spirit, Hawtrey, Niemeyer, and Blackett espoused economic policies that would directly impose abstinence on the working classes, thwarting any unwillingness to sacrifice. Fiscal, industrial, and monetary austerity served exactly this purpose.

Fiscal Austerity

During the summer of 1919, under direct advice of his Treasury experts, Chancellor Chamberlain offered a public ultimatum: "If we cannot balance revenue and expenditure next year, our credit—national and international—will be seriously shaken and the results may be disastrous" (July 26, 1919, T 171/170).

This call for budgetary rigor was a step (and pretext) toward sowing the behavioral shift among the "unruly" majority, with a goal of curing inflation.[41] It also served as justification for increasing (regressive) taxation and cutting government expenditure; both policies curtailed consumption for the majority and incentivized savings/investment for the minority.

TAXATION TO IMPOSE THRIFT

"Taxation," Hawtrey wrote, "by reducing people's resources, gives them an inducement to reduce their consumption of commodities" (Hawtrey 1919a, 351). In a moment in which overextending taxation to the working classes faced peak opposition, Hawtrey praised taxation's ability to force abstention on the people.

During the war period, mounting workers' movements opposed the state's extractive measures, which had increased the tax base to include much of the working classes for the first time.[42] High inflation after the war exacerbated the contentious and political nature of such reforms, with unions demanding a reduction of the tax burden to account for increased cost of living.[43] After the war, and still facing popular demands, the Treasury refused to pay the high financial price of restoring prewar-level exemptions in real terms (i.e., to take account of inflation), a measure which would have freed 2.2 million of 3.4 million income-tax payers from this form of hardship.

To impose "compulsory thrift"[44] upon the classes who, in the view of experts, were structurally incapable of saving/investing, indirect taxation—that is, taxation on consumption goods—was the most effective means. Indirect taxation was at once less visible (thus less contestable) and more pernicious. It transferred purchasing power away from people whose earnings were too small to be liable to the income tax but who could still not do without basic goods. It was the definition of regressive taxation: "the smaller the income, the larger is the rate upon it which the taxes represent" (HMSO 1927, 211–13).

Spurred by the advice of Treasury experts, in his budget of April 1920 Chancellor Chamberlain introduced a further tax increase on working-class consumption goods such as tobacco, beer, and spirits, all of which had already risen during the year prior.[45] As table 6.1 shows, the weight of indirect taxes grew throughout the decade.

Hawtrey repeatedly cited how regressive measures like these suited the priorities of capitalist recovery. "It is only by financial methods, such as drastic taxation, which tend to curtail the expenditure of the

Table 6.1. Distribution of taxes in Britain

Year	Direct Taxes (in percentage)	Indirect Taxes (in percentage)
1919–20	75.1	24.9
1924–25	66.9	33.1
1929–30	64.2	35.9

Source: Chancellor of the Exchequer, Budget, vol. 1, 1924-25, T 171/232, 235; and Inland Revenue, Budgets of April and September 1931, IR 113/42.

individual upon consumable commodities, that deflation and capital expenditure can both be encouraged" (Hawtrey 1919a, 351).

Indeed, once utilized with the purpose of repaying debt and interest on debt, regressive taxation *did* serve to avoid demand-driven credit expansion and induced the virtue of investment through transfers of wealth "from the poorer to the richer" (HMSO 1927, 99). Between 1921 and 1932, the largest item in the chancellor's budget was in fact debt service, which meant that the nation was shifting tax revenue to holders of the national debt—the portion of the community that, according to our technocrats, was more "inclined" to save, and thus invest.[46]

In October 1921, Niemeyer sent a note to the chancellor in which he made this economic logic very explicit: "When debt is repaid out of money collected by taxation from the *citizens at large* it is used to pay off loan holders, that is that portion of the community which is *more inclined to save* than the rest and the tendency will be for the investor who is paid off to reinvest his money in other securities. In other words, debt repayment *extracts money* from those who are not likely to save and invest and makes it available to those that are more likely to do so" (T 176/5, part 2, fols. 39–40, my italics). In other words, the state extracting money from the working classes was the key to capital accumulation.

Once again, Niemeyer's words echoed those of Hawtrey, who in 1920 had written, "taxation for debt redemption takes money from people who might otherwise spend it on themselves and uses it to increase the resources of the capital market" ("Mr McKenna on over-taxation," GBR/0014/HTRY 1/14, Churchill Archives Centre). Still in 1932 Blackett had very similar thoughts: "Sinking fund payments may indeed be a useful method of assisting to build up capital for productive purposes" (Blackett 1932, 236).

With the same goal of rewarding the saver/investors, experts conceived of ways to lower taxation for the wealthy classes. Here again the rationale was simple: since the wealthy classes have a natural propensity to save, high direct taxation on these classes would check savings and discourage investment. Niemeyer wrote: "The level of taxation must not be inconsistent with the economic life of the country and with the accumulation of fresh capital" (T 176/39, fol. 62). Higher death duties and "Capital Levies [taxation on capital] mean a much more serious loss to the country at large" (Niemeyer, March 13, 1926, T 176/39, fol. 59) since, as Blackett put it, the levies would "trench" on "the nation's capital" (Blackett 1932, 240).

This wording illustrates the subtlety of austerity's political message, one that rationalizes and justifies the shift (or extraction) of resources from the many to the few. These virtuous few were wealthy not only because of their individual moral qualities; they also operated to fortify capital accumulation, which was assumed to be in the national interest.

This thinking, which remains pervasive today, was successful in defeating the many radical redistributive reforms on taxing wealth that had arisen in the immediate aftermath of the war. Introduced in April 1920, the corporation tax was reduced by half as early as 1923, and was ultimately abolished in 1924. It would return to the House of Commons only after World War II. Similarly, the 1915 Excess Profit Duty—a major victory for British trade unions—was completely eliminated in 1921. Even more emblematic of the triumph of austerity was the fate of the capital levy. Deemed the battle horse of the Labour Party[47] after the war—uniting a widespread attack against profiteers—by the mid-1920s the idea of it was dead and buried. The Committee on National Debt and Taxation voiced the novel social internalization that justified profit-making and the riches of the capitalist class. The capital levy, it was suggested, "involved a penalisation of thrift which is both unjust and also economically indefensible" (HMSO 1927, 402).

Of course, when operating under the guise of budgetary rigor, the state could lower taxation on the few only if it curtailed public expenditure. A thrifty state was to technocrats the ultimate mantra to overcome the postwar crisis.[48] The majority of the population had to be forced to abstain not only from individual consumption but also from public consumption at large, grossly subverting the postwar reconstructionist trend. Blackett warned of the dangers of the government's complicity in supporting citizens to live beyond their means: "The attempt to maintain standards of living for everyone, above those which the economic activities of the nation justified, by means of government expenditure out of taxation is in part responsible for the breakdown" (Blackett 1932, 240). For our experts, such excesses were no longer tolerable.

THE ATTACK ON SOCIAL EXPENDITURES

Hawtrey had set it in stone in *Currency and Credit*: in addition to taxation, reduction of public expenditure was vital to curtail consumers' income and redirect resources for private capital investment.

By the summer of 1920 the Treasury was pressing all departments to provide a progress report in order to cut expenditure within a fortnight.[49] Later, in December 1920, the cabinet explicitly gave in to these anti-reconstructionist pressures: "Whilst recognising that there are many reforms that are in themselves desirable in order to improve conditions in the United Kingdom . . . to the extent that such reforms involve further burdens upon the Exchequer or the Rates the time is not opportune for initiating them or putting them into operation" ("Draft Resolutions on Economy," December 8, 1920, CAB 23/23, ff. 196). The cabinet therefore instructed that all "schemes involving expenditures not yet in operation are to remain in abeyance" (ibid.).

The Treasury's fiscal austerity went well beyond curtailment of the reconstructionist plans discussed in chapter 2. Its greatest victory came in the unprecedented Geddes Axe of 1921—a legend in British politics, as it represented the country's largest expenditure squeeze in the twentieth century.[50] It beat even the renowned cuts of the Thatcher Administration in the late 1970s and 1980s. The Geddes legislation sliced an additional £52 million from the public budget beyond the £75 million that the Treasury had already planned in the summer (see table 6.2). The two combined were a remarkable reduction in historical perspective, amounting to about 20 percent of central government spending (Hood and Himaz 2014, 8). A telling indicator of austerity's actual objectives, the axe gashed the British population even though Britain had already attained a primary surplus the year before. Britain's governing body for social budgeting, the Committee of National Expenditure, or the "Geddes Committee," was a technical body working closely with the Treasury. The chancellor and his experts kept the budget-cutting priority alive through numerous briefs that guided the committee's work (see Blackett's note in T 171/202, fols. 34–39).[51] In his speech for the House of Commons in March 1922 Chancellor Robert Horne expressed profound gratitude to the "highly capable body of men" (T 172/1228 part 3, fol. 3) who had "discharged the very onerous task" that the Treasury had "laid upon them" through "unremitting labour." He valorized this effort to economize, calling it the "most valuable services to the community" (ibid., f. 2). Such a "service" to the "community" consisted in bulldozing all postwar emancipatory proposals.

The British citizens faced the defeat of the public housing program—the existence of which many Treasury officials had opposed since the program's inception.[52] Of course, with the curtailment of government subsidies and a vigorous policy of sale of public housing came the defeat of the building guilds movement examined in chapter 3. Christopher Addison, the champion of the Housing and Town Planning Act of 1919, resigned from government in protest,[53] while the minister of health, Sir Alfred Mond, was left to lament this turn of events as inimical to "the housing needs of the community. . . . There will remain many cases of serious overcrowding and evil slum conditions in many places" (June 22, 1921, T 161/132, fol. 51).

Citizens also watched the burial of the plan for universal health care, which would ultimately have to wait until after World War II to be revamped. It was instead supplanted by a proposal for a 15 percent cut for the Ministry of Health, which coincided with the renunciation of the educational gains promised by the 1918 Education Act—including the plan for universal continued education until the age of sixteen—that ultimately remained only on paper. The Board of Education was a particular nuisance to the Treasury, as it was "determined not to allow political pressures for the economy on public expenditures" to "halt the normal growth of educational provision." The board took a blow when the Geddes Committee proposed £18 million in cuts, a 32 percent decrease from the previous year; the government ended up cutting more than £16 million for education. Such slashes strangled the education system by closing small schools, reducing salaries, and increasing class sizes (T 172/1228 part 7, see fols. 4–5). The teachers were docked

Table 6.2. Spending cuts in Britain for main budget categories between 1922 and 1923 (in £m)

	Defense	Education	Social Security	Health	Foreign	Salaries	Total (in £m)
Nominal cuts	79	15	13	12	20	6	162
Real cuts (1922 prices)	85	16	14	13	22	7	176

The cuts in real terms are even more impressive than those in nominal terms because of the effect of falling prices between 1922 and 1923. I represent the cuts in real terms to highlight the severity of the already deep cuts. Note that prior to the Geddes Committee's involvement the chancellor had already planned £75m in cuts. The Committee recommended additional cuts, totaling £87m.

Source: Hood and Himaz (2014).

5 percent of their salary. It goes without saying that the ambitious plans for critical adult working-class education (studied in chapter 2) were choked by these cuts, to the point that the Central Labour College shut down in 1929 for lack of funding. Central government expenditure on education and on health insurance remained below the 1921–1922 level for the rest of the decade (see Peden 1985).

These impacts reverberated among people across the empire. The Geddes Committee prescribed reductions in services to colonies, making explicit that "the assistance which can be given by the British Exchequer to our African Dependencies must be limited to the most urgent requirements which those Dependencies can show themselves to be unable to meet out of their own resources" (HMSO 1922d, 12).

By 1922, all sectors of social policies were unable to resist the economy drive: the state's priority of debt reduction propelled a constant flow of resources from the working classes to the creditor classes of society. In fact, the large primary surplus reached a peak of 9 percent of nominal GDP in 1923; the surplus was used mainly to finance the redemption of debt. The amount the British state spent (as a share of nominal GDP) to pay creditors was almost double the amount spent for social measures (specifically, the sum spent on health and education) for each year of the decade starting from 1921–22.[54]

It is telling that the only expenditure that did not fall during these years—and in fact skyrocketed—was unemployment insurance.[55] This was the result not of greater generosity in the subsidies, but of a quadrupling of unemployed workers from 1920 to 1921, with an unemployment rate above 10 percent of the insured workforce for the whole decade. It can be argued that unemployment was the most emblematic measure of austerity-induced social sacrifice. As the reader will learn in the following pages, this social calamity was an expected and even intentional outcome of the austerity doctrine of the British technocrats.

In fact, the two companions of fiscal austerity—industrial and monetary policies—actively collaborated to worsen the employment possibilities, and thus the wages, of British workers. Again, this population was forced into financial abstinence.

Industrial Austerity

The Treasury's technocrats knew that the defeat of inflation and the rehabilitation of capital accumulation could not occur without industrial austerity. Industrial austerity came in the form of privatization and legal measures to discipline and repress labor.

PRIVATIZATION AND DEPOLITICIZATION: THE CROWDING-OUT ARGUMENT

The state's large-scale dismantling of its wartime control facilitated the depoliticization of the country's economy—a process to shore up the pillars of private property and wage relations and to protect the investing classes.

The Treasury fervently supported a privatization drive, which in part took the form of eradicating all "superfluous ministries."[56] This included the Ministry of Reconstruction, the Ministry of Transport, the Ministry of Munitions, the Ministry of Shipping, and the Ministry of Food, all abolished in 1921. The Ministry of Labour was also under Treasury's brutal attack and barely survived the cut.

It goes without saying that austerity targeted public employees, too. In the summer of 1919 the chancellor complained loudly: "the number still employed in the public services have, in the aggregate, hardly decreased perceptively since the war. That cannot be defended. . . . Everything in excess of this must be ruthlessly cut down. In the interest of economy we must be willing to content ourselves with the second best where the best is too costly" (August 28, 1919, T 170/171, fol. 2).

The Treasury's demands were satisfied. In 1920 and 1921 total civil employment fell from 19,537,000 to 17,417,000 (Feinstein 1972, Table T-126), meaning that the government laid off 11 percent of all public employees in a single year. The Geddes Axe also contributed its share, saving the Treasury 5 percent in GDP through layoffs and cuts in wages.

Certainly, economy of resources was the explicit pretext. More fundamentally, these policies derailed the alarming postwar social processes that were detailed in chapters 3 and 4, in particular their tendency toward upward pressure. The "grandiose ideas of departments" (April 6, 1925, T 176/21, fol. 10), as Niemeyer put it, had to be formally opposed, since only once "their appetites [were] definitely checked" would the appetites of their employees also be checked (ibid.). The austerity logic was impeccable: once people lost their jobs in the public sector, they would be thrown into the unrestrained private labor market, and thus would have to abide by its incontestable laws of supply and demand. Economic necessity disciplined workers; it subdued potential for political misbehavior.

These insights explain the Treasury's fierce opposition to any public plans to contest the country's rising unemployment. Noteworthy is the Gairloch episode in the autumn of 1921, in which some Liberal ministers met in the Scottish village under the aegis of Prime Minister Lloyd George to pressure the Treasury to embrace an expansive policy of loan-financed public works to create new jobs.[57] The Treasury was bombarded with proposals: from the Gairloch Scheme for a national development loan (T 172/1208, fols. 43–45), to a railway electrification plan (ibid., fols. 85–86), to a plan of the minister of health for the utilization of war savings money for unemployment relief works (ibid., fol. 87). Blackett and Niemeyer strongly opposed these and other "wild cat schemes" (ibid.), warning the chancellor that "the national financial position makes it therefore imperative to limit assistance to something near the barest minimum needed to prevent starvation" (ibid., fol. 143).[58]

Just as privatization disciplined workers to accept their place in the vertical relations of production, it also benefited the saver-investor classes. The controllers' agenda was immovable: the state had to release all possible resources in favor of private enterprise. In Niemeyer's words: "Industry could not permanently prosper while the state was absorbing the greater part of investible savings" (T 176/21, fol. 26). In 1922, Blackett used the same terminology: "the fund of investible capital is reduced by the lending to the government of what might otherwise be lent to trade" (T 171/202, fol. 23). Here lies the crux of the crowding-out argument: the government is accused of diverting private savings from the investment market—money that would otherwise be invested in more productive private enterprises.[59]

At least until 1924, Keynes shared these austere beliefs. When starting work on his *Treatise on Money*, he had no doubts that "[a] supply of new capital can only come into existence insofar as those who have claims on the community's flow of income are willing to defer their claims, i.e., out of savings. The expenditure, on the production of fixed capital, of public money which has been raised by borrowing, can do nothing of itself to improve matters; and it may do actual harm if it diverts existing working capital away from the production of goods" (Keynes 1971, vol. 13, 19–23).[60]

The evils of public works did not stop there. Public works could also be inflationary. This was because the government did not always borrow from "genuine savings" (i.e., taxes or Treasury bonds), but rather financed its investment through novel credit expansion—a wartime practice that our technocrats abhorred. Cheap money was the greatest of Hawtrey's peeves since it propelled an inflationary upturn that increased employment, and ultimately boosted wages and working-class consumption—which in turn triggered monetary instability and escalated the threat to capital accumulation.[61]

The Treasury did not abandon the crowding-out argument later, even in the face of the social crisis following the 1929 crash. In 1929, Stanley Baldwin's conservative government's pleas for public works to confront the "miserable condition"[62] of the 1.5 million unemployed British citizens fell on deaf ears. Indeed, austerity was the mantra with which the Treasury pressured the government to approach the Great Depression, even after the fall of the gold standard in 1931 (see Peden 1996, 69–88).

WAGES, UNEMPLOYMENT, STRIKES

A fundamental plank of austerity dogma is that a drastic reduction in wages can cure any economic downturn.

Higher wages not only lead to excessive consumption; they also produce the parallel problem of higher production costs. Technocrats after the Great War knew that the increased bargaining power of organized labor (T 172/1208) meant that inflation would not act as a device for reducing real wages; it would merely escalate costs of production that would result in rising export prices (T 176/5, part 2, fol. 35).

The need to lower prices in order to boost exports is repeated time and again in the notes and memoranda of the two controllers (see T 176/21, fol. 27; February 19, 1923, T 172/214, fol. 4). Niemeyer was explicit: "It is generally admitted that if British trade is to compete in the markets of the world, the price of British goods must come down. This in effect means that the wages of British labour must come down" (Niemeyer, T 175/5, part 2, fol. 36).

The "recipe for the long-term general interest" was the people's dual sacrifice of decreased consumption (which would reduce internal demand and prices) and decreased wages (which would permit lower costs of production and thus improve competitiveness). As Blackett put it, the "period of painful process to return to sound conditions will begin to be succeeded by a revival of industry on a new basis of reduced wages and reduced prices" (June 8, 1921, T 175.6, part 1, fol. 1).[63]

Hawtrey had anticipated these thoughts in his talk to the British Association for the Advancement of Science in 1919: "deflation also inevitably involves a reduction of wages. This is an indispensable condition both of the reduction of cost of production and of the reduction of effective demand. . . . By facing a period of tribulation we can get back to a sound currency, and shall reap our reward in having a clear future before us" (Hawtrey 1919b, 433–34).

To these experts, unemployment was not a feature of market capitalism, but rather a temporary phenomenon. If the unemployment lasted too long, it would be attributed to workers' failure to be virtuous citizens. Thus, unemployment was another indicator of the true culprits of the economic crisis: the majority of citizens who were earning too much, thus spending too much—leading as we know to expansion of credit and thus an inflationary spiral. The correlation drawn between unemployment and excessive wages is lucid in Niemeyer's account: "If present wages are to be maintained a certain part of the population must go without wages. The practical manifestation of which is unemployment" (Niemeyer, T 176/5, part 2, fol. 37).[64]

Of course, lower wages as an "indispensable condition" for capital rehabilitation was the opposite of what people were demanding. And once again, these experts were aware of the class conflict in the offing. Hawtrey wrote: "It seems not unlikely that the difficulty of reducing [wages] again will be the determining factor in the settlement of the future monetary units."[65]

Fortunately for the economists, the economic downturn greatly reduced these difficulties. Starting in the summer of 1920, unemployment rose swiftly and spectacularly as the tide began to turn against the workers. Nevertheless, workers continued to strike at a massive scale throughout the year. As the historian James Cronin observed, "perhaps the best evidence of depth of class antagonism in 1919/20 is how long it took to abate" (Cronin 1979, 127). Clearly, with high levels of labor organization the release of coercive market forces required political boosting. Hence, industrial austerity, as put into practice by the British government, envisaged techniques of legal action to curtail workers' bargaining power and their freedom of association. Ironically, Treasury officials did not condemn state intervention when it came to matters of law and order; in those cases it was a reason to rejoice.

The October 1920 Emergency Powers Act was the first restrictive legislation in response to the great wave of strikes. It allowed the government to declare a "state of emergency" whereby it could exercise wide, even repressive powers as it deemed necessary for any "purposes essential to the public safety and the life of the community" (Emergency Powers Act, 1920, Section 2.1 [Regulations], HC Deb. vol. 199, 28 September 1926, cc 409–508).

The government widely adopted such prerogatives during the general strike of 1926, and its new legal latitude equipped it to break the strike in a little over a week. In August 1927, Parliament passed the Trade Disputes and Trade Unions Act "to vindicate the authority of the state and protect the liberties of the citizen," as characterized by Attorney General Douglas Hogg (HC Deb 2 May 1927, vol. 205, cc 1307). The American economist H. A. Millis, who published a long analysis of the legislation in the *Journal of Political Economy* in 1928, summarized the unforgiving nature of the Trade Disputes and Trade Unions Act.

> The new legislation changes [the] situation in several respects: (1) by placing restrictions upon the right to strike, and to lock out; (2) by imposing further restrictions upon "picketing"; (3) by striking at the financial support of the political activities of labor; (4) by requiring the organizations of civil servants to divorce them-selves from, and to remain out of, affiliation to other trade unions and the Labour Party, and also to refrain from political activities; and (5) by placing limitations on pro-labor local governments and other public authorities. (Millis 1928, 306)[66]

In the name of general interest, the authorities protected themselves from the recurrence of general strikes by outlawing any sympathetic stoppages and any political strikes, including those strikes that stood for a general amelioration of workers' labor conditions (beyond a specific occupation) and those demanding nationalization. In a nutshell, it was possible to strike for a clause, but not for a cause. Incitement to participate in an unlawful strike became a criminal offense, punishable by imprisonment for up to two years; the attorney general was empowered to sequester the assets and funds of unions involved in such strikes. In this way the British state put a final nail in the coffin of labor solidarity and demands for social change.

Even Millis had to admit that the act was a unique episode in British history, inasmuch as it "curtailed the rights of labour on both the industrial and the political fields" (Millis 1928, 315). The results were immediate. The average number of disputes in 1927 and 1928 fell to half of those in the years 1924 to 1925 (Mitchell 1998, Table b.3, 176). Even more impressively, as Miliband put it, "while the average number of workers involved in strikes and lock-outs in each of the three years 1919–1921 was 2,108,000, in each of the thirteen years 1927–1939 it was 308,100—and not by any means because Labour lacked major grievances in those years, or achieved notable successes by the use of its parliamentary strength" (Miliband 1961, 148–49). By 1930 union membership had halved with respect to 1920 (going down from 8.4 million to 4.8 million participants—see chapter 9, figure 9.4).

This momentous turn of events, from labor empowered to labor defeated, cannot be fully explained without an investigation into the workings of monetary deflation—the queen of all austerity policies in Britain—without which the subjugation of the British workers could not have been achieved.

Monetary Austerity

DEAR MONEY AND SAVINGS

The Treasury controllers stood fast on Hawtrey's main theoretical principle: credit was "unruly," or "a peculiarly unstable and sensitive phenomenon," as Blackett wrote in a note to Chamberlain. This theory had a weighty policy implication. Credit's lack of self-regulation and its constant expansionary tendencies required "national control" over its supply (Hawtrey 1919, 50). Hence, rather than a hands-off monetary policy, British experts wholeheartedly endorsed monetary management through the manipulation of the bank rate in order to achieve the desired economic "equilibrium" (Hawtrey 1919a, 24).

A return to currency stability, Hawtrey wrote, entailed "a painful and laborious journey," and "the painful and laborious journey must be travelled, after every indulgence in inflation . . . after the debauch comes the headache" (Hawtrey 1919a, 375). Once more the burden of this journey fell primarily on the workers through reduced incomes and restricted consumption—both necessary for monetary management to be successful.[67]

In Hawtrey's model, a rise in the interest rate was very effective to this end[68] since it discouraged merchants from borrowing, meaning a reduced circulation of credit. With merchants halting the credit machine, manufacturers would reduce production and reduce employment, curtailing the income of wage earners and hence their expenditure, further slowing down the economy, since merchants had even less incentive to borrow to replenish their stock. In a few words, dear money meant less employment and less income in the pockets of consumers.[69]

Facing opposition but holding fast to their Hawtreyan economic theory, the Treasury and the Bank of England put into action an unprecedented dosage of dear money. By April 1920, Governor Norman and the Treasury had agreed on a 7 percent rate that was maintained for over a year.[70] For the first time, a high bank rate was used to satisfy the objective of stabilizing domestic prices.

This "swift and severe dose of dear money" was supported by the most commanding minds not only of the Treasury but also of British academia more generally. Both Pigou and Keynes rooted for an even higher rate. Pigou's influential article in *The Times* (March 1, 1920) pushed for an 8 percent rate, while Keynes[71] went further by advising the chancellor in a private letter that "the rate for money should be put to 7 percent and then again soon after to 8 percent. The results of this action would have to be watched. But as a personal opinion I should not be surprised if 10 percent would be required to achieve the necessary results."[72] These drastic prescriptions were the outcome of the catastrophic diagnosis that all British technocrats shared: inflation was understood not merely as an economic problem, but as an existential threat to the capitalist order. Indeed, rising prices would exacerbate workers' demands for higher wages and greater social redistribution, and could even light a revolutionary charge. In his 1919 bestselling book *The Economic Consequences of the Peace*, Keynes paraphrased Lenin to caution: "the best way to destroy the Capitalist System [is] to debauch the currency" (see Mann 2017, 235).

In August 1920, Hawtrey was still advocating even dearer money. Prices had fallen, but not enough. "The problem before the country is to reduce prices by something between 20 and 25 per cent" ("The Government's Currency Policy," August 4, 1920, GBR/0014/HTRY 1/13, Churchill Archives Centre). A year later, Hawtrey proudly affirmed that the deflationist policy was finally effective. He wrote, "[w]hat actually happened in this country was a combination of high bank rate, budget surplus and an agreed restriction of credit by the banks" ("The Credit Situation," July 1921, GBR/0014/HTRY 1/13, Churchill Archives Centre; also in T 176.5, part 1, fol. 6b).

Niemeyer defended deflation on pedagogical grounds. During the inflationary boom, "people were living in a fool's paradise." In 1921, he was of the conviction that "[w]e have, after all, made one big step in advance. We have all realised that after four years of devastating war the country is and must be poorer than before" (T 176/5, part 1, fol. 17b). Niemeyer sought to position this shift as long-term, cautioning that the government would lose the "educative effect" of deflation if the country reverted to cheap money: "People will say: scarcity is over: money is cheap: there is no need for economy: and rush down the steep place for inflation until the shilling goes the way of the franc and the mark" (February 3, 1920, T 176/5, part 2, fol. 70).

As with taxation, technocrats viewed deflation as effective because it operated differently on the different classes of society. While deflation forced workers to abstain, it rewarded the creditor classes of society with a higher return on capital. The latter were thus encouraged to save.[73]

Certainly, a rise in the exchange rate was detrimental to export-oriented British businesses due to a fall in international competitiveness. But experts saw it as a short-term adjustment. The pressures of unemployment caused by deflation also served to lower production costs, which in turn made British exports even more competitive.

By October 1921 Niemeyer could proudly state: "There is already a tendency for some wages to fall as the consequence of the credit restriction which has already taken place. Nothing should be done to check this tendency" (Niemeyer, October 5, 1921, T 175/5, part 2, fol. 37). This harsh dear money policy coincided with the end of the postwar boom and was certainly the main factor in thrusting the British economy to its lowest real GDP of the century in 1921.[74] The slump was severe—the 1919 gains in production and income over their wartime levels were lost within a year and unemployment reached a peak of 18 percent in December 1921 (Howson 1975, 10).

What some economists today would characterize as a mistake of economic management had clear political advantages. The evil of unemployment was not so evil for the long-term survival of exploitation, a principle upon which capital accumulation rested. Unemployment weakened workers' position, silenced demands for greater economic democracy, and guaranteed lower labor costs (see chapter 9). As Cronin put it: "The astronomical levels of unemployment in some of the most militant and strike prone industries must have served to lower the expectations of workers and erode the bases of workshop organization" (Cronin 1979, 129). Indeed, technocrats got what they wished for: wages fell tremendously as a consequence of the austerity-induced slump. Average money wages and retail prices plummeted by 30 percent between 1920 and 1923, a remarkable degree of flexibility (Peden 1985, 68). The *Economist* estimated that by 1922 working men lost three-quarters of their wartime wage increases. The loud demands for workers' management of just a few years prior were reduced to a whimper. Moreover, the consequent weakening of labor, and the shortage of revenue in the state coffers (due to less tax income during a downturn), provided the political conditions to stifle the reconstructionist plans of expansionary fiscal policies.

Once high bank rates deflated domestic prices, those high bank rates had to persist in order to achieve an even costlier objective: returning to the gold standard at the prewar parity of 1914. This amounted to a long haul of deflation, as the sterling needed to be raised from $3.40 in 1920 to $4.86 in 1925—a 10 percent price deflation (see Peden 2000, 128–89).[75]

In fact, after 1921, Hawtrey expressed concern regarding a prolonged spell of deflation;[76] however, the concern was never high enough to swing him from his loud advocacy in favor of returning to gold at its prewar par. Once more, Hawtrey made clear how, even if burdensome for the workers, the gold standard meant a protection to those who he thought really counted for capital accumulation: the creditors—"the class of non-speculative investors who play so considerable a part as the sleeping partners of the modern capitalist system" (Hawtrey 1919a, 357). For this reason, he explicitly opposed the widespread proposal to restore gold at a lower par; it would have entailed an unquestionable "injustice so long as the capitalist system continues" (ibid.).

For the Treasury and the Bank of England, returning to gold, so costly in terms of unemployment and social sacrifice, had a further invaluable political payoff that was worth *any* economic sacrifice. The gold standard buttressed the exemption of monetary policy, and consequently also of fiscal policy, from political discussion and intervention.

This depoliticization of economic matters—or rather, the de-democratization of the economy—guaranteed the system's prioritization of capital accumulation, of which monetary and fiscal austerity were necessary elements. More specifically, Treasury officials knew that once monetary policy was linked to the maintenance of a fixed exchange rate, politicians would no longer be free to determine the supply of money or the level of interest rates.[77] The same held true for budgetary policy, as it could not run counter to the constraint of the balance of trade. In this way, the gold standard provided a final indissoluble buffer to any expansionary programs. And of course, most important of all, gold would function as a mechanism to permanently discipline workers into accepting lower wages. In the case where they were not going to accept such discipline, the repercussion would be to their own detriment. Clearly, these coercive effects were in the interests not merely of financial capital but of industrial capital as well:[78] they were foundational for an overall rise of profit rates. Indeed, starting in 1926 profit rates became much steeper than they had been in the previous five years (increasing from 18 percent to 27 percent between 1926 and 1928—see chapter 9, figure 9.3).

Niemeyer could not have been more explicit in responding to criticism: "for a time no doubt our current difficulties will be attributed to a return to gold. It is so much easier to do than to grapple with our real problem, how to reduce the cost of production and to cease thinking that we can consume more than we can produce" (T 208/105, fol. 5). As it turns out, Niemeyer's argument brought things back to where they started: in order to keep credit in check, the golden recipe of lower consumption and greater production prevailed.

If the British people were to abstain, then where would demand for British goods come from? Blackett, like his colleagues, had a simple answer: "the fact is that the only form of demand which will really help the situation is demand from abroad. An artificial stimulation of the home demand will merely mean encouraging people in this country to take in each other's washing and waste their energy in so doing" (Blackett, June 8, 1921, T 175.6, part 1, fol. 15). In this framework, exports were to be at once the driver of economic growth and the key to a virtuous balance of payments.[79]

Ironically, experts regarded a return to gold not "as a class question" but as a decision taken "from the standpoint of the general interest" (T 208/105, fol. 4); or, in Governor Norman's grandiose terms, gold represented the interest not of one class of one nation but of the "world." These thoughts should not come as a surprise, since they are indicative of the austerity logic that is still pervasive today—the underlying assumption that rationality *itself* coincides with the rationality of capital accumulation. There is nothing else as important.

With the gold standard, austerity could pass as a technical, natural, and unavoidable mechanism; yet in truth, as we have shown, the gold standard was not an automatic mechanism after all, given that it required austere practices—both to return to it and to maintain it.[80]

Hawtrey was very explicit that the gold standard *in itself* was not sufficient to prevent inflation. His call at the Genoa conference was for a *managed* standard. The "great Central banks of the world" ("Draft Resolutions," T 208/28, fol. 5) were to take absolute charge of monetary policy and, in so doing, enjoy full "discretion." These words, which might at first sight appear innocuous, deserve to be investigated in their full political significance.

The Technocratic Project

Blackett, Niemeyer, and Norman were "fanatically attached" (Sayers 1976, 523) to the Genoa doctrine—a vision of technocracy operating at a global scale, where the British model would be followed by the rest of the world.

The resolutions of the Genoa conference came from Hawtrey's pen and are worth recalling: "The return to sound currency will be assisted if reliance is placed on the international cooperation of the banks of issues rather than on direct government action" ("Draft Resolutions," T 208/28, fol. 2). As "private corporations," central banks have to be "free from political pressure and should be conducted solely on lines of prudent finances" (T 176/13, fol. 26; T 208/28, fol. 4).

These resolutions reveal an unabashed faith in a technocratic project, one that places the hub of economic decisions in the hands of a body that has absolutely no democratic liability. In this sense, and as Hawtrey explicitly put it, "the Government must answer criticism, for its tenure depends on popular support." The central bank, on the other hand, "is free to follow the precept: 'Never explain; never regret; never apologise'" (Hawtrey 1925a, 243).

Never apologizing, the neutral expert could act unimpeded to ensure the proper functioning of the market. Though popular among technocrats, these views were being largely contested and required protection. During the turbulent years of deflation and unemployment, British citizens were not blind to the profound impact monetary policy was having on their lives. In 1925, the Independent Labour Party launched a popular campaign in favor of central bank nationalization. In a frenzy for rebuttal, Hawtrey wrote a full-fledged defense of the technocratic nature of central banks.

Monetary management, he declared, is "a technical task which is the field of the expert" (ibid., 239), and thus has to be "made the subject of intensive scientific study of a kind that would be inappropriate to broad political decisions" (ibid.). No exception could be made regarding the requirement "to separate the central bank, as the expert body, from the executive Government" (ibid.). In Britain, Hawtrey told the reader, the separation had been fully accomplished: "the Bank of England is the property of its share-holders, and the governors and directors are responsible to no one else." He then added: "It is thoroughly understood, however, that their position is one of trust for the public interest" (ibid.).

Undoubtedly, in this framework, what was good for the central bank was also good universally and for the public at large. Any faint doubt that, as a private institution, the central bank could work in favor of the ruling class was strongly disregarded, since "the only defence against inflation is to be found in the wisdom of the financial world in general, and of Finance Ministries and central banks in particular" (ibid., 240–41).

Hawtrey was adamant that it was precisely in a "democratic age" that technocratic exemption from democracy was "an advantage." One had to escape "ill judged pressure at critical times," and especially any opposition to deflation on the part of workers and business. Indeed, until "a healthy public opinion could ever be evolved on the subject of credit control"—and Hawtrey declared himself agnostic on whether it would ever be possible—"the welfare of the community" depended "vitally upon the technical efficiency and enlightenment of those who administer the great central banks of the world" (ibid., 244).

The eliteness of scientific knowledge thus became the means to justify the undemocratic nature of an institution with immense social power and impact on everyone's lives. Hawtrey's innocent parallel between the workings of the central banks—which he admitted would "intimately [affect] the entire economic life of the country"—and the colonial office governing a colony betrays the fundamental antidemocratic or even repressive content of the austerity project.

Keynes agreed heartily. He wrote: "My own view is in complete accord with that of Mr. Hawtrey, that this activity is one which should be pursued by a semi-autonomous body not subject to political interference in its daily work" ("Discussion by Prof. J. M. Keynes from the Chair," in Hawtrey 1925a, 244). The common ambition was impeccable: the economic sector must be depoliticized.

It is in the light of this long-term and potentially irreversible project of detaching the economic from the political that one should understand the effort of Hawtrey, Blackett, and Niemeyer to get rid of the anomalous wartime involvement of the Treasury in monetary policy, whereby as Bradbury recalled, "the Bank would have to regard itself as a department of the Treasury and he [Lord Cunliffe, Governor of the Bank] always took the line of receiving orders from the Chancellor of the Exchequer."[81] The austere fiscal agenda of the Treasury, especially in the form of redeeming the floating debt, had a precise political significance: it allowed the Bank of England to gain back its full autonomous control over monetary policy.[82]

On February 17, 1929, now in his role as director of the Bank of England, Blackett proudly testified his past efforts: "I arranged with the Chancellor of the Exchequer soon after April 1920 to revert to the prewar practice of either not informing the Chancellor of the Exchequer in advance of an intended change in the bank-rate or letting him know only at about 10:30 or 11 of the Thursday" (T 176/13, fol. 25). As a government representative, the chancellor did not have, and ought not to have, any official role with respect to the bank rate. Setting the bank rate, Niemeyer commented, was to be the decision of a "private corporation" (T 176/13, fol. 26).[83]

As a private corporation, the Bank could put economic priorities over all social concerns; in the meantime, the Treasury could happily escape all accountability for the social sacrifice, especially in the form of unemployment, that austerity measures were inflicting on the British population.

When, in March 1921, Chancellor Chamberlain was asked about the "vital importance of this fall in Bank rates upon unemployment, which is the most vital question we have to consider today," he batted it away, saying, "the price of money is wholly outside government action" (T 176/13, fols. 9–10). Two years later, upon similar contestation, the secretary of the Treasury, Sir William Joynson-Hicks, blatantly stated: "in accordance both with the tradition in this country and the unanimous advice of experts at the Brussels and Genoa Conferences, control of the Bank Rate rests with the Central Bank and not with the Government" (T 176/13, fol. 10). In March 1925, Chancellor Churchill defended the "depoliticized" deflationary policies as a matter of etiquette: "I think it would be an inconvenient practice if the Chancellor of the Exchequer were to set the precedent of expressing approval or disapproval of decisions taken at any time by the Bank of England" (T 176/13, fol. 11).[84]

The message was clear: political criticism had no place under technocracy. Niemeyer and Blackett further exercised great effort in sowing this austere ideology outside of Europe. In his mission to India, Blackett succeeded in creating an independent central bank (which commenced its operations in 1935), while Niemeyer found success in Brazil (in 1931) and Argentina (in 1935), where governments established central banks under his blueprint.

In his notes to convince the Brazilian government to abide by these technocratic principles, Niemeyer used his old talking points. He admonished that, if technocratic independence was not institutionalized, "political considerations and the pecuniary exigencies of the Government rather than considerations of sound monetary economy are likely to sooner or later become dominant. . . . The risk of excess issues, inflation, and depreciation of the currency is constant" (Niemeyer 1931, 17). To avoid such outright disaster, of course the solution was a no-brainer: the central bank must be "an entirely private Commercial undertaking" (ibid., 18), led by private agents independent of any sort of political representation. The technocratic counteroffensive that began in Britain had by this time established itself on a global scale.

Technocracy as the rule of experts had as its basis an assumption of epistemic superiority. In this sense, the experts were the guardians of untarnished objective knowledge on how to properly stabilize credit and run the market economy. As we have explored in depth in the preceding pages, such knowledge prescribed the austerity motto—produce more and consume less. Hence, it emerges that austerity was not only an anti-democratic project, but, at its core, a repressive one: it forced people to sacrifice without criticism.

Conclusion

This chapter explored how austerity was an anti-democratic and fundamentally repressive project emerging out of an epoch of unprecedented democratic demands. In a moment when the scope of social alternatives broadened and citizens were no longer willing to sacrifice their livelihoods in the name of economic rigor, experts deployed Hawtreyan economics to impose on people ever greater sacrifice for the purpose of stabilizing the economy.

Sacrifice came in the double form of decreased consumption (which would reduce internal demand and prices) and decreased wages (which would reduce costs) to boost production and economic competitiveness. Such was the "recipe for the long-term general interest."

A fundamental step in this direction was to depoliticize the economy—that is, to abolish any form of state control so that wages would again be subject to impersonal market pressure rather than be prone to political contestation. Looking closely, it emerges that the fixation of the experts on balanced budgets and on curbing inflation had a *deeper* goal: reconfiguring the indisputability of capitalist relations of production, based (as we know) on the pillars of private property and wage relations.

Indeed, the Treasury and the Bank of England prolonged their dear-money policies even after inflation was curtailed. Furthermore, the British state did not loosen its fiscal belt even after budgetary surplus was achieved in 1920. The austerity-induced downturn and consequent unemployment was no economic mistake, but rather a powerful means to cool the collective temperature of an embattled working class, to create the pathway to dismantle reconstructionist plans and shift resources to the creditor classes of society.

The British experts were of course aware of the non-neutral class impact of austerity. A 1920 memorandum of the Bank of England read: "The process of deflation of prices which may be expected to follow on the check to the expansion of credit must necessarily be a painful one to some classes of the community, but this is unavoidable" (Bank Memorandum, February 10, 1920, T 172/1384, fol. 30b). These lines disclose how austerity proceeded to normalize class repression through the idea of "unavoidable" and "natural" economic truths that only our experts could deliver.

Protest, however, did not easily subside. The normalization of sacrifice required a further process of depoliticization: the insulation of economic policies from any form of public scrutiny. The ideal was an economy run by "expert guidance free from political interference" (Blackett 1931). The main contribution of Hawtreyan economics was to fortify the concept of monetary management (or *austere* management) of the market economy and to assign managerial command to a technocratic institution. As a private body, Hawtrey told us, the Bank of England was "free" to inflict austerity without ever having to "explain," "regret," or "apologise." In this sense it emerges that there was nothing more political than the technocratic mission to depoliticize.

Audacious as the British case may be, it had little on the Italian experience of austerity, where its political and repressive nature was ever more glaring in its weddedness to Fascism.

CHAPTER 7

Austerity, an Italian Story

> The directives of domestic policies are summed up in these words: thrift, work, discipline. The financial problem is crucial: the budget has to be balanced as soon as possible. Austerity regime:[1] spending intelligently: the support to the productive forces of the Nation: ending all war controls and state interferences.
>
> Benito Mussolini, first speech in Parliament on November 16, 1922 (in Mussolini 1933, 22)

Following months during which Fascist squads waged violent attacks on leftist opposition, Benito Mussolini officially seized power on October 29, 1922.[2] More than a coup, Mussolini's infamous March on Rome was a ceremonial display of strength: Italy's Fascist leader had been called upon by King Vittorio Emanuele III to resolve the postwar political crisis, and Mussolini had executed his orders.

In his first speech in Parliament as the newly nominated prime minister, Mussolini spoke the language of austerity: "thrift, work, discipline," he said, pledging to depoliticize the nation's economy by putting an end to all "state interferences."

Mussolini delivered on his promises. Fiscal and industrial austerity (1922–1925), followed by monetary austerity and continued industrial austerity (1926–1928), bulldozed hard-won social reforms and workers' aspirations. These policies served to enact a common purpose: the rehabilitation of the fundamental pillars of capital accumulation—

nowhere better observed than in the regime's capacity to secure brisk "industrial peace." A year into the new regime, the minister of finance, Alberto De Stefani, could toast to labor's defeat: "In 1920/21 the loss through strikes was 8,201,000 working days and in 1921/1922 7,336,000 days. From 1st November 1922 to 31st October 1923 the loss has been only 247,000 [days—a 97 percent drop in two years]. Profits and revenues are increasing" (Summary of Financial Statement, Italian Senate, December 8, 1923, FO 371/8887, fol. 68).

Austerity required Fascism—a strong, top-down government that could impose its nationalist will coercively and with political impunity—for its prompt success. Fascism, conversely, required austerity to solidify its rule. Indeed, it was the draw of austerity that led the international and domestic liberal establishments to support Mussolini's government even after the *Leggi Fascistissime* [literally: "very Fascist Laws"] of 1925–1926 that installed Mussolini as the nation's official dictator. Liberal experts in Italy,[3] Britain, and the United States were quick in observing that a central strongman with "full powers" was the most effective means of safeguarding Italian capitalism from its multifaceted "enemies." While chapter 8 explores the international appeal of Fascist austerity, this chapter delves into the intimate association between Italian liberals and authoritarianism—a connection with which the canonical literature has failed to grapple.

Austerity's Italian enablers were some of the country's best-established economists and champions of the emerging paradigm of pure economics—a direct precursor of today's mainstream neoclassical economics.[4] Two of them, Alberto De Stefani and Maffeo Pantaleoni, were prominent Fascists. The other two, Umberto Ricci and Luigi Einaudi, identified as liberal. They joined forces—and found notable common ground—under the banner of austerity. For each, austerity served a highly functional role: it was both the expression of a system of domination and a means of reinforcing it.

These economists' facilitation of austerity (and accordingly, their support of Fascism) leaves an important question: how much were their austerity policies motivated by the principles of pure economics, and how much was tied to their political participation in Italy's class war? Also: was pure economics really so pure? Or was it rather that it had at its foundation a profoundly classist disposition? If no definitive answer can be given, certainly an investigation into the thoughts and actions of these four economists can provide insights to illuminate these questions.

None of this is to claim that the intellectual antecedent of today's mainstream economics was the *only* driver for 1920s Fascist economic policy; nationalism and the safeguarding of financial-industrial interests are also to blame, and they are both extensively discussed in the literature.[5] On the other hand, the drivers that will be explored here—economic expertise and austerity—have been wholly disregarded or ignored. Perhaps this is because of the light they might shed on the repressive nature of today's economic science.

A focus on austerity also offers a new lens to historically evaluate Italian Fascism and its economic agenda. Indeed, while traditional historiography stresses the discontinuity between the first laissez-faire period (1922–1925) and the corporativist period that followed (with the latter usually understood as the real expression of Fascism), I suggest that a continuity can be drawn between the two: austerity. Whatever its historiographic period, austerity was always much more than laissez-faire; it embodied the active intervention of the state against capitalist crisis.

The Experts in Power

On December 3, 1922, only a month after the formation of his new cabinet, Mussolini issued a royal decree granting full powers to his government for the reform of the tax system and public administration.[6] It inaugurated the so-called Period of Full Powers, which endowed Italian economic experts with unencumbered authority to foist austerity measures on the Italian public.

Alberto De Stefani, Maffeo Pantaleoni, Umberto Ricci, and Luigi Einaudi were successful professors of economics who traveled in the highest academic circles.[7] The four professors were (or eventually became) members of the *Accademia dei Lincei*, the nation's most prestigious honorary institution for scholars. Their commitment to academic debates at national and international levels was complemented by a deep engagement in current affairs. The four professors regularly partook in policy discussions and contributed to domestic and foreign newspapers.[8] The degree of their involvement in actual policy *making*, however, varied.

The stern-faced Alberto De Stefani took the lead in shaping Fascist economic legislation. In 1921, at age 42, after the violent militancy at the dawn of the Fascist movement, he became a member of parliament as member of the Fascist Party. The circumstances of his transition into electoral politics signaled the strength of his commitment to Fascism: rather than identifying as a member of the "National Bloc," a coalition that included Liberals and nationalists, he demanded and was granted identity solely as a Fascist. He became the sole Fascist deputy elected in 1921, representing his hometown of Vicenza.[9] From then on, his political career skyrocketed. Two days after the March on Rome, the king called on Mussolini to create a new government. Mussolini nominated De Stefani to run the Ministry of Finance, which soon merged with the Ministry of Treasury (Royal Decree 1700, December 31, 1922, in Camera dei Deputati 1929). De Stefani held that position of power until June 1925,[10] pushing for unprecedented austerity under his constant motto: "nothing for nothing: for every hundred billion of greater state income, a hundred billion less expenditures" [*"niente per niente"; per ogni cento milioni di maggiori entrate, cento milioni di minori spese*] (De Stefani 1926b, 8). During those years of fervidly sowing a new national economic identity, De Stefani's closest technical advisors were two of his most admired colleagues: Pantaleoni, his primary mentor; and Ricci, who had been a guide and supporter of De Stefani's academic career.

A founder of pure economics as a school of thought,[11] Pantaleoni was surely the most renowned Italian economist at the time. His fame extended worldwide, and his classic book *Principi di economia pura* (1889) had been translated into English in 1898. Pantaleoni shared the spotlight with the famous founders of the neoclassical-economic movement, including William Stanley Jevons, Hermann Heinrich Gossen, Alfred Marshall, and Léon Walras. Pantaleoni's magnum opus represented a true methodological turning point for economic studies in Italy, paving the way for much of today's standard theory (Barucci 1980) and inspiring generations of younger economists (including the polymath Vilfredo Pareto,[12] who helped evolve economics from a philosophical field to a more quantitative one; the two became close friends and collaborators). As we know from chapter 5, Pantaleoni's reputation for rigor is what earned him a post among the selected advisors at the Brussels Financial Conference of 1920.

His political career was just as intense. A parliamentarian in the early 1900s and a committed Nationalist,[13] Pantaleoni eagerly joined the Fascist movement upon its inception in March 1919; in 1920 he joined the leader Gabriele D'Annunzio in the irredentist occupation of the Croatian town of Fiume, where Pantaleoni briefly helmed the Ministry of Finance. In 1923 the Fascist regime rewarded his accomplishments with a seat at the Senate. Here Pantaleoni's collaborations with Minister De Stefani became more intense. Ricci described his colleague's eagerness to work for austerity policies: "Pantaleoni was a spotless and fearless citizen, a champion of many battles, which sometimes provided him with bitter enemies. . . . I had the fortune to collaborate with him in more than one commission, in particular the one for the reduction of public expenditures in Italy, that had him as president. I saw him work without pause, day and night" (Ricci 1939, 19).[14] Pantaleoni's political influence and scholarly international fame were at their peak at the time of his death in 1924.

Despite being perhaps the most committed liberal of the four, the bespectacled Ricci was crucial for the growth of Fascist economic policy. In 1923, Mussolini sent a letter to the minister of education, Giovanni Gentile, personally asking for the young Ricci's recusal from many of his duties as a professor in order to serve the government full-time. A 1925 memorandum of the Ministry of Finance summarizes Ricci's fervent activity in those years:

> Professor Umberto Ricci, successor of Pantaleoni in the chair of political economy at the Royal University of Rome, has been at the disposal of His Excellency, the Minister of Finance, from June 1923 to February

1925. During this period Professor Ricci, apart from taking part in commissions of less importance has carried out his activity 1) as a member of the *Commissione Censuaria Centrale*; 2) as member of the Commission for the Revision of Balances and the Reduction of Public Expenditure; 3) as member first and then president of the investigative committee for the technical organization of the Ministry of Finance. Moreover, Professor Ricci was a member of a) the board of directors of the National Railways and b) the board of directors of the National Institute of Insurance (Istituto Nazionale delle Assicurazioni).[15]

Ricci acted with determination: as we shall see, the national railways were among the institutions most affected by cuts, while the Fascist government also privatized the National Institute of Insurance. But Ricci proved to be more austere than even Fascism could satisfy. In the name of a strict defense of austerity, he ended his service to the government in February 1925. Indeed, the polemic that distanced Ricci from the regime had little to do with breaching political freedom and everything to do with breaching "economic freedom"—the freedom of the market. This rift escalated in 1928, costing Ricci his academic post in Italy.[16] At age 46, he relocated to Egypt to continue his scholarly life as an academic in Cairo, where he also played a role as government advisor. In a 1941 pamphlet the professor proudly recalled holding a seat in the Egyptian Fiscal Commission, giving influential speeches, and reporting in Egypt's major newspapers "to illuminate the Egyptian public opinion on institutions of greater financial control."[17] The expert's mission was to transplant the Italian and British austerity frameworks, and especially to build an "independent organ to keep finances in check" (Ricci 1941, 53).

The last of the four economists was the prestigious liberal professor Luigi Einaudi, an Italian senator since 1919 and one of Mussolini's initial candidates for the position of minister of treasury. Though the final offer never materialized, and in fact Einaudi never served in the Fascist government, he still played a crucial role in building consensus for Fascist austerity at home and abroad. After the 1924 murder of the socialist politician Giacomo Matteotti,[18] Einaudi opposed Fascism politically; however, based on his interventions in the Liberal newspaper *Il corriere della sera*, and especially his copious work as a correspondent for the *Economist*, Einaudi's fervent support of Fascist economic policy throughout the 1920s is undeniable.[19]

After Fascism was defeated in the second world war, Einaudi became the leading representative of the Liberal Party in the Italian Constitutional Assembly (1946) and was Italy's first elected president of the Republic (1948–1955). In these roles he embodied a tacit institutional continuity between the establishment that had supported the rise of the dictatorship and the new democratic republic. To this day, Einaudi is revered as one of the most respectable public figures in Italy. Universities, avenues, and cultural foundations across the country bear his name. In addition to the University of Turin, during his life Einaudi also taught at Bocconi University, fortifying its long-lasting legacy as a hub of neoclassical economics; even today Bocconi remains the home institution for influential austerity hawks. For example, the economist Mario Monti, the long-standing president of the university, led the "tear and blood" austerity reforms in his role as a non-elected prime minister of Italy between 2011 and 2013. There is also Francesco Giavazzi, who as of 2022 is the economic advisor of Mario Draghi's non-elected technocratic government and who, together with his famous colleague Alberto Alesina and other so-called "Bocconi boys," advised European and international institutions—such as the Ecofin (the Economic and Financial Affairs Council, made up of the economic and finance ministers from all European member states), the ECB, and the IMF—to commit to austerity after the 2009 financial crisis.[20]

Einaudi's relationship to Fascism—including his persisting support of the austerity that the Fascist government enacted—has been downplayed, if not forgotten, in contemporary histories and narratives. However, his relationship to it raises one of the main themes of this book. Ricci and Einaudi—celebrated as Italy's most authentic ambassadors of liberalism—had one priority during the postwar crisis: deploying austerity to guard the market economy against an imminent collapse. Such austerity was embodied in the Fascist policies of the 1920s, with repressive politics as an integral component. Ricci and Einaudi didn't have to declare loyalty to Fascism to be of service to it; austerity weaved Fascism and liberalism together in a shared, coercive pursuit.

If one focuses on these four men's economic beliefs, the ideological differences between the two Fascists and the two Liberals disappear. Their contemporaries seemed aware of this connection. In 1921 De Stefani himself declared to the Fascist newspaper *Il popolo d'Italia*:

> I would, for example, bestow the Fascist membership card to Vilfredo Pareto, to Maffeo Pantaleoni, to Umberto Ricci, to Luigi Einaudi. The Fascist *Vademecum* is exactly in the works of these men; it would be good if Fascists were educated in their works in order to acquire that bright unity of thought that must guide intelligent actions. (De Stefani, "L'orientamento del Fascismo secondo il pensiero di Alberto De' Stefani," *Il popolo d'Italia*, September 21, 1921, 3, interview by Mario Zamboni)

Once in office, De Stefani confirmed these views in an open letter in *Il popolo* addressed to his "illustrious friend," Luigi Einaudi:

> When my young and bold comrades ask me how to develop a Fascist mentality, also in the technical field of social, economic and financial problems, I direct them to the works of four great Italian Fascists, who are non-militant and without a party card: Vilfredo Pareto, Maffeo Pantaleoni, Umberto Ricci and "last but not the least" Luigi Einaudi, whom I plead my comrades to forgive if he propagandizes for Fascism on the columns of the *Corriere della sera*. (De Stefani, "The Financial Program of the National-Socialist Party, Open Letter to Senator Luigi Einaudi," *Il popolo d'Italia*, January 14, 1922)[21]

Were these unwarranted associations? Political opportunism? Popular interpretations and commentaries usually argue "yes." The remainder of this chapter explores how these forgiving characterizations are incorrect—and how, on the contrary, De Stefani's descriptions were based on his peers' austerity bona fides. These foundations are evident in their actions and journalistic and academic writings.[22] Indeed, theirs is a set of cases in which political and academic endeavors—two lanes that scholars usually evaluate separately—are in profound harmony. With these four economists as their ambassadors, austerity policies found useful means of dissemination in the communication of economic theory. Indeed, the dual motto of austerity—consume less and produce more—was driven by these economists' will to implement and "make real" the ideal models of a virtuous, capitalist society that presupposes the subordination of the working class.

Pure Economics and the Technocratic Project

In their efforts to restore the primacy of capital accumulation, Alberto De Stefani, Maffeo Pantaleoni, Umberto Ricci, and Luigi Einaudi faced two battles.

The first, which had already begun at the turn of the century, proceeded within the realm of academia. The four economists joined forces with their Switzerland-based colleague, Pareto, in a lengthy and successful campaign to subvert the Italian historical tradition of economic thought, acting instead "to do justice against all false schools and proclaim pure economics sovereign" (Ricci 1939, 44). To this end, Pantaleoni's purchase and management of *Il giornale degli economisti*—the most influential journal of economics in Italy—in 1910 was a crucial step toward building the hegemony of a new scientific paradigm.

In parallel, the four men battled strenuously to shape public opinion at a moment in which it had "gone astray." After the war this second battle took primacy. Indeed, in the wake of World War I the unthinkable was upon them: capitalist values and social relations—the very preconditions for pure economics to exist as canon—had to be defended from the incursions of society at large.

Regarding the effort to fend off the masses, Ricci spoke of economists as "struggling to make the public understand that trains could not depart to the moon." The public, the economists claimed, were uneducated about economic truths and thus acted against their own interests. Alas, these economic truths had been mined by experts in such exquisite terms that they were "no longer intelligible," not only to the masses but to any non-specialist, including parliament deputies. It was the lofty status of pure economics that lent a superior aura to its practitioners, who were burdened with the arduous task of educating humanity regarding correct economic behavior in order to bring about economic equilibrium and progress. As Ricci explained, the economist acted selflessly for the good of the whole. In this crusade he sacrificed his "interest as individual, group or class to the interest of the collective" (Ricci 1926, 2). The pedagogic mission was, in Pantaleoni's mind, so "great and difficult" that it required "much work, exceptional energy, indomitable civil courage and subtle acumen" as well as access to a newspaper that is "greatly diffused and financially independent" (Pantaleoni 1922, 222).

Ricci gave two important speeches on the matter. The one he delivered in Pisa, for the opening of the academic year 1921–1922, was titled "The Alleged Decline of Political Economy" [*Il preteso tramonto dell'economia politica*]. The other, which he gave at the University of Bologna in January 1922, was titled "The Unpopularity of Political Economy" [*L'impopolarità dell'economia politica*]. On both occasions he conceded that ignorant and opportunistic masses hated economists and viewed them as public enemies (Ricci 1926, 72). He couched the public's disdain as resentment—economists, after all, were the thing keeping society from collapsing under its own indolence: "By proclaiming the principle of universal taxation, promoting the shutdown of useless public offices, the dismissal of redundant employees, the abandonment of public works, the economist surely doesn't make new friends" (Ricci 1926, 102).

An economist should never be discouraged, Ricci cautioned, because an economist is the purest human force:

> Not always [the economist's] words are listened to, not always the conscience of accomplishing his duty is accompanied by the joy of the result. But if sometimes he is affected by the sorrow of having spoken in vain, *a reward awaits him*, one that no human force may subtract from him. As he progressively climbs the ivory tower, and abandons at each floor his prejudices and interests, his vision gets ever more refined, his horizon is enlarged; eventually, when the high summit is reached, he

discovers the *unity in the truth, the order in the disorder* . . . and the spectacle from the high tower becomes even more marvelous when, in the exchanges among firms, groups, classes and nations, one is capable of distilling *rigorous and elegant laws*, worthy of competing with the laws of celestial mechanics. This vision of beauty is the economist's sovereign reward. (Ricci 1926, 104–5, my italics)

All four of austerity's Italian economists shared this intellectually elitist position, not to mention a tendency toward self-adulation. It was a set of conceits expressed through Ricci's religious metaphor, by which the "contemplation" of "the divine science" of economics is "the privilege of the few" and "does not always appear as beautiful, true and good to the profane public" (Ricci 1926, 72).

Pure economics is imbued with this manner of positivism. (I use the present tense here with a nod to how this continues with present-day neoclassical theory.) Over time, the discipline achieved a reputation for rigor and epistemic legitimacy that equaled that of other hard sciences. In Ricci's evocative words: "The socialist and the protectionist are to the economist like the astrologist to the astronomer, the alchemist to the chemist, the sorcerer to the doctor" (Ricci 1926, 25). De Stefani and Ricci paid homage to their teacher Pantaleoni; they hailed him as "an archangel with a flaming sword," battling against all historicism to proclaim that "there must be a theoretical part of economic science, a nucleus of doctrines, that are independent of opinions, as well as of ethical, political and religious predilections. Something similar to physics and mathematics . . . this is 'Pure Economics'" (Ricci 1939, 44).

In 1923 De Stefani recounted his exhilaration on first discovering pure economics when he read Pantaleoni's *Principles* and Pareto's *Cours d'economie* in a bookstore: "I was seduced by an analysis in which the useful and the harmful, the pleasure and pain and all the most complex facts of our economic order were conducted through calculus formulae and described through graphic representations. . . . The equilibria became intersection points of curve systems and numbers that resolved systems of equations. The human spirit found quietude in those formal truths" (De Stefani 1923, 1187). Economists proclaimed the objective status of pure economics through a forceful, highly narrated separation of society's economic and political realms. They drew a strict boundary line: *the economic is transcendent, an isolated system in abstraction from other elements of the sociopolitical sphere.* In this way, pure economists diverted their gaze from historical questions like the origins of property ownership or class relations; these things were understood as falling outside the economist's domain, and considered naturally occurring givens.[23] Economists' claims of objectivity are fortified by their quantitative methods: numbers can't lie, so how can economics?[24]

Pure economics aspired to be something like the Platonic form of social inquiry. Just as ideas for Plato were the authentic essence of existing phenomena, so too economic ideas were more *real* than reality itself. They were the true model, the archetype that reality played out. Its self-described "purity" did not stem from a detachment from the real world; to the contrary, economics had an undeniable and practical end game. Like Plato's philosopher, the economist had to return to the cave and rescue the unenlightened from their ignorance. The four professors had as their ambition to eradicate the impurities of the real world so that it would conform to the purity of their mathematical models.

Ricci summarized the famous passages of Pantaleoni's *Principles* that center economic theory as a prerequisite for policy making:

> First of all, one must be well-read in pure economics, then trained in applied economics, that is, pure theory; finally, one can embark on the resolution of concrete economic problems, that is, the peculiar and contingent issues that everyday reality puts under our eyes and whose core is economics. (Ricci 1939, 45–46)

More explicitly, models and theorems had not only to dispense practical economic knowledge; they had to command people's obedience. As Ricci spelled out: "It is the honest desire of any good theorist of political economy that theoretical constructions be deemed not merely a luxury of the intellect, but necessary to explain and forecast events, and essential to *tame men*" ("*ammaestrare gli uomini*," Ricci 1908, 389, my italics).

After the war it was indeed the majority of citizens that required taming, since they had revolted against the authentic essence of things.

The models of these four economists captured just such an essence—a society in which capital, not labor, was the engine of the economic machine.

The Virtuous Saver and the Unruly Worker

In 1920 Luigi Einaudi wrote a polemic in the Liberal newspaper *Il corriere della sera* bemoaning Marxist economists and their labor theory of value: "Why should a capitalist profit only because the machine is his? Why shall he live without doing anything? Is it not obvious that his profit comes from the exploitation of someone else's labour?" he asked, sarcastically. "This is the celebrated and vulgar sophism of Marx's *Capital.* . . . But it is enough to ask: how much would be produced if the savers did not produce capital? The answer: nothing. Without capital, labour produces zero."[25]

De Stefani offered a similar explanation to his students: "Capitalism is the phenomenon of a class that lives on the specific productivity of capital, it depends on the right of property and heredity, not on a subtraction at the expense of the workers." It was, he specified, "a result of savings and conservation, useful actually to the very working classes" (De Stefani 1919, 164).

At a moment when workers endorsed economic theories that put labor as the source of capital formation, these highly visible national experts championed an opposing set of theories: it was actually the saver-investors who held the keys that propelled the system. In this manner, economists provided scientific grounds to naturalize a class society—and thus to justify its inevitability, and ultimately its fairness. They did so by equating the members of the bourgeoisie with the concept of the *homo economicus*—a rational agent who acted out of self-interest.[26]

A mathematical notion of economic virtue—still used in neoclassical models today—lent rigor to Ricci's analysis: a so-called virtual cost of economic abstinence. It is measured, then and now, by the subjective discount rate, which is based on the psychological rule that, all other things being equal, goods now are preferred over goods in the future. In this thinking, a virtuous agent will have a lower subjective rate of interest and will be more prone to save:

> The subjective discount rate is low for men who have an acute foresight ability and can vividly foresee future joys and needs, for energetic and disciplined men, who can endure the restraints they impose on them-selves . . . for men raised with sober customs. All these moral virtues—farsightedness, self-control, love for your offspring, moderate habits—together with the certainty of a long life—may render the discount rate extraordinarily small. (Ricci 1999, 33)

Indeed, in this individual-virtue framework, *any* economic agent could potentially practice the virtuous behavior of the *homo economicus*. But the reality, at least according to Ricci, is that "amongst the tools with which man elevates his degree of civilization, individual abstinence [*l'astinenza*] is both the most effective and the least widespread" (Ricci 1999, 7). Indeed, *only a select few* had the propensity to abstain, to live within their means, and few actually did: "The businessman is thrifty, a thinker and a calculator, it is this real man who most resembles the ab-stract man pictured by economists, who does not fuss like a sissy [*don-nicciuola*] of a hardship to come" (Ricci 1999, 23). Pantaleoni agreed emphatically that unlike others, the entrepreneur was not a "sissy." He spoke of the entrepreneur's virtues in evolutionary terms:[27] the ability to preserve the species through rational self-interested behavior. It was the entrepreneurs who "realise almost perfectly the type of the *homo economicus*, and who therefore know, and take advantage, of every opportunity that presents itself of earning a profit" (Pantaleoni 1898, 259). Examining these ideas together, neither Pantaleoni nor Ricci en-visioned a clear-cut conceptual distinction between the saver and the entrepreneur: both roles embodied rational economic agents by virtue of maximizing their individual utility.

This core conceptual murkiness squares well with the economists' adherence to Say's law, an economic principle that was scripture, too, among British experts of the era. According to Say's law, all savings in an economy are transformed into productive investment.[28] For Pantaleoni, this transformation was exactly what the capitalist process was all about, and it was foundational to society's economic progress (see Pantaleoni 1923). In this sense, for pure economists, the self-interest of the *homo economicus*, whether in the form of the saver or the entrepreneur, personifies the interest of society as a whole. In Pantaleoni's and his colleagues' models the market economy benefited everyone: the optimal performance of economic relations, delivering optimal results with respect to prices, quantities, and the allocation of resources and commodities.

Accordingly, private savings and private accumulation never clashed with the general interest. On the contrary, public interest depends on these private "virtues." These principles remain embedded in the standard economics textbooks of today; they are so ingrained that our protagonists' exhaustive defense of them seems overboard.

On the other hand, Pantaleoni's public interventions demonstrated his belief that the economic status of the working classes reflected their lack of social and economic merits: "all considered, it seems obvious that the classes with lower incomes are significantly deficient in qualities with respect to others. *So that this deficiency [deficienza] is the cause of the lower income and not the lower income the cause of the deficiency*" (Pantaleoni 1922, 36). Members of the working classes were such because they suffered from incurable vices, such as wasteful consumption, and were hangers-on to a more perfect economic system populated by savers. Being poor or working-class was a choice and a pathology.

Pantaleoni's characterization of the Italian working class was conspicuous in its timing: war had brought "undeserved" wealth to the Italian workers thanks to higher nominal wages and government price controls on foodstuffs and other social services. In Pantaleoni's telling these same workers, rather than saving, had indulged themselves to a point of moral and economic degradation (1922, 58):

> The working classes basically don't save and spend everything in plea-
> sures [*godimenti*], with the consequence of a remarkable decay of their
> moral qualities. . . . This is the outcome, first, of the pressure of the war,
> and, then, of the pressure of socialism and Bolshevism.[29] This state of
> affairs will necessarily lead to collapse, because it is exasperating [*paras-
> sitico*] to capitalism and an obstacle to new savings and the growth of
> production.

He reiterated, this time with evocative imagery and with a further nod
to the insidious influence of the Russian Revolution:

> Thanks to Bolshevism, the modesty in the standard of living that char-
> acterized Italians has vanished. It has disappeared in both the working
> class and the peasantry. It is disgusting to witness the masses of workers
> that are drunk in all our cities . . . the notable increase of wages was not
> accompanied by greater civilization so that the worker and his spouse
> live like pigs [*porci*] in their homes in order to waste the greatest part of
> their income in wine at the tavern. (Pantaleoni 1922, xiv)

The purportedly more liberal Einaudi also demonstrated a highly classist attitude—with a special nod to alcohol expenditures:

> It is well known that the wages of workers in the industrial and com-
> mercial areas of Italy have increased noticeably . . . *the evidence being the
> conspicuous increases in unnecessary consumption of alcoholic drinks, of
> sweets, chocolate, and biscuits.* (Einaudi 1920, 96–97, italics in original)

Ricci joined, too: "The darlings [*beniamini*] of economic policy during
the war and after have been the workers of the great cities. In other
words, the savers were punished, and the squanderers rewarded" (Ricci
1921, 450).

The economist architects of Italian austerity distrusted, and perhaps
despised, the working classes for their ineptitude in the vital action of
economic growth: saving. While it is impossible to ascertain whether or
not pure economics was the *primary* source of the economists' classist

convictions, it is safe to assert that pure economics at least *reinforced* their classism.

Of course, one could always attempt to educate these unruly workers. All four economists consistently preached sacrifice, abstinence, frugality, and self-restraint. Einaudi was certainly the most passionate on the topic, which he had taken seriously since the start of the war.[30] His op-eds in *Il corriere della sera* were relentless: "The Duty to Save" (July 7, 1919); "The Fever to Live and the Necessity of Renunciations" (April 11, 1919); and "Don't Buy!" (June 19, 1920),[31] which read:

> If the newspapers preached abstinence and penitence to the nouveau riche, the peasants and to the workers they would undertake an action that is morally worthy and socially useful. (Einaudi 1920, 174)

These campaigns' resemblance to the endeavors of Blackett and Niemeyer on the British savings committee is striking. More than in Britain, however, the Italian economists were convinced that after the war the situation in their country had gotten completely out of hand. For all their core ineptitude, workers had actually gained economic and political power. It was clear that only a strong government could set things straight for capital accumulation. Here entered the Mussolini dictatorship.

Austerity, Technocracy, and Authoritarianism

> With Bolshevism in Government . . . it is impossible to produce and save.
>
> Pantaleoni (1922, iv–v)

Fascist and Liberal economists shared a belief in the power and good of a government made up of economic experts—a technocracy. They also agreed that the policies necessary to ensure sound economic principles were neither political nor pursuant of any partisan interest; they were simply true. It is the role and the duty of experts to define and implement them.

This technocratic ethos permeated De Stefani's 1927 speech in front of an audience at the English Institute of Bankers: "We still judge of sound finance by the strict adherence of government practice to those laws that are *not political* but *natural* and human; and in all countries the people are inexorably forced to pay the penalty for *disobeying* them" (De Stefani 1927, 316, my italics).

Of course, after the war "disobedience" had reached unthinkable highs. The four experts viewed the postwar political situation as horrific and saw no possibility for a spontaneous or painless economic redemption. Pessimism seeped from Pantaleoni's memorandum at the Brussels conference:

> The probability of Governments stopping their interference and taking again to their proper business, which is to furnish the general conditions for unfettered private activity, is very small, because public opinion supports them on the wrong line. . . . (Pantaleoni in Brussels 1920, vol. 5, 103; reprinted in Italian in Pantaleoni 1922, 51)

Similarly, during a public lecture at the University of Rome, Ricci opined: "moral preaching is of little benefit," since the two major austerity "remedies"—consuming less and producing more—were trumped by their exact opposite. He continued, "all abandon themselves with a shortsightedness [*imprevidenza*] equal to impudence [*sfacciataggine*] to a consumption frenzy [*gazzarra di consumi*] . . . people adore strikes, British Saturdays, the shortening of the working-day, the slowing down of labour intensity" (Ricci 1920, 7–8).

In this heated moment, a technocratic government was necessary to advance the agenda of hard austerity. It was, however, not entirely sufficient. The Italian government had to be strong, too. And by *strong*, the Italian economists did not mean a government with economic leverage; they envisioned an authoritarian, "law and order" government, one that would never hesitate to use repression against the population in order to protect the market economy and its natural laws (Pantaleoni 1922, 47–48).

Pantaleoni's inclination toward violence is well documented (Michelini 2011a). In speeches and conversations, he frequently invoked the notion of a "Fascist stick" to oppose working-class movements, and he even spoke of "extermination war" [*guerra di sterminio*] against the internal enemy: the "Bolshevik leaders."[32] His condoning of violence to advance an anti-socialist agenda was often interspersed with anti-Semitic remarks, associating Jews with the anti-capitalist conspiracy.[33] It is telling that even the liberal Ricci similarly and explicitly called for repression during the tumultuous postwar years in Italy. Concerning the popular uprisings against inflation, Ricci polemicized: "To repress [the revolt], or better, to oppose the vandalistic fury, would have been easy, at least at the beginning. Instead, public forces were left with no instruction" (Ricci 1920, 11).

Einaudi joined Ricci in complaining about the weakness of Giolitti's and Nitti's postwar, pre-Fascist governments. To him, Italians were "oppressed by the absolute rule of an old, ineffectual, compromising, sceptic set of politicians" (Einaudi in the *Economist*, November 27, 1922, reprinted in Einaudi 2000, 267). To succeed against antagonistic social forces, austerity measures needed an overhaul. Action had to be quick and ruthless, and the inefficient democratic process could not fit this purpose. But the Fascist movement seemed up to the task.

Einaudi's newspaper columns reveal how the deep continuity between austerity and political repression was true not only for Fascist economists, but also for austere Liberals.[34] Indeed, in *Il corriere della sera* he silently glossed over the murderous behavior of the Fascist action squads, who were beating, killing, and torturing political opponents throughout the country,[35] to express profound gratitude toward Fascism for "giving the decisive blow to Bolshevik tyranny and folly" (Einaudi 1959–65, vol. 6, 771). Einaudi's articles attacked the attempts of the moderate socialists to collaborate with the government to reestablish constitutional legality and prevent the rise of Mussolini. Einaudi accused them of "seeking power to control the military and the royal guard and use this power against Fascism and against the nation" (Rossi 1955, 295).

In a similar vein, Einaudi wrote in the *Economist*:

When the worst happened, in September last, and the occupation of factories by armed workers and the institution of Soviets in factories

> seemed to point to an imminent Communist revolution in Italy . . .
> [y]ouths of the middle class, returned men and officers, in indignation
> grouped themselves into "Fasci." . . . The communists are everywhere
> defeated. . . . This renewed feeling of hope in the future of our country
> is not the least important cause of the better tone in foreign exchanges.
> (March 24, 1921, in Einaudi 2000, 191–92)

The four professors thought of Fascism as the new political class, as
"another set of politicians: young, energetic, full of vigor and of patrio-
tism" (Einaudi, November 27, 1922, in Einaudi 2000, 267), who would
finally prove determined enough to go against the will of the masses
and impose austerity. The questions Einaudi posed on the exact day of
the March on Rome (October 28, 1922) are very telling:

> The important question is, what is the economic platform of the new
> party? Signor Mussolini, the chief, is not an economist. Passionate and full
> of vigor, he is able to commit his party to headlong plunges into unknown
> seas. For the moment, he has uttered at Naples only one economic sen-
> tence: "Italy needs at the helm a man capable of saying no to all requests
> of new expenditure." So far, so good . . . public opinion was seriously and
> gravely warned of the necessity of putting an end to the increase in public
> expenditure, and of reducing even useful expenses. . . . Will the new Party
> have the will and the power to redress the awkward financial situation of
> the State . . . ? (October 28, 1922, in Einaudi 2000, 263–64)

These questions were practically rhetorical based on Einaudi's profound
optimism for the Fascist state. A few days earlier, in *Il corriere della sera*,
Einaudi had praised the economic agenda of the National Fascist Party
(PNF) that De Stefani presented at the party's congress in Naples, October 22–24, 1922. Einaudi testified that De Stefani's orthodox ideas were
exactly the ones he had been calling for. He concluded with a phrase
of full endorsement of the Fascist Party: "We ardently desire a party,
and be it the Fascist one if the others can't do better, who can use the
appropriate means to reach the objective of the spiritual and economic
grandeur of our homeland [*patria*]" (Einaudi 1959–65, vol. 6, 921).

Einaudi's enthusiasm for this so-called Bill of Full Powers stemmed from the policy's promise to "suppress this or that public service, to transfer railways and the other industrial State concerns to private hands; to reduce, simplify, or increase existing taxes." Einaudi enthused: "Never was such absolute power entrusted by a Parliament to the Executive. . . . The renunciation by Parliament of all its powers for so long a period was received with general cheers by the public. Italians were sick of talkers and of weak executives" ("Italy—Absolute Government in Italy—Taxes to Be Simplified—Working of the Succession Tax—A New Excise?" *Economist*, December 2, 1922, 1032ff.).

It seems clear that the austerity economists were not infatuated with Mussolini's charismatic figure *per se*, but rather saw him as the right man at the right time to implement the principles of pure economics. And indeed, the economists did not hesitate to criticize Mussolini's policies when the policies did not conform to austerity principles. For example, in an article in *La vita Italiana* (1921), Pantaleoni condemned Mussolini's mistakes when *Il Duce* was found sympathizing with socialist parties (Pantaleoni 1922, 215–16); Einaudi too was troubled by some initial, seemingly Bolshevik maneuvers of the Fascist Party (Einaudi 1963, vol. 6, 898). Nevertheless, the worries of the experts were soon quelled: *they* were the experts who would surround and advise Mussolini.

With De Stefani steering the Treasury,[36] austerity policies imposed savings and hard work upon the working classes, allowing market forces to work under the best possible circumstances to reinitiate capital accumulation and guarantee stable conditions for profit. Let us investigate a bit further how.

Austerity in All Policies

FISCAL AUSTERITY—THE RETREAT OF THE STATE

The objective of budget-balancing fiscal policy, at least as far as the Fascist Party and its economists were concerned, was to reestablish the best economic behaviors for the resumption of capital accumulation.[37]

The majority of citizens would have to curb their consumption to release resources in favor of the saving-investing classes. In one of his public speeches, De Stefani left no ambiguity about what he characterized as the universal benefit of such an austerity agenda:

> We need to speak plainly: a finance based on criteria of persecution of capital is a mad finance . . . instead of impeding the amortization of capital by pressing on savings that can be reinvested and that have been contended from the state to private economic action, it is better to press on consumption and this in the true and definitive interest of the disadvantaged populations. (De Stefani 1926b, 12)

As the Italian economists told the story, the true interests of the "disadvantaged population" depended on capitalism; people could only prosper if capitalism prospered. But this prosperity came at a cost, and the sacrifices in that enterprise were to be distributed unevenly. Fiscal austerity managed the revenue and the expenditure side of the budget, respectively, through regressive taxation and budget cuts. The two worked in unison to ensure "compulsory thrift" among the people and to bolster capital investment among the virtuous elite.

Taxes

De Stefani and his colleagues warred against the "confiscatory progressivity" of the postwar period. The most renowned tax expert of the four, Einaudi, stoutly opposed the "fiscal lewdness" [*scelleraggini tributarie*] of the postwar governments and their irrational tax policies that "banished capital in favor of labour."[38]

The centrist-liberal prime minister Giovanni Giolitti had won the 1919 elections on promises of progressive taxation of "war profiteers" and the wealthy,[39] while the Socialist Party campaigned for expanding the inheritance tax—with their spokesman, Giacomo Matteotti, proposing a fiscal reform to reshape the social structure in favor of the working people via a widespread redistribution of resources from profits to wages (Matteotti 1919).[40] Even the Fascist Manifesto of 1919 reflected the spirit of the times, as it announced "[a] strong progressive tax on capital that will truly expropriate a portion of all wealth."[41] These were dangerous times, as Einaudi put it, when no progressive taxation could satisfy the "cupidity" of the masses (Einaudi 1927).

However, in his speech in May 1923 at the Scala Theatre in Milan, De Stefani announced a turning point: "The politics of persecution of capital has been suddenly arrested thanks to our action" (De Stefani 1923, 226). Tellingly, his speech was delivered not in front of the people's representatives in Parliament, but rather in front of the elite of Italy's financial capital, who sat comfortably in the cushioned seats of the majestic theater. The minister took the occasion to emphasize that the state should release private capital from fiscal pressure to promote its "natural" use in private investment (De Stefani 1923, 210), to stimulate ever greater savings, and attract foreign capital.[42] Indeed, the Fascist state exempted international financial capital from taxation.[43] (As chapter 8 will detail, these measures gained the regime great popularity in international financial circles and secured profuse credit.)

The new taxation principle was labeled *produttivista* [productivistic]. It prioritized the accumulation of wealth over any "aim of social justice or more egalitarian redistribution of wealth" (Einaudi 1927, 490). The redistributive rationale was inherently classist (and akin to the system in Britain):[44] when the state taxed, it collected resources from the whole community, then used that revenue to pay back the possessors of state bonds, i.e., the creditor classes of society (De Stefani 1928, 195).

De Stefani's 1923 fiscal reforms expanded the tax base to impose greater tax control over the lower classes. These tax brackets were subject to the *imposta di ricchezza mobile* (the tax on income) for the first time.[45] De Stefani was triumphant: "I found an army of 600,000 contributors for the *imposta di ricchezza mobile* . . . a new fiscal conscription of wage earners has come to close with 100 thousand enrolled . . . the nation has understood the necessity of the state" (De Stefani 1923, 206).[46]

Far from a conscription of riches, De Stefani had actually managed to constrict wages. Moreover, to further (and silently) extract resources from the poorer members of society, the Fascist government steadily increased consumption taxes throughout the decade. The ratio between direct and indirect tax revenue dropped from 0.94 in 1922 to 0.72 in 1925, and to 0.61 by 1929—an even more pronounced trend than in the British case. More specifically, duties on basic commodities grew between 1922 and 1925 by approximately 5 percent per year in real terms (Toniolo 1980, 48). Meanwhile the government managed to abolish "vexatious taxation on luxury goods" (Einaudi 1927, 490).

In line with the principles of austerity, Italy's medium-high income brackets benefited from tax relief through the abolition of all progressive war and postwar taxation. This included, for example, the long-contested taxes on war profits and the mandatory declaration of ownership of financial assets [*nominatività obbligatoria dei titoli azionari*] (Rossi 1955, 75–90).[47] The abolition of the *nominatività dei titoli* effectively curtailed any possibility to progressively tax capital income.[48] Moreover, the technical findings of Pantaleoni's earlier study on inheritance taxes buttressed De Stefani's July 1923 orders, effectively eliminating taxation of inherited wealth altogether.[49]

De Stefani's reforms also provided structural facilitation of tax evasion at the top (see Gabbuti 2020a, 28–29). Out of an estimated 18 billion lire of total tax evasion in Italy by 1934, no less than 8 billion were dividends and interests on public bonds—financial channels pursued almost exclusively by the nation's wealthy. The minister himself had to admit that "between 50 and 75%" of the income tax was evaded, with "greater evasion at the top" (De Stefani 1926b, 211). This loss for the state coffers was, however, irrelevant with respect to what really counted: the reestablishment of capital order.

Social Policy

Along with taxation, a reduction in public expenditure was key to shifting resources from public consumption to private capital investment.

At the peak of his administrative powers, in December 1922 De Stefani appointed his own "commission for the revision of balances and the reduction of public expenditures," taking cues from the successes of Britain's Geddes Committee. Through this commission, De Stefani worked unremittingly to revise and slash all items in the state budget. Pantaleoni chaired the commission, and Ricci was one of its leading figures. The latter expressed fond memories of it: "Minister De Stefani has imposed on himself as a supreme duty [*supremo dovere*] the reduction of expenditures; it is for him such an ardent preoccupation to be blamed as an obsession. He put together a small committee in which he himself intervened daily, and the committee, working day and night for three months, has reviewed the budget entry by entry and proposed economies that were agreed-upon by the individual ministries" (Ricci 1923, 612).

The results of this "new will" [*volontà nuova*] performed "miracles to curb expenditures" (Ricci 1923, 612). De Stefani was fond of using the euphemism "the spirit of the Minister of Finance hovers [*aleggia*] in all administrations" (De Stefani 1923, 212). Pensions and subsidies for war veterans and their families were the first to go. From 1923 to 1924 total state expenditures were cut by a third (Ragioneria Generale dello Stato [RGS] 2011), with redistributive expenditures suffering the most.[50]

In the *Economist*, Einaudi cheered the reforms achieved by the committee, adding that their self-evident merits "call[ed] for no comment" (May 1923, in Einaudi 2000, 289). The efforts to "increase the powers of the Italian Treasury," he wrote, took direct inspiration from Britain: "Signor De Stefani laid great stress on the efficacy of the British Treasury in checking expenses and controlling expenditure departments" (ibid., 290–91).

The experts' counter-reforms reversed the three major reformist postwar victories detailed in chapter 2—insurance against disabilities and old age, insurance that covered accidents in the agriculture sector,[51] and mandatory unemployment insurance.[52]

A final, devastating volley against the wartime economy came with the abolition of the Ministry of Labour and Social Insurance in April 1923—a blow to all Italian workers who had just recently won their twenty-year battle for the Ministry's creation.[53]

By June 30, 1925, the budget was balanced: the amount of public expenditure (excluding defense and debt payments) as a percentage of nominal GDP reached the level of the prewar years (13 percent in 1912), a considerable drop from the almost 29 percent of 1922.[54] The grip of fiscal austerity did not loosen from there. Social expenditure in particular continued to fall throughout the decade and beyond, reaching its lowest point in 1934 (by which time the amount spent on social intervention had dropped by more than a quarter compared to 1924).[55] In the meantime, the amount the state spent on debt and interest payments was more than double the amount spent on social programs, and continued to rise through the whole of the 1920s and most of the 1930s (RGS 2011). If we were to think of the austere Fascist state as a disciplinarian father, then it had a clear bias: while it was thrifty toward the majority, it was willing to be quite generous when it came to the habits of its entrepreneurial children.

For evidence of the fiscal priorities of the austere Italian state, the famous bailout of two major industrial-financial consortia[56]—Ansaldo/Bank of Rome and the Ilva/Credito Italiano—is telling. In the canonical understanding of Fascism, there would seem to be a conflict between these interventionist measures and De Stefani's laissez-faire Fascist policies (see for example Toniolo 1980). But through a lens of austerity, one can observe and appreciate the common ground between budget cuts and bailouts: both actively reinforced capital accumulation. In this sense, it is clear that austerity is much more than simple laissez-faire; it is a lever of power for a society's upper crust. It is telling, then, that this seemingly discordant set of policies remains the go-to policy intervention for governments dealing with financial crises today.[57]

Ultimately, the curtailing of social expenditures was undertaken with a more insidious objective than merely curbing the deficit. It was about sound relations of production, and specifically about disciplining the workers. Here Ricci left no doubts when he attacked social reforms for "protecting hustlers [*faccendieri*] and troublemakers [*facinorosi*]" (Ricci 1926, 15). He was especially critical of unemployment benefits that quelled the market's force over labor: "When there is a government that gives out subsidies to the unemployed, the temptation is born to become unemployed [*nasce la tentazione di disoccuparsi*], to take the subsidy, to work less, and produce less" (Ricci 1926, 22). Cuts in state

expenditure worked hand in hand with industrial austerity to free entrepreneurs from the hindrance of workers' political demands.

INDUSTRIAL AUSTERITY

Privatization

Ricci spoke for his colleagues when he repeatedly called the state "a
terrible [*pessimo*] producer and a terrible administrator"[58] (Ricci
1921, 229).

The scorn for the state's economic ineptitude was grounded in a deep
anxiety: the melding of the economy and politics did not allow for the
class-appropriate behavior of the economic agents. The financial flourishing of lower classes amid government interventions did little to help
the private sector. In this way, the saving-investing classes were being
"chased away" [*scacciati*] (Ricci 1920, 8).[59] This crowding-out argument,
taken from the British Treasury, was a common narrative among the
Italian experts. In this economic understanding, wealth is effectively
zero-sum; as De Stefani wrote on the pages of *Il corriere della sera*, "the
public body is a competitor of the private entrepreneur in the use of
currency and of national wealth. The miracle of the multiplication of
bread and fish has been done only once" (De Stefani 1928, 24).

On the other hand, a socialist economy was portrayed as giving the
working classes a "free ride" to work less and consume more. For Italian
economists it was understood that, once hired by the state, employees
degenerated in their behavior, becoming the antithesis of the virtuous
homo economicus. Public employees became immoral "loafers" [*fan-
nulloni*] because they lost the sound economic incentive of the unfettered market (Ricci 1926, 13). "The employee is brought to consider
the fixed stipend as an acquired right, a guaranteed pension [*pensione
di garanzia*] in exchange for which there is no obligation to give anything," Einaudi argued. He scolded, "the duty to work arises when overtime begins, since it's uncertain and is paid according to the work done"
(Einaudi 1959–65, vol. 5, 233). Such critical observations are common
within the economics literature today. The celebrated Italian economist

Alberto Alesina, who studied economics as an undergraduate at Bocconi before a career at Harvard, bemoaned public-sector jobs as creating a "culture of dependency" whereby "residents in the South [of Italy] demand more public employment in order to take advantage of a large income premium and a greater job security" (Danninger, Alesina, and Rostagno 1999, 3–4). To Alesina and others before him, public employment was synonymous with individuals who were unprepared to "face the market" (ibid.). In other words, citizens were unwilling to accept high enough exploitation.

Alesina's thoughts resonated with Pantaleoni's earlier statements, with the latter arguing that without progressive government interventions "the entire population, and especially the low-income classes would have on the one hand suppressed luxury expenses and on the other offered more labour" (Pantaleoni 1922, 47–48). Under Fascism, technocrats had the tools to "redeem" the Italian population.

The financial year 1922–1923 marked a major turning point for public works expenditures. Just one year prior, public works were at their historic peak. De Stefani's administration began a drastic retrenchment, to the point that in 1924–1925 and 1925–1926 expenditures reached figures that were lower than the prewar fiscal years[60] (Cecini 2011, 333). More Italian people would depend on the impersonal laws of the market for their livelihoods. In this way, industrial austerity collaborated with fiscal austerity (especially in the form of cuts in welfare measures) to intensify people's market dependence, and thus quiet people's dissenting political voices.

A 1923 reform of bureaucracy (Royal Decree 2395, November 11, 1923, in GU 270 Supplement [November 17, 1923]) pursued efficiency through layoffs: the regime fired more than 65,000 Italians (De Felice 1966, vol. 1, 397). Workers of the publicly owned postal and railway sectors were most targeted.[61] De Stefani made clear that their high deficits depended primarily on "an exaggerated expense for personnel," a workforce he characterized as "too numerous and well remunerated" (De Stefani 1923, 215).

Between 1923 and 1924, the Fascist state removed 27,000 railway workers (15 percent of the total employees) and made arrangements to dismiss a further 13,000 and to curtail sick leave. The British ambassador to Italy, Sir Ronald William Graham, described the events as "the introduction of iron discipline and the strictest application of the eight-hour day."[62] In the meantime, in the name of greater revenue, a regressive rise in ticket fares forced workers to choose between giving up the service or paying the higher fares and thus "consuming less" in their other daily expenditures.[63]

Large-scale privatizations were the permanent solution to impose the other half of the austerity motto, "produce more."[64] Stripped of the state's wartime monopolies, workers would be disciplined into competing within the free labor market—a competition so fierce that strikes would become "impossible," Pantaleoni exaggerated.[65] While the railways proved too tough to privatize, the Italian experts found success in other important sectors, to the extent that scholars speak today of these events as "the earliest case of large-scale privatisation in a capitalist economy" (Bel 2011, 939).

These privatizations were everywhere. The state had served as the main provider of telephone services since 1907, having nationalized services previously owned by private firms. In February 1923, a Royal Decree established the conditions to grant franchises to private providers, and by 1925 the government had fully privatized the telephone sector. The Istituto Nazionale delle Assicurazioni (Institute of National Insurances) had been established in 1912 to provide life insurance, previously controlled by foreign firms, to the Italian public. In April 1923, the state relinquished its monopoly, and a de facto duopoly with private companies (Assicurazioni Generali and Adriatica di Sicurta) began. Also in 1923, the state gave up the control of match sales, which it had assumed in 1916. Private firms also took over the building and management of motorways (see Bortolotti 1992, De Luca 1992).

Wages, Strikes, Corporativism

Austerity's effort to reconstitute the divide between the economic and political domains guaranteed that "*the direction of the labour of the masses*" would rest once again "in the hands of the *men of talent and personality whom selection makes into entrepreneurs*" (Pantaleoni 1922, 47–48). Pure economics had dispelled the possibility of class antagonism within industry. The vertical relation between capital and labor was portrayed as harmonious and to the benefit of the workers themselves. In fact, workers' livelihood and productivity depended on the capacity of a select few—those who most resembled the *homo economicus*—and their capacity to save/invest.

In this model, workers lost economic agency, bringing their work in line with the definition of labor in Pantaleoni's *Pure Principles* as a "complementary commodity." This concept of labor stresses the priority of capital over labor, a priority also reflected in the wage-fund theory—again, an important building block of pure economics. This theory presupposes that wages are always and necessarily paid out of the entrepreneur's capital—not as a portion of the surplus he has reaped from workers' labor, but rather as something that is made possible only because of the entrepreneur's virtuous savings. The entrepreneur anticipates wages with his disposable capital and plays the vital task of disciplining/directing labor, insofar as the latter lacks the capacity to self-manage: "The entrepreneur disciplines labour and discipline means coordination . . . this coordination is a difficult problem that few know how to resolve, and the one who knows how to resolve it is called entrepreneur . . . the entrepreneur does not tell the worker to work but to work in a certain way: you know how to organize without him? Go ahead [*fate pure*]" (Pantaleoni 1910, 230).

No economic theory could be more distant from the thoughts and practices of the *Ordinovista* movement detailed in chapter 4. For Gramsci and Togliatti, workers' political agency emerged from the centrality (and potential autonomy) of their labor. Instead, in the world of these four economics professors, workers' loss of economic agency ensured their loss of political agency: understood as any other commodity, economists saw labor as a thing to be exclusively priced through the laws of supply and demand.[66]

In his academic lectures, Pantaleoni asked students: "what wage can the entrepreneur give to the worker?" He answered: "as much as he is worth. He certainly cannot pay him more than what he is worth, and by competition, he will not be able to pay him less . . . the rule that labour is paid how much it is worth [*tanto quanto vale*], nothing more nothing less, holds" (Pantaleoni 1910, 204).

Clearly, the concept of exploitation as a social class relationship (i.e., the idea that surplus value is actually reaped from unpaid labor time) is eliminated from such a framework. The focus lies exclusively on "equal" market transactions and on the fair remuneration of labor according to the rule that, under market competition, the price of labor is equal to its marginal productivity. For Pantaleoni and his colleagues, this rule had been dramatically broken in the postwar momentum and legal protection of labor. Unlike economic laws, political laws had no inherent limits and could be pushed to a frightening extreme: unemployment benefits, minimum wage, and hour regulations brought wages "much above their marginal efficiency"[67] (Pantaleoni, Memorandum, Brussels 1920, vol. 5, 106).

The Fascist state passed coercive labor laws that reduced wages and forbade unions, coming to the defense of true economic laws. The paradox here is stark: economists, so adamant in protecting the free market against the state, had little problem with the state intervening in the labor market. This reflects another core assumption underlying austerity: in a moment of crisis, the "pure economics" of capitalism cannot be resurrected on its own.

Starting at the end of the factory occupations in the fall of 1920, Fascist violence against workers' organizations became a constant. However, workers remained resilient even after Mussolini's rise to power. For example, during the 1924 elections in Turin for the renewal of the industrial committees, workers voted predominantly for the CGdL, a party antagonistic to Fascism. The Fascist unions, meanwhile, which preached the defense of production in the national interest, received only a few votes.

The austere Fascist state overcame these difficulties through legal means. In October 1925, the Pact of Palazzo Vidoni suppressed workers' internal factory committees altogether and placed all organized labor under the exclusive control of the Confederation of Fascist Corporations, which espoused—and enforced—industrial peace in Italy.[68]

Royal Decree 563 of April 3, 1926 (in GU 87 [April 14, 1926]) formalized the pact and refused to legally recognize independent unions. The remaining Fascist unions became nothing more than an extension of the Fascist Party and the Fascist state. The regime declared strikes and lockouts illegal while reenacting the compulsory arbitration that had militarized the workforce during the Great War. The right to strike was replaced by a power to appeal through a Fascist union to a labor magistracy with the idea that "impartial justice of the State replaces the ruinous struggle between opposing parties" (Functions of the New Labour Magistracy in Italy, March 25, 1927, FO 371/12202, f. 91).

The abolition of unions fit the agenda of the liberal economist Ricci, who repeatedly spoke publicly against the unionist logic, portraying them as a threat to both state sovereignty and capitalist production: "The union is a monopolistic organization. The monopolist aims at maximizing its gain and it obtains it with a contraction of the quantity sold, and in the last instance of the quantity produced" (Ricci 1926, 22–23).

The final defeat of workers' aspirations came with the Labour Charter of 1927, which suppressed any chance for class conflict.[69] The charter codified the spirit of corporativism,[70] the object of which, in Mussolini's words, was "to unite within the sovereign state the pernicious dualism of the forces of capital and labour" that were no longer "regarded as necessarily opposed to one another but as elements which should and can aim for a common goal, the higher interest of production" ("The Circular to all Syndical Associations," March 25, 1927, FO 371/12202, f. 91).

This birth of the new Italian corporations sanctioned a legal association between employers and employees representing the "unitary organizations of production" to "maintain the discipline of production and work, and promote its perfection."[71] These syndicates, as Einaudi wrote in the *Economist*, "are obliged to exercise a selective influence amongst workmen, so that their technical capacity and moral standard can be indefinitely increased" ("Italy's Labour Charter," *Economist*, May 14, 1927, 1008ff.). De Stefani hailed the charter as an "institutional revolution," [*rivoluzione istituzionale*] while Einaudi justified its "corporativist" wage-setting as the only means to mimic the optimal results of the neoclassical competitive market (Einaudi 1931, 316).[72]

Once labor became a social obligation, workers were subdued into fulfilling "the development of national strength."[73] This rhetoric, which became common among the technocrats, was the most powerful means to mask increasing exploitation. Emblematic of this trend of greater extraction of surplus value was the widespread deployment of the so-called "system Bedaux," an American post-Taylorist method of work measurement and scientific management that Fiat first introduced in Italy in 1927. (The Bedaux system also found solid footing in Britain in those years.[74]) Even the Fascist unions were compelled to denounce these intensified labor efforts, which quickly resulted in fatigue and ill health among workers. The unions went so far as to raise concerns about the "integrity of future generations" [*l'integrità della stirpe*] (Musso 2002, 167).

The continuity and coherence between austerity and Fascist corporativism[75] is visible not only in the process of labor coercion,[76] but also in the explicit priority of the principle of capitalist production over any other political principle, and the explicit safeguard of the principle of private ownership of the means of production. Article 7 of the charter read: "The corporative State considers private initiative, in the field of production, as the most efficient and useful instrument of the Nation," which meant that "state intervention in economic production may take place only where private initiative is lacking or is insufficient."[77]

Thus, austere corporativism conceived the "interest of the nation at large" ("Italy's Labour Charter," *Economist*, May 14, 1927, 1008ff.) as having the interests of the owner-investor class at its core; it also regarded the subordination of the majority to capital order as a part of the national interest.[78]

Through these authoritarian measures, the Fascist regime was able to achieve a key objective of austerity: an unparalleled slashing of wages. By 1929 there had been a 26 percent drop in nominal daily wages compared to 1926 (Scholliers and Zamagni 1995, Table A.6).[79] Thus, throughout the 1920s industrial growth and increasing labor productivity went hand in hand with a severe decline in real wages (see chapter 9, figure 9.7).

Indeed, unlike the British case, industrial austerity under a dictatorship did not need to rely on an economic downturn to suppress wages:
real wages had dropped significantly between 1923 and 1925, even while
the country was experiencing economic growth. As we shall see in the
next section, politically induced wage suppression became ever more
central once monetary austerity and its goal of achieving the gold standard kicked in.

MONETARY AUSTERITY

> If the national government defends the lira, it is doing so in the interest of
> the savers.[80]
>
> Volpi, speech in Parliament on December 9, 1926 (in Cotula and Spaventa
> 1993, 579)

The Italian professors had not been introduced to the complexities of
Hawtreyan monetary theory—especially Hawtrey's belief that inflation was an inherent threat stemming from the very functioning of the
market economy. The four Italians' understanding of inflation was the
most orthodox kind, rooted in a basic idea that price disequilibrium—
like any form of economic disequilibrium—was due to external, and
especially political, interferences. Thus, in the Italian case of inflation
following World War I, it was simply the result of the government's
increase of currency circulation, which was necessary to fund the
war effort.

As inflation worsened, the Italian government sought to abate it
through price caps. This did nothing but worsen the situation: as Pantaleoni bemoaned, "[t]he artificially low price of commodities merely increases its consumption,"[81] further increasing the scarcity of goods. Instead, Pantaleoni wrote in his Brussels memorandum, if the state were
to halt new currency expansion, "an equilibrium of nominal prices
would be settled by itself. . . . Private commerce can in no possible way
trouble equilibrium prices" (Brussels 1920, vol. 5, 104).

For this self-equilibrating approach to work required an introduction of austerity policies, the same sort enacted by the British Treasury.

In other words, the Italian government needed to decrease liquidity in its economy, and to do that it had to decrease borrowing[82]—measures that would moderate spending among the general population while boosting resources for creditors. In doing so, savers/investors could gain confidence instead of worrying that monetary uncertainty—inflation—would "mow down their income" [*falcidierà il loro reddito*], as Ricci put it (Ricci 1919, 33).

In their manipulations of the economy, Italy's stewarding economists were willing to tolerate domestic sluggishness if it meant taming inflation. They likewise took solace in a belief that the lower domestic prices they were engineering would increase foreign demand for Italian goods. They were wrong, but not egregiously so: the lira had proven remarkably stable during the early years of the Fascist government, offering a reasonable basis for the economists to bank on what today's economists call *export-led growth*. Like their British colleagues in chapter 6, the Italian economists were betting on external demand for cheap Italian goods.

However, for a secondary power like Italy, engagement in international markets was often not enough. During the spring of 1925, the lira's fate turned around dramatically, a fall that *The Times* attributed to "a bad attack of speculation fever"[83] ("Italian Finance," *The Times*, April 9, 1925, 9), since "the economic situation of Italy . . . does not justify the recent decline in the value of the Lira" (ibid.).[84] The episode demonstrated how, even if a country's fundamentals were sound, international pressure on an unpegged currency could be devastating. In response, Mussolini became hell-bent on achieving the gold parity and combatting Italy's worsening exchange rate. His famous Pesaro speech of August 1926 publicly inaugurated the so-called Battle of the Lira. Mussolini ordered "combined effort and sacrifices made by all classes in the highest spirit of discipline and responsibility" (August 18, 1926, OV 36/22, f. 123A, 8) in order to defend the Lira (ibid., 10). Here again, the working classes would pick up the tab.

Einaudi, Ricci, and De Stefani (who resigned from his post in July 1925[85] and was succeeded by the financial expert Giuseppe Volpi, Count di Misurata) were loyal soldiers in Mussolini's lira battle. And like the

Duce, they presented it as a matter of shared class burden and "national" interest, especially in its virtuous objectives. As a practical matter, the popular classes shouldered the national burden.[86] The government's objective was to cement what much of the public had fought against just a few years back: the bourgeois economic order and its values. Einaudi, speaking plainly in the *Economist*, wrote that "some suffering is the inevitable accompaniment of the revaluation of the lira," yet it would guarantee "the elimination of the unfit" and of course, "prudence and restraint," and the "best roads towards recovery and future prosperity."[87]

As in the case of Britain, dear money meant a decrease in note circulation (a 21.4 percent drop between 1925 and 1929), and especially a rise in the bank rate. As his last hurrah as finance minister, in June 1925 De Stefani increased the interest rate from 3 to 6.5 percent, then further to 7 percent,[88] to chase "the recent increase in Bank rate in England and the United States."[89]

By December 1927, Mussolini could proudly announce victory: the lira was pegged to the exchange rate against the British pound at *Quota Novanta* (92.46 lire to the pound sterling and 19 lire to the dollar). Such a revaluation of the lira (an increase in value of 39 percent with respect to its value in August 1926) required extraordinary efforts to adjust prices and wages. The *Duce* gave a meticulous summary of what got them there:

> 9) A rigid discipline and hard work by the Italian people; b) The balancing and surplus of the budget; c) The unification of the right to issue bank-notes; d) A considerably reduced currency; e) Settlement of foreign war debts and consolidation of the floating debt; f) Favourable balance of international payments; g) The actual stability of the exchange for eight months; h) The adjustment of salaries, cost of production and prices; i) A large gold cover in the circulation on the basis of the new gold parity. (December 21, 1927, FO 371/12198, f. 234, 2)[90]

Mussolini's list of thank-yous laid bare a symbiosis of monetary, fiscal, and industrial austerity that were the core of Fascist economic policy;

his comments also acknowledged the selective sacrifice that the trinity enforced.

For all the pomp of Mussolini's announcement, ongoing revaluation of the lira—which had the potential to reduce exports due to the ensuing price changes—made it imperative that Italy bolster its fiscal austerity.[91] In short, export shortfalls demanded compensation through a decrease in domestic consumption.[92]

In this spirit, De Stefani especially advocated for the reduction of the subsidies for public employees as a "provision of vital economic importance" for the country's revaluation policies (De Stefani 1928, 99). In the same spirit, Count Volpi declared his "determination . . . to secure economies in all possible directions,"[93] even in a moment of budgetary surplus.[94] Economizing took the evocative form of the mandatory sale of coarser bread, called "grey bread." The British embassy reported, "the press exhorts all Italians to take pride in using this war bread as a contribution towards victory in the present economic struggle" (August 6, 1926, FO 371/11387, fol. 154).

To compensate for a lack of competitiveness owing to the country's appreciated currency, lower consumption went hand in hand with higher production at lower costs. A stronger lira required lower nominal wages,[95] which could secure lower prices on the international market and thus reestablish the country's competitiveness abroad, which in turn had the potential to improve the national balance of payments.[96] In this sense, revaluation of the lira ushered in an unprecedented degree of industrial austerity.

Once the Labour Charter eradicated all labor opposition, the Fascist state could take daring steps to reduce wages by legal decree. In May 1927, all public employees, including those in the railways and other autonomous administrations, lost the bonus they were due to compensate for the high cost of living (without the cost of living having decreased). That same month there were wage cuts of around 10 percent for agricultural and industrial labor. In October another generalized reduction of nominal wages, in the magnitude of 10–20 percent, ensued (Toniolo 1980, 114).[97] As Volpi had put it to the Italian Senate in February 1928, by this time the country was "unified under iron discipline," having made "admirable efforts" to "facilitate the adjustments of wholesale and retail prices to the value of the lira" (February 17, 1928, FO 371/12947, fol. 163, 20).

Industrialists accepted monetary revaluation on the grounds that drastic cuts in labor costs fully compensated for the fall in the prices of manufacturing outputs.[98] The short-term losses of profits due to deflation—which raised the cost of production by increasing the price of borrowing and hampered competitiveness—represented a minimal toll. It opened an expressway to stable, structural exploitation (see figure 9.2). Indeed, as was illustrated in Britain, increased unemployment subordinated the workforce into accepting hierarchical relations of production—the vital prerequisite for profit-making.

Official statistics denied increases in unemployment, but sources suggesting otherwise leaked abroad. In October 1926, the British embassy reported on layoffs at Fiat: "there are serious rumours of thousands of workmen having been dismissed and production cut down" (October 29, 1926, OV 36/1, f. 18, 2).[99] By the end of 1928, high unemployment and low labor guaranteed a swift economic recovery and a rise in profits. Capital's reward was visible in the profit rate data (figure 9.3): Between 1927 and 1930, the overall profit rate jumped from 8.68 percent to 16.6 percent.

Clearly the process of "rehabilitation" of the lira was not merely a monetary operation, but something even more foundational for postwar capitalism: the sealing of a class system into stable hierarchies under the name of necessary national efforts for economic redemption. During an interview with the *Daily Mail* on July 1, 1926, Mussolini discussed the new legal authorization that kicked to the curb the 8-hour workday law—one of labor's most significant postwar reformist victories. Ambassador Graham reported:

> Sig. Mussolini is stated to have said that the new restrictions [of a 9-hour working day] will be received, not only without opposition, but with enthusiasm, that if he had invited the Italians to work 10 hours instead of nine, he knew they would have agreed, because they are conscious

of the fact that the innovation is not a caprice of the Government but is dictated by national necessity. (July 2, 1926, FO 371/11387, fol. 104, 5)

In sum, the gold standard in Italy, as in Britain, did not merely represent the endpoint of much-suffered austerity. It was rather a device to enforce its "naturalization," since under the gold standard austerity constraints were no longer politically disputable. The legacy of "golden" austerity was not short-lived. To avoid losing the gold parity after the 1929 downturn, the country was confronted with more restrictive fiscal and credit policy combined with a decree that cut wages by another 8–12 percent in December 1930 (Cotula and Spaventa 1993, 889). Indeed, austere theories continued to dominate the understanding of the possible causes and solutions to the Great Crash of 1929, both among Liberals and among Fascist economists in Italy. If the primary cause of the crisis was diffused "moral decay" and "overconsumption," the solution was to be more wage deflation—in other words, the usual motto: consume less, produce more.[100]

Conclusion

This chapter has set out to explore the birth of austerity in Italy under the "impartial" guide of four renowned professors of economics. Despite their ideological divergence, the four shared a deeper set of beliefs and a precise mission: they worked in concert as guardians of a universal economic science—a science that, despite its purported purity, had the intrinsic practical aim of "taming" citizens to consume less and produce more. The emerging Fascist regime endowed the professors with the opportunity of a lifetime: to actually mold society to correspond to the ideal of their models.

In a moment when war collectivism challenged the efficiency of market performance, these professors were steadfast regarding its idealization and protection; in a moment of heightened class struggle, the four set out to deny class antagonism through their "classless" models. Indeed, pure economics operated to depoliticize economic theory by expelling class analysis, only to reintroduce classist assumptions covertly in their rigorous microeconomic calculations. In this manner, any class difference was the outcome of a difference in the extent of individual rational economic behaviors.

One need only step away from the abstractions of their academic works to attain a full view of their classist beliefs. Pantaleoni was the most explicit: "Bourgeois is whoever has the moral and intellectual value required to be such: he who lacks talent, activity, perseverance, control of his own passions and impulses, stops being a Bourgeois; these qualities are all required to emerge amongst comrades and dwell in a class that is not that of the plebes [*volgo*]" (Pantaleoni 1922, 109).

Under a strong government, austerity policies—fiscal, monetary, and industrial—served just such a purpose of protecting the wealthy capitalist minority in its capacity to save, invest, and ultimately profit while forcing the majority to consume less and work more.

In sum, as in the British case, the experts' move toward an *apolitical* theory had the *political* aim of subordinating the majority of citizens to the logic of capital accumulation. Going back to De Stefani's La Scala speech, we may now grasp the full meaning of his use of the word "austerity." He employed it to encourage individual sacrifice and, in particular, the giving up of social protections in the name of the nation's more important financial needs:

> In the speech of the 25th of November, I reminded the Parliament that, right after the march on Rome, the awareness of the financial necessities of the Nation were widespread, even in the humblest part of the Italian population. Today, as yesterday, I need to place on the national agenda the conscious renunciation of the rights gained by the crippled, the invalids, the soldiers. These renunciations constitute for our soul a sacred sacrifice: *austerity*. (De Stefani 1926b, 34, my emphasis)

These may remind us of the words of the British Treasury officials who, though more soft-spoken when addressing the working classes, also invoked the notions of "sacrifice" and "enforcing abstinence" (Hawtrey 1919a, 230). Indeed, the Italian story more explicitly discloses dynamics and goals that were already apparent in chapter 6 regarding British austerity. Economic theory—be it Hawtreyan economics or pure economics—provided consensus for coercive policies, disguising them as beneficial to society at large. We have shown how our experts concealed the relations of domination behind abstract economic principles only to buttress these relations of domination via austerity policies.

Chapter 8 delves deeper into the interconnection between the two stories: Fascist austerity was widely applauded and supported by the British establishment.

Italian Austerity and Fascism through British Eyes

When Italy has well considered these fundamental truths, when she has convinced herself that her only hope is in herself, that others will not grant her credits unless she shows herself to deserve them by her *austere* and quiet behavior, the lines to follow are simple and obvious . . . an economic policy framed to stimulate production; a home policy of order and a better understanding between the classes; a financial policy of economy. Above all the fundamental truth is always the same, however unpleasant and inflexible: *consume less* and *produce more* . . . what is more necessary than anything else is to restore the confidence of capitalists . . . the principles of recent English legislation must be adopted.

"Translation of extract from a speech delivered at Melfi on March 12, 1922 by Signor Nitti" (FO 371/7669, fols.198–200, my emphasis)

After World War I, Britain and Italy passed sweeping austerity legislation on the same timeline and with many of the same component policies. Britain was a long-standing parliamentary democracy with well-established institutions and orthodox Victorian values. It had enjoyed centuries of global financial and economic hegemony. Italy, on the other hand, was economically backward, fresh from Bolshevik revolutionary surges and civil strife during and after the war. Why, then, were two very different countries seemingly operating in tandem to reconfigure their domestic economies?

The British and Italian stories are actually profoundly intertwined. The nature of austerity is such that its domestic policies are set with an outside view in mind: the Italian economists in particular sought to make Italian goods and currency valuable and accessible to foreign markets, especially Britain, which would in turn facilitate capital accumulation within Italy. Economic technocrats in both countries sought to sow austerity beyond their borders so as to guarantee the stability of capitalism as a global economic system—a system that had been unprecedentedly shaken by the war. Domestic welfare was not a component of their thinking. The relationship between Fascist Italy and Britain is emblematic of a perverse partnership in which traditional ideological boundaries—including those between liberalism and fascism—were bridged in the name of economic necessity.

For Italy, the lesser of the two economies, it is worth asking: was austerity really a sovereign choice? In a way it undoubtedly was. As discussed in chapter 7, Italy's economic experts had a lucid understanding of austerity policies as a weapon against internal class struggle and a means of securing capital accumulation among the virtuous savers/entrepreneurs. To these ends, and for these few, austerity was successful. Italian austerity was backed by the commanding domestic tradition of pure economics and household names such as Pantaleoni, Pareto, Ricci, and Einaudi. These professors, however, did not limit their gaze to Italy. They were also engaged with, and inspired by, technocrats from British political economy. The Italian economists were, as the British embassy repeated, "deeply imbued with the classical British tradition" (July 10, 1925, FO 371/10784, fol. 37).

Moreover, to fully explain why austerity thrived in Italy, we need to tell another side of the story: how foreign interests influenced—and in some cases defined—the rebuilding of a country that had teetered on the brink of Bolshevism. By the 1920s Italy was a country with substantial war debt, and was heavily reliant on imports of goods and raw material. In other words, it was a country beholden to others: fundamentally dependent on foreign capital and credit for its economic investment and development. Italy's position of dependence meant that international creditors could exert strong pressures—including pressures that would open Italy to foreign investment, even at the expense of the Italian people. This came in the form of austerity.

This chapter's epigraph is taken from a 1922 speech by the economist and Italian prime minister Francesco Saverio Nitti, who explicitly calls for "austere and quiet behavior" from the Italian people in order to restore the "confidence of capitalists"—in particular, credit and investment. Nitti cautioned that any such credits from foreign countries would be illusory until the government changed economic policies to reflect the "unpleasant truth" of austerity: "consume less and produce more."

Britain had stakes in the game, too. As in the Italian case, these stakes were at once political—to prevent revolution—and economic—to increase profitable venues for its capital and commodities. Indeed, an increase of exports to Italy was crucial in the mind of the British technocrats, who were all betting on the expansion of external demand to compensate for their austerity-induced suppression of internal consumption.[1] Under austere Fascism, trade between Italy and Britain intensified considerably relative to the prewar period. England was second only to the United States as the primary supplier of imports to Italy, especially coal and wool. A substantial share of Italy's exports, especially silk and motorcars, went to Britain.[2]

British technocrats understood that the groundwork for insulating capitalism in Italy would take the form of austerity, and implementing that austerity would require a strong government. The British found those conditions in the form of Mussolini's dictatorship; Fascism imitated the principles of austerity. The British were not alone in this. Similarly to the austerity motives of liberal economists within Italy they reflected a wider international consensus that proved fundamental in order for Fascism to gain legitimacy and consolidate its rule.

This chapter builds on the 1971 classic book by Gian Giacomo Migone, *The United States and Fascist Italy: The Rise of American Finance in Europe* (translated in English in 2015), which documented the substantial hand that American financiers—especially those at J. P. Morgan—lent to Mussolini's rule. Indeed, as Migone explores, Fascist Italy acted as a key agent for the expansion of American capitalism in Europe after World War I. Unlike all other European countries, America was not weakened after the war, but strengthened: the US had doubled its gross national product and its exports and held a credit balance with the rest of the world of $12.562 billion (Migone 2015, 2). After the war, through substantial industrial austerity, the US subordinated its working classes, preventing "organized workers from obtaining a substantial redistribution of profits within American society and stopped them from building any international networks that might be a resource for strengthening their autonomy" (ibid., 15). The country was sitting on an overabundance of liquid capital and an ever-greater quantity of goods and services that were ready for export. Given the isolationist tenor of US politics in the 1920s, the expansion of American capital in Europe and the relationship between Europe and the US was left to informal channels; "these channels, of course, were dominated by the New York financial establishment, and in particular by the House of Morgan" (ibid., 136).

The following pages explore how the influence of American and British capital over Mussolini's economic policy was specifically focused around austerity, with the particular objective of sealing capitalist class relations under an international order.

This arc began with the capitalism crisis leading up to Mussolini's ascent, then extended to the international establishment's views on the necessary relationship between austerity and a strong state, which in turn coined the elite establishment's rationalization of political violence. It concludes with an exploration of the thorny issue of Italy's war debt settlement and the effort to achieve the gold standard—two cases where the international pressure for austerity was profound and the benefits for the Italian people were nonexistent.

The Problem of Italian Dependence

After the war, Italy was not economically self-sufficient. Italian bureaucrats articulated the country's problem of foreign dependence explicitly: "Unlike France, or even Germany, Italy cannot isolate herself without perishing. She either lacks all together, or only possesses in insufficient quantities, all the more necessary raw material, she has an enormous adverse balance of foodstuffs and fats, and she lacks iron, coal, fertilizers, textiles, etc." (FO 371/7669, fol. 196).

Italy's crisis of trade imbalance escalated. The armistice in 1918 brought an end to both the fighting and the wartime agreements around exchange rates and the decontrol of currencies. The likely excess of imports over exports that followed would immediately degrade the exchange rate for Italian currency.[3] A devalued lira not only meant an increase of the country's burden of external debt; it also promised more expensive imports, an increase in domestic prices, and a setback of industrial activity based on a lack of raw materials.

In January 1919, Italian minister of industry Giuseppe De Nava wired an anxious message to the British prime minister, David Lloyd George. Italy's lack of coal, De Nava warned, was hampering "industrial reconstruction and the solution of the already serious labour problem" (T 1/12343/10710/19). The British ambassador to Italy, Sir J. Rennell Rodd, projected bleak consequences: "The closing down of the great factories in the North of Italy, with the cost of living at its present prohibitive price and the inflammable condition of the popular mind, would bring the menace of revolution perilously near . . . unemployment and shortage of food may make desperate the most amenable of mankind."[4]

More than just coal, wool and meat were also missing. As a Treasury file of 1919 revealed, "there are many other commodities, equally important to the economic life of the country, which are not imported at the present time, merely on account of lack of finance" (T 1/12343/10710/19). A continuation along the vicious spiral of high indebtedness—which discouraged creditors and worsened monetary instability—could even result, many feared, in a full-blown monetary breakdown in which the lira lost all purchasing power.

While appreciating the difficulties facing the Italian people, British chancellor of the exchequer Andrew Bonar Law made plain that the British Treasury had "great difficulties to face itself" (ibid.). In February 1919, Britain announced that it would curtail the credits previously allowed to Italy, occasioning real and profound panic among Italian bureaucrats. After intense financial negotiations between the two treasuries, an agreement was reached that secured for Italy a substantial public loan. The agreement specified that the loan was to be "used in the first place for repaying all outstanding debts due to British departments" (T 1/12367/35323),[5] and would be followed by another stream of credit in August 1919, which Niemeyer and Blackett had approved.

Given Italy's grave and worsening dependence on foreign credit, the 1919 British loans were not enough. Italian leaders continued desperately to call for aid to prevent a complete political breakdown—a breakdown, they stressed, that would not go unfelt by their British allies.

In April 1920, Sir Edward Henry Capel-Cure, commercial counselor of the British embassy in Rome, reported on his conversation with the Italian minister of finance, Signor Carlo Schanzer (a man who would later participate in the Genoa conference and profusely endorse austerity). In Capel-Cure's interview—which was immediately transmitted to the British Treasury—Schanzer warned that the financial condition of Italy was "almost untenable" given the high costs of imports. He lamented how "expenditure at this rate could mean nothing short of national bankruptcy and, what was more, revolution" (April 14, 1920, T 1/12551/1). Capel-Cure emphasized to those at home that Schanzer's warnings were not to be underestimated: "The minister repeated the word ['revolution'] several times, and it is the first occasion, in my fairly intimate personal knowledge of him, on which I remember his not having veiled an expression of this description." Capel-Cure recapped Schanzer's preoccupations in the meeting—"The revolution, he said, would undoubtedly spread to France and to Switzerland . . . the Bol[s]chevistic element was only too painfully apparent" (ibid.). The urgent message was clear, as Capel-Cure conveyed: it was in England's interest to take the burning question of Italy's exchange into "immediate and most serious consideration" (ibid., 2).[6]

Meanwhile, the Italian minister of Treasury Signor Luzzatti stressed to others outside Italy that granting credit was no mere charity, but rather a matter of mutual interest in preventing revolution. Italy was a nation "whose dire stress might be the means of producing a conflagration," Luzzatti warned, noting that such developments "might spread to England herself" (ibid., ff. 4). British financiers were aware that the stakes in Italy were inextricably economic and political. A memorandum written by the banker Sir Herbert Hambling, for example, was adamant that political chaos would not only threaten capitalist civilization generally, but would bring the immediate loss of British capital already invested.[7]

Given the British Treasury's reluctance to contribute further, Italy's financial hope rested in private hands—that is, American and British private banks. Of course, this would not come at zero cost. Capel-Cure reported as part of his conversation with Schanzer: "As a matter of fact I have been told a few days ago, by the head of the bank that tried to raise the ten million for Signor Schanzer in August, that the city of London would probably not entertain any proposal from Italy [to raise a private loan] until the [public] subsidy was taken off bread, and other betterments of the finances began" (April 14, 1920, T 1/12551/4).[8] Capel-Cure here planted an early seed of austerity: Italy needed to cut its public subsidies if financial assistance were even to be considered. This type of imperative, as we know, would multiply.

The Italian and British establishments coalesced around a shared narrative of the problem: to understand the Italian economic crisis, "the political reason was to be put in the first line" (April 12, 1920, T 1/12551/1). Italy's economic problems could only be solved after addressing its political problems. After all, strikes and redistributive policies were primary factors "in the nervousness shown abroad towards Italy's finance," and moreover, foreign financial observers understood notions like taxes on profits or luxury goods as an expression of "the selfishness and the cupidity of individuals and classes" in Italy (ibid.). Here again, the blame fell on the majority of the population—backward masses who consumed too much and produced too little.

By the summer of 1922, economic conditions in Italy had not improved. On July 4, the office of the British commercial counselor wrote to the British ambassador to Italy, Ronald William Graham, to inform him about "an interesting article" published in *Il messaggero*, titled "Foreign Criticism of Italian Financial Policy" (July 4, 1922, FO 371/7656, fols. 267–69). The article discussed the "widespread and growing distrust" toward Italy in foreign financial circles. It suggested that foreign interests were particularly "alarmed at the methods of taxation, and at the readiness which the Italian Government shows to impose burdens on foreign money invested in Italy, and at its alleged disregard to its obligations." Special reference was made to a capital levy [*tassa sul patrimonio*]. Disparaging conclusions followed: "the result may be not only to prevent foreign capital from coming to Italy, but also to induce those who have already invested in the country to realize their holdings and take their money away."[9]

Later that July, Capel-Cure expressed deep dissatisfaction with the country's lack of resolve: "The Italian government has to cope with a number of white elephants. Their railways, posts, and telegraphs present a continuously increasing deficit to be met sooner or later by the taxpayer" (July 21, 1922, FO 371/7656, fol. 283). Capel-Cure argued that wage increases were a central part of the problem: "government officials and employees who are organized under trade unions have been able to exact from the state a considerable amount of salaries and wages." The British commercial counselor warned that this trend could spread to non-unionized workers and further deplete state finances (ibid.).

The British Foreign Office joined the choir of criticism of Italy: "The central government is weak and embarrassed; the administration inefficient; the civil service disloyal; the army in a state of chaotic reorganization . . . the agrarian situation is menacing . . . the internal and external prestige of the Italian government has seriously declined" (June 22, 1922, FO 371/7669, fol. 191, 6).

These critics agreed that the only way out for Italy was British-style austerity.[10] In light of this dictum, the right man at the right time was soon to grapple with the problem of Italian financial dependence.

Austerity and the Strong State

SIGNOR DE STEFANI: THE GOOD SOLDIER OF AUSTERITY

As Capel-Cure had noted earlier, the "political complexion" of Italy mattered to its financial rehabilitation (FO 371/7656, fol. 284). On October 27, 1922, the day before the March on Rome and the establishment of the Italian Fascist state, British ambassador to Italy Ronald William

Graham reported to his superiors on the worsening state of the lira-sterling exchange, framing it as a political problem: "the sudden depreciation of the value of the lira is attracting special attention in the Italian press and the comments are gloomy. In nationalist quarters it is ascribed to the internal state of the country and a need of a strong government" (October 27, 1922, FO 371/7656, fols. 287–88).

The ambassador's next dispatch—written a week after Mussolini's seizure of power—took a more optimistic tone: "I have the honour to report that the political events of the last week appear to have had a favourable effect on the Italian exchange" (November 3, 1922, FO 371/7656, fol. 290). The reasons for optimism were straightforward. Once in power, Mussolini quickly set the capital-friendly priorities straight. On November 10, 1922, the British embassy announced that in Italy plans were afoot for guaranteeing investments of foreign capital, and in particular for ensuring that such capital would not be subject to taxation in either Italy or the country of origin.[11]

The Times discussed how the attracting of capital offered a compelling case "for the complete abolition of succession and death duties." Such priorities should remain without limit, even, the newspaper argued, if it meant "a considerable and immediate reduction in the revenue."[12] This argument was in line with the crux of austerity's logic: balancing the budget served as a pretext for the actual objective of shifting resources in favor of capital accumulation. This objective took precedence over anything else.

Only a year later, in December 1923, British ambassador Graham reassured British observers that the previously broken trust was being mended. "Foreign capital had overcome the not unjustified diffidence of the past, and was once again coming to Italy with confidence."[13] Graham contrasted the incapacity of Italy's decadent postwar parliamentary democracy, in its instability and corruption, with the efficient economic management of De Stefani's ministry.

Indeed, the foreign liberal press extolled De Stefani. He attracted praise from American and British financial circles for two compelling and interrelated reasons: first, his resoluteness as an *expert*—"too often lacking in a professional politician"—and second, his laudable commitment to British-style austere values. *The Times* introduced him as an Italian version of "an Oxford don," a man whose collaborators were "soaked in the English economists." These virtuous Italians' "unconcealed ideal" was "to apprehend and copy the British system of public finance" ("Fascismo," *The Times*, July 2, 1923, 13).[14] In the *Economist*, Luigi Einaudi[15] wrote an article titled "An Italian Geddes Committee" that highlighted how "Signor De Stefani laid great stress on the efficacy of the British Treasury in checking expenses and controlling expenditure departments."[16] Similar praises came from the British Embassy in Rome. Graham spoke of De Stefani as "a theoretical economist by training and profession" who had framed for himself "a programme which practically consisted in balancing the budget and declining all temptations to inflate the currency" (July 10, 1925, FO 371/10784, fol. 37).

Both *The Times* and the *Economist* stressed that one of De Stefani's greatest virtues was "the courage to brave unpopularity," which allowed him to pursue austerity measures with "a dogmatic certainty of opinion" ("Fascismo," *The Times*, July 2, 1923, 13).[17] And indeed, De Stefani's willingness "to tame men" in the face of popular opposition was a hard-won impulse born of his training in pure economics. The professor's bravery came from his school's self-proclaimed mission of realizing "rigorous and elegant [economic] laws" (Ricci 1926, 104–5).

De Stefani's alacrity was also doted on by the liberal press: "he lives, sleeps, eats in the ministry, and his day is 8 to 8 with half an hour for lunch, for seven days in the week. I suspect that this superactivity is due to his not unnatural mistrust for the officials whom he has inherited."[18] Of course, as the press also knew, but seemingly refrained from writing, De Stefani's ability to ignore social demands was only partially due to his resolute personality: the expert could use his "firm hand" because he was part of the firm grip of an authoritarian state.

THE INVINCIBLE DUO: AUSTERITY AND AUTHORITARIANISM

In the weeks that followed Mussolini's seizure of power, foreign observers noted the remarkable effectiveness of state power in implementing austerity. On November 3, 1922, a dispatch from British ambassador Graham emphasized a breakthrough that had already occurred in both economic policy and political power. He described plans for privatization and reductions in public services, concluding that "[the] government is much stronger than its predecessors for enforcing measures of the above nature" (FO 371/7660, fol. 185).

The Times, meanwhile, defined Fascism as "an anti-waste government"[19] in the same breath in which it covered Mussolini's opening speech to the nation—a speech that was steeped in themes that were objectively authoritarian and austere: "the guiding motives of our internal policy . . . may be summed up in three words—economy, work, discipline. We must attain budgetary equilibrium as speedily as possible. . . . Respect of the law will be enforced at all costs. The State is strong, and will display its force against all. . . . Whoever turns against the State will be punished."[20]

In Mussolini's senate address on June 8, 1923, the *Duce* asserted that "the dominant fact in 1919–1920 . . . the occupation of the factories, the continual and permanent strike of state employees" had been eliminated and punished, thanks to the Fascists' replacement of a state "devoid of virility" with one that "was growing stronger and stronger and could impose discipline upon the nation" (ibid., fol. 75). The British embassy described this speech as "convincing": "his speech shows the Fascista movement in its true light as the reassertion of 'authority' against 'liberty' as the idea of government . . . the complete subordination of the rest to the Fascisti" (FO 371/8885, fol. 73).

The tone of British observations during the early days of the Fascist regime was not condemnation, but a nodding appreciation for the Fascist leader's good sense. Graham, for example, said that for Italy, "the chief failure lay in 'parliamentarianism'" (FO 371/7660, fol. 198). With its factious dynamics, parliamentarism—or democracy—only increased ungovernability at a moment when grave economic necessity and revolutionary threat called for something stronger.[21]

Even Montagu Norman, the governor of the Bank of England, who expressed wariness of the fact that under Fascism "anything in the way of otherness" was "eliminated," and "opposition in any form [was] gone," added in the same breath: "this state of affairs is suitable at present and may provide for the moment the administration best adapted for Italy." He continued:

> Fascism has surely brought order out of chaos over the last few years: something of the kind was no doubt needed if the pendulum was not to swing too far in quite the other direction. The *Duce* was the right man at a critical moment. (Letter to John Pierpont "Jack" Morgan Jr., November 19, 1926, G1 307, fol. 27)

The international establishment's support for a strong state was not an outlier or an aberration.[22] These sentiments pervaded British diplomatic circles and the British liberal press: Fascist dictatorship was an unavoidable and necessary means to govern a turbulent country and achieve sound economic objectives.[23] Oliver Harvey, second secretary of the British embassy in Rome, left no doubt as to the criterion for this judgment: "the Mussolini experiment should stand on its merits as a pure and unadulterated dictatorship, like that of Cincinnatus, to be justified or otherwise by the gravity of the situation and by success" (October 22, 1923, FO 371/8886, fol. 46). Dictatorships were only bad when they were wrong.

After the regime's first year in power, the embassy and the international press continued to rejoice at Mussolini's triumphs.[24] He had succeeded in uniting political order with economic order, the very essence of austerity.[25] In Graham's 1923 general report, circulated to the prime minister, the ambassador continued to give high marks:

> Eighteen months ago, any instructed observer of national life was bound to come to the conclusion that Italy was a country on the downgrade. . . . It is now generally admitted, even by those who dislike Fascismo and deplore its methods, that the whole situation has changed . . . a striking progress towards the stabilization of State finances . . . strikers [decreased] by 90 percent and working days lost [decreased] by over

97 percent, and an increase in national savings of 4,000 [million lire] over the preceding year; indeed they exceed for the first time the pre-war level by nearly 2,000 million lire. (FO 371/9946, fol. 246, 16)

These messages left no doubts: any preoccupation with Fascist political abuse dwindled under the successes of its austerity. The chairman of the British Italian Bank, J. W. Beaumont Pease, put it simply: auster-ity's success was about "strenuous work and thrift" under "the highest conception of state authority."[26]

The Fascist state's use of political repression and violence in its pur-suit of capital accumulation would seem to offer a final test for the lib-eral approvals around Mussolini and his regime. In their glossing over and defending these abuses, the liberal establishment would quickly, and thoroughly, fail that test.

POLITICAL REPRESSION AND THE INTERNATIONAL DOUBLE STANDARD

The celebrated successes of austerity in Italy—counted in terms like industrial peace, high profits, and more business for the Brits—had a repressive face, too, one that went far beyond such high-level develop-ments as institutionalization of a strong executive and bypassing of Par-liament. In Italy, Mussolini did not seek to shield his repressions from public view; after all, he noted, "the measures adopted to re-establish public order are, above all, the suppression of the so-called subversive elements."[27]

International observers were aware, for example, that the Fascist Squads, notorious for their cold-blooded violence during the turbulent years of 1919–1922, had been made an integral part of the state appara-tus, reinforcing the military character of the government.[28] In July 1923, amid public claims of unconstitutionality, the Grand Fascista Coun-cil announced that these so-called Black Shirts formed "a formidable and indivisible army destined to guarantee the continuance of the Fas-cista government" ("Summary of Proclamation," FO 371/8885, fol. 201). This full-blown federal militia was a "large force to overawe his [Mussolini's] political opponents," necessary "so long as the state shall not have become entirely Fascista" (July 30, 1923, FO 371/8885, fol. 184).[29]

The British embassy reported on a variety of these proceedings: the continuous aggression against political opponents;[30] the burning of socialist headquarters and of chambers of labor; the driving out of office of various socialist mayors; electoral frauds or explicit intimidations of voters at the polls (prior to elections being eliminated altogether after three years of the regime);[31] the execution of political enemies; the arrest of communists;[32] and several notorious political homicides—most importantly the murder of the Socialist deputy Giacomo Matteotti, who had opposed the government and its elections.[33]

The American and British financial circles' treatment of the "Matteotti Affair" is emblematic of the prioritization of economic results over political freedom (and seemingly over concerns around political violence). *The Times* and the *Economist* both treated the killing as the Italian government's occasion "to clean up the Ministry of the Interior" and to rid Mussolini's government and party of disgraceful elements.[34] Mussolini could strengthen and normalize the party by expelling its extremist fringes (Migone 2015, 55), which would be justified if it gave better footing to the financial orthodoxy of Mussolini and De Stefani.[35] Elsewhere, in a campaign speech during the height of the Matteotti crisis, US Secretary of State Andrew Mellon ignored the accusations of Mussolini's abuse of power. Instead he spoke highly of the leader's capacity to achieve a balanced budget and to free industry from government regulation while ridding the country of the nefarious influence of socialists (ibid., 56).[36]

In the midst of the Matteotti crisis, the chairman of the British-Italian Banking Corporation, Beaumont Pease, explicitly defended the Fascist government against any rumor of instability, calling instead for its assistance and "cordial sympathy."[37] Pease claimed that in his position—"unique" in England—as the leader of the only "British banking institution dealing almost exclusively with Italian affairs," he could ascertain not only the flourishing of his *own* profits but more generally "the industrial prosperity established by Mussolini" and the "resulting benefit to British Industry." He declared: "By trusting the Italians we have secured a great deal of business for British manufacturers which would otherwise have gone to Germany, America and elsewhere, and never once have we been let down financially" ("The British-Italian Banking Corporation, Limited," *Economist*, March 21, 1925, 559ff.).

The chairman's main justification for austerity was the usual one: "there is no responsible Italian who does not deplore the excess and misdemeanors which have been committed [by Mussolini]," yet "there is hardly one who would not admit the benefit the country has derived from the policy of the present government." Of course, such supposed national benefit came in the form of industrial, monetary, and fiscal austerity. These policies were anything but beneficial to the majority of Italian citizens.

Pease's words are remarkable and bring forward a mode of rationalization that was typical of the British liberal establishment: "It seems to me that there is no particular cause for anxiety. . . . We can well disregard such of their internal methods as may be unpalatable to us, and trust them to find their own means of working out their salvation, towards which they have already gone a long way." The intellectual maneuvering here was explicit: economic and political considerations were separate and distinct—and unequal—realms of judgment. However uncomfortable an authoritarian political setting might be, it was the necessary one to achieve economic success. And it was also the case that economic recovery was the sole universal standard upon which to judge the Fascist regime; the ends might yet justify the means. Furthermore, one had to be tolerant: the political regime was up to the Italians to handle.

Observers ultimately agreed that what was inadmissible in a country with a democratic tradition—especially an Anglo-Saxon country—was instead well-suited for the Italian citizen after World War I.[38] *The Times* articulated this double standard: "It seems improbable that under his [Mussolini's] system[,] democracy, in the British sense, can survive in Italy. But critics do not always realize how totally different is the meaning of democracy in the two countries, and frequently forget that before Signor Mussolini came into power the position of the Italian Parliament was one of deep humiliation."[39]

Governor Norman agreed: "Italy is not a free country in the usual sense of the word, and certain things are lacking which in a liberal country like England are apt to be missed, for instance, freedom of speech, freedom of the Press, freedom of politics and so on. But the fact remains that she has made economic and financial progress. . . ."[40] Italian people were different from British people, and the former were not going to miss democracy or other liberal values.[41]

At the Bank of England, an anonymous handwritten document from 1925 titled "Fascist Italy—Fascist Methods" articulated this double standard in stark terms. The document contained an inventory of Fascist oppression in its human terms, including the firings of all public servants "who might be inclined to indulge in anti-fascist activities" (OV 36/1, fol. 17), the dissolution of all non-Fascist municipalities, and the complete control over those municipalities by the *podestà* (central government officials who superseded elected local authorities). Moreover, it noted, "apart from bludgeoning and castor-oil, murder has been resorted to on a large scale—not only in the early days, but since the party came into power, for the purpose of suppressing obnoxious adversaries" (ibid.). The memo ended with a list of the regime's major political murders. However, far from being denounced, these facts of political abuse were reported with a tone of "realism" regarding the inferior conditions of Italians:

> [T]he Italian people are the descendants of Roman slaves. After the decay of the Roman power, they remained for some fourteen centuries under the domination of various warring sets of foreigners . . . slave peoples are generally incapable of governing themselves . . . so it is that democratic government in Italy, which has never been a conspicuous success, broke down utterly when the strain of the great war had produced exceptionally severe moral degeneration among the unstable Italian people . . . the nation was ripe for bolshevism . . . but the nation—or perhaps its non-latin-rulers?—was not ripe for suicide. . . . Mussolini and his Fascists seized power and restored order. They rule the country today by force according to their own will, and the people are reduced to the servitude which had been their lot for a score of centuries. (ibid.)

The argument in favor of Mussolini's dictatorship thus took various shades: there were bluntly racist remarks like those above, alleging the ultimate incapacity of "Latins" to be democratic; or a slightly milder line that played on cultural relativism and pragmatic good sense. Nothing else, it seemed, could save such a cursed country.[42]

Indeed, if observers raised doubts, they were not out of concerns for democracy, but rather for what would happen in the absence of Mussolini. This worry was palpable within the Bank of England, with its 1926 memo: "if that system fails . . . anything could happen, including civil war and chaos" (November 13, 1926, G1/307, fol. 22). In June 1928, Einaudi wrote in the *Economist* that he worried about a lack of political representation, but that he worried more about a lack of capital order.[43] He spoke of the "very grave questionings" in the minds of the Englishmen: "When, again, in the inevitable course of nature the strong hand of the great Duce is removed from the helm has Italy another man of his calibre? Can any age produce two Mussolinis? If not, what next? Under weaker and less wise control may not chaotic revulsion follow? And with what consequences, not merely for Italy, but for Europe?" ("The Corporative State in Italy," *Economist*, June 23, 1928, 1273ff.).[44]

Even in that summer of 1928, the ghosts of the earlier capitalist crisis years still loomed large. In commemorating former prime minister Giovanni Giolitti's career, the *Economist* focused on a dark spot therein: "Unhappily he was a partisan of the 'wait and see' policy up to the point of not interfering when workmen, in September, 1920, invaded industrial establishments and rural workers occupied private lands" ("The Late Signor Giolitti," *Economist*, August 4, 1928, 228).

The liberal international establishment was so enamored of Mussolini's implementation of austerity that it rewarded the regime with the financial resources to further solidify the country's political and economic rule—in particular through settlement of its war debt and stabilizing the lira. As US Federal Reserve governor Benjamin Strong affirmed in 1927, Italy's display of "self-discipline and capacity for sacrifice" granted the country the right to be supported in its plan to achieve the gold standard (see Migone 2015, 189).

These rewards from liberal institutions elsewhere ignored that Italy's bootstrapping self-discipline was, in reality, the authoritarian rule of Mussolini. The prime minister's agenda to impose "self-sacrifice" upon the working classes—including the suppression of their wages, working rights, and sheer livelihood—amounted to deflation by violent means.

Debt and the Consolidation of the Lira

British and American financiers were more than just supportive spectators of Fascist austerity. Their acceptance of Mussolini's regime within the capitalist international order was crucial for the regime's consolidation.

In a letter to his finance minister during the early summer of 1925, when international speculative attacks continued to ravage the lira,[45] Mussolini displayed full cognizance of the unavoidable interdependence with international capital:

> We must realize that we are confronting the whole financial world's lack of faith in Italian finance, a lack of faith that explains and provokes speculation lowering currency value. As long as this lack of faith did not have internal consequences, the situation presented no imminent danger; but the day that politics crosses the border (and in the long run it is inevitable), the distrust will spread throughout the country and cause depositors to withdraw their funds (which amount to $51 billion), and the regime would have no power to stop the collapse. (Migone 2015, 179–80)

Mussolini's message was clear: international financial confidence could make or break the Fascist regime. Settling the war debt and achieving the gold standard were the surest paths to guaranteeing the durability of that confidence. Notably, this agenda of Mussolini's presupposed proving the country's creditworthiness through austerity.

Ever since the end of the Great War, the US and British Treasuries had denied Italy's pleas for war-debt cancellation.[46] Thus, from the onset of the Fascist regime, the Anglo-American financiers unanimously described Mussolini as being "most anxious to come to an agreement as to Italy's debt at the earliest possible moment."[47] Of course, debt repayment involved the outflow of large amounts of capital and required a relatively large percentage of government revenues, requiring further fiscal austerity. The *Duce* offered reassurances that his country had good credentials in this respect given his haste in improving the budget and guaranteeing industrial peace.

In the years preceding and following the debt settlements, the British embassy, the Treasury, the Bank of England, and these institutions' American counterparts obsessively monitored Italian finances.[48] These watchdogs were happy with what they saw. Following a meeting in 1926 with Italian finance minister Giuseppe Volpi to discuss the war debt, British chancellor of the exchequer Winston Churchill remarked: "I have been greatly impressed by the immense progress made by Italy under the present regime—a budget balanced under considerable surpluses, as industry rapidly increases in importance, a favorable balance in the international payments . . . an orderly and progressive government, a *thrifty* and *industrious* population and an almost complete absence of unemployment"[49] (T 176/40, fol. 5, my italics). Notably, Churchill's praise for the tidiness of a once problematic nation included a checklist of austerity measures.

The debt settlements with the US and Britain of 1925 and 1926, respectively, were necessary for Italy to achieve the gold standard because they opened up access to further credit.[50] Indeed, the collaboration of the Bank of England and the US Federal Reserve—the two institutions that controlled the mechanisms of the stabilization procedure—was contingent on debt settlement, which had the added benefit of granting Italy access to foreign capital markets.[51] Immediately after Italy dealt with its dues, J. P. Morgan Chase Bank signed off on a loan of $100 million to support the stabilization of the lira.[52]

The Fascist state zealously publicized its compliance with the international code of austerity, to the point that De Stefani arranged the "regular transmission of the publications of a financial character" to the British Foreign Office (October 15, 1924, FO 371/9936, fol. 96).[53] Theirs was a tenacious application of austerity, one that convinced international markets to shift from speculating downward to speculating upward in favor of the revaluation of the lira, starting in October 1926.

The "British experts [*tecnici*] . . . are our most shrewd critics,"[54] Volpi wrote to Mussolini in 1926. The day after the regime announced gold parity, Chancellor Churchill wrote to offer his "heartiest congratulations" for an achievement that "crowns the great work you have done for the re-establishment of Italian finances" (December 26, 1927, FO 371/12198, fol. 236). The great work of austerity included a forced reduction of internal consumption to improve the balance of trade.[55] By 1927 the government reported that "imports have fallen by 21%, exports have increased in quantity" (FO 371/12947, fol. 163). This meant a "patriotic cooperation of the Italian people" (September 1, 1926, OV 36/1, fol. 16)—who consumed less and worked harder in a labor market that the state had purged of any independent representation.

Indeed, international financial experts explicitly pressured Fascism to defeat labor's demands. For example, while examining Italy's request for a stabilization loan, Fed governor Strong urged Italy to maintain its balance of trade with a further reduction of cost of living and wages, which the governor of the Bank of Italy, Bonaldo Stringher, gave assurance he would achieve.[56] The defeat of labor was such that, as the British Embassy reported, "the leaders of the General Confederation of Labour (the C.G.L), in view of the fact that their organization now only exists on paper and as a name on a letterhead, have decided on its dissolution" (January 28, 1927, FO 371/12202, fol. 71). Ambassador Graham concluded: "there is obviously no room for such an organization as the C.G.L in the labour system developed by the present government, and its existence could hardly be expected to continue" (ibid., fol. 72).[57]

By exacting sacrifices on the working classes, Italy could finally participate in the international capitalist order. After gold stabilization, the *Economist* announced that it expected "foreign capital, mainly for the United States and Great Britain," to "seek more freely temporary or permanent investment in Italy." The article praised the anti-inflationary actions of the newly created central bank: "the Banca d'Italia will take the necessary steps to prevent an inflow of foreign capital from resulting in credit inflation and affecting the price levels."[58] As chapters 5 and 6 showcased, the technocratic project of an independent central bank to keep inflation at bay was a central pillar of British austerity. It was the only pillar that Fascism struggled to achieve.

An Independent Central Bank?

In the course of Italy's austerity rehabilitation, the institution of lower wages required a strong intervention by the Italian state on the labor market. While international technocrats commended this melding of economics and politics for its capacity to discipline the rebellious Italian workers, the melding of the economic and the political as it related to monetary policy was less appreciated.

As part and parcel of its austerity efforts, Italy had followed the 1922 Genoa code that prescribed the formation of a central bank. The Banca d'Italia, in existence since the nineteenth century, was granted status in May 1926 as Italy's central bank and the country's sole bank of issue.[59] At that moment all of the gold or equivalent reserves were transferred to it, along with a substantial increase of capital from the J. P. Morgan loan.

Bank of England governor Montagu Norman had received accounts of the Banca's deflationary measures since 1922.[60] Following the bank's transition to being Italy's central bank, Norman was profoundly troubled by its formal and substantial lack of independence. The Bank of Italy, just like the British one, was a joint-stock company—a private body; however, it was still subject to political control. Its new statute read: "The Minister of the Treasury has permanent supervision on the Banca d'Italia, verifying annually the balance sheets and accounts, the metallic reserve and so on." Moreover, the Banca was formally obliged to advance money to the government and could only change the bank rate by order of the Minister of the Treasury (OV 36/22, fol. 108). Governor Norman was disquieted by such an "attitude of Fascism" being extended to Italy's monetary systems (October 28, 1926, G1/307, fol. 9, 2). On various occasions and in letters to other central bankers, Norman lamented the political subjugation of the Italian Banca's governor, Bonaldo Stringher,[61] to the point of questioning his own support for the lira's stabilization.[62] His concerns matched those of other technocrats in Britain, including Hawtrey, Blackett, and Niemeyer.

In a letter to US Fed governor Strong on March 4, 1926, Norman outlined his dissatisfaction with Finance Minister Volpi's attitude toward the Bank of Italy. After being admonished about the requisite independence of the Bank for the purpose of "stabilization and cooperation,"[63] Volpi had reaffirmed that "he himself was going to direct Central Bank policy," which Volpi regarded as a part of general finance policy (G14/95, 1–2). Later, in November 1926, Norman wrote to his colleague Hjalmar Schacht at the German Reichsbank: "Stringher is about 70 years old and I guess has no more independence than a tail of a kite. If he is a wise man he is probably happier without it, for the power exercised by the fascisti leave no room for independence and seem to extend further and to become more inquisitorial each time that a gun is fired at the Duce" (November 5, 1926, G1/307).

Note that Norman's problem with authoritarianism was not about the deprivation of worker's rights and liberties, but rather about the prospect of stewarding the central bank via the whims of politics, which could create "uncontrollable and unpredictable future circumstances," especially in the dreaded case of Mussolini's financial experts changing their minds regarding orthodoxy. The governor's thoughts contained no negative judgment of the regime's political or economic choices. He merely pointed out the problem of monetary policy not being "knave proof" to a possible change of the regime's austere orientations. Norman's dilemma again highlights the double standard typical of the international technocrats: political questions only mattered insofar as they started to knock at the pearly gates of the economic domain.

For their part, J. P. Morgan and other bankers "were anxious" that "stabilization should proceed whenever possible and Italy should naturally be [the] next place"—i.e., whatever interventions were necessary to stabilize the currency should be taken (cable of J. P. Morgan to Norman, November 8, 1926, G1/307, fol. 15). US Fed governor Strong was also determined to move ahead. He responded firmly to the doubts of his British colleague Norman, expressing a belief in the rightness of prioritizing stabilization over Norman's "conception of orthodox independence" (November 26, 1926, G1/307, fol. 31). He gave reassurances that the Italian finance minister had changed his tone: "Volpi has expressed the view to others," he wrote, "that as rapidly as possible the bank should be freed from political or state control" (ibid.).

Warmed by this reassurance, Norman wrote in October 1927, "I do not think one should complain, especially if, as seems possible, the measure of their independence is increasing"; and he announced a forthcoming "comprehensive and cooperative account and understanding" between the British and Italian central banks. And to secure the credit necessary for stabilization, the Italian regime set out to reinforce the façade of an independent central bank. By the autumn of 1927 Strong was convinced: "I have received Signor Stringher's assurance," he told Norman, "[that] the Banca d'Italia is established in a position of independence and financial control" (November 29, 1927, G14/95).[64]

Volpi, reading the room, had turned away from his previous stubbornness. A 1928 speech articulated his belief that "the position of the Bank of Italy as controller of the money market is also clearly defined: a sound capital situation, ample reserves, independent management, and the possession of means for protecting the currency and controlling the money market."[65] Ultimately, the international financiers were willing to believe this narrative because Italy was delivering on their austerity agenda.

Technocracy prevailed in the matter of Italy's central bank, even if it didn't exactly match the British case. For Hawtrey and his colleagues at the Bank of England, the main reason for demanding an independent central bank was to avoid any possible democratic supervision of economic policies, thereby steering clear of people's tampering with austerity. The Italians achieved the same immunity from public criticism with different methods. Rather than relying upon experts within long-standing technocratic institutions, the Italian economic professors propped up strong and coercive executives who could deliver on implementing their economic models.

Conclusion

This chapter scrutinizes the external forces that pushed for austerity in Italy after World War I. In short, the commitment to austerity by international financial experts was so great that they were willing to rely on a bloody dictatorship to reinstate the crumbling pillars of capital accumulation. All eyes turned toward Mussolini, whose dictatorship was strong enough to finally tame the Italian people into being "disciplined, silent, and peaceful."[66]

In this light, foreign onlookers evaluated and judged Fascism solely in terms of its economic performance. These international experts were agnostic when it came to political methods. To them, a violent dictatorship was akin to "Roman baroque architecture":[67] it would offend in a different democratic climate, but in Italy it actually suited the country and people quite well.

The explicit connection between austerity and political repression—so evident under Fascism—reveals how the economic treatment of Italian citizens was not in fact so different from the treatment the British experts envisioned for their own people. Indeed, as chapter 6 has emphasized, British technocrats pushed hard for a nondemocratic implementation of economic policy through the independence and authority of central banks. Even if different in nature, the Italian and the British versions of technocracy shared a common end: creating systems that imposed sacrifice on the majority of the public, then insulating those systems from political interruption.

The consolidation of the Fascist regime coincided with the culmination of its austerity triumph, which was announced with Italy's entry into the "Gold Standard Club" in December 1927. This political consolidation, however, did not mean the liberation of the country from its dependence on Anglo-American capital. On the contrary, Italian monetary policy was now tied to a continuation of austerity in order to maintain its gold parity—a bind that ultimately served the interests of foreign financial capital, forevermore. In fact, budgetary equilibrium and the gold standard guaranteed the subservience of the debtor, Italy, and allowed Anglo-American capitalists to elude competition with a devalued lira that would otherwise enable Italy to export cheap products to the American and British markets.

These dynamics might sound familiar, as they were a precursor of the relationship that the experts at the International Monetary Fund (IMF) contrived and enact with most of the peripheral countries in the world today: loans conditional upon austerity; a focus on "economic freedom" rather than political freedom; and the compulsion to open a country's economy to international scrutiny.[68] The Italian story helps us to scrutinize other, more recent austere cases with a sharper eye. On closer examination, these austerity-based adjustment programs disclose the same underlying aim: taming the population to produce more and consume less in order to safeguard capital accumulation.

The following chapter will provide empirical evidence of the "success" of austerity in enforcing hard work and abstinence. The trends of the 1920s provide insights on the reasons for the persistence of austerity in the twenty-first century.

CHAPTER 9

Austerity and Its "Successes"

Austerity was, and remains, a shrewd endeavor. By critically studying its origins and architects, we see again and again that austerity was conceived, and succeeded, as a counteroffensive: it functions to preserve the primacy and indisputability of capitalism in times when capitalism is under political threat. And it does so by introducing structures—policies—that shift resources from the working majority to the saver/investor minority. The immediate distributional impacts have the important long-term function of disempowering the majority and thus reinforcing the general acceptance of the pillars of capital accumulation: private ownership of the means of production and wage relations. You get what the boss gives you.

The Italian and British experts who ushered in austerity achieved a great victory: they rehabilitated their capitalist economies through models and policies that justified the economic superiority of a small minority as the only road to economic recovery. This chapter provides a critical summary of the achievements of these two austerity initiatives—with "achievements" in this usage not necessarily being synonymous with "things that are good."

What's clear is that austerity is particularly effective not in stabilizing economies, but in stabilizing class relations. After all, austerity has historically never been about curbing inflation and budget control; its manipulations of aggregate demand have always been a means to a deeper end. Austerity secured the best possible conditions for profits to soar, while the majority—the politically underserved—were forced to relinquish all fledgling projects of economic democracy and to "live harder" through lower wages and lower consumption. Austere capitalism produces losers and winners, and it always has.

The study of class shares (i.e., wage share versus profit share) provides a clear sense of the losers and winners of austerity, and in turn its political implications. Class shares measure the portion of GDP that goes to labor and to capital—the most immediate indicator of the balance of forces between a society's two main classes. The reassertion of capital order, i.e., the primacy of capital over labor, is foundational to promoting capitalist investment: capital does better when workers are subordinated, wages are low, and regulation is minimal. Following World War I, austerity's knack for collapsing the wage share was vital in a moment when the wage share had reached an unprecedented high, stirring among workers great expectations of a breakaway from capitalist exploitation. Thus the political utility of austerity becomes obvious. A rescue of the hierarchical labor-capital split meant an escape from the capitalist crisis (and the egalitarian impulses that came with it) triggered by the Great War.

To give a sense of who was part of "labor" and who was part of "capital," it is useful to recall that in 1921 the British working classes encompassed more than 60 percent of the population, while the "owner class" was roughly 7 percent (Gómez León and de Jong 2018). In Italy, the propertied upper class (bourgeoisie) constituted only 1.7 percent of the entire population, against a working class (in both agriculture and industry) that was almost half of the population (Sylos Labini 1975, Table 1.2). Given these tiny fractions of society that benefited from austerity, the movement's losers extended well beyond wage workers: these groups comprised most of the middle classes that made up the populations' middle grounds—public employees, independent farmers, soldiers, shopkeepers, and other professionals. While it is true that the value of these professionals' pensions and savings increased with deflation, that same deflation also spurred a loss of employment and a loss of social benefits.

Measuring austerity's economic effects in Britain and Italy also corroborates one of the main claims of this book: that there is a profound parallelism between austerity in a democratic setting and austerity in a Fascist setting. In the 1920s, the repressive nature of British austerity primarily took the form of market coercion: workers were forced into compliance with the logic of capital accumulation after the Treasury and the Bank of England devised policies that triggered high unemployment and curtailed welfare rights. Increased economic necessity brought workers to their knees. The Italian version of austerity did not need to rely on unemployment as such, since it was accompanied by Fascist state interventions that slashed nominal wages by decree and annihilated genuine worker's representation.

The two forms of austerity, Fascist and democratic, aligned in their success at thwarting dissent. This can be seen in the similar rise-and-fall patterns of worker strikes and the rise-and-fall patterns of compensation and wage share. The data presented in this chapter illustrate how the repressive drive of austere Italian Fascism behaved much the same as austerity in the British parliamentary democracy, both after World War I and today.

Class Shares, Exploitation, and Profit Rates

To grasp the political (and economic) implications of austerity, there are three main timelines to consider: the wage share of national income, the ratio of non-wage to wage incomes (known as the rate of exploitation), and the profit rate.

Figure 9.1 shows the wage share—the portion of GDP that goes to wages (i.e., the income of the working class) as opposed to profits (i.e., the income of the capitalist class). In essence this relation is zero-sum: what is taken from one class is gained by the other.

The similarity of these patterns in Britain and Italy is striking.

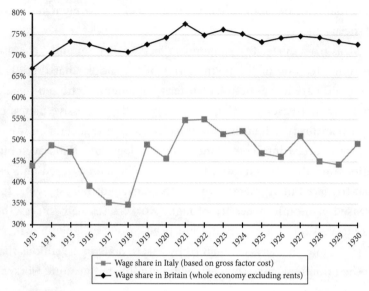

9.1. Wage share of national income for Italy and Britain. The wage share is calculated by subtracting from the total nominal GDP the portion of GDP that constitutes the income from profits. (Sources: Gabbuti 2020a [for Italy] and Thomas and Dimsdale 2017 [for Britain].)

Britain's maturity as an industrial society came with a century-long tradition of industrial militancy which entailed that its workers enjoyed a higher level of national income compared to their Italian counterparts. Moreover, the war years had a different impact on the workforce of the two countries. In Italy, the wage share dropped dramatically—from 44 percent in 1913 to 35 percent in 1918, a shift of 9 percentage points of national income from workers to capitalists. Meanwhile, in Britain the wage share actually increased from 67 percent in 1913 to 71 percent in 1918 (see figure 9.1). This phenomenon illustrates a dynamic described at length in chapter 1: the Italian labor force experienced a greater degree of militarization, whereas British unions retained a firmer voice in their role of collaboration with/opposition to the state.

The years of postwar capitalist crisis saw a common surge of the wage share, a fact of unprecedented and deep historical importance.

Never had workers in either country gained such a high proportion of the national output. During these red years, the Italian wage share grew to 49 percent in 1919 from 35 percent in 1918, and peaked at 55 percent in 1922. This was a huge increase even compared to the prewar levels (44 percent in 1913). It meant that in 1921, capital reaped fewer fruits from economic growth than labor, something unseen until that moment. Capital share dropped from 65 percent in 1918 to 45 percent in 1922.

Though more moderate, the British case still looks quite impressive. Wage share rose from 71 percent in 1918 to 78 percent in 1921. This was an unprecedented increment with respect to the prewar years (in 1913 it was at 67 percent). Even if the surge is numerically not as striking as the Italian case, two factors must be kept in mind to evaluate the potentially explosive effect of the British circumstances. First, British workers were in possession of a significant amount of the GDP, a measure of their strength, which gave them a greater voice in settling economic agendas; second, that power had still increased like never before. The troubles for capital were embodied in a 7-percentage-point drop in profit share between 1918 and 1920 which swept away the war gains. The postwar profit share was one-third of the prewar amount. As in Italy, these class gains were also fuel for a movement to nationalize and give British workers a central, potentially independent role in the production process.

The austerity counteroffensive had an unequivocally uniform impact on both countries: it reversed both countries' labor gains dramatically. Under Fascist austerity the gross wage share of Italian workers tumbled throughout the 1920s, reaching a new low in 1929 when it touched the level of 1913. Capital had gained back its dominant position. British labor experienced a similar fall: by 1929 workers had lost all of their postwar gains in share of national income.[1]

Another way to visualize austerity's dramatic impact on class relations is to look at the ratio between profits and wages, a tangible measure of the trend of *exploitation*. As figure 9.2 shows, in Britain exploitation increased by 32 percent over the decade, while in Italy—from

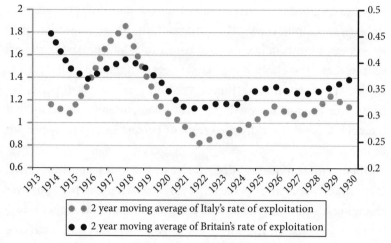

9.2. Rate of exploitation in Italy and Britain. The rate of exploitation is calculated as the ratio between profit share and wage share. Note that the two countries have different axes: the vertical axis on the left depicts the Italian rate of exploitation, the one on the right the British rate of exploitation. (Author's calculations.)

the start of Fascist austerity in 1922 until 1928—exploitation surged by 54 percent.[2] Here again these similar trends in the two countries strongly counteracted the trends of the red years.

Higher exploitation is also reflected in productivity growth, which combined with a decline in real compensation delivered a larger surplus to the capitalists. In Britain this trend was strong in the early years of austerity: between 1920 and 1922 labor productivity per head grew from 18 percent to 20 percent, while real wages stagnated.[3] In Italy the dynamic of declining real wages and increasing productivity (up by 20 percent from 1922 to 1926)[4] was pronounced until 1926, when the instability of the lira promoted a price deflation that was faster than the fall of nominal wages.

This increase in exploitation brought a surge in profit rates.[5] Figure 9.3 shows that the profit rates for capital grew throughout the 1920s in both countries. From 1920 until the end of the decade, the profit rate more than tripled in Britain. A similar increase occurred in Italy, where profit rates surged from 4.9 percent in 1920 to 8.3 percent in 1926.[6]

In 1924, *The Times* reported on the success of Fascist austerity: "the development of the last two years have seen the absorption of a greater proportion of profits by capital, and this, by stimulating business enterprise, has most certainly been advantageous to the country as a whole" (OV 36/22, f. 22). This type of narrative is typical, and is essential in the selling and sticking of austerity doctrines throughout history: consensus for public and popular sacrifice is built through the rhetoric of the good of the whole.

Repression of internal demand in Italy was compensated by export-led growth thanks to a strong world demand and a devalued lira. Indeed, Italy's 9.3 percent growth in real GDP in 1923 opened the doors to three years of economic boom. The ensuing deflation in 1926–1927 had a negative impact on exports and real GDP (which dropped 3 percent during 1927), but this fall in business was compensated by wage suppression that guaranteed the endurance (and in this case, the quick reversal) of profit rates. Italy's real GDP growth was back to 6.3 percent in 1928 (Gabbuti 2020b, 256).[7]

A similar compensatory dynamic characterized the British case, where the austerity-induced economic stagnation[8] that lasted throughout the 1920s was accompanied by stagnating nominal wages. Accordingly, sluggish economic growth did not preclude the enrichment of business owners. Rather, the austerity-induced downturn was *vital* to

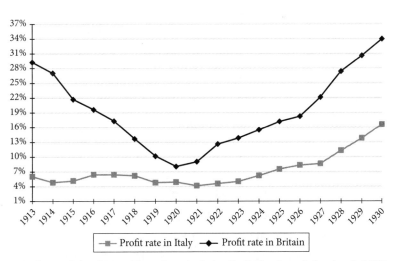

9.3. Profit rate in Italy and Britain. The profit rate is calculated by dividing the profit share (nominal GDP minus wage share) by the nominal value of the non-dwelling capital stock. (Author's calculations.)

securing a turnaround in the relations between capital and labor, which in turn secured the existing wealth of the capitalist class.

On the Operation of Austerity

In Britain in 1920–1922, monetary deflation, combined with a colossal cut in government expenditures (detailed in chapter 6), "defeated" inflation through a massive economic downturn that ushered in a period of unprecedented unemployment. In 1921 national unemployment skyrocketed from 2 percent to 11.3 percent.[9] Almost 2.5 million people left the labor force (Feinstein 1972). In the manufacturing sector alone, Britain lost almost 1.3 million jobs that year—almost one-fourth of the entire manufacturing sector.[10] From then on, the number of the officially unemployed averaged around 1.7 million throughout the decade, a number at least twice its prewar levels. This figure is even more striking considering that Britain during the war was approaching full employment, with the unemployment rate as low as 0.3 percent in 1916.

An immediate consequence of Britain's austerity-induced downturn was the wave of economic coercion that overtook British workers. Amid rising unemployment, organized labor lost much of its political power. By the end of the decade, only one-fourth of the working population was unionized, down from almost 40 percent after the Great War (see figure 9.4).

The number and intensity of British strikes (i.e., the percentage of strikers relative to the labor force as a whole) are a good yardstick to capture the strength and militancy of labor in the postwar years.[11] As illustrated in figures 9.5 and 9.6, both metrics tell a similar story around union participation. In 1919 there were around 2,600,000 workers (12 percent of the labor force) participating in strikes; by 1927 there was almost a twofold drop (a 96 percent decrease). In that year worker strikes reached rock bottom, with only 108,000 workers on the picket lines (that is, 0.5 percent of the labor force). The 1926 general strike interrupted this trajectory, but at a larger cost: the general strike is widely

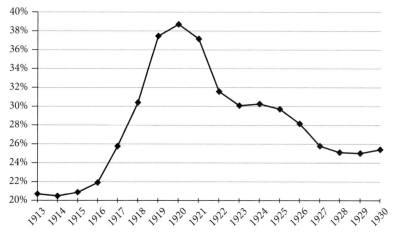

9.4. Trade union membership as a percentage of employment in Britain (Thomas and Dimsdale 2017).

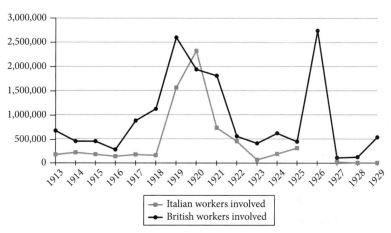

9.5. Workers involved in strikes in Italy and Britain (Mitchell 1998, table B.3, "Industrial disputes").

regarded as sounding the death knell of class struggle in Britain.[12] Among the casualties of this defeat were the many experiments for alternative forms of economic organizations that were detailed in chapters 3 and 4, from the building guilds to the plans for nationalization and workers' control in mining and other sectors.

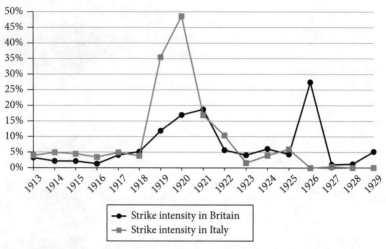

9.6. Strike intensity in Italy and Britain. The strike intensity is the number of striking workers expressed as a percentage of the total industrial workforce. (Mitchell 1998, table B.3, and Thomas and Dimsdale 2017 [for Britain] and Lay et al. 1973 and Mitchell 1998 [for Italy].)

The arcs of strike occurrence and intensity in Italy are even starker in their illustrations of how, through austerity, workers were disarmed of their tools for social change. Workers' demonstrations reached their peak in 1920, with more than 2.3 million workers in agriculture and industry on strike,[13] a number that represented 12 percent of the entire workforce and 48.5 percent of the labor force in capitalist-productive sectors.[14] Similar to its British equivalent, the great mobilization of Italy's two red years occurred at a time when the labor market was favorable to workers: unemployment rates were low. Even if the workers' momentum began declining prior to Mussolini's rise to power (and it did: the economic downturn of 1921 increased the number of Italy's unemployed), it is indisputable that the effects of Fascist industrial austerity—with the state actively intervening to suppress workforces and wages—were devastating.

In 1923 the British ambassador to Italy, Sir Ronald William Graham, reported back to his betters in the UK: "[T]he first year of the Fascista Government has shown, in comparison with the preceding twelve months, a decrease in strikes of 75 per cent., in strikers of 90 per cent., and in working days lost of over 97 per cent., resulting in a gain for the nation of 7,089,418 working days and of the continuous employment of 469,750 more men" (Italy Annual Report 1923, FO 371/9946, fol. 246, 39).

The international domestic and liberal establishment celebrated the newly found "industrial peace" described by Graham. His dispatch displayed a sense of contentment: "The firm rule of the government has not only maintained order, but has given the innate good sense of the country the opportunity to assert itself . . . it may be said that twelve months of tranquility is a solid achievement which can justifiably be regarded with satisfaction" (ibid., 38–39). By 1927 the Fascist Labour Charter sanctioned the full authoritarian control of the Italian labor force (see chapter 7). It is no coincidence then that, according to the official statistics, strikers were almost extinct the following year (3,000 strikers overall in 1928).

Mussolini's industrial austerity forced underpaid work on Italy's population through a form of political coercion that was unthinkable in Britain: the *Duce* outlawed independent unions and slashed wages by decree. However, intersections between the two examples are abundant. In fact, the austere British government did not fear enacting explicit, repressive labor laws against strikers to complement the economic coercions imposed by the market. On the other hand, once unemployment rose, the Italian state's violent political attacks on dissenting workers were complemented by the economic coercion of impersonal market forces. Notwithstanding the rapid economic growth of the first years of the Fascist regime, in 1924 unemployment in Italy was still higher than in 1920.[15] Moreover, as we know from chapter 7, the regime's deflationary turn of 1926–1927 combined with further cuts in public budgets represented another blow to the working classes.[16]

The political defeats of organized labor in Britain and Italy immediately translated into economic losses. As economic slumps go, these would not have provoked panic from either country's leaders: wage compression was the central aim and consequence of each state's austerity agenda, and losses in other metrics were part of the process.[17]

In Italy there was an uninterrupted fall in real wages that lasted for the whole interwar period, a unique trend among industrial countries (Zamagni 1975, 543). In the 1920s alone, the drop in real daily wages in Italy was almost 15 percent (see figure 9.7).

The success of Fascist austerity in suppressing wages is particularly striking relative to the country's gains in the immediate postwar period. After the 1919 eight-hour-day law, in 1921 daily real wages were 50 percent higher than in 1918, and 35 percent higher than in 1913. There was an even bigger jump in hourly real wages: in 1921 these wages had almost doubled relative to prewar years (1913).[18] But by 1923, when Mussolini informally abolished the working hour limit so that employers could begin enforcing longer days of work, the statistical 4 percent fall in daily real wages in just two years didn't fully capture the more marked fall in hourly pay (reaching a 13 percent decrease from 1922 to 1926). Workers were working more hours, and netting less pay.

While real wages reflect the purchasing power of workers, they don't do justice to the actual cuts in Italian paychecks, and with them the lived experiences of the Italian people: especially the power dynamic between capital and labor. Figure 9.7 maps real wages in Italy from before the war through the 1920s, seemingly telling a story of a predictable leap during the country's red years followed by a plateau, give or take, with the onset of austerity. Wage cuts during this period would have been partially offset by deflation's even more pronounced drop in the prices of consumer goods (and hence would not have been reflected in the metric of real wages). But between 1926 and 1928, Italian workers were *also* forced to accept a drop of 26 percent in nominal daily wages, thereby undercutting the consumer spending-power benefit of deflation.[19] The contrast here with respect to 1921, when Italian workers achieved a 400 percent increase in nominal industrial daily wages with respect to the prewar years, is mind-blowing.[20]

The same set of factors applies to the British case. Given the economic downturn and deflationary spiral that occurred in Britain, the social implications of austerity—and its capacity to offset the impact of workers' mobilization after the war—are underrepresented in historical

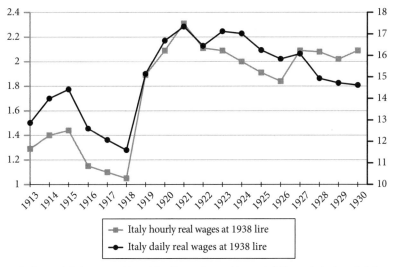

9.7. Real wages in Italy, expressed in 1938 lire (Zamagni 1975, tables 1 and 2). The vertical axis on the left depicts the hourly real wages, the one on the right depicts daily real wages.

records of real wages. This fact has skewed the telling of this chapter in Britain's history.

Indeed, the drop in real wages starting in 1920 (see figure 9.8) corresponded to an even greater drop in the disposable income of British households. The concrete impact of austerity is apparent in how quickly the trend in nominal wages was reversed: by 1920 nominal weekly wages for British manual workers had soared 178 percent from prewar levels (reaching £3.70, from £1.33 in 1913), but then the bulk of such gains were lost within two years. By 1923, when monetary austerity and the cuts of the Geddes Axe had taken their toll on expenditures in public health and education, there was a 29 percent drop in average weekly earnings, with wages stagnating around £2.61 for the rest of the interwar years.

Once the population was deprived of key social benefits, many workers lost their jobs, and even those who were able to keep their posts were forced to work harder at lower wages. Here the second axiom of austerity—consume less—found concrete realization: most of the country had no choice but to consume less. The reduction in

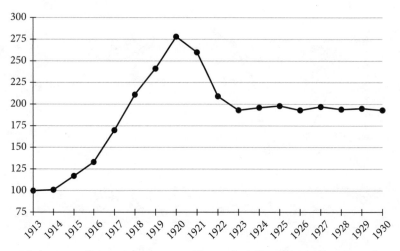

9.8. Real average weekly wages in Britain, expressed in 1913 pounds (Feinstein 1972, table 65, T140–41).

living standards for the majority of the public is illustrated by the measured consumption patterns around basic goods, which declined from already precariously low levels. Statistics of the time reveal that British and Italian citizens *really did* practice abstinence as their technocratic overlords advised. In Britain, the increase in consumption that occurred during the war years was lost in the years that followed, with no rebound in consumption of basic popular goods (including alcohol and tobacco) for the entirety of the 1920s. Mirroring a trend in Italy, British housing expenditures—which grew by over a third from 1920 to 1930—were the only exception to this larger trend.[21] The difference, of course, is that housing expenses were not a choice, but rather an obligation in light of increased rents. More generally, British domestic consumption demand dropped dramatically in the early years of austerity: from 1919 to 1923, there was a 40 percent drop that was never regained during the interwar period (Sefton and Weale 1995).

The violence inherent in austerity was reflected in poverty rates of the period. While Fascism "did not recognise (nor use) the category of 'poor'" (Preti and Venturoli 2000, 731),[22] Vecchi (2017) calculates that during the 1920s the percentage of the Italian population in absolute poverty increased to almost 30 percent—reversing a trend of decreasing poverty that had been ongoing since 1861.[23] In Britain, even the country's modest social inquiries produced alarming results (which were skewed by their stringent criteria for calculating poverty). For example, the Social Survey of Merseyside of 1928, carried out by Liverpool University, reported 16 percent of the population in poverty, only 2 percent of whom received any public assistance. Similarly, the New Survey of London Life and Labour carried out in 1929–1930 found that approximately 14 percent of the population in East London were "subject to conditions of privation which, if long continued, would deny them all but the barest necessities and cut them off from access to many of the incidental and cultural benefits of modern progress" (report in Thane 1996, 157–58).

The devastating effects of austerity with respect to wages, unemployment, and living standards offer a strong case to question the legitimacy of the endeavor.[24] That it was never questioned reflects the fundamental political motives that drove it: the subordination of the majority was an essential prerequisite to safeguard the smooth function of capital accumulation and especially to allow the ruling minority to reap the benefits of a return to unadulterated capitalism.

Austerity promoted income concentration, filling the pockets of the elites of British and Italian societies.[25] In Italy from 1925 to 1930 there was a noticeable growth in share of total income garnered by the few, with the income of the top 1 percent growing by 9.6 percent, the top 0.1 by 29 percent, and the top 0.05 by 41 percent.[26] Growth in income concentration continued, even through the onset of the Great Depression in 1929 (Gabbuti 2020b, 274). Such is the rule in the recent history of capitalism. Income data from the two most recent global recessions, the 2008 financial crisis and the 2020 COVID-19 crisis, indicate how, rather than being levelers of income distribution, economic crises only serve to enrich the few and impoverish the many. This is ever more the case when the crises are managed through policies that, under the guise of stimulating the economy, actually perpetuate the old logic of austerity: shift resources from the many to the few.

Conclusion

Austerity and its repression of domestic demand were undertaken to defeat more than a simple economic shock. Indeed, the austerity decade that followed World War I in Britain and Italy fully consolidated the bourgeois social order.

The economic statistics collated in this chapter corroborate the argument that austerity worked (and still works) to restore the optimal conditions for capital accumulation, primarily through higher unemployment, lower wages, increased exploitation, and an increase in profit share. Austerity produces the large-scale scarcity that aligns workers with owners' interests. In this sense, austerity's "inflation-targeted" policies might be better described as "rate-of-exploitation–targeted."[27]

As Michał Kalecki's 1943 classic article "Political Aspects of Full Employment" pointedly theorized, a dosage of unemployment is imperative to secure the balance of forces between capital and labor that perpetuates social relations favorable to capital investment, in particular a sufficient discipline of the workforce. Government spending programs and monetary expansions instead challenge this precondition by fostering a tighter labor market. As Kalecki writes, "Under a regime of permanent full employment, the 'sack' would cease to play its role as a disciplinary measure . . . [creating] political tension" (Kalecki 1943, 3).[28]

The gains of austerity came primarily in the form of replacing political tension with a shallow notion of political stability, which in turn enabled the resurgence of investment. The parallel and intertwined stories of the British and Italian cases reveal that, notwithstanding their institutional differences, the technocrats in both countries were capable of achieving the same results, as illustrated by the fall in wage shares and consequent rise in profit shares in both countries. While the British Treasury officials mostly relied on the economic coercion of impersonal market forces, the Italian professors benefited from the political coercion of a Fascist dictatorship that guaranteed immediate wage repression—by force where needed. In both countries, the restoration of capital accumulation came with greater income concentration at the top and lower consumption everywhere else.

Of course, as many Keynesian and Marxian economists point out, the repression of internal demand may be problematic for capital accumulation in the long run, as a lack of public and private demand hinders the realization of profit, and thus investment.[29] But if this book highlights one thing, it's that the perpetuation of austerity to this day should not be reduced to a matter of irrationality or bad economic theory from the experts who run economies. Austerity is a tool to maintain capitalist social relations of production—to maintain class. In an austere capital order, popular protests may arise, but the protesters face a political landscape that structurally disempowers them: it's hard to protest capitalist austerity when you have to depend on capitalism to survive. As we shall explore in the concluding pages of this book, with the resurgence of austerity in the late 1970s, surges in profit shares and exploitation have been a constant in most countries of the world.

CHAPTER 10

Austerity Forever

[The Federal Reserve] needs to remember that their priority is the macroeconomy. When I see them say that they won't raise rates until diversity groups' unemployment rates are appropriate, I get nervous. . . . If they take inflation seriously, monitor [it] closely and are prepared to cause pain, they will be able to control inflation.

Lawrence Summers, interview for *Bloomberg Wall Street Week*, March 5, 2021

If one subscribes to the argument that austerity is a tool for managing a capitalist economy, as Keynesian economists did and do, then one might believe that the continued deployment of austerity across societies and economies is a form of political irrationality—a wrong economic policy based on wrong economic theory that has never succeeded in achieving its stated ends. Take, for example, the events depicted in this book. Against its promise to stabilize the world economy, the austerity project of the 1920s was a spectacular failure: its reduction of aggregate demand—an effect its designers *intended* to introduce—is cited by many as a cause of the Great Depression that began in 1929 and was only really resolved with the economic stimulus of, ironically, another World War. The same assessment of failure can be drawn from near countless economic downturns that have followed austerity revolutions in Latin America and Europe over the past several decades.[1] Argentina's complete economic meltdown in 2002 followed a decade of austerity, one with all the industrial, fiscal, and monetary trappings of the 1920s including large-scale privatization, exorbitant social cuts, and an interest-rate jump from 5.8 percent in 1996 to 9.4 percent in 2001.[2] These outcomes seem to affirm the Keynesian view that austerity fails in its purported objective to boost economic growth. But as this book illustrates, austerity's capacity to impose and reinforce class structure is the true measure of its efficacy; it was a servant to, and indeed the primary safeguard of, capital order. In this sense, it was never an irrational calculation. This underlying rationale became evident based on the timing of its emergence, a moment in which capitalism had been challenged at its core. In the war's aftermath alternatives to capitalism were enticing citizens, not just in Eastern Europe but, as our book has explored, also at the continent's heart, in countries such as Britain and Italy. New economic institutions threatened to destroy the very concept of "wage-worker" and private capital. Austerity was a bulwark against these nascent threats.

In the originating cases in Britain and Italy, as in more recent examples, an activist technocratic minority intervened in what they regarded as a world out of order. Under the guise of curtailing inflation and balancing the budget—talking points that remain cornerstones of the expert rhetoric today—economists worked then and now in service of a more essential objective: the subordination of the majority to a prevailing economic order.

In other words, when economists peddle austerity as a means to "fix the economy" their goal is something more insidious. In describing the austerity-induced economic downturn of 1921, the British economist G. D. H. Cole (who did not favor austerity) captures the essence of how austerity moves and shapes a society: "The big working-class offensive had been successfully stalled off; and British capitalism, though threatened with economic adversity, felt itself once more safely in the saddle and well able to cope, both industrially and politically, with any attempt that might still be made from the labour side to unseat it" (Cole 1958, 419).

Far from irrational, austerity was a wily counteroffensive that protected capitalism and its relations of production against the inroads of democracy. To be sure, austerity successfully disempowered the majority.

The Austerity Trinity: Back in Action

The interwoven devastations of fiscal, monetary, and industrial austerity smothered all forms of class-based activism in 1920s Britain and Italy. In Britain, a handful of remaining strikes sought only to achieve sectional industrial interests, not the full-blown recasting of the organization of production; in Italy strikes disappeared altogether. Alberto De Stefani expressed pride in this rapid calming, remarking in 1926 that "during the last four years, the Fascist regime has balanced the budget, restored discipline in the labour world, and faced, notwithstanding the sacrifices it entailed, the settlement of war debts" ("Italian Monetary Policy," *The Times*, October 22, 1926, 17).

This successful precedent made austerity a popular and recurring toolkit for economies around the globe. This was especially the case starting in the late 1970s, when austerity again came into fashion in the majority of capitalist countries, including Britain and Italy.

A full-blown exploration (or autopsy) of this later period—especially one that does justice to the many cases of IMF-backed structural reforms in the global South[3]—would require a book of its own. However, even a superficial study of the more high-profile cases reveals the persistence of the austerity logic—and the tendency of history to repeat.

State intervention and public welfare were back in vogue after World War II.[4] In the war's aftermath, both British and Italian organized labor strengthened and bolstered their political sway. The inflationary pressures of the mid-1970s only amplified workers' voices; union ranks grew, strikes mounted, and so did calls to break away from the presiding capital order.[5]

Wages and labor rights continued to flourish throughout the decade. In Italy, the years 1970–1977 saw real wages rise at an annual average of about 7 percent (Levrero and Stirati 2004, 2), with the wage share increasing and reaching a high of 70 percent in 1977. Similar trends were on display in Britain, where workers' activism in the postwar decades brought the national wage share as high as 79 percent in 1975.[6] During the country's so-called winter of discontent—from October 1978 to February 1979—strikes occurred on a scale unseen since the General Strike of 1926. In 1979 alone, 4 million people were withholding labor, a figure equaling the combined number of strikers during 1919 and 1920.[7]

But 1979 also saw the rise of Prime Minister Margaret Thatcher, who famously dismissed workers as "idle, deceitful, inferior, and bloody-minded" and rejected talk of class in favor of a focus on "personal responsibility." Thatcher inaugurated austerity's comeback in Britain, this time under the counsel of a team of experts that included members of the famed Mont Pelerin Society[8]—an intellectual community regarded by many as the originators of neoliberalism, organized around a commitment to defend the "central values of civilization."[9]

Nigel Lawson, Thatcher's chancellor of the exchequer from 1983 to 1989, spoke in terms similar to his 1920s predecessors, extolling virtues like "firm monetary discipline, buttressed by a prudent fiscal stance" (HC Deb 15 March 1988, vol. 129, cc 995). In his 1988 budget speech, Lawson enthusiastically recounted the effects of his major business taxation reform of 1984: "[It] has given us one of the lowest corporation tax rates in the world [35 percent]. This has encouraged overseas companies to invest in Britain" (ibid., cc 999). On that same occasion he also announced a further extension of regressive taxation, including an abolition of capital duties and a substantial increase in consumption duties, including those on cereals, cigarettes and hand-rolling tobacco, beer, cider, wine, and spirits[10]—policies, he said, that would tax "the bad habits" of the working public. Meanwhile, British industrial austerity proliferated. Between 1982 and 1986, experts at the Treasury oversaw more than 22 privatizations of large public-sector companies, including the car maker Jaguar, British Telecommunication, and British Gas; public utilities such as water and electricity were also put up for sale.[11] In 1988 Lawson bragged, "[s]ince 1979 we have privatised getting on for 40 per cent of the state-owned sector of industry," before adding, "privatisation benefits the company, its employees and the economy as a whole" (HC Deb 11 February 1988, vol. 127, cc 487). New laws also allowed employers to sack strikers and reduce dismissal compensation. They forbade workers to strike in support of others and threatened to seize union assets in cases of the perpetuation of "unlawful" strikes.[12] The first to face a blow were the steelworkers in 1980, who lost a thirteen-week strike battle and paid the price with thousands of jobs. Then in March 1985 came the emblematic capitulation of the miners after a titanic year-long strike. The collapse of the most powerful group of workers in the country changed the face of British labor relations. If, in 1979, half of all British workers were trade unionists and 4.6 million people participated in strikes, by 1998 union members were reduced to less than a third of the workforce, and only 93,000 still partook in strikes.[13] From 1975 to 1996, rates of economic exploitation almost doubled. In those same years the profit rate grew from 21 percent to 32 percent.

Following the advances of labor in Italy during the 1970s, austerity was reintroduced and was predictably successful in quieting and disciplining the majority. It began with the first adjustments to adhere to the European Monetary System (EMS) in 1979, and from then was vastly strengthened with Italy's commitment to adhere to the 1992 Maastricht Treaty—the founding document of the European Union, steeped in the economic principles of austerity. With the Maastricht Treaty, the EU's twelve member states assumed permanent austere obligations as a matter of "multilateral surveillance."[14]

Among the men who guided Italy's effort to meet the conditions for EU membership[15] was Mario Draghi, who headed the Italian delegation of the intergovernmental conference that gave shape to the Maastricht Treaty. Since then, Draghi has been at the forefront of Italian technocratic power. He served as director general of the Italian Treasury (1991–2001), governor of Banca d'Italia (2005–2011), and president of the European Central Bank (2011–2019). On February 5, 2021, Draghi was sworn in as Italian prime minister—appointed not via elections, but via direct nomination from the Italian president of the Republic.

Draghi continued a trend of non-elected technocratic prime ministers in post-Maastricht Italy, led by senior officials of the Banca d'Italia Carlo Azeglio Ciampi (1993–1994) and Lamberto Dini (1995–1996). Together these men implemented austerity reforms[16] that targeted the Italian welfare state and tilted the relationship of power to favor capital over labor. While the Italian government drastically reduced expenditure for social interventions, the wage share steadily declined beginning in 1983 (when it was 70 percent of GDP), reaching a low of 61 percent in 2001.[17]

The Italians also introduced industrial austerity measures to promote greater wage and price "flexibility." These efforts culminated in the abolition in 1992 of the *scala mobile* (the Italian system of wage indexation introduced in 1975, and an emblematic victory for labor; see chapter 9, note 5). The state also initiated a groundbreaking privatization campaign to restore the country's budgets, "increase efficiency," and boost its standing as an EU member. Most national banks and public enterprises, including IRI (the Institute for Industrial Reconstruction), ENI (petroleum and natural gas), and ENEL (gas and electricity), were sold off. The establishment of the Euro as Italy's currency, which in effect eliminated the country's capacity to regulate its own currency, has increased the country's tendency toward fiscal and industrial austerity measures to meet its economic ends. As with the gold standard during the interwar years, this loss of monetary sovereignty reinforced the necessity to shape people's behaviors through other means and according to an austere political order.

All of this came to a head in June 2011, when the Italian people turned out in record numbers to vote on a referendum to halt the privatization of all public utilities, including water, with the objective of transforming them into common goods. It had been more than fifty years since the country had successfully utilized its constitutional instrument of direct democracy in this way. Many read the episode as a significant manifestation of popular agency, or perhaps more radically a step toward a modified organizing of Italian social life. Two months later, and as had been the case in Italy for nearly a century, the austerity reflex kicked in.

On August 5, 2011, at the peak of the debt-market crisis, Italian prime minister Silvio Berlusconi received a highly confidential letter signed by the president of the European Central Bank, Jean-Claude Trichet, and his designated successor, Mario Draghi. The letter declared "the gravity" of the hour, and called for "necessary" and "bold" action—"essential to restore the confidence of investors" (see letter in *Il corriere della sera*, August 5, 2011). The ECB had leverage on its side: if Italy softened on its austerity reforms, then the central bank would stop buying back Italian bonds. The bank's demands were clear: Italy was to display harsh fiscal rigor (to achieve a public deficit equal to 1 percent of the GDP as early as 2012) and, the letter suggested, undertake constitutional reform that would "make budget rules more stringent." The letter called for "privatization on a large scale" of local public services, including public utilities and water (the very things the people had just opposed). It also demanded an overhaul of restrictive rules on hiring, firing, and wage bargaining, and required Italy to reduce the cost of its public employees by curbing wages "if necessary."

Whereas Mussolini's government succeeded in 1922 at implementing the international austerity agenda largely conceived by foreign interests, Berlusconi was less successful at achieving similar goals in 2011. The pressures from the ECB, combined with the financial markets' speculation on Italian bonds, forced him to resign that November. He was succeeded as prime minister—though again, not through election—by Bocconi University economist Mario Monti, who sought "substantial restructuring of the roots of [Italy's] economy in favor of productivity and competitiveness."[18] Monti's actions bring to mind those of De Stefani, who in 1922 was willing to sacrifice anyone— especially the weaker members of society—to gain financial credibility abroad. While De Stefani invoked the "conscious renunciation of the rights gained by the crippled, the invalids, the soldiers," so, in similar fashion, did Monti cut the funds of those suffering from amyotrophic lateral sclerosis (ALS). When asked about the social impact of this reform, his answer was simple: it was nothing but the consequence of resource constraints due to the immoral behavior of the Italian citizens who, up to that moment, "had protected their privileges" [*tutleato i propri privilegi*] and "acted cunningly" [*furbizia*].[19] The refrain sounds familiar: crises are attributed to people living beyond their means and refusing to work productively.

Ensuing governments, including those led by the Italian Democratic Party (PD), pressed on with austerity. For example, Matteo Renzi's Jobs

Act of 2014 reversed the historic rights of the 1970 Statute of the Workers, making it legal to fire workers at any time for "economic reasons." As precarious forms of work and underemployment boomed, real wages plummeted by 4.3 percent between 2010 and 2017.[20] The impact of these austerity years on the standard of living of the Italian population is visible in the official data on real per capita consumption, which fell rapidly between 2011 and 2014—a 7 percent drop.[21]

Italian austerity was far from an externality imposed by the economic troika (ECB, European Commission, and IMF). Within Italy, the intellectual hold of the country's austere economists—the so-called "Bocconi boys"—continues to dominate debates around politics and economy, both domestic and international. That Bocconi University proudly maintains the tradition of Luigi Einaudi, who taught public finance there from 1902 to 1925, is no small part of this. Like their predecessors in the 1920s, Italian economists such as Alberto Alesina, Silvia Ardagna, Carlo Favero, Francesco Giavazzi, and Guido Tabellini have served as prominent advisors to the IMF, the World Bank, and the ECB, entrenching a core belief that economic growth requires a public majority to accept working harder for lower wages.[22]

Disempowering "Apolitical" Theory

The economic experts at the Brussels and Genoa conferences would not have envisioned themselves as subordinating the will of the majority *as such*. Rather, in the dissonance that is common among economists, they would have seen their reforms as grounded in an elevated understanding of how the world works. These fathers of today's mainstream economics presented austerity policies as the outcome of theory that was objective and neutral, a worldview that transcended class relations. Their stated urge to "tame men," in turn, was not domination, but rather a necessity for an organized society—something above mere politics or class. Such is the manner of depoliticization: it served (and still serves) to conceal economic coercion under the guise of building consensus—in this case, as elsewhere, for the disempowerment of the many.

However, a theory that masquerades as being above class is also a theory that fails to account for class in its theoretical framework. That austerity came to exist in the shadow of the Great War—a "class-agnostic" economic framework deployed for a moment of unprecedented class conflict—demonstrated the imperiousness, and deniability, of its originators.

Economists re-naturalized capital as a social relation by walling off its alternatives. While *L'Ordine nuovo* theorized labor as the source of value for employers and criticized exploitation as a structural trap for workers, economists portrayed these relationships as equal exchanges among equal individuals—a road to prosperity for all those who demonstrated a rational capacity to optimize. Economists modeled the market society as one in which all people, if sufficiently rational and virtuous, could potentially thrive. This seemingly emancipatory insight was actually among the most classist: social hierarchies were reflections of individual merit, meaning that those who weren't at the top didn't deserve to be. The saver-entrepreneurs' profits were the products of their virtuous behavior, the same behaviors that signed workers' paychecks and propelled the economy.

No physical weapon could have been as powerful as this theoretical framework in removing agency from workers and justifying private profit. The message is one that today we have all internalized: if enough effort is exercised, we can elevate ourselves to become part of the saving-and-investing class. Those who fail to do so can blame only themselves.

Current economic models continue to reinforce our passive acceptance of this capital order. In the example of the "Bocconi boys," the set of influentially austere Italian economists whose profiles were ascendent starting in the late 1970s, their theories reflect an assumption that savers-investors hold the key to economic prosperity. It remains the through line in their theories.[23]

It follows logically that the purpose of economic policy is to shift resources from the majority to an economic minority. Cuts in social spending, Alberto Alesina wrote, "signal that tax rates won't have to rise in the future, thus spur investors to be 'more active'" (Alesina 2012).[24]

Specifically, to boost profit expectations, governments have incentives "to cut the *most politically sensitive* components of the budget: [social] transfers and government wages and employment" (Alesina and Perotti 1995, 12, my italics). The overall message here is explicit: cuts in social spending and labor costs not only boost the profits of the select few; they also serve as a control over the majority, who otherwise would slack off (the same kind of slacking that keeps them from being savers and investors).[25]

The interconnection between fiscal and industrial austerity (what economists call *supply-side reforms*, including privatization and labor-market deregulation)[26] assures the maximum disciplinary effects of market forces. Here again Alesina and colleagues offer a playbook for economic control: "[A] decrease in government employment reduces the probability of finding a job if not employed in the private sector, and a decrease in government wages decreases the worker's income if employed in the public sector." In both cases, they note, "the wage demanded by the union for private sector workers decreases, increasing profits, investment, and competitiveness" (Alesina and Ardagna 2010, 5). The experts are clear: in the name of the good of the whole, "wage moderation"; "no more Christmas-related extra payments" (Alesina and de Rugy 2013, 15); and a higher retirement age were all desirable policies. As Alesina once mused, "If the French think that they can keep retiring at 60, they're kidding themselves" (Alesina 2012).

Unlike austerity's early architects, whose theories were framed as operating on a level above class, these latter-day austerity hawks demonstrate awareness of how their policy prescriptions affect the working class. "Fiscal adjustment may increase income inequality," wrote Alesina and Roberto Perotti in 1995, noting also that "the share of profits in the business sector increases" and that the "wage share falls during the adjustment and remains lower after, relative to before" (Alesina and Perotti 1995, 21). These class effects correspond to the most efficient conditions for capital order.

Buried in the technical jargon and technocratic publishing outlets where these policy statements are made, Alesina and his colleagues demonstrate the same distrust for the working classes that Luigi

Einaudi and Maffeo Pantaleoni displayed after the Great War. In one scientific paper written for the International Monetary Fund, Alesina denounces the "culture of dependency" of people in the south of Italy, a trait he argues is enabled by expansionary policies that further discourage entrepreneurship: "the less individuals are prepared to 'face the market,' the more they prefer public jobs. Furthermore, it generates a powerful constituency of public employees and their unions who are typically opposed to market-oriented policies and more flexibility in the labor market" (Danninger, Alesina, and Rostagno 1999, 4).

Austerity has been animated since its beginnings by anxiety about the wills and actions of "entitled" citizens. In the words of its bard, Alesina, austerity arms experts and leaders with the tools to "protect" economic decisions from people's "unavoidable political pressures to pursue short run expansionary policies" (Alesina and Grilli 1991, 14).

Anti-Democracy and Authoritarianism

As Pantaleoni put it bluntly in 1920, economic policy making could not be "at once popular and exact." The problem of political democracy was that people did not understand what was in their best interests; they had to be kept away from economic decisions for their own good. Today's austerity politics remain grounded in a drive to shield economic governance from popular opinion—to keep the economy from getting political.

In Italy, where political successions already proceed in anti-democratic ways, the anti-democratic ideas of 1920s technocrats continue to be reinvented with new sophistication. As part of an ongoing and tireless academic effort that began in the early 1980s and is still underway, austerity-hawk economists have advanced a notion that electoral democracies (especially those with proportional representation) have an intrinsic tendency toward accumulating debt and are therefore economically inefficient. In the words of one noteworthy paper, "[l]ack of fiscal discipline is almost exclusively found in countries governed by representational democracies" (Grilli et al. 1991, 359). These sentiments evoke Pantaleoni's at the 1920 Brussels conference:

"where Socialism is strong, where democracy is strong, public finance will go the wrong way" (Brussels 1920, vol. 4, 109).

While the Italian professors under Fascism found immunity from democratic liability in an authoritarian government that allowed them to directly implement their models, the British version of technocracy centered on a campaign for economic management in the hands of independent central banks—a campaign that was then exported all over the globe. Blackett's efforts with the Indian Central Bank were matched by Niemeyer's similar efforts in Eastern Europe, Australia, Brazil, and Argentina.

The universal link between austerity and political repression that went unconcealed under Fascism but was buried in policies elsewhere reveals how the economic treatment of Italian citizens was not so different from the one that the British experts envisioned for their own people. Even if different in implementation, the Italian and the British technocrats shared a common purpose: imposing sacrifice on the majority of the public. Both did so without any real rebuke.

Once people were removed from the decision-making process, the models of pure economics could reassert the primacy of the market, letting it function as it should—i.e., unabated and free from worker demands. In their view, economic freedom was more important than political freedom—especially the political freedom to manage the economy democratically. In fact, these economists understood economic freedom not in the Gramscian sense, where economic freedom meant emancipating the majority from exploitation (as detailed in chapter 4), but rather as the protection of the saving-and-investing minority and the unfettered free market in which this minority operated. In other words, economic freedom meant the operation of capital accumulation, which required the economic coercion inherent to wage relations and thus the unfreedom of the popular classes. The technocrats' conception of economic freedom was indeed incompatible with any empowerment of the majority.

The British Treasury experts could forgo physical violence because they used interest rates and the budget to knock workers out of their jobs and social securities. Even in settings of elite liberal capitalism, experts are still protective of the power to tweak the dials of macroeconomic management, and they develop similar strategies to hide them from popular view. The insulation of central bank independence is a trope of the austerity project to this day; a vast literature almost unanimously praises the "social desirability" of excluding citizens from monetary decisions, favoring instead "an agent whose preferences are more inflation averse than are society's preferences" (Alesina and Summers 1993, 151).

The constitution of the European Central Bank (ECB), which since 1999 has served as the sole issuing institution of all European member states, represented a huge achievement for the technocratic austerity set. The ECB operates with a mandate and structure that draws on the Hawtreyan template of the 1920s. Since the Maastricht Treaty, the ECB retains formal "independence from elected officials," so as to operate "without prejudice" in favor of price stability—its primary mandate. This constitution also forbids European council representatives from being a part of the ECB's Council (Article 15.1, in Alesina and Grilli 1991, 13). It also "explicitly forbids" the ECB board to "receive any instruction from either community or national political institutions" (ibid., Article 7).[27] Political independence is accompanied by economic independence:[28] the ECB has no obligation to finance the member nations' public deficits, thus heavily restricting expansionary fiscal policy within its states.[29]

The EU era has also given austerity hawks a window to advance institutional reforms that explicitly strike at the foundations of democratic principles—political guardrails that, especially in Italy, were formalized to mark a distance from the country's Fascist past. Similar to Fascist economists in the early 1920s, these contemporary figures advocate for electoral reforms to diminish proportional representation (and thus favor stronger governments) and to rewrite countries' constitutions to include an obligation to a balanced budget. Italy implemented both policies in the 2010s.

In times of greater popular contestation against capital order, the only route to accomplish these austerity ends was the endorsement of authoritarianism. The script of austere Fascist Italy was replayed under

Augusto Pinochet's military dictatorship in Chile (1973–1990), which was ushered in by the bombardment of the Palacio de la Moneda on September 11, 1973, to remove Salvador Allende, the socialist president who was then the leader of a popular struggle for social redistribution and resocialization of large sectors of the economy. The coup opened the doors for the "Chicago Boys"—a select group of Chilean economists trained at the University of Chicago under neoclassical gurus Milton Friedman and Arnold Harberger—to implement their *Ladrillo*: a brick-like document outlining a fierce austerity plan that successfully smothered the Chilean alternative to capitalism. Chile's Museum of Memory and Human Rights, opened in 2010 in Santiago, commemorates the human costs of a regime enabled in order to enact Chilean austerity: more than 40,000 people died, disappeared, or suffered repression during Pinochet's dictatorship. When asked about these incidents, Chilean economist Rolf Lüders, himself a Chicago boy and a former minister of finance under Pinochet, lucidly pointed to the connection between austerity and political coercion: "And if you ask me if you justify the human rights violations? No, I find them awful. But it seems to me that it would not have been possible to make the change that was made in Chile without an authoritarian regime" (in the 2015 documentary, *Chicago Boys*). The "change" he refers to brought about the usual proceedings of austerity: a surge of unemployment (32 percent in 1983), accompanied by a rise in exploitation, which from 1971 to 1985 almost doubled (from 0.62 to 1.28). In those years the share of corporate profits rose from 31.4 percent to 42.4 percent.[30] The proportion of wages decreased by 17.6 percent while the proportion of profits increased by 10 percent. The poverty rate increased from 20 percent to 44 percent.[31]

The mingling of authoritarianism, economic expertise, and austerity is a recurring trend in modern history. It is seen in the case of the Berkeley-trained economists working under Suharto's dictatorship in Indonesia (1967–1998), as well as the dramatic story of the assertion of *capital order* in Russia after the dissolution of the USSR. In that instance, the government of Boris Yeltsin effectively declared war on Russian legislators who opposed the IMF-backed austerity agenda that Yeltsin courted to stabilize the Russian economy. The peak of Yeltsin's assault against democracy came in October 1993, when the president called in tanks, helicopters, and 5,000 soldiers to rain fire on the Russian Parliament. The attack killed more than 500 people and left many more wounded. Once the ashes settled, Russia was under unchecked dictatorial rule: Yeltsin dissolved the "recalcitrant" Parliament,[32] suspended the constitution, disbanded the constitutional court, shut down newspapers, and jailed his political opposition.[33]

Much as it did with Mussolini's dictatorship in the 1920s, the *Economist* had no qualms in justifying Yeltsin's strongman actions as the only path that could guarantee capital order: "Mr. Yeltsin had to choose between smashing his rival with force or seeing himself, his government and any prospect of reform destroyed. . . . Mr. Yeltsin's opposition was a bizarre coalition of extremists of every kind, more than a few of whom, to western eyes, seem downright crazy. . . . The threat, in the end, was extreme—and so, necessarily, was the response." The article concluded, "These gains—the restoration of Mr. Yeltsin's power to govern and renewed progress in economic reform—are great indeed."[34] In the months that followed, as the *Economist* doted on the rapid privatization of Russian industries, data from the World Bank showed that unemployment had reached double digits.[35] If, in 1987–1988, 2 percent of the Russian people lived in poverty (i.e., survived on less than $4 a day), by 1993–1995 the number reached 50 percent: in just seven years half the Russian population became destitute.[36] In the same period, non-wage income rose from 5 percent to 23 percent of GDP.[37]

These immediate, devastating effects of austerity were no surprise. They were the scripted results of the "economists' consensus," as Lawrence Summers defined it in 1994 while he served as a Treasury official during Bill Clinton's administration. Summers was adamant that, for Russia, "the three '-ations'—privatization, stabilization, and liberalization—must all be completed as soon as possible. Maintaining the momentum of reform is a crucial political problem."[38] As a foreign interest, the United States was keen to solve this crucial problem: President Clinton passed billions in aid to Yeltsin,[39] and USAID lavishly funded the Harvard Institute for International Development, directed by the economist Jeffrey Sachs, to advise Yeltsin's austerity project.

In her essay "What Is Authority?" the twentieth-century political theorist Hannah Arendt wrote: "The search for the best form of government reveals itself to be the search for the best government for philosophers"—the people doing the search—"which turns out to be the governments in which philosophers have become the rulers of the city" (Arendt 1961, 114). For austere economic experts imposing their wills on transitional economies since the 1920s, the process is very much the same: at the very moment their supposedly pure knowledge of transcendent economic ideas is applied to governing the real world, it quickly becomes clear that economic ideas are not really transcendent after all. While these economists may refute the suggestion of an agenda in these moments, their keenly political interventions reveal them, no matter how they may want the story to be told, as inescapably party to a struggle to preserve capital order—seemingly the only form of social order they can conceive of.

The austerity impulse is present even where it appears otherwise. So far in the twenty-first century, two financial crises have been met with economic responses labeled "Keynesian" for their decisions to spend rather than cut. But some old habits don't die. After 2008, governments took care to save financial institutions first, thereby draining resources from the public in the years that followed. The rationale for such activities perfectly matched those that we have encountered in this book: a shift of resources from the many to the few.

The same austerity pattern emerged during the response to COVID-19. Public resources were lavishly spent to fund financial institutions and large-scale corporations, while the public majority was left with meager crumbs. In the US, the CARES Act of April 2020 allocated $790 billion as loans and guarantees to large businesses and tax breaks—an unprecedented amount. Meanwhile the funds allocated for the 160 million American households that qualified for direct payments was less than a third of that.[40] Amid mounting unemployment—the global shortfall in employment increased by 144 million jobs in 2020[41]—downward pressure on wages grows and the prospects for private profits are revived. Inequality reached unprecedented new highs during the pandemic, and in June 2021 the International Labour Organization reported that "relative to 2019, an estimated additional 108 million workers [globally] are now extremely or moderately poor, meaning that they and their family members are having to live on less than US$3.20 per day in purchasing power parity terms."[42] An analysis from the Institute for Policy Studies around the same time showed that between March 2020 and March 2021 the world's 2,365 billionaires enjoyed a $4 trillion boost to their wealth, increasing their fortunes by 54 percent.[43] As austerity takes more sophisticated forms, it remains a boon for a predictable few.

Soaring public deficits that have mounted due to COVID will call for harsher austerity in the near future. In February 2021, the Harvard economist Summers, speaking at Princeton University about the inflationary risks of the Biden administration's proposal to issue a cash stimulus to the American public, told the audience "there is no compelling economic case for a stimulus" (interview for *Bloomberg Wall Street Week*, March 5, 2021, min. 55). If governments were to provide households with "more than what they need," those households' spending would throw off the delicate stasis of the economy: "the spending propensity out of [middle-class households] would be far greater than the spending propensity economists usually estimate from wealth which is driven by fluctuations in the stock market."[44] Spending by people who shouldn't spend, Summers warns, would cause inflationary harm to the economy of the wealthy.

A century after Ralph Hawtrey, Summers's fears and predictions match the Hawtreyan scoldings that undergird much of this book's arguments. These ideas are neither wrong nor irrational, per se. They are merely the expression of a very clear worldview, one whose global primacy is maintained by a century-long project in economic austerity. It is grounded firmly in the most dismal parts of the dismal science, those that keep people entrenched within a status quo.

This book has detailed a set of influential economic patterns that are pervasive across the globe and that shape our daily lives. Contrary to what the proponents of austerity would have us think, however, the socioeconomic system we live in is not inevitable, nor is it to be grudgingly accepted as the only way forward. Austerity is a political project arising out of the need to preserve capitalist class relations of domination. It is the outcome of collective action to foreclose any alternatives to capitalism. It can thus be subverted through collective counteraction. The study of its logic and purpose is a first step in that direction.

Afterword

By telling the story of post–World War I reconstruction through a new lens of austerity, *The Capital Order* transcends the canonical disciplinary boundaries between political economy, economic history, and history of economic thought, as well as labor and social history. If these efforts are successful, then the result would expand, critique, and sometimes depart from entrenched scholarly conversations. In addition to its central contribution of offering an alternative understanding and approach to austerity, this book requires a rethinking of the relationship between Keynesianism and neoliberalism; the history of neoliberalism; the history of the interwar period; and especially the history and nature of Italian Fascism.

In the first place, the lens of austerity is a powerful tool by which to reassess the history of political economy in the twentieth and twenty-first centuries. It provides fertile grounds to begin a reappraisal of the all too familiar narrative of the century-long confrontation between two opposing economic traditions: the Neoliberal tradition and the Keynesian tradition. If we focus on austerity's primary objective—that is, the foreclosure of alternatives to capitalism through depoliticization—commonalities emerge.

These commonalities can be traced back to Keynes himself, who, as we know, was a prominent interlocutor of the experts at the British Treasury and whose insights on effective demand were heavily influenced by Ralph Hawtrey. We've seen how, after the Great War, Keynes shared with his fellow austere British experts a real terror of the collapse of the capital order. The book *In the Long Run We Are All Dead* (Mann 2017) articulates how this "existential" anxiety is a constant of contemporary Keynesianism, given that no other social order outside of capitalism is really conceivable.

Certainly, Keynes did break with the Treasury's orthodoxy on the grounds of his rejection of Say's law. Indeed, the downturn of the 1930s—when the world financial system was in collapse and unemployment was rampant in most of the industrial countries—deeply affected his thinking, to the point that he describes the *General Theory* as the outcome of "a long struggle of escape from habitual modes of thought and expression" (Keynes 1964, viii). He theorized the need for state intervention to boost effective demand, boost macroeconomic stability, and thus secure adequate investment of entrepreneurs' available private savings. However, Keynes never strayed far from the deepest kernels of the austerity project.

Keynes endorsed the most fundamental technocratic impulses. Like his austere colleagues, Keynes's economic theory expelled the notion of class conflict and concealed class repression. By disregarding the labor theory of value and the importance of exploitation to explain capital accumulation, Keynes's model accepts the principle that the engine of the economic machine is the entrepreneur and his economic investments, the key to the prosperity of all. In the *General Theory* deficient effective demand is ultimately due to a lack of investment on the part of entrepreneurs. It follows that the objective of macroeconomic management is to create an optimal investment environment, i.e., "a political and social atmosphere that is congenial to the average businessman" (Keynes 1964, 162). Unlike many of the radical reconstructionists studied in chapter 2, Keynes's advocacy for state intervention was not the advocacy to emancipate political priorities from economic ones. Quite the contrary: the domain of the political was *functional* to the reproduction of the *capital order*, an *order* led by the virtuous few.

Thus, in line with the very foundations of austerity, in the Keynesian framework workers lose economic primacy in the reproduction of capitalism. This loss of economic agency entails a loss of political agency that is handed over to the economic experts. Like his austere colleagues, Keynes is confident that economists are the guardians of classless truths, that they know what is good for the people and should be in charge of economic decisions on their behalf. This means that problems of poverty and unemployment—which deeply affect the concrete lives of people—are exempt from the political discourse, and are understood as a technical issue to be addressed "in the expert realm of reason and reasonableness" (Mann 2017, 10). Thus, the urge to depoliticize the economic domain persists as a key solution to preserve the social order. Once the capitalist state is neutralized as a suprahistorical institution in the hands of experts who can manage the economy for the good of the whole, the state is no longer viewed as the terrain of class struggle, but as the instrument of illuminated technocrats. It is fascinating to note that the very foundation to speak about a big break of Keynesianism with respect to austerity, i.e., the support of a greater role for the state as an economic actor, emerges from the same technocratic intuition: the pillars of capitalism have to be safeguarded, and people should accept the rule of experts.

The consequences of a technocratic approach to economic knowledge are visible in the New Keynesian stream of thinkers. For example, the 1984 article by the eminent economists Carl Shapiro and Joseph Stiglitz, "Equilibrium Unemployment as a Worker-Discipline Device"—tellingly formulated at the height of the Reagan-Thatcher crusade against organized labor—"naturalizes" unemployment. The disciplinary equilibrium rate of unemployment ensues as the natural product of the rational decisions of representative agents, certainly not the outcome of the exercise of capitalist power or class conflict. Given the informational asymmetry, and given the tendency of workers to shirk, the status quo is vindicated as a rational economic outcome. In line with the mainstream neoclassical framework, New Keynesian economists model workers as being selfish, opportunistic, and lazy. It is a short leap to incorporate in the theoretical framework to remove the necessity for workers to accept economic sacrifices, especially wage compression and monitoring, for the cause of the greater good.

If the lens of austerity permits one to put in question the separation of the Keynesian and neoliberal frameworks, it also certainly makes room for a reassessment of neoliberalism's history and its origins that Quinn Slobodian's *Globalists* (2018) recently revamped. Indeed, reconstructing the austerity project in the immediate aftermath of the Great War allows us to shift the conversation about the longue durée of neoliberalism into the terrain of class struggle and think of the history of capitalism of the twentieth and twenty-first century in this light.

One crucial and often neglected element is the magnitude of the existential threat to capitalism immediately after the Great War—reconstructed in the first half of this book. Slobodian emphasizes the effort to guarantee international economic integration and "global governance" via a legal institutional framework in the face of a crumbling Habsburg empire. Unlike *Globalists*, this book studies how, outside of Eastern and Central Europe, it was class conflict rather than new nation-states that challenged the existing order to its core. Under the guidance of economic experts, austere states actively intervened through economic policies that were key to secure the material disciplining of the majority through an expropriation of resources and wage curtailment. These policies, and the economic theories that justified them, were vital to revive a smooth functioning of capital accumulation, guaranteeing a flow of goods and property rights, both domestically and globally.

By telling the story of post–World War I reconstruction through the lens of austerity, this book has demonstrated how austerity was, and remains, an elaborate exercise in class domination. It is unquestionably more pernicious than the traditional telling of this story, one in which an international coalition worked to reestablish the gold standard after the war with the operating intention of securing and stabilizing global international exchanges. (Barry Eichengreen's well-known 1992 book *Golden Fetters* tells this story most notably.) As this book shows through archival and newly translated material, this "gold effort" was a surface manifestation of something deeper: a technocratic collaboration that successfully foreclosed alternatives to capitalism.

The dramatic events of the 1929 economic crash and the Great Depression that followed have attracted no shortage of scholarly attention, a focus that has obscured some of the political and ideological dynamics of the years before the Depression and following the Great War. The choice to focus this book on the early 1920s to the exclusion of later years does not take away from this period's relevance to understanding the Depression; as readers will find, a study of austerity serves to untangle the precipitating factors that promoted the crash and exacerbated the Depression. This is true for Britain, for Italy, and also for the United States—a country that remains in the background of the story but deserves more scrutiny to fully complete the puzzle of the origins of the austerity project as one of class repression. Montgomery (1987) and Migone (2015) provide good grounds to continue such excavation.

Finally, this study contributes to debates and reassessments around the history and nature of Italian Fascism (1922–1945) as well as its economic agenda—especially timely given the centennial anniversary of Mussolini's rise to power in October 1922. Traditional historiography envisages a discontinuity between Fascism's initial laissez-faire period (1922–1925) and the corporativist epoch that followed in Italy (usually understood as the "real" expression of Fascism). By viewing this same period through a lens of austerity, in terms of both economic policies and economic ideology, one can observe greater coherence across these two different phases. Austerity, in fact, is the thing that ties the two together. It embodied the active intervention of the state to reinforce capital accumulation through privatizations, bailouts of financial-industrial complexes, monetary deflation, and especially coercive control of labor. Speaking broadly, the nationalist slant of Fascist austerity emerges through the sacrifice of the majority for the saving/investing minority, who purported to represent the interests of the whole nation. Our story supports the notion that the interwar economy's truly Fascist element was its coercive control of the labor force (see Toniolo 1980, xii–xiii; and Ciocca 2004, 198–99). Recent scholarship points in a similar direction: it departs from the common understanding of the

1930s as different from the 1920s because of greater social spending. Indeed, it traces the continuities in Fascist policies across the 1920s and 1930s by highlighting the gaps between the propaganda of social policy intervention in the 1930s and the paucity and ineffectiveness of state redistributive policies, which actually worsened the living standards of the population (Espuelas 2015; Gabbuti 2020b; Giorgi and Pavan 2021).

Of course, this discussion about Fascist economic policies is closely connected to debates on the nature of Fascist economic theories, too. In this domain, my work further corroborates the scholarship of the Italian political scientist Luca Michelini (2011a, 2011b, 2020), who writes: "the relationship between Fascism and economic science cannot be identified with the issue of the birth and affirmation of corporativist doctrine, although that was of considerable importance. No less important, however, was the part played by the 'Fascist right,' starting with its founder, Pantaleoni, and passing through those authors and journals that wanted to adapt their theoretical and political teaching to the changing times" (Michelini 2020, 52). Indeed, the "Fascist right" is what I call austere Fascism. Such an austere strand of Fascist economic theory took direct inspiration from the fathers of pure economics. Moreover, it did not just inform the first "liberal" years of Fascist economic policies; its influence continued during the corporativist phase, as is reflected in the regime's economic policies. The classist corporative state would safeguard private profit and guarantee the subordination of workers—the core objectives of Pantaleoni's and Pareto's austerity project. Such a historical enquiry into the relationship between pure economics, austerity, and Fascism is all the more important if we keep in mind that pure economics constitutes the grammar of present-day mainstream economic thought.

Acknowledgments

The Capital Order is the result of much personal sacrifice and profound solidarity among a vast transatlantic community of scholars. Thinking about the many years that went into completing this all-consuming project, my heart is warmed at the thought of so many mentors and friends who have filled my life with encouragement, insight, and joy. I would like to thank a few of them in chronological order.

First and foremost, I am grateful to Professor Giorgio Lunghini, my first academic mentor, who introduced me to the history of economic thought when I was studying philosophy at the University of Pavia and who pushed me to pursue a PhD in economics. It was in fact during my years as a doctoral student at the Sant'Anna School of Advanced Studies, Pisa, that the inspiration for this book first emerged. In 2013, a time when my country was undergoing profound austerity restructuring, I first encountered Gianni Toniolo's *L'Economia dell'Italia Fascista*. It occurred to me that the parallels between Mussolini's time and our own, while striking, were unexplored. I am grateful to each member of the Sant'Anna scholarly community for keeping me motivated at the earliest and therefore most daunting stages of my research. I am perhaps most indebted to Giovanni Dosi, my main supervisor in Sant'Anna, for innumerable fruitful discussions and for his critical spirit that challenged me to keep searching for the right approach to my work. I cherish the enriching conversations with Alessandro

Nuvolari, Andrea Roventini, Alessio Moneta, and Francesco Lamperti. The exchanges with the historians of economic thought Riccardo Faucci and Luca Michelini made a difference in those years. However, I would have never found the strength to persist in my work, even in the moments of deeper confusion and self-doubt, especially concerning my eclectic approach that never fit in any disciplinary canon, without the crucial help of Nicola Giocoli and George Peden, both of whom "adopted" me as a thesis supervisee. Their passionate scholarly conversations and generous help in revising and editing drafts was a most precious gift. I have fond memories of my time in Callander as a guest of George and his wife Alison, when I was well fed and learned how to best approach archival research while taking long walks in the Scottish plains.

During my two-year stay in Rome, where I undertook much of the archival work that informs this book, the regular mentorship of Pierluigi Ciocca was the biggest honor I could have hoped for. The almost weekly visits in his magnificent office filled with books in Corso Vittorio inspired both personal and scholarly enthusiasm for the project. Thanks to Pierluigi's support I was able to access the library of the Banca d'Italia, a magical environment where the rarest books can be retrieved. In those years, the encounters (which still continue today) with Gianni Toniolo and Robert Skidelsky, two leaders of their field, were another immense scholarly treat.

The support of the Young Scholar Initiative (YSI) of the Institute for New Economic Thinking, which generously funded conferences and workshops, boosted my enthusiasm for this research immeasurably. I would like to thank all of the members of the YSI community for all the exciting intellectual exchanges, in particular Robert Johnson and Jay Pocklington for their dedication to a project that deeply inspires young thinkers.

This book would never have taken the form it has without the life-changing experience of being hired in 2016 as an assistant professor in the economics department of the New School for Social Research, where I refined (and continue to refine) a Marxian perspective in political economy. I am enormously grateful to everyone involved in the hiring process, and especially to Anwar Shaikh, who believed in my work from the moment he read the first draft of my PhD thesis. Indeed, persistent interlocution with my colleagues Anwar Shaikh and Duncan Foley was crucial for refining my theoretical lens. I am especially grateful for Duncan's dedication in the latest book-writing process: his meticulous comments on every chapter and our regular lunches on the Upper West Side to discuss the material are among my best memories of this intellectual adventure. Of course, I cannot go without thanking my colleagues Ying Chen, Teresa Ghilarducci, Paulo Dos Santos, Willi Semmler, Mark Setterfield, Sanjay Reddy, and Will Milberg for their insights and especially for their professional support.

Among the most remarkable characteristics of the New School for Social Research is the tightly knit scholarly and human community that goes well beyond the department and the discipline. The conversations with philosophers Cinzia Aruzza, Richard Bernstein, and Sandro Mezzadra (visiting for a year from Bologna); historians Aaron Jakes, Emma Park, and Julia Ott (Director of the Robert L. Heilbroner Center for Capitalism Studies, which helped support my research); political scientists Andrew Arato, Quentin Bruneau, Carlos Forment, and Andreas Kalyvas have been eye-opening and tremendously joyful.

The academic year I spent at the Institute for Advanced Studies in 2018–2019 was a blessing: a temporary escape from hectic New York life in which I could find the peace of mind that allowed me to transform scattered pieces of research into systematic chapters. Munirah Khayyat, Rima Majed, Daniel Aldana Cohen, Maggie Hennefeld, David Bond, Didier Fassin, Nicola di Cosmo, and Myles Jackson are great scholars and friends who have made my experience at IAS unique. Special thanks are due to Marcia Tucker, head librarian at IAS, whose professionalism and devotion allowed me to systematically uncover hidden research material. I am grateful for all the Monday mornings Marcia and I spent discussing weekly research goals and the primary sources to investigate. Her capacity to find the most precious archival material, up until the very end of the writing process, is what made this book as rich as it is. During that academic year I received an invitation to participate in the Remarque Institute's Kandersteg seminar titled

"Revisiting 1919," where the conversations with Susan Pedersen and many other participants left a positive trace.

I would like to recognize the indispensable role of Sam Salour, who in the year at IAS and beyond has been the greatest source of inspiration: an intellectual and emotional pillar in my life and a true comrade. With him I was able to transform my research into a systematic intellectual endeavor. The full extent of my gratitude for his care, dedication, and patience is beyond verbalization.

In January 2020, when I was back in New York, overworked by teaching and immensely worried about my tenure process, I received a life-changing email from Chad Zimmerman, brilliant executive editor at the University of Chicago Press, inquiring into my work. In addition to his unbridled enthusiasm for the project, Chad's editorial and intellectual sagacity made the book what it is. I cannot thank Chad enough for his constructive and creative engagement, but most especially for his unwavering support. I am immensely grateful to Zvi Ben-Dor Benite for his kindness and generosity during the earliest months of the editorial process.

In the last phases of writing the manuscript, a couple of workshops with close friends and colleagues gave me indispensable input. For their friendship and dedication I thank Basma N. Radwan, Alex Zevin, Luca Falciola, Carlo Invernizzi, Amana Fontanella-Khan, Quentin Bruneau, Aaron Jakes, Nick Mulder, Jeremy Kessler, Barnabie Reine, Siavash Radpour, Andreas Kalyvas, and Teddy Paikin. Special thanks to Homa Zarghamee, whose input, especially for the book proposal, was vital, and to Adam Tooze, who not only sparked one of the most exciting historical discussions at my manuscript workshop, but whose influence over these last years has been of incalculable value for my intellectual development. I am most grateful to James Galbraith for his friendship, unequivocal intellectual prowess, and encouraging feedback throughout these years of research and writing. Thank you to Stephen Meardon for his generosity in friendship and intellectual collaboration, to Susan Howson for having read and commented on my manuscript with important critical insight, and to Giacomo Gabbuti whose feedback and expertise, especially for the quantitative chapter, was invaluable. Giacomo organized a workshop in Oxford in October 2019 on the Italian economy under Fascism that opened the door for a holistic exchange of ideas among scholars in the field. A special thanks to Professor Roberto Marchionatti, an authority in the history of economic thought, for enriching and thorough conversations in his office at the Fondazione Luigi Einaudi in Turin, the center he runs. I also thank all of the staff of the Fondazione for their prompt practical help in the research.

My deepest and most sincere thanks go to my graduate student Aditya Singh, a brilliant up-and-coming political economist, whose daily support made the final writing process a joyful experience and without whose presence this book would never have been delivered with the timing that it was. I also thank Lauren Sweger-Hollingsworth, Cesar Garcia, Ricardo Hernandez, Lauren Johnston, Penelope Kyritsis, and Marc Triller, my talented graduate students at the New School, whose critique and feedback was most timely.

A final word on Gianfranco Mattei. At the young age of twenty-seven, Gianfranco was already a professor of chemistry at the Polytechnic School of Milan and collaborating with his comrades in the GAP (a partisan unit operating in Italian cities) at their secret site at Via Santa Giulia 25 bs, Rome, to design bombs to be used against the Fascists. It was not long before a whistleblower compromised him and his comrades. He was taken to the infamous prison of Via Tasso, where the Fascist militia brutally tortured members of the political opposition to obtain information about the mounting anti-Fascist resistance.

Gianfranco is my great-uncle, child of my great-grandmother Clara Mattei, whose name I carry. Following two days of constant brutalization, Gianfranco hanged himself with his belt rather than betray his comrades in the resistance. His last words, written on the back of a check and surreptitiously passed to his cellmate, were for his parents: "*Siate forti, sapendo che lo sono stato anche io*" (Be strong, knowing that I also was).

The memory of his courageous sacrifice to protect his comrades, his resolute battle against the oppressor, and his selfless dedication to changing the world for all animates my life with personal and political purpose. To my great-uncle Gianfranco Mattei, and to revolutionaries everywhere, I dedicate this book.

Notes

Introduction

1 Luis Ferré-Sadurní and Jesse McKinley, "N.Y. Hospitals Face $400 Million in Cuts Even as Virus Battle Rages," *New York Times*, March 30, 2020, https://www.nytimes.com/2020/03/30/nyregion/coronavirus-hospitals -medicaid-budget.html.

2 Camila Vergara, "The Meaning of Chile's Explosion," *Jacobin Magazine*, October 29, 2019, https://www.jacobinmag.com/2019/10/chile-protests -sebastian-pinera-constitution-neoliberalism.

3 "Third Greece Bailout: What Are Eurozone conditions?" *BBC News*, August 21, 2015, https://www.bbc.com/news/world-europe-33905686.

4 See Peter Coy, "Why are Fast Food Workers Signing Noncompete Agreements?," *New York Times*, September 29, 2021, https://www.nytimes .com/2021/09/29/opinion/noncompete-agreement-workers.html.

5 Saez and Zucman (2019).

6 Throughout this book the term "state" is preferred over the term "government." This is because while the words are often used interchangeably, the state is more than just governments (understood as particular executives in charge). The state is embodied in a plurality of institutions and is the sum of all of these—legislative bodies (parliaments), judiciary bodies (the courts), executive bodies (government in charge: ministers, or other elected officials), administrative bodies (state agencies concerned with the management of the economy, such as central banks), and law enforcement bodies (police, etc.). In Ralph Miliband's words: "What 'the state' stands for is a number of particular institutions, which, together, constitute its reality, and which interact as parts of what may be called the state system" (Miliband 1969, 49).

7 Blyth (2013, 203).

8 For a full-blown economic analysis of the dynamics of the capitalist system

as one driven by profit, and thus real competition amongst private businesses to attain such profit, see Shaikh (2016).

9 Gallacher and Campbell (1972, 12).

10 Einaudi (1959–65, 904); Togliatti (1919b).

11 "Reconstruction in Europe," *Manchester Guardian Commercial*, May 18, 1922, p. 66.

12 For a history of austerity policies that European empires implemented in their colonies, see Park et al. (2021). The history of austerity practices in European colonies does not figure in this work because, as I explain, the mode of austerity described herein depends on practices of democratic contestation which were only legible by virtue of actors' legal equality, which (by virtue of politico-legal arrangements) was nonexistent in European colonies.

13 Maffeo Pantaleoni (Brussels 1920, vol. 4.107).

14 Milanović (2019, 2).

15 Skidelsky (2009); Krugman (2015).

16 *The Collected Writings of John Maynard Keynes*, vol. 10, 1971–1989 (Cambridge: Cambridge University Press), 446–47.

17 Mann (2017) argues that the legacy of Keynesianism is haunted by the potential collapse of civilization that is inevitably understood as the capitalist civilization: "As Keynes' theory of civilization makes clear, because the bourgeois cannot imagine a non-bourgeois society, it cannot conceive of its own end as anything else but the end of the world" (Mann 2017, 23). Mann's reflections find even sturdier grounds if one places Keynes in the context of the aftermath of the Great War.

18 To be sure, while central to explaining the downturn, austerity policies were not the *only* factors that contributed to it. Simon Clarke, for example, stresses overproduction and a lack of global competitiveness as important reasons for the break of the British postwar boom (Clarke 1988, 209–10).

19 Pigou (1947, 43). Average weekly earnings for all manual workers dropped from £3.7 in 1920 to £2.61 in 1923 (see Scholliers and Zamagni 1995).

20 Dr. Alfred Salter, 161 Parl. Deb. H.C. (March 7, 1923), cols. 627–75.

21 For example, in a 2020 analysis (https://www.oxfam.org/en/blogs/virus
-austerity-covid-19-spending-accountability-and-recovery-measures
-agreed-between-imf-and) Oxfam finds that 76 out of the 91 IMF loans negotiated with eighty-one countries since March 2020—when the pandemic was declared—push for belt-tightening that could result in deep cuts to public healthcare systems and pension schemes; wage freezes and cuts for public sector workers such as doctors, nurses, and teachers; and cuts to unemployment benefits, like sick pay (see also https://www.oxfam.org/en/
press-releases/imf-paves-way-new-era-austerity-post-covid-19).

22 To be sure, I am not claiming that austerity is the *only* factor to explain wage repression, let alone to explain inequality. For example, global move-

ment of capital in search of cheaper labor and technology shifts are factors that have attracted the majority of the workforce within service sectors characterized by low productivity and precarious work hours (see Taylor and Ömer 2020).

23 See Istituto Nazionale di Statistica (June 16, 2021). The level of absolute poverty is calculated as the monetary value at current prices of the basket of goods and services that are considered essential for each family, based on the age of each of its members, geographical allocation, and the place of residence (Istituto Nazionale di Statistica [February 2, 2021]).

24 Inman and Booth (2019). For official statistics see Department for Work and Pensions, "Households Below Average Income (HBAI) Statistics," https://www.gov.uk/government/collections/households-below-average-income-hbai--2.

25 Shaikh (2016, 60).

26 See Wartzman (2020); for the RAND working paper Wartzman references, see Price and Edwards (2020).

27 Stein (2006).

Part I

1 On the history and the development of early capitalism and its entrenchment see Wood (1999), Polanyi (1944), North and Thomas (1973).

Chapter One

1 Caracciolo (1969, 163–219).

2 Under pre-war laissez-faire capitalism, the state had a limited role: for example, in Victorian Britain, considered the epitome of laissez-faire, the state had a say in three limited economic spheres: social policy, finance, and commercial relations with foreign powers: "[G]overnment, apart from the Post Office and a few naval and military establishments, did not own or administer business undertakings, did not concern itself with the organization of industry or the marketing of its products, did not attempt directly to influence the course of trade, and rarely intervened, except as a borrower, in the money or capital markets" (Tawney 1943, 1).

3 J. A. Salter formulates a description that can be applied to the whole control mechanism developed during the war: "it is important to remember that control was extended step by step by the compelling forces of circumstances. It was already almost complete before it was adopted as a deliberate policy. Each new extension was normally undertaken reluctantly as the only method of meeting an immediate emergency" (Salter 1921, 62).

4 These rates, circulated as a government document or "Blue Book," were arbitration prices settled by a committee of seventy-two, representing the government, shipowners, cargo owners, the marine insurance business, deck officers, and seamen; the owners, with twenty-four, formed the largest group. As set, they yielded an average annual profit of over 10 percent on the book value of the ships. Sir Leo Chiozza Money notes that "Liberal as they were, however, the Blue Book Rates were far below the extravagant market rates caused by the shortage of tonnage" (Chiozza Money 1920, 73).

5 Until the war, both Britain and Italy loyally embodied the balanced budget tradition: expenditures were minimal and matched revenues. However, by 1918, Britain's central government expenditures had soared to nearly fourteen times their 1913 level, and Italy's had risen by almost nine times (Mitchell 1998, Table G-5, 820–21). Revenues could no longer keep pace.

6 For an explanation of the mechanism of the gold standard, see Barry Eichengreen's 1992 classic, *Golden Fetters*.

7 During the war, Britain's exchange rate was supported by foreign borrowing and formal or informal restrictions on gold movements (Moggridge 1972, 18). No longer under the grip of the gold standard, the state could increase credit circulation and imports without fearing a reflexive outflow of gold and a currency devaluation that would instigate a credit contraction to avoid unpegging from the standard. The state could also borrow from banks who, free from the "golden fetter," could issue credit beyond the nation's gold reserves. For a detailed analysis of war finances in Britain see Morgan (1952) and Peden (2000); on Italian war finances see Einaudi (1933, 27–57), Frascani (1975, 1–85), Forsyth (1993).

8 Britain and Italy declared a "state of exception" so as to give much greater powers to the government, increase military powers in the civil sphere, and shorten administrative procedures. However, while the British Parliament maintained a function of control, in Italy the parliament was stripped of all its powers. Indeed, on May 22, 1915, a law of full powers granted the government power to legislate (through *decreti legge*) without passing through parliament in all matters "regarding the defence of the State, the safeguard of public order and the urgent and extraordinary needs of the national economy." Overall, the British chamber had 423 sessions between 1915 and 1917 while the Italian chamber gathered only 158 times (Procacci 1983, 44).

9 In the case of Italy, for example, Article 7 of the royal decree of June 26, 1915 (Royal Decree 997, in GU 177 [June 26, 1915], 4296), reads: "industrialists cannot refuse the production and distribution of the necessary material for war. In the case in which they ask for prices that are excessively high, they will have to accept the payment that will be established by the administration" (Franchini 1928, 81).

10 With the Treasury Agreement (that gave life to the Munitions Act) workers' unions had successfully obtained a munitions levy on the controlled

establishments of 100 percent on all profits above a prewar "standard" plus 20 percent. However, this tax was easily evaded by capital expenditure, wear-and-tear allowances, and other methods which made the concept of standard meaningless. Its yield was negligible (Pollard 1969, 64). The Excess Profits Duty (EPD) introduced in the second budget of 1915 (which also applied to firms other than controlled establishments) was more successful. It encompassed a quarter of the British war revenue. Its average rate during the war was 63 percent, yet only around 34 percent was actually collected due to much evasion, delay, and fraudulent taxes. Munitions firms were actually exempt from EPD until 1917. On war taxation see Daunton (2002, 36–59).

11 In the age of steam, coal had become the key source of power. Further, in 1913 Britain was still by far the largest exporter of coal. During a national mining conference held in London in July 1915, Prime Minister Lloyd George gave an apt characterization of the centrality of coal in Britain: "In time of peace coal is the most important element in the industrial life of this country. The blood which courses through the veins of industry in the country is made of distilled coal. In peace and in war King coal is the paramount Lord of industry. It enters into every article of consumption and utility; it is our real international coinage. When we buy goods, food and raw material abroad we pay not in gold but in coal" (Redmayne 1923, 2). On the coal industry during and after the war, see Armitage (1969, 101–58), Hurwitz (1949), Kirby (1977). About the control of coal in Italy, see Franchini (1932, 39–40).

12 For a thorough description of state wool purchase and manufacture in Britain see Lloyd (1924, 125–48).

13 On the British Ministry of Munitions and its technology research, see Wrigley (in Burk 1982, 47–49). In Italy, the results of industrial innovation research were diffused through the *bollettino del comitato generale di mobilitazione industriale*.

14 For a detailed analysis of the role of the Italian regional committees, see Franchini (1928).

15 Agriculture commissioners at the provincial, municipal, and intramunicipal levels [*commissari agricoli privinciali, comunali*, and *inter-comunali*] coordinated the public management of agriculture (see De Stefani 1926a, 109). Through these institutions, the state also imposed forced labor in the fields [*obbligatorietà delle prestazioni*] and hired military men and war prisoners for agricultural work.

16 See the royal decrees of May 10, 1917, n. 788; October 4, 1917, n. 1614; and February 14, 1918, n. 147. See also De Stefani (1926a, 112–13).

17 On the complex institutional structure that dealt with Italian food policy, see De Stefani (1926a, 257–71) and Bachi (1926, 151–65).

18 "At the outbreak of the War, Britain imported from abroad four-fifth of

the cereals consumed, two-fifths of the meat, three-quarters of the fruit, besides all the sugar and colonial products and substantial proportions of other food-stuffs" (see Pollard 1969, 58). Like Britain, Italy too was highly dependent on imports for much of its food necessities. During the war, 15–20 percent of Italian imports came from Britain (Zamagni 1990, 280). To tackle the war emergency, the royal decree of August 31, 1918, "granted to the State no less than the imports of all military and nonmilitary material necessary for the country and their redistribution to the commercial and industrial bodies through rationing" (Porisini 1975, 57). For details on the regulation of international and local import and export see De Stefani (1926a, 206–23).

19 According to state official Leo Chiozza Money, "If the bulk purchases had not been made and if the buying had been left to the ordinary private enterprise agencies, our raw materials would have cost us several times as much, if we had got them at all" (Chiozza Money 1920, 128).

20 In Britain, "4,970,000 men were enlisted in the army, 407,000 in the navy, and 293,000 in the air-force out of a total male labour force of some 15 million" (Wrigley 1987, 23). Only a year into the war, voluntary enlistment had already caused an immediate shortage of labor: "By July 1915 the estimated drop in total occupied male population employed in coal and other mining was 21.8 percent, iron and steel 18.8 percent, engineering 19.5 percent, electrical engineering 23.7 percent and shipbuilding 16.5 percent" (Wrigley 1987, 24).

21 The 1911 census suggests a total male labor force (occupied and unoccupied) of 15,093,000. Given that around 5,670,000 were recruited during the war, the available male labor force was around 9.5 million. This calculation does not consider the change in the sex composition of the labor force that occurred during the war. More women were employed in industries during the war. For example, while in 1914 the proportion of women in the industry and transport sectors was 23 percent, it rose to 34 percent by 1918. The number of women considered gainfully employed grew from slightly under 6 million in July 1914 to 7,311,000 in July 1918, or from 31 percent to 37 percent of all women and girls over the age of ten. (For details on women and the labor market during the war see Pedersen 1993, chapter 2, 72–133.)

22 On the vast topic of state repression of the working class in Italy during the war, which extended well beyond the factory, see Procacci 2013; Procacci 1999; Procacci and Corner 1997; and Procacci (ed.) 1983, in particular the chapter titled "La legislazione repressiva e la sua applicazione," 41–59.

23 L'Internazionale di fronte allo scoppio della guerra was a pamphlet commissioned by the Socialist parliamentary group (written by Giuseppe Emanuele Modigliani in 1916) to explain the reasons for the socialist opposition to the War. See Vivarelli 1967, 56.

24 See Luigi Tomassini, "Gli effetti sociali della mobilitazione industriale: industriali, lavoratori, Stato" in Menozzi et al. (eds.) 2010, 25–57.

25 For details on the militarization of the Italian labor force, see Franchini (1928), Labanca and Procacci (2018), Tomassini (1991).

26 A law passed on November 5, 1916, that strictly defined crimes and punishment. The state punished the abandonment of work with military incarceration for 1 to 2 years, and it punished the unauthorized movement of labor with jail for 2 to 6 months. Refusal to obey corresponded to jail for up to 1 year and assault against a superior could lead to a 15- to 24-year jail sentence. Einaudi remarks that "the results achieved with the methods of military coercion were remarkable. The absences from work, that touched 8.40% before militarization, decreased to 4.88% immediately after" (Einaudi 1933, 113).

27 For a detailed analysis of the various means the state used to discipline labor for war production in Britain and of unions' compliance with these means, see Rubin (1987, chapter 7, 178–202).

28 In Italy, factory committees were born at the beginning of the century, more as spontaneous forms of workers' representation to deal with industrial disputes than as permanent organs of representation. With the war, their role was *de facto* legitimized even if *de jure* this occurred only in 1918 (see Spriano 1960, 467–71).

29 See statistics in Franchini (1928, 123). On Italian women labor force during the war see Camarda and Peli (1980, 21–42) and Isnenghi (1982, 237–48).

30 Other techniques for expanding the pool of labor included the suspension of migratory rights, the exemption of soldiers (especially skilled workers) from the front to work in war industries, the employment of colonial manpower, and the compulsory enlistment of war prisoners or inmates.

31 Scholars note that Italy's enhanced productivity in the war industries did not derive so much from technological advancement in industrial organization as from an increase in employment and especially an intensification of the exploitation of the workforce (see Alessandro Camarda, "Salari, organizzazione e condizioni di lavoro," in Procacci [ed.] 1983, 166).

32 In just the auxiliary factories of Milan in 1916, more than half a million working days were lost due to accidents (see Renzo Paci, "Le trasformazioni ed innovazioni nella struttura economica italiana," in Caracciolo 1968, 52–53). On the issue of workplace accidents see Camarda and Peli (1980, 65–71) and "Il problema sociale dell'infortunio sul lavoro" in *Il bollettino del comitato centrale di mobilitazione* (February-March 1918, 96–103). In Britain the registered accidents increased from 14 percent to 48 percent, while professional illnesses increased significantly in all countries. For example, production of explosives caused increases in workplace exposure to toxic substances. On the Italian phenomenon of the so-called *lunedianti*—that is, those who would not show up to work on Mondays— see Camarda and Peli (1980, 72–83).

33 The priority of productivity impacted a wide range of factory services.

The state ran and subsidized them. In controlled establishments, factory canteens provided cheap hot meals (by the end of 1918, 900 canteens were expected to be feeding an industrial population of close to one million—see His Majesty's Stationery Office 1918a, 195), and the state had established health centers and drinking facilities as well as better sanitary and washing facilities. Regarding the canteens, the 1918 report states that the Munitions (Food) Committee recorded its judgment that the canteen's "high value as an agency of improved nutrition, and therefore increased energy and output is beyond doubt. Not only must this value be retained and enhanced, but steps should be taken to encourage an extension of the movement in all practical ways" (ibid.).

34 On piecework and how it changed the wage structure in Italy see Camarda and Peli (1980, 121–33).

35 The 1920 Committee of Enquiry into the work of the employment exchanges attests the extended role of these institutions in controlling labor during the war. In its report we read: "Much additional work fell upon the Exchanges during the war. Very many workers and employers were under obligation to go to the Exchanges during this period, and the average daily number of vacancies filled rose to 4,713 during the first six months of 1916, and to 5,071 during the first six months of 1918" (Ministry of Labour 1920, 6).

36 Another telling example of the power wielded by the state in directing labor mobility across the nation is the recruitment of Italian civilian labor to work on the front line in the logistical services. This was a relevant experiment in terms of organized migrations: in 1916 and 1917 the state displaced more than 210,000 workers from southern regions (Sicily, Calabria, Abruzzo, Puglia, Campania) to the areas behind the front (see Ermacora 2007; see also Ermacora 2005, 53–54, 63–64, 89–92, 134).

37 To read more on dilution in Britain during the war see Wolfe (1923, chapter 9, 148–73); Cole (1923, chapter 6, 83–114; chapter 8, 129–41). For a good discussion of the process of dilution in Italy and skilled workers' loss of autonomy, see Bezza (1982, 75–78).

38 For an analysis of the malfunctioning of the bargaining process in Britain at the beginning of the war and the gradual push to state intervention, see Cole (1915, chapter 6, 138–67).

39 The Committee on Production (founded in February 1915) remained in place until the end of the war, and was then reappointed as a Court of Arbitration under the Wages (Temporary Regulation) Act of 1918.

40 One of the first acts of Lloyd George as prime minister was the creation of the Ministry of Labour in December 1916. It was formed by removing the board of trade's semi-autonomous labor departments (the employment department dealing with employment exchanges and unemployment insurance; the chief industrial commissioner department, with responsibil-

ity over the conciliation and arbitration services; and the Trade Boards Department responsible for overseeing minimum wages in nine trades) and combining them under a new ministry. In 1917 the ministry created two divisions: a labor intelligence division to prepare a weekly report on the labor situation for the war cabinet, and a Joint Industrial Councils division to promote the establishment of Whitley councils throughout the industry. For details on the ministry and its administrative difficulties, see Rodney Lowe's "The Ministry of Labour, 1916–1919: A Still, Small Voice?" in Burk (1982, 108–35).

41 The government extended arbitration beyond the auxiliary establishments to industries in the war zones and to those that "were important for the economic life of the country." For details on the Italian arbitration procedure, see Franchini (1932, 162–66).

42 The 1918 report also states: "Meanwhile, despite the heavy claims in 1918 of the Army, the Navy, munitions, shipbuilding and transport, the output was well maintained, and in some cases remarkably increased, in the two other great fields of production, namely, raw materials and food" (His Majesty's Stationery Office 1919, x).

43 Sir Leo Chiozza Money writes that, difficult as it was, "The soldiers obtained their food, munitions and supplies. The civilian population was maintained in a fair degree of comfort. Essential trades such as the cotton industry had proper consideration, and were given such supplies of material as to preserve their existence" (Chiozza Money 1920, 89).

44 "New Ideals in Politics," *The Times*, November 18, 1918, 4.

45 "A Nationalization Proposal," *The Times*, December 11, 1918, 16. Winston Churchill was a Conservative from 1900 to 1904; he then joined the Liberal Party from 1904–1924, and finally reverted back to the Conservative party from 1924 until the end of his political career.

46 The original enquiry on war expenditures 1920–1923 is republished in Crocella et al. (2002).

47 "Le ricerche statistiche per la mobilitazione industriale e gli ammaestramenti per il dopoguerra," in *Il bollettino del comitato centrale di mobilitazione industriale*, October 1917, 130.

48 The *Economist*, which represented the epitome of pure liberalism, was strongly against state intervention in the economy, of course. For example, as early as December 21, 1918, it exhorted the government to stop its practice of paying "people for putting difficulties in the way of private enterprise." For an excellent long-term historical study of the position, ideology, and impacts of the magazine, see Zevin (2019).

49 Italy's industrial mobilization apparatus was dismantled soon after the armistice and, after a brief parenthesis, so was the state's control over agricultural production and prices (see Paola Carucci, "Funzioni e caratteri del ministero per le armi e munizioni," in Procacci 1983, 60–79). As for Britain,

the largest part of its decontrol process coincided with the extensive austerity measures of 1921 that we will study in the second part of this book. That
year the Ministry of Munitions, the Ministry of Food, and the Coal Control
Department were dissolved, as well as the Railway Executive (see Tawney
1943).

50 *Daily Herald*, July 10, 1919, p. 1 (late London edition); *Daily Herald*, August
26, 1919, p. 5.

51 "Profiteering Is a Plague: How It Has Reduced the People to Poverty and Is
Building Up a C3 Nation," *Daily Herald*, August 25, 1919, 5.

52 In fact, the state acted to limit the priorities of profit in the national interest: "it assumed control for the duration of the war over a great number of
the larger private undertakings, it has limited profits by imposing an 80 per
cent excess profits tax, and it has intervened to prevent profiteering in the
essential requirements of the nation" (HMSO 1918a, xvi). Further, employers were subjected to managerial interference, governmental scrutiny, and
oversight (see Pedersen 1993, 84; Rubin 1987, 20–23).

53 For example, in Britain, the Ministry of Munitions cooperated with the
home office to promote civic recreation schemes. Most importantly,
between 1914 and 1918 there was a major expansion in welfare services
for mothers and infants. The Maternity and Child Welfare Act of 1918
consolidated and extended previous schemes: the appointment of health
visitors, maternity and child welfare centers, midwifery service, and
maternity homes and hospitals for nursing mothers and babies. Creches,
day nurseries, and homes for orphan or illegitimate children multiplied
to allow women to go out to work (HMSO 1919a, 286). Local government
boards were in charge of protecting the welfare of the blind, supervising
the treatment of tuberculosis, and preventing infectious and epidemic
diseases. In 1917, the state introduced the free treatment of venereal disease
for civilians as well as for soldiers. Scholars have described this measure as
"the first installment of a free national health service" (Titmuss 2018, 48).
We will discuss this subject matter further in chapter 2.

54 The literature on the nature of the development of the Italian industrial
sector during the war years is extensive. Luciano Segreto (1982, 146–47)
provides a good overview of both the productive and technical achievements the dark side of such expansion. Many scholars have studied the
processes of vertical and horizontal integration that occurred between the
financial and industrial sectors in those years (see in particular Romeo
1972, 115–26; Castronovo 1982, 139–46; Castronovo 1995, 203–7; Grifone
1971, 22–31).

55 For a detailed enquiry on the frauds and abuses, see "L'inchiesta parlamentare sulle spese di guerra (1920–1923)" in Crocella et al., eds. (2002).

56 For example, in 1914 Fiat had 4,300 workers; that number grew to more

than 40,000 in 1918. In 1914 it produced 4,800 automotive vehicles, and by 1918 its production rose to 70,862, of which 63,000 were for the Italian government. The aeronautic industry, practically nonexistent in 1913, employed by the end of the war around 100,000 workers. The chemical and textile industries also developed impressively, especially because of large state subsidies and direct intervention to support their technical apparatus, for example with the formation of the committee for chemical industries [*Comitato per le industrie chimiche*] (see De Stefani 1926a, 151–53).

57 Zaganella (2017, 190). The declared profits of the public limited companies jumped from 4 percent on the eve of the war to 8 percent in 1917. The profits of iron and steel industries jumped from 6 percent to 17 percent, automobiles from 8 percent to 31 percent, and wool from 5 percent to 19 percent (Porisini 1975, 34).

58 On the decline of real wages during the war, see Zamagni (1991, tables 2 and 3, 140–47). Severe rationing, low agricultural production, and inflation were such that by 1917—when imports were limited by the German submarine war—working classes in the big Italian cities were at their survival limits (Bachi 1926, 159). In the countryside, the absence of male workforce and food requisitioning for the army made conditions all the more unbearable. The words of Ernesto Ragionieri are telling: "Perhaps due account has not been given to the fact that the excess of deaths in the civilian population during the war surpasses six hundred thousand with respect to the prior period matching the number of the dead at the front" (in Fava 1982, 176). For a detailed analysis of the social impacts of inflation and the worsening living conditions of workers in different sectors of the economy, see Frascani (1975, 59–83).

59 Unlike Italy, in Britain the state's efforts in maintaining the levels of agricultural production and imports of consumption goods, rationing, and rent control raised the living expectations of the poorest, while public health and food quality improved (Procacci 2013, 48). While in Italy average real daily earnings decreased during the war years (falling continuously from 1915 to 1918), in Britain the average weekly real wages increased over the same period (rising continuously from 1913 to 1919). See figures 9.7 and 9.8 in chapter 9.

60 Regarding Britain, Pedersen writes: "The preservation of working-class organization in Britain meant that the labor movement was, from the beginning, aware of its strength and able to set some conditions for its cooperation in the prosecution of the war" (Pedersen 1993, 82).

61 Under the war government of Lloyd George, Labour MP Arthur Henderson joined the War Cabinet. John Hodge, the secretary of the Steel Smelters, and George Barnes, the former secretary of the Amalgamated Engineers, took the new posts of minister of labour and minister of pensions,

respectively. Thereafter, trade union views were regularly expounded to the Cabinet. Several other Labour MPs—also former trade-union officials—were appointed to junior offices.

62 For example, in 1916 *La mobilitazione industriale* appointed "*la commissione cottimi*," which involved the participation of trade unions.

63 Gramsci recalls an impressive episode that took place in 1917 in Turin: "When in July of 1917 the mission to Western Europe of the Petrograd Soviet arrived in Turin, the delegates Smirnov and Goldemberg, who presented themselves before a crowd of fifty thousand workers, were greeted with deafening cries of 'Long live Lenin! Long live the Bolsheviks!'" (Gramsci [1921], https://www.marxists.org/archive/gramsci/1921/03/turin _councils.htm).

Chapter Two

1 I owe the term "reconstructionists" to P. B. Johnson, who uses it in his fascinating 1968 study, *Land Fit for Heroes*, on social reform after World War I (see Johnson 1968, 220).

2 A century later this line of thinking has seen a resurgence in popularity in "modern monetary theory" and its related thinking about the relation of the state to the economy. See for example, Taylor (2019) and Kelton (2020).

3 Ministry of Reconstruction (1918, 28–29). Hall's words were then partially reprinted in Ministry of Reconstruction (1919, 6–7).

4 Filippo Vassalli, Genoa University, inauguration of the academic year 1919–1920, republished in Pavan (2016, 180).

5 Regarding the Italian case, Ilaria Pavan stresses that the years 1917–1919 represented "the real starting point" in which the welfare state was born (see Pavan 2019, 835).

6 Amongst the most notable reforms of the Liberal government (1905–1915) we have the Education Acts of 1906–1907, which enabled local authorities to provide subsidized school meals and required medical inspections for school children. In 1908 old-age pensions were granted on a noncontributory, means-tested basis. The National Insurance Act of 1911 was by far the most important achievement: it provided for state-supervised contributory insurance schemes against ill health for wage earners, and against unemployment for some trades that were more subject to fluctuations in the trade cycle. For a more detailed survey of the welfare measures at the beginning of the century see Peden (1985, 16–35) and Thane (1996, 49–94).

7 As the War Cabinet stressed: "Welfare work, as now understood, was little known in British industry before the war" (His Majesty's Stationery Office [hereafter HMSO] 1919a, 289).

8 Haldane to Escher, December 26, 1918, Haldane papers, folder 103, in Johnson (1968, 245).

9 "Mr. Lloyd George on his Task," *The Times*, November 25, 1918, 13. In that same speech Lloyd George remarked: "Slums are not fit homes for the men who have won this war or for their children . . . therefore the housing of the people must be a national concern."

10 Jason [pseud.] 1918, 5–6. Hammond detailed that before the war "the whole life of a nation was to be subordinated to this imperious demand [of the production of wealth] . . . consequently, the most terrible conditions were tolerated as the alternative to the loss of trade. Children became hereditary factory slaves, towns grew up in hideous form, and men and women were reduced to the utmost degradation, and the triumphs of our industry all over the globe left the great mass of our working population less free than the inhabitants of a Red Indian village. This conceptual value and purpose in national life did not satisfy everybody, but it satisfied the ruling class as a whole" (ibid.).

11 See Addison's biography, Morgan and Morgan (1980).

12 Cabinet memorandum, February 25, 1919, GT 6887, Cab 2; reprinted in Clyne (1970, 169).

13 Lloyd George had made explicit that "a vigorous community, strong, healthy men and women, is more valuable even from the commercial and industrial point of view than a community below par in consequence of bad conditions—treated if you like not as a human proposition, but as a business proposition" ("Mr. Lloyd George on his Task," *The Times*, November 25, 1918, 13).

14 The Whitley Councils (see chapter 1) well embodied their reconstructionist industrial principles. They provided the institutional grounds for a "better spirit" (HMSO 1919b, 152) whereby class antagonism could be replaced with "the cooperation of all classes" in "the interest of the community" (Ministry of Labour 1917, 9). The 1918 British legislation that prohibited wage cuts for a period of six months after the armistice in order to avoid the worst consequences of war demobilization and the resulting surge in labor supply was an important component of the reconstructionist industrial scheme.

15 For a good survey of the struggle of Italian workers' organizations to achieve global welfare coverage before and during the war, see Rigola (1918) and Cherubini (1977, 236–54).

16 Both countries provided for war pensions and family allowances to soldiers. Furthermore, as already mentioned in chapter 1, the need to maintain a high level of productivity in the labor force informed a complex apparatus of factory welfare services. The state established industrial canteens, health centers, and drinking facilities as well as better sanitary and washing facilities (HMSO 1919b, 285–98). In this way the state shouldered much of the cost of the social reproduction of the labor force. On the

war welfare measures in Italy see Procacci (2013) and Pavan (2016). On war welfare measures in Britain see Pedersen (1993, 79–133) and Pedersen (1990). Pedersen stresses the gendered logic behind the British welfare system and its long-term impact on British postwar society.

17 Once the ministry was born under the direction of Leonida Bissolati, it "controlled *all* forms of assistance benefiting *all* those affected by the war" (Ministero per l'Assistenza Militare 1919, 28), thus adopting a framework that was labeled "proto-universalist" (Pavan 2019, 840). It is interesting to note the progressive spirit of this form of welfare, whereby cohabiting partners had the same rights as a spouse. This was the case also for the free state-sponsored life insurance designated for soldiers that allowed partners, illegitimate children, or even "old friends" to be named as beneficiaries in the event of the bearer's death. In the words of Nitti, of the Ministry of Treasury: "Every soldier in the trenches, on the front lines, or in any part of our land is entitled to write in the name of someone dear to him, be it a brother, wife or lover, mother or illegitimate child, or an old friend, or a far-off person who in some way is close to his heart, and he may do as he likes with the sum that the state puts at the disposal of its combatants" (in Pavan 2019, 843).

18 As Tommaso Tittoni, president of the Italian Senate at the time, put it, "In the grave riots that have exploded in various parts of Italy, I was impressed by the fact that, to muster sufficient forces to face the storm, it was necessary to send for Carabinieri and police from other districts that thus remained unprotected. I have often wondered what the government would have done if revolt had broken out simultaneously throughout the peninsula" (Tittoni 1930, 278–79—in Tasca 1965, 27).

19 The Chambers of Labour, founded at the end of the nineteenth century, were a territorially based labor organization that regrouped the members of the various unions.

20 Nitti, in Pavan (2019, 846). Originally: "nelle trincee e sui campi" "pieno diritto di cittadinanza." In Atti Parlamentari, Camera dei Deputati, XXIV Legislatura, speech of October 20, 1917, 14792.

21 Letter written to Nitti by Vittorio Cottafavi, MP (senator from 1924), exponent of the Liberal Constitutional group and a member of the rich property-owning class of the *modenese* region (ACS, Presidenza del Consiglio dei Ministri, 1920, fol. 6.2.690, in Pavan 2016, 186).

22 The functions of the Ministry of Reconstruction, which began operations in August 1917, were defined as follows: "To consider and advise upon the problems which: may arise out of the present war and may have to be dealt with upon its termination, and for the purposes aforesaid to institute and conduct such enquiries, prepare such schemes, and make such recommendations as he thinks fit" (HMSO 1918a, 202). The department was divided

into branches dealing respectively with commerce and production (including the supply of materials); with finance, shipping, and common services; with labor and industrial organization; with rural development; with the machinery of government, central and local, health, and education; and with housing and internal transport.

23 Major L-Col David Morgan, HC Deb 7 April 1919, vol. 114, cc 1756. Hereafter parliamentary debates will be cited by speaker's name, House (HC or HL), date, and location (e.g., cc 1756).

24 "There are in this country at the present time at least 70,000 houses quite unfit for habitation, and a further 300,000 which are seriously defective. . . . There are about 3,000,000 people living in overcrowded conditions, i.e., more than two in a room, and in the area covered by the London County Council, their return showed 758,000 living under these dreadful conditions" (Clarke 1920, 234). Bad housing was understood as the primary cause of infant mortality, which was hitting the working classes almost four times more than the middle and upper classes (John Davison, HC Deb 7 April 1919, vol. 114, cc 1746). Infectious diseases like tuberculosis were endemic and their spread unstoppable when "In the vast majority of cases not only were one or more persons sleeping in the same bed, but there were other beds in the same room, in some instances four other beds in the same room" (Dr. Addison, HC Deb 7 April 1919, vol. 114, cc 1715).

25 The Housing Act granted local authorities the power to acquire land and houses, and was intended to overcome private enterprise, deemed "dead as far as building houses for the working classes is concerned" (Ernest Pretyman, HC Deb 7 April 1919, vol. 114, cc 1772), in favor of "bringing the action of the State and of the public utility societies to bear." Public utility societies included "the co-operative building societies and the other societies which work for a strictly limited dividend and not for speculative building" (Captain William Ormsby-Gore, HC Deb 7 April 1919, vol. 114, cc 1800). As we will explore in detail in the next chapter, under these reforms the building guilds were given the chance to prosper. This first Act was soon bolstered by the Housing (additional powers) Act of December 1919 (known as the Addison Act from the name of the minister of health), which extended the power of the newly created minister of health to aid local authorities to undertake housing enterprises.

26 The Women's Cooperative Guild gained a large representation in the local maternity committees that flourished after the Maternal and Infant Welfare Act of 1918 discussed in chapter 1.

27 That same year, the cabinet agreed to a substantial increase in old-age pensions in order to cope with the deplorable problem of poverty among the elderly. The new measures endorsed the recommendations of the 1919 Ryland Adkins Committee, such as a doubling of the pension to 10s. per

week. Various conditions and qualifications were relaxed in favor of applicants. Income limits were increased, with the effect that around 220,000 additional pensioners came onto the books (see Macnicol 2002).

28 See Peden (1985, 51) and HMSO (1919a, 296).

29 Ministry of Reconstruction 1919b, Cmd. 321, 5. This public education drive was a true revolution. In 1917 Viscount Richard Haldane attested: "when I was in charge of the War office, I found that a surprising number of recruits could not read or write" (Haldane, "National Education," p. 85, included in Dawson 1917).

30 The declarations of the committee read: "Adult education will clearly thrive only under conditions which allow of the fullest self-determination on the part of the students as regards the studies to be pursued, the choice of the teacher, and the organisation of the class. Our proposals, therefore, are framed with a view to ensuring the maximum liberty to students and establishing the right relation between the students, the teachers and the bodies providing education—a relation which should be one of co-operation" (Ministry of Reconstruction 1919, Cmd. 321, 168). The same report remarked that "study and discussion grow more easily among groups of students who have considerable freedom in organising education for themselves and who are assisted to experiment on their own lines rather than bound to follow any prescribed system" (ibid., 117). Great stress was put on denying any "censorship" or interference "with the freedom of the students to work out the type of education which suits them best" (ibid., 118). Most importantly, "The State should not . . . refuse financial support to institutions, colleges and classes, merely on the ground that they have a particular 'atmosphere' or appeal specially to students of this type or that. All that it ought to ask is that they be concerned with serious study" (ibid., 118).

31 Regarding the popular education movement, the committee reports: "The movement, in short, is neither esoteric nor superficial, neither the foible of a few select individuals nor the evanescent fashion of a moment. It is a natural development which has its roots deep in popular needs, and which falls into its place as a logical stage in the development of education in Great Britain" (Ministry of Reconstruction 1919, Cmd. 321, 36).

32 The explicit auspice was: "that their work, now necessarily sporadic and disconnected, may be developed and find its proper place in the national educational system" (Ministry of Reconstruction 1919, Cmd. 321, 5).

33 Ministry and Transport Act of 1919, https://www.legislation.gov.uk/ukpga/Geo5/9-10/50/contents/enacted.

34 The underlying principle of the bill was to bring under one minister and one department the functions connected with health "which are at the present moment scattered among at least half-a-dozen Departments in

Whitehall" (Major Astor, HC Deb 26 February 1919, vol. 112, cc 1910). The parliamentary secretary to the local government board, Major Waldorf Astor, used an evocative military metaphor: "to use in the great fight against the disease the same principle which has enabled us to defeat the other enemy on the Continent. That is to say, we want unified command, one staff to look ahead, plan a campaign, and then carry it out" (ibid., Major Astor, cc 1909).

35 In the words of another MP: "This Bill is an urgent public necessity and as it is conceived in a bold, comprehensive spirit, I feel sure that when its principles are carried into effect it will have the result, not only of improving the general health of the community, but of adding very considerably to the comfort of the people themselves" (ibid., L. Colonel Nathan Raw, cc 1896).

36 The Socialist Party conference of October 1916 in Rome drew up a plan for universal and mandatory social insurance for illness, invalidity, and old age. Less than a year later the national council of CGdL unanimously pushed for an extension of insurance to safeguard maternity and protect against work accidents and poverty (Cherubini 1977, 225ff.).

37 The system was funded by joint contributions from workers, employers, and the state, with considerable aid from municipalities and local charities, which increased their function and financial autonomy.

38 Cermenati was adamant that "The worker's right to social assistance, in all cases, is guaranteed. His old age is safe from penury and indigence, he can be certain to receive proper support in times of involuntary unemployment, and soon enough, there will also be provisions for what most concerns the working classes, that is, aid in the event of illness" (Minutes of the Consiglio Superiore della Previdenza e delle Assicurazioni, meeting of December 2, 1919, in INPS, 1962, 352, quoted from Pavan 2019, 851).

39 Reforms of mandatory insurance against accidents and insurance for old age and invalidity (Regent's Law Decree 670, April 29, 1917, in GU 184 [August 4, 1917], 3497) had already been crafted during the war, and found more far-reaching explication during the postwar years.

40 Regent's Law Decree 603, April 21, 1919, in GU 104 (May 1, 1919). Local administrators had an extensive role in exercising these welfare objectives (see De Stefani 1926a, 388–91).

41 For details see Bartocci (1999, 226). See also Cherubini (1977, 194–211). Cherubini's book is particularly illuminating as regards the class struggle that unfolded around these reforms.

42 Pavan (2019, 848); ACS, Presidenza del Consiglio dei Ministri 1918, fol. 5.1.607.

43 Note that it did not include domestic workers, civil servants, or those who worked from home. The insurance was based on subsidies from workers

and employers with a substantial annual state contribution. For details see "Decree no. 2214 of October 19, 1919" in Pavan (2019, 859–60) and Cherubini (1977, 218–24).

44 In 1920 the Unemployment Insurance Act extended the 1911 scheme to cover most industrial workers. It expanded coverage "from 2-3 million in 1912 to over 12 million" people (Peden 2000, 168). After the summer of 1920, when unemployment in Britain tripled in just a few months, reconstructionists pushed for many proto-Keynesian proposals of loan-financed public works to keep people in jobs; in their means and objectives these projects deeply contrasted with prewar budgetary orthodoxy (see chapters 3 and 6).

45 The ministry was in charge of i) the supervision on the part of the Cassa Nazionale of insurance against work accidents, ii) the application of the law on mandatory insurance against disability and old age, and iii) collection of labor statistics and coordination of the office of employment exchanges [l'Ufficio nazionale per il collocamento e la disoccupazione] established in October 1919. The first minister of labour, Mario Abbiate, was a progressive Liberal, known for his devotion to the problems of labor and his important enquiries on workers' labor conditions. Under his purview the protection of workers' welfare became a legal prerogative.

46 In Marucco (2008, 181), originally in ACS, Atti Parlamentari [AP] Camera, Leg. XXI, 1a sessione, Discussioni, 2a tornata del 15 maggio 1901, 3867.

47 Marucco (2008, 183), originally in ACS, AP Camera, Leg. XXIII, 1a sessione, Discussioni, tornata del 12 maggio 1910, 6789.

48 On Nitti's productivist reformism see Barbagallo (1984, 119–26).

49 This function of social control of welfare is especially important in times of economic downturn when the labor force is separated from its primary system of control (that is, the labor market). The idea is that welfare inhibits workers' inclination to break with the system as they still have something to lose.

50 The radicalization of the moment in Italy was also expressed in the radical behavior of the CGdL (traditionally reformist), which, on July 15, 1920, was signing a pact in Moscow "for the triumphs of social revolution and of the universal republic of the Soviet" (see Tasca 1965, 124).

51 Benito Mussolini, "The Crisis of Their Authority" [la crisi della loro autorità], Il popolo d'Italia, July 29, 1920.

52 In Marucco (2008, 186), originally in ACS, AP Camera, Leg. XXVI, sess. 1921, Documenti, n. 2, Relazione della commissione parlamentare d'inchiesta sull'ordinamento delle amministrazioni di Stato e sulle condizioni del personale, presentata il 18 gennaio 1921, 260.

53 The Ministry of National Economy—already responsible for a wide array of functions—also took on the main responsibilities of the abolished Ministry of Labour. This was a clear regression to the prewar situation where

the problems of labor were in the hands of the Ministry of Agriculture, Industry, and Commerce. For the history of the Ministry of Labour see Marucco (2008).

Chapter Three

1   Cole had used very similar words: "[A]fter the fall of the Habsburgs, the Hohenzollerns and the Romanoffs, after the coming of Soviet Russia, and for a time, of Soviet Hungary, who, whatever his attitude towards these things, will dare to affirm that revolutionary social changes are impossible in his own country? Who will hold an untarnished faith in the permanence and inviolability of the old order?" (Cole 1920a, 9) or, "the control of Capitalism over Labour is breaking down" (ibid., 20).

2   In Britain, a proportion of women over thirty years of age was also enfranchised. More specifically, women over thirty who either occupied property of no less than five pounds yearly value or were married to a man similarly entitled. Section IV of the Act read: "A woman shall be entitled to be registered as a parliamentary elector for a constituency (other than a university constituency) if she—(a) has attained the age of thirty years; and (b) is not subject to any legal incapacity; and (c) is entitled to be registered as a local government elector in respect of the occupation in that constituency of land or premises (not being a dwelling-house) of a yearly value of not less than five pounds or of a dwelling-house, or is the wife of a husband entitled to be so registered" (Terry 1918, 14). On the subject see Terry (1918) and McKibbin (1990, 66–101).

3   Historians debate about the nature of the socialist ideology of the Labour Party, expressed in the famous clause IV of the 1918 constitution printed in *Labour and the New Social Order*. The clause committed the party "to secure to the workers by hand and by brain the full fruits of their industry and the most equitable distribution thereof that may be possible, upon the basis of the common ownership of the means of production and the best obtainable system of popular administration and control of each industry and service." Most scholars tend to agree with Cole (1958) and Miliband (1961), who understand the constitution as a Fabian blueprint that was general enough to attract union consensus. While it did not propose to abolish private property *in toto*, it *did* call for the nationalization of land and much of the strategic industries together with radical social measures. Thus "even though the implementation of the Labour's programme would not have ushered in a socialist society, it would have made a vast difference to the character and texture of the old one" (Miliband 1961, 62). McKibbin (1974) brings this pragmatic reading of clause IV further, arguing that rather than an ideological conversion it was a matter of sensitivity to the structural

changes brought about by World War I. In this sense the socialist objective was primarily a response to the fear of bolshevism and the need for a powerful parliamentary and socialist alternative. It was also a measure that allowed Labour to establish a break with the Liberal Party and to attract the professional middle classes who had matured socialist tendencies (see McKibbin 1974, 95–97).

4   The Italian Popular Party (or the People's Party) was founded on January 18, 1919, by Luigi Sturzo, a Sicilian Catholic priest. It was inspired by Catholic ideas of social justice and pushed for redistributive social reforms and women's suffrage. On its origins and agenda see Invernizzi-Accetti (2019). Its activities died out in 1926 once the Fascist dictatorship took full control.

5   The socialist party won the administrative elections with the following manifesto: "The *comuni* cannot be conquered but with the objective of seizing them and paralyzing all powers, all mechanisms of the bourgeois state with the objective of accelerating the proletarian revolution and the establishment of a dictatorship of the proletariat" (in Tasca 1965, 204).

6   At the Socialist Party congress of Bologna in October 1919, the "maximalist" current affirmed its victory over the reformist current and joined the Third International. The radicalization of the Italian Socialist Party had begun after the defeat of Caporetto in fall 1917 (when the "Intransigent Revolutionary fraction" of the Socialist Party was born). The revolutionary line gained the majority in the official meetings in Florence in November 1917 and dominated the party for many years afterward. In 1919 the reformist agenda was defeated in favor of the most maximalist program in all main local party elections [*congresso provinciale*]. Even in Milan, homeland of the reformist tradition, the intransigent faction won the March 1919 elections for the directive council hands down. The sprouting of many revolutionary local newspapers mirrors this radicalizing trend. In Naples, Amadeo Bordiga, the future communist leader, founded the weekly magazine *Soviet*. In Florence, *La Difesa*, the weekly of the Socialist federations, was a champion of most extreme lines.

7   The leaders of CGdL were reformist members of the socialist party. The pact of allegiance of 1918 reaffirmed the decisions of 1907 (CGdL was founded in 1906), which assigned leadership of "political" strikes to the "party" and "economic" strikes to the CGdL. Ludovico D'Aragona, the leader, laid out the plan in January 1919: it included "highly progressive taxation," "cultivation of land and execution of public works by workers united in cooperatives in the interest of collectivity," and the "right of workers to control factory management" and "the whole fruit of labor to whom produces it." The plan also included "global insurance against unemployment, work accidents, illness, and old age" (in Nenni 1946, 13). Over half of the CGdL members were industrial workers; more specifically, they were distributed in the following way: 200,000 construction workers, 160,000

metal workers, 155,000 textile workers, 68,000 in the gas industry, 60,000 state employees, 50,000 in chemicals, 50,000 private employees, 30,000 woodworkers, 25,000 railway workers, 23,000 leather workers, 22,400 workers in the building crafts, 22,000 tramway men, and 21,000 paper workers. CGdL also organized 890,000 agricultural workers.

8   In Britain, for example, among women workers, the growth of unionization was on the order of 130 percent between 1914 and 1920 (Burgess 1980, 165). In the metallurgical sector the major craft unions grew by 76 percent between 1914 and 1918. On the other hand, the two largest trade unions of less skilled workers organizing in the industry—the National Union of General Workers (NUGW) and the Workers' Union (WU)—grew by 216 percent and 137 percent respectively (Hinton 1973, 49–50).

9   The source of these figures is Dataset 1: Labour disputes annual estimates, UK, 1891 to 2018; Office of National Statistics (ONS).

10 *Memorandum on The Causes of and Remedies for Labour Unrest, Presented by the Trade Union Representatives on the Joint Committee Appointed at the National Industrial Conference* (held at the Central Hall, London, February 27, 1919). Reprinted in Cole (1920a, 247).

11 On the police strikes, see Critchley (1978) and Morgan (1987). Regarding the unrest in the armed forces, the general revolutionary scare, and the reaction of Lloyd George to labor unrest, see Wrigley (1991).

12 Coercive powers of the state were also mobilized in full during the 40-hour strike on Clydeside in January–February 1919. On the government's military response against British workers see, among others, Morgan (1987).

13 The number of working days lost in a year is calculated by multiplying the total number of working days lost due to strikes by the number of workers involved. See Ministero dell'Economia Nazionale (1924), Supplemento 38, "Bollettino del lavoro e della previdenza Sociali," page 15 for industrial strike data and page 278 for agricultural strike data.

14 Note that this number does not include the 450,000 occupying workers and the 6 million days of lost work during the factory occupation between August 30 and September 20, 1920—an episode we will explore at length in chapter 4. Zamagni documents that in Italy the level of mobilization during the red biennium was "really exceptional" with respect to other countries: industrial disputes involved 30 percent of the labor force, while the percentage in other countries was around 20 percent (see Zamagni 1991, 151–52). For strike data see chapter 9 of this book, figures 9.5 and 9.6.

15 See Ministero dell'Economia Nazionale (1924, 177), Supplemento 38, "Bollettino del lavoro e della previdenza Sociali." Metalworkers accounted for the lion's share: in March 1920, the metalworkers had 70,270 strikers with 1,448,209 days lost (ibid., 176). During the whole of 1919, almost 400,000 striking metalworkers contributed to a loss of over 11 million working days (ibid., 154). However, the workers who carried out these strikes came from

all social categories, even those traditionally distant from direct action, including priests, schoolteachers, and judges.

16 In 1919 the textile industry had the highest percentage of strikes of all, even more than metalworkers (18 percent, compared to 12 percent for metalworker strikes). Gender distribution in the other industrial strikes in 1919 were as follows: in chocolate factories, 386 men to 1,106 women; shoe factories, 38 men to 9018 women; leather factories, 8 men to 330 women; button factories, 1,189 men to 2,446 women; tobacco, 83 men to 263 women. Source: Ministero dell'Economia Nazionale (1924, 156–82).

17 Data from that time show that in 1919 and 1920 there was a surge of "wins" over losses for the workers. See Ministero dell' Economia Nazionale (1924, 28–29).

18 Real daily wages increased by 53 percent (see chapter 9, figure 9.7).

19 See Scholliers and Zamagni (1995, 258, Table A.23—Average Weekly Earnings, Manual Workers, 1780–1960 [£s], Assuming Full Employment).

20 The struggle was widely popular throughout the British labor movement, which launched a strong campaign for "hands off Russia." Starting in January 1919 and covering the issue daily, Labour tried to convince the government to withdraw troops from Russia. At the Labour Party conference of June 1919, the speech of the chairman invoked the official stance of the Labour Party: "We must resist military operations in Russia"—(A Voice: "And Ireland")—"and the perpetuation of conscription at home. There can be no peace so long as we continue to indulge in military adventures in Russia. Russia must be left free to work out its own political salvation, and it would be far better to send to the people the means to stabilise and consolidate the democratic growth of the country than the means for one section to destroy another or perhaps also the Revolution itself" (Report of the Nineteenth Annual Conference of the Labour Party, June 25, 1919, 113, at https://babel.hathitrust.org/cgi/pt?id=msu.31293500351923&view=1up&seq=14&skin=2021&q1=Russia%20must%20be%20left%20free%20to%20work). The campaign was ultimately successful. On July 30, 1919, Churchill announced that "our troops will be withdrawn from Russia before the winter" (*Daily Herald*, July 30, 1919, 1). For details, see Macfarlane (1967, 126–52).

21 The memo on the causes and remedies of industrial unrest was drafted by the trade union representatives on the occasion of the National Industrial Conference of February 1919 (reprinted in Cole 1920a, 271). This enquiry echoed in many respects the 1917 governmental enquiry.

22 In another passage Hodges gives a good idea of the revolutionary situation: "We are confronted with an increasingly educated working class; a class which more and more rejects the imposition of external will and authority over it; a class which yearns for the status of responsible manhood in industry and which rebels against any cramping institution which thwarts its aspirations for freedom. The purpose of life is becoming more generally

manifest as the enjoyment of freedom. For generations it has been believed by the working classes that the only institution which stood in the way of freedom was political in character. The freedom of political democracy is a magnificent accomplishment, but it is now realized that the slavery of industry is harsher than the slavery of the unfranchised serf. Hence the impulse of industrial freedom. The struggle to shake off the imposition of external wills because the instruments of production are owned by the possessors of such wills is the most remarkable phenomenon of the age" (Hodges 1920, ix–x).

23 The peasants were also granted recognition in the form of an elected representative—a fiduciario—to oversee the correct application of the new labor agreement and to form a council of fiduciari.

24 These demands for economic democracy were springing from diverse industries: miners, railway men, construction workers, engineers, and shipbuilders, as well as workers in the post office and the civil service. For example, the NUR (National Union of Railwaymen) put forward an articulate request for nationalization and joint control of the railway system, while the union of post office workers drafted a very comprehensive scheme for transforming the postal service into a self-governing service on Guild socialist lines. For discussion of the Railway workers in connection with decontrol, see Armitage (1969, 46–100).

25 The other half of the twelve-member commission consisted of three coal owners (Evan Williams, R. W. Cooper, and J. T. Forgie) and three representatives of industry (Arthur Balfour, Sir Eric Duckham, and Sir Tony Royden). The first stage of the hearings concerning working wages and hours occurred March 3–20, 1919; the second, regarding the broader issue of nationalization, was concluded in June 1919.

26 It is interesting to note that this sentiment of condemnation of private capital was also shared by the commissioners representing capital, such as Sir Arthur Duckham, president of the Institution of Civil Engineers. Duckham submitted his official final report in June, the first two points of which read: "I. The private ownership of minerals has not been and is not in the best interests of the community, II. The providing of the country's mineral resources should not be left to private enterprise" (Great Britain, Royal Commission on the Coal Industry 1919b, xxii).

27 Between the first and the second stage, 163 witnesses were heard, comprising a plurality of voices: miners' wives, economics professors, civil servants, engineers, secretaries of local miners' federations, representatives of industry, colliery owners, etcetera (see Great Britain, Royal Industry on Coal Industry Commission 1919a, xxiv; 1919b, xxix–xxxii).

28 William Straker, the secretary of the Northumberland Miners, commented in his precis that "During the first stage of this Commission the old ways of mine management and control were shown to be so beaten into mud, that

the Report, known as the 'Sankey Report,' and accepted by the government, declared that 'the present system stands condemned'" (Great Britain, Royal Commission on Coal Industry 1919b, 944).

29 Meticulously gathered firsthand evidence highlighted class division and social injustice: the miners' disgraceful working and living conditions, which were "in the majority of cases, nothing less than scandalous" (Great Britain, Royal Commission on Coal Industry 1919a, xiv). The industry's deadly work accidents and decreases in real wages since 1914 were put side by side with owners' excessive profits, which had quadrupled during the war. "The life standards, the homes, and the colliery conditions of men who give this indispensable toil, afford the most crushing case against the continuance of the present system" (Hodges 1920, v).

30 For example, in his deposition, Mr. William Straker denounced the antagonistic and individualistic vision of society as an outdated fixation that must be overcome: "Those against nationalisation evidently hold that competition is the very soul of progress. Life, to them, is an antagonism, each individual struggling for supremacy; and out of this struggle the fittest will survive. This means that out of selfishness, scientifically applied, will come the greatest good to the greatest number. This seems to me to be a primitive idea belonging rather to an early form of society than to the 20th century civilization. On the other hand, those in favour of nationalisation hold just as strongly that life is not necessarily an antagonism, and that mutual aid, applied scientifically, must give the best results. This is a conception which mankind arrives at after getting away a considerable distance from the primitive. Selfishness is the root cause of all wrongdoing; therefore any system which is an outgrowth of selfishness must be wrong. That which is morally wrong cannot be economically right. Systems based upon this great truth ought to be encouraged, as such must produce a better citizen. Systems based on the desire for selfish gain ought to be discouraged, as making for all that is worst in individual and corporate life. That which draws men together in co-operative activities makes for progress and human welfare; that which keeps men in a hostile attitude one to another wars against welfare and progress" (Arnot 1919, 29).

31 Divided ownership, it was pointed out, meant huge loss of coal used for barriers, wasteful shaft development and unnecessary underground haulage, undue expense in draining and even the impossibility of a systematic provision for drainage, inefficiency in marketing, extra expense in railway wagonage, and so on. For an analysis of the technical and specific discussion about coal see Sankey's June 20 final report on the second stage of the inquiry, in Great Britain, Royal Commission on Coal Industry (1919b, iv–xiii, v–viii) or Chiozza Money's evidence in Arnot (1919, 25–27).

32 The call for radical economic democracy was already present in the 1912 syndicalist-inspired program *The Miners' Next Steps*. The unrest in the pits

of 1919 also produced the pamphlet *Industrial Democracy for the Miners: A Plan for the Democratic Control of the Mining*, published by the industrial committee of the South Wales Socialist Society, which offered a detailed scheme for the implementation of workers' control. For details on these rank-and-file movements see Ives (2016, 58–75).

33 Commissioners gave lengthy technical reports on the workings and economic benefits of nationalization: the unification in production, in buying and selling, in transport, and in distribution would result in enormous economies and far greater efficiency in the coal mines, securing "a cheap and adequate supply of coal" (Great Britain, Royal Commission on Coal Industry 1919b, vi). In his report, Sidney Webb summarizes the rationale behind the experts' view: "Nationalisation is called for (1) as the only means of adequately improving the position of the miners with regard to housing, accidents and special disease and infantile mortality; (2) as the only means of dealing economically and efficiently with the nation's coal resources; and (3) as the only means of ensuring that the coal is supplied to the consumers with regularity and at the lowest cost" (Great Britain, Royal Commission on Coal Industry 1919b, 478). The potential merits of nationalization were considered even by orthodox economists such as A. C. Pigou. In his deposition to the commission in April 1919, Pigou stated that "under full nationalization there are *possibilities* of results better than any other plan can offer" (Great Britain, Royal Commission on Coal Industry 1919b, 417). Nationalization was thus understood as a guarantee of efficiency and the common interest; it was going to benefit the nation, not just the miners. As John R. Clynes, Labour MP, put it: "National ownership is advocated not for a trade, or a class, or a sectional benefit. Gain for the community inspires the demand made for immediate changes in both the terms of service, and the conditions of ownership of this great property" (Hodges 1920, iv).

34 Drafted by William Straker and officially submitted to the commission on May 23, 1919.

35 Each report gave a different view of the managerial weight of the workers in the production process. Sankey's scheme put the minister of mines (responsible to Parliament) in supreme control, with the obligation to consult the National Mining Council on "all questions connected with the operation and management of industry." On the other hand, the miners' scheme understood the National Mining Council itself—the minister of mines being a member—as the supreme authority. In this scheme, half of the Mining Council was composed of members elected in Parliament (including technicians, experts, and managerial workers), and the other half was elected by the workers. The Council would engage in all activities of production, distribution, and export of coal (*Miners Bill*, reprinted in Arnot 1919, 37–47). In July 1919, even with some reservations regarding the

supposedly limited degree of workers' representation, miners' representatives decided to endorse Sankey's proposals to send a strong message to the government.

36 "Subject to a general superintendence, and the necessity of making the industry self-supporting, they [mining councils] may pursue their own policies with a free hand and a free purse. Their finances are to be kept 'entirely separate' from one another" (Henderson 1919, 266). Importantly for our story, financial independence from the Treasury was envisaged: "The Treasury shall not be entitled to interfere with or to have any control over the appropriation of moneys derived from the industry. The said moneys shall be kept entirely separate and apart from other national moneys, until the profit accruing from the industry is periodically ascertained and paid into the Exchequer" (Report by The Honourable Mr. Justice Sankey, G. B. E. [Chairman]. In Great Britain, Royal Commission on Coal Industry 1919b, xi).

37 *The Times*, for example, published the reports in full. See "State Coal," *The Times*, June 23, 1919, 19–20.

38 The connection between monetary austerity and unemployment was clear in the minds of Treasury officials such as Ralph Hawtrey, who on multiple occasions affirmed that "it was true that unemployment was due to a contraction of the supply of the means of payment." For details, see chapter 6.

39 Viglongo (1920, 75–76).

40 Ibid., 76.

41 Workers were paid for their labor. The surplus was divided between the reserve fund and payment for the different shares of workers' capital as well as for any extra labor. These cooperatives were by law "open," that is, they had "to admit members limitlessly keeping in mind the development capacity of the cooperative." This meant acceptance until there was labor for its members (see Buffetti 1921, 85–86).

42 See Ministero per il Lavoro e la Previdenza Sociale (1923, 218–31).

43 The president was in charge for two years; councillors served for two years, half of the four (or more) of them being up for election each year. See the template of the co-op statute in Buffetti (1921, 43–54).

44 Like the Sankey proposals for miners' joint control, the guilds too were organized nationally in a three-tier structure. The guild committee functioned as the board of directors. The district or local guild committee was the core of the guild network. It comprised at most two representatives of each craft so as to assure an equal voice in the activities and transactions of the guild. These representatives served for one year, were subject to recall, and were eligible for reelection. In July 1921, the national conference of district guild committees adopted a constitution for a national building guild, envisaging, in addition to the local level, also regional councils and a national board.

45　During the period from October 1920 to March 1922, the London guilds "lost an average of 4.7 days per man through sickness, about half the number lost each year by uninsured workers in the United States, about half the number lost in 1915 by insured workers in Germany, and about half the number lost in 1913 by insured workers in Austria" (Joslyn 1922, 111).

46　At the same time, given the uncertainty of the business, the Cooperative Wholesale Society (the second largest dealer in building materials after the government, which provided initial capital and material) withdrew its finances, leaving guilds without capital, which was ever more necessary if they were now to build not for public but for private customers while competing with private producers.

47　For details on the Geddes Axe see chapter 6.

Chapter Four

1　"Two Revolutions" [*Due Rivoluzioni*], *L'Ordine nuovo* 2, no. 8 (July 3, 1920): 57.

2　Ibid. Gramsci envisaged the factory council as a first nucleus of a classless society: "The factory council must be formed according to the principle of organization by industry; it must represent for the working class the model of communist society, at which it will arrive through the dictatorship of the proletariat; in this society there will not exist divisions of class, all social relations will be governed according to the technical requirements of production and of the corresponding organization, and will not be subordinated to an organized state power" (Gramsci 1921).

3　J. T. Murphy was considered the brain of the British Shop Steward Movement. He was active in the Sheffield wing of the Shop Steward Movement, which emerged in engineering factories during the war. In 1916 Murphy joined the Socialist Labour Party and was one of the founding members of the British Communist Party in 1920. For his memoir, see Murphy (1941).

4　The movement remained faithful to its radical position, so that in January 1920 the national conference of shop stewards took a firm stance, officially declaring full control of industry to be its ultimate objective, while repudiating joint control or any other bourgeois scheme: "This Conference, while urging the rank and file of the working class movement to support the miners or any other body of workers in their fight against the employing class, declares that the nationalization of any industry which leaves the capitalist class in power will not emancipate the workers and calls on the organized labour movement to strive for the confiscation of the mines, railways and other means of production and distribution in the interest of labour. Therefore the conference declares that all schemes of joint control, whether embodied in the Sankey Report, Whitley Report or any other capitalist scheme, are detrimental to the best interests of the working class and urges the workers to reorganize themselves for the purpose of independently taking control of the industrial and social machinery in the interests of the exploited masses" (*The Worker*, February 14, 1920, reprinted in Pribićević 1959, 140).

5 This episode has been extensively documented by contemporaries from Giolitti to Albertini, from Salvemini to Einaudi, Buozzi to Nenni, Gramsci, Togliatti, Tasca, and Bordiga, and has been debated by historians.

6 US Department of Labor (1917, 9).

7 Prior to 1914 the elected shop stewards were few, had limited representative tasks and belonged mainly to skilled organizations. With the war a new type of steward, unofficial (no longer appointed by trade unions, but chosen by groups of workers in each establishment) and with considerably wider powers, took the leadership in every industrial dispute within the trade.

8 US Department of Labor (1917, 9).

9 Scholars have produced a few (yet detailed) studies expanding on the strike actions and militancy of the various shop steward groups, especially on the Clydeside, exploring their successes, their repression, and their political weaknesses (see Gleason 1920, Kendall 1969, Hinton 1973, Pribićević 1959).

10 Antonio Gramsci (1891–1937) is to this day among the most influential thinkers of the twentieth century. Born in Sardinia, he studied philosophy at the University of Turin. He was an active and militant intellectual until his imprisonment in 1926 by the Fascist regime. He spent the rest of his life in prison, and died at the age of 46. The literature on Gramsci is extensive. We only mention a few. On the evolving relation between Gramsci and the Liberal tradition see Michelini (2011b). For a multifaceted reconstruction of Gramsci's biography and thought see Giasi (2007), which contains the contributions of the conference of the Fondazione Istituto Gramsci on the occasion of the author's seventieth death anniversary. On a recent reconsideration of Gramsci's philosophy in the *Prison Notebooks* see Thomas (2009).

11 To give a sense of the city's red spirit, one can note that the first issues of the local edition of the Socialist *L'Avanti* in December 1918 started out with 16,000 copies; in just a few months the local circulation had reached 50,000 (see Spriano 1971, 16–17).

12 Gramsci recalls the incident: "The insurrection exploded on 23 August 1917. For five days the workers fought in the streets of the city. The insurgents, armed with rifles, grenades and machine guns, managed to occupy some quarters of the city and attempted three or four times to possess the city centre where the government institutions and military commands were located. . . . The people erected barricades, dug trenches, surrounded some

districts with barbed wire and electric current and held back for five days all the attacks of the troops and the police. More than 500 workers fell, more than 2000 were seriously injured. After the defeat the best elements were arrested and deported and the proletarian movement lost revolutionary intensity. But the communist feelings of the Turin proletariat were not extinguished" (Gramsci 1921). For a detailed description of the political actions of those months, including all the rallies and meetings, see the archival documents of the *magistratura militare* on the judiciary investigation reprinted in Zucaro (1960).

13 The internal commissions were grievance committees elected by union members within the factory to handle everyday problems of discipline, arbitration, etcetera. The project of the factory councils was to vastly extend the internal commission's competence and its level of inclusivity, elect factory commissars from among the workers who would then elect a factory committee as the executive body of the factory council. In Gramsci's words: "Today, these commissions have the task of curbing the power the capitalist exerts within the factory, and they perform an arbitration and disciplinary function. In the future, developed and improved, they should be the organs of proletarian power, replacing the capitalist in all his useful managerial and administrative functions" (Gramsci with Palmiro Togliatti, "Workers' Democracy" [Democrazia operaia], *L'Ordine nuovo*, June 21, 1919, I, n. 7, 47). The commissars' duty was representing the workers against the capitalists, and crucially, "studying and pushing the other comrades to study the bourgeois system of production." Indeed, apart from the administrative functions (which had also been proper to the internal commission), the factory council was involved in "intense revolutionary preparation" [*intensa preparazione rivoluzionaria*] and actively framed itself in the general political action, aiming at the dictatorship of the proletariat (Assembly of the factory commmisars of Turin, "The Programme of the Department Commissars" [*Il programma dei commissari di reparto*], *L'Ordine nuovo*, November 8, 1919, I, n. 25, 193).

14 "Discussion on the Factory Councils" [*Discussioni sui Consigli di fabbrica*], *L'Ordine nuovo*, November 22, 1919, I, n. 27, 212, signed: a group of organized workers from Fiat Centro [*firmato: Alcuni operai organizzati della Fiat Centro*].

15 Immediately after the war, Gramsci recounts, "The problems of the revolution, economic and political, formed the object of discussions in all the workers' assemblies" (Gramsci 1921).

16 Ibid.

17 Hamon (1919, I, n. 19, 145).

18 "Work Plan" [*Programma di lavoro*], *L'Ordine nuovo* 1, no. 1 (May 1, 1919): 2.

19 See "Letters from England" [*Lettere dall'Inghilterra*], *L'Ordine nuovo*, September 6, 1919, I, 17, 133; October 11, 1919, I, n. 21, 166; February 7, 1920,

I, n. 36, 287; March 27, 1920, I, n. 42, 338; June 12, 1920, II, 5, 36; and July 17, 1920, II, n. 10, 80.

20 [*lugubre scienza dei fatti economici*] Togliatti 1919a, 71.

21 Gramsci, "Two Revolutions" [*Due Rivoluzioni*], *L'Ordine nuovo* 2, no. 8 (July 3, 1920): 58, reprinted in Gramsci (1994, 171).

22 See for example Mankiw (1997).

23 This principle represented a big shift with respect to the war industrial committees: no longer were the commissars picked by unions, who—as the worker Arturo Jacchia remarked—"took care of picking the members of the committee from the workers who were agreeable to the administration." Instead, "Today it is preferable that [the commissars] belong to socialist organizations" (Jacchia 1919, I, n. 9, 66).

24 For a good critique of intellectualism, see Gramsci against Tasca in Gramsci 1920a, I, n. 12, 95.

25 Gramsci 1920a, I, n. 12, 95. And again, in his *Prison Notebooks* he would remember the journal as follows: "This editorial board was not abstract, did not consist of repeating mechanically scientific or theoretical formulae . . . it applied to real men, formed in specific historical relations, with specific feelings, ways of life, fragments of conceptions of the world . . . this element of 'spontaneity' was not neglected nor despised: it was *educated* and directed" (Gramsci in Spriano 1971, 136).

26 Gramsci 1919a, I, n. 18, 140.

27 "Cultura e Socialismo," *L'Ordine nuovo*, June 28–July 5, 1919, I, n. 8, 55–56.

28 The full "Second Thesis on Feuerbach" reads: "The question whether objective truth can be attributed to human thinking is not a question of theory but is a *practical* question. Man must prove the truth—i.e., the reality and power, the this-sidedness of his thinking in practice. The dispute over the reality and non-reality of thinking that is isolated from *practice* is a purely scholastic question." See Marx and Engels ([1888] 1969, vol. 1, 13–15).

29 The metaphor of the school appears often in *L'Ordine nuovo*. For example, the idea that the factory councils "are a school of life in which the new class that will direct the destiny of humanity is educated and acquires responsible consciousness" ("International Political Life, a Destruction and a Genesis" [*Vita politica internazionale, uno sfacelo ed una genesi*], *L'Ordine nuovo* 1, no. 1 [May 1, 1919]: 7).

30 "The Instrument of Labor" [*Lo strumento di lavoro*], *L'Ordine nuovo* 1, no. 37 (February 14, 1920): 289.

31 Courses ranged from "Anarchy and the Theory of the State," taught by Angelo Tasca, to "Economics and Socialism," taught by Togliatti, to a series on the French Revolution, taught by Terracini. For a detailed description of the school, see "The Program of the School of Socialist Propaganda" [*Il programma della scuola di propaganda*], *L'Ordine nuovo* 1, no. 28 (November 29, 1919): 216.

32 "The Programme of the Department Commissars" [*Il programma dei com-missari di reparto*], *L'Ordine nuovo* 1, no. 25 (November 8, 1919): 194.

33 Zini (1920, I, n. 38, 301–2). The shop stewards were thinking along the same lines. Workers were "realizing that the right to vote for parliament, once in five years, is of little value compared with the right to vote on the way industry should be carried on" (Gallacher and Campbell 1972, 3). Murphy suggested that for this reason economic emancipation held absolute politi-cal priority: "Real democratic practice demands that every member of an organization shall participate actively in the conduct of the business of the society" (Murphy 1917, 8).

34 "The type of proletarian State is not the mendacious [*menzognera*] bour-geois democracy, but the proletarian democracy; not parliamentarism, but the self-government of the people (masse) through representative institutions of their own" (untitled, *L'Ordine nuovo* 2, no. 16 [October 2, 1920]: 124).

35 The revolutionary strategy of the Italian councils put at center stage the connection between the economic and the political. The British movement, which arose from a syndicalist tradition, initially lacked this insight as it underestimated the role of the worker party. After 1920 many of the leaders of the British movement realized the need for a party; many of the people who founded the Communist Party of Britain in 1921 came from this group of leaders (see Hinton 1973). On his end, as early as 1919 Gramsci rebuked any accusation of syndicalism and of "economism." To him, political organization was intrinsic to the organization of the production process through the councils (see Gramsci 1919c, I, n. 25, 191). Moreover, for Gramsci and Togliatti the revolutionary breakthrough could be put into motion at the level of the factory but required a central connection with the political role of the party. The party had to be actively integrated and transformed to be "rooted in the workplace, had to be inserted in the 'connective tissue' of the factory." Only through the tight interconnection with the councils can both the unions and the party be transformed from bureaucratic institutions that are distant from the proletarian masses into institutions that can "involve actively and consciously the great proletarian masses in the revolutionary process . . . a party that lives within the prole-tarian masses that is its clear and definite consciousness and will" (Gramsci 1920b, I, n. 43, 340). Once actively integrated with the new proletarian or-ganization of the councils, the party provided essential organizational lead-ership. Coherently with the Leninist tradition, the *Ordinovisti* understood the party as the vanguard for the seizure of political power, indispensable to defeating the capitalist state.

36 The first general meeting of department commissars put forth some guidelines but refused to formalize a "definitive program," highlighting that

it was to be seen as a "practical experiment"—one that would be "open to continuous and radical innovation" ("The Programme of the Department Commissars" [*Il programma dei commissari di reparto*], *L'Ordine nuovo* 1, no. 25 [November 8, 1919] 193).

37 For example, see Murphy 1917; Gallacher and Paton 1918; Gallacher and Campbell 1972; Dingley 1918, Walsh 1920; Pratt 1917. The central philosophy was that "These committees should not have any governing power, but should exist to render service to the rank and file, by providing means for them to arrive at decisions and to unite their forces" (Murphy 1917, 10).

38 [*Tutti i commissari hanno obbligo di indire frequenti referendum nei loro reparti su questioni sociali e tecniche e tenere frequenti comizi*] ("Programme of the Department Commissars," *L'Ordine nuovo* 1, no. 25 [November 8, 1919]: 194). As for the workers' representatives—the commissars—their very daily experience escaped bureaucratic estrangement, since they lived in immediate contact with the working masses and secured this connection with a concentric set of commissions. Elections ran by closed ballot during the working day, and the final counting of votes occurred immediately and publicly. On the other hand, the "executive committee of the factory council" [*il comitato esecutivo del consiglio di officina*] was elected by the commissars as the "maximum organ of proletarian self-government" [*massimo organismo dell'autogoverno proletario*] that held "executive mandate within the factory and representative mandate in the councils' assemblies." The executive committee of Fiat Centro had its long-term objectives clearly laid out: "We will be able to build a gigantic octopus whose tentacles will infiltrate in all the wrinkles of modern industrial life, embracing and coordinating all the productive and revolutionary activities. We will in this way be able to build a formidable instrument of struggle to direct for the achievement of our ends and for the establishment of proletarian power" ("The Opinion of the Executive Councils on the Workshop Committees" [*il parere del C.E. sui Consigli d'Officina*], *L'Ordine nuovo* 1, no. 42 [March 27, 1920]: 335).

39 "To the Department Commissars of the Fiat Centro and Brevetti Workshop" [*Ai commissari di reparto delle officine Fiat Centro e Brevetti*], *L'Ordine nuovo* 1, no. 18 (September 13, 1919): 140.

40 The National Advisory Council, founded in July 1919, represented the metal industry at the national level and envisaged a national council with the ultimate object of coordinating the movement of all the British workers as one body. In 1921, faithful to the intention of uniting all rank-and-file movements beyond metal workers, the movement did receive a new constitution, changing its name from Worker Control and Shop Steward Movement to National Workers' Committee Movement (NWCM).

41 The socialist party of Turin wrote to invite peasants to participate in the congress of workers' councils of 1920, declaring: "Peasants, we invite you to

participate in the work of the congress of the factory commissars, because you too are oppressed by the heavy capitalist order that the workers want to sweep out" ("For the Congress of the Factory Councils, to the Industrial Workers and Peasants of All Italy" [*Per il Congresso dei Consigli di Fabbrica, Agli operai e contadini di tutta Italia*], *L'Ordine nuovo* 1, no. 42 [March 27, 1920]: 331). According to Gramsci, the proletarian revolution would solve the pernicious "southern question," as the industrial workers would break the chains of "capitalist slavery" and eliminate at once the colonization of the south of Italy by the northern bourgeoisie.

42 Gramsci (1921).

43 Speech of Gino Olivetti to *confindustria*, reprinted in "The Opinion of the Industrialists on the Factory Councils" [*l'opinione degli industriali sui Consigli di Fabbrica*], *L'Ordine nuovo* 2, no. 2 (May 15, 1920): 15.

44 *L'Avanti*, Piedmont edition (May 1, 1920), reprinted in Spriano (1971, 101).

45 The Turin section of the local socialist party, which had been left on its own to confront the offensive of the repressive forces of the state, passed a motion (prepared by Gramsci) for the renovation of the socialist party and the expulsion of the "nonrevolutionary communists." It put at center stage the role of leadership and coordination of a fully revolutionary party, grounded in the factory and understood to be an expression of proletarian vanguard. A couple of months later, at the second congress of the third international, Lenin approved this motion, in both its criticism and its practical proposals, as fully responding to the principles of the third international. For the isolation of *L'Ordine nuovo* and the immobilism of the CGdL and the PSI, see Spriano (1971, 97–98).

46 Obstructionism was initiated in every engineering and metallurgical factory and every naval dockyard. In general, for a well-documented account of the whole episode of the factory occupation, see Spriano 1975.

47 Santhià (1956, 120).

48 "Many working-class families had been without wages since the end of August; their situation was getting desperate. . . . Urgent needs were met by subsidies from the cooperatives, above all popular solidarity, in 'communist kitchens' and a thousand gestures of aid and fraternity" (Spriano 1975, 83).

49 Testimony in Natoli (2017, 194).

50 Ibid.

51 See Rocca 1920, 221–52.

52 Anonymous editorial, "The Symbol and Reality" [Il simbolo e la realtà], *L'Avanti* [Piedmont], September 3, 1920.

53 The representatives in Rome were: D'Aragona, Baldesi, and Colombino for the CGdL; Marchiaro, Raineri, and Missiroli for FIOM; Conti, Crespi, Olivetti, Falck, Ichino, and Pirelli for the confederation of industry.

54 The press used the word "capitulation" to describe the agreement, while the majority of industrialists called it a diktat coming from the govern-

ment and widely criticized their representatives at the conference (see ACS, Ministero degli Interni, direzione generale di ps, affari generali e riservati, D. 13, busta 74, n. 2958, in Spriano 1975, 195).

55 Missiroli 1924, 172, reprinted in Spriano 1975, 104.

56 [*la vittoria dei metallurgici non ha l'eguale in tutta la storia del movimento operaio internazionale*]

57 Contemporaries as well as historians have endlessly debated on the contentious issue of whether or not the summer of 1920 represented a "true" revolutionary moment, and whether the objective conditions were preempted by a weak subjective factor: the "lack of decisiveness" of the party and the union. The complexity of the debate, which is bound not to find a resolution, is beyond our investigation here. What is clear is that many in the establishment were certain that a major blowup was near at hand. In Luigi Einaudi's words from 1933: "The situation would really have become revolutionary if the leaders of the socialist movement had exploited the revolt of the factory workers and moved to an assault on the regime" (Einaudi 1933, 332).

58 ACS, Ministero degli Interni, direzione generale di ps, affari generali e riservati, D. 13, busta 74, n. 2936, reprinted in Spriano (1975, 190).

59 *La gazzetta del popolo*, October 3, 1920, reprinted in Spriano (1975, 123).

60 Salvemini (1929, 22).

61 The manifesto of the Milan chamber of labor read: "Workers! Ours is a truce. Don't disarm, only demobilize, don't let the distrust sap your spirit. Our hour will come and it has to find us strong, ready for it all. We wait because we can, we want, we have to win!" (*L'Avanti*, September 22, 1920). In the following days *L'Avanti* used a tone of a revolutionary future: for example, in *L'Avanti* of September 24, 1920 an article appeared titled "workers, proceed united, for the new battles, for the certain victories!"

62 Gramsci repeated that the "factory councils have demonstrated to be the revolutionary institution most historically vital for the proletarian class" (Gramsci 1920c, 121). And in October he wrote: "the Italian proletariat can be determining for the world revolution" ("The political week, international discipline" [*La settimana politica, la disciplina internazionale*], *L'Ordine nuovo* 2, no. 18 [October 16, 1920]: 138).

63 The engineer Pietro Borghi agreed: "in substance the experience of the past September was excellent" (Seassaro 1920, 134) and now it was all about reaping its fruits for future action. Fiat employee Mario Stagiotti also noted: "They had to prepare for the decisive moment . . . everything will have to fall in front of the formidable force" (in Spriano 1971, 142).

64 See also Serpieri (1930, 328–33).

65 For a dramatic reconstruction of the years of the civil war and the attacks of the Fascist squads, see Tasca (1965, 143–221) and Salvemini (1966, chapter 19).

66 The book's aim is in no way to claim that austerity was the only reason for

the defeat of the socialist proposals, as such a claim would entail counter-factual analysis and a robust investigation of the internal weaknesses and strengths of these very movements, which is not our objective here.

Chapter Five

1 In Genoa all the powers of Europe participated, including Germany, Russia, Austria, Hungary, and Bulgaria. The US was invited to both conferences but declined to attend officially.

2 Luigi Facta, former Italian prime minister, at the first Genoa meeting, quoted in Medlicott et al., eds. (1974, vol. 19, 305).

3 The outstanding issue of the Genoa conference, the one that caught the most media and public attention, was Russia and its economic relations with the West—the focus of the first committee. The reconciliation effort failed because it left the Russian questions of recognition, credits, property, and debts unanswered and because it failed to address the problem of a new reparation crisis with Germany. The deep political opposition between nations on certain issues (for example, that of France and Britain on reparations, the recognition of the Russian government, Upper Silesia, disarmament, and so on) did not undermine their unanimous consensus on austerity—formalized by the commission on finance.

4 In 1922 the *Economist* noted that "Genoa, like Brussels, suffers from the drawback that it cannot deal with the problems of reparations and war debts or with political questions such as disarmament" (see "The Eve of the Conference," *Economist*, April 8, 1922, 661ff.). On the fundamental problem of reparations and debt, see for example "A Critical Conference," *Economist*, December 9, 1922, 1063ff.; see also the economist Gustav Cassel, who laments "the narrow limits drawn up in advance for the deliberations of the Genoa conference . . . the conference was required to make recommendations for the recovery of a sick world without touching some essential causes of the illness" (Cassel 1922, 140). See also other articles within the same issue of the *Manchester Guardian Commercial*: J. M. Keynes, "The Genoa Conference," 132–33, and Francesco Saverio Nitti, "The Genoa Conference," 134–36.

5 I defined technocracy in the introduction to this book as the rule of economic expertise, both in the historical form of economists advising and implementing economic policies and in the epistemic form, whereby the economist achieves a classless and neutral standpoint and posits universal value-free truths about an unchanging object. Such an object is never understood as historically constructed by human practice, but rather as a given, a fact of this world.

6 Preparing for the conference, the secretariat of the economic and finan-

cial section of the League of Nations compiled fourteen preparatory
documents, containing empirical data and expert advice. The statistical
documents dealt with "Currency Statistics," "Public Finance," and "International Trade." They are collected in Brussels 1920, vol. 4. These statistics
were discussed thoroughly in the *Economist* (see for example "Some Recent
Budgets," *Economist*, November 3, 1923, 783ff.). For a description of the
documents see Siepmann (1920, 437–39).

7 Davis continued: "The volumes of statistics are not merely collections of
crude figures. On the contrary, the data are selected, worked up, and care-
fully presented as a basis for interpretation" (Davis 1920, 350).

8 The members of the Advisory Committee (appointed by the secretary
general of the League of Nations) were Jean Monnet (Chairman, France);
Joseph Louis Avenol (France); Alberto Beneduce (Italy); R. H. Brand
(Great Britain); Dudley Ward (Great Britain); José Gonzales (Spain); W. T.
Layton (Director of the Secretariat of the Conference, Great Britain); and
Carel E. Ter Meulen (Holland).

9 *International Financial Conference, Monetary Problems XIII: Joint Financial
Statement of the Economic Experts*, reprinted in Brussels 1920, vol. 5, 2–3.

10 His Majesty's Stationery Office (HMSO), "Reports of the Committee of
Experts Appointed by the Currency and Exchange sub-commission of the
Financial Commission," 1922, London, cmd. 1650.

11 Amongst the many "financial ills from which the world is suffering" they
emphasized: the "enormous volume of both internal and external debt";
an increase of government expenditure; the "enormously increased" paper
currencies leading to runaway inflation; worldwide "shortage of capital";
and the breakdown of international trade (Brussels 1920, vol. 1, 4–5 and
vol. 3, ix).

12 "The Cooling Lava," *Economist*, November 13, 1920, 857. *Revival of Marxism*
was a book by Joseph Shield Nicholson published in 1920.

13 Brussels 1920, vol. 5, 7.

14 The League of Nations put its pedagogic aims into practice by preparing
pamphlets and periodicals of comparative financial positions, which it continued publishing for years afterward. Furthermore, the Brussels financial
conference was sensitive toward public opinion and inaugurated "its own
economic news-sheet, called the *Conference Forum* or the *Tribune Libre*"
(Siepmann 1920, 441).

15 As discussed at length in the conclusion of this book, the literature of neoclassical political economy normalizes the distrust for political institutions,
which therefore have to be reformed to give as much influence to independent (non-elected) economic bodies as possible. See for example Vittorio
Grilli et al. (1991), Alesina and Summers (1993), and Alberto Alesina and
Vittorio Grilli, "The European Central Bank: Reshaping Monetary Policy in
Europe," in Canzoneri et al. (1992).

16 In the words of Brand, vice president of the financial committee in Brussels, "revenue should at least be sufficient to meet all ordinary recurring expenditure, including interest and sinking fund on debt" (Brussels 1920, vol. 2, 19). Lord Chalmers went so far as to speak of a "universal" and "imperative" principle: individuals "must pay their way" (ibid., 25).

17 One of *The General Theory*'s main points of contention against the mainstream framework was the rejection of the idea that investments = savings (the so-called Say's law). For Keynesians, what capital accumulation needs is not more (potentially idle) savings, but rather an incentive for investors to invest—that is, high enough profit expectations. High profit expectations come with the expectation of selling more goods that can be guaranteed by high aggregate demand—especially more government spending.

18 See chapter 4 for the episode of the factory occupation.

19 The Genoa resolutions reaffirmed that to achieve currency stability "the reduction of Government expenditure is the true remedy," since "in order to gain effective control of its own currency, each Government must meet its annual expenditure without resorting to the creation of fiduciary money or bank credits for the purpose" (Report of the Second Commission [Finance], Resolution 7 and Resolution 11, in Gordon and Montpetit 1922, 68–70). Moreover, a reduction and consolidation of public debt would diminish the liquidity of the economy, since debt holders would be unable to use maturing bonds as means of payment.

20 This diagnosis of inflation runs counter to the Keynesian argument developed in the 1930s, by which inflation is not caused by public deficit spending *per se*, but rather emerges when the economy reaches full capacity and demand structurally outstrips supply. Thus, in the Keynesian argument deficit spending does not provoke inflation until full employment.

21 Lloyd (1925). In its critical tone the article clearly specifies the pitfalls of deflation. The rise of the value of the pound necessarily involved: "1) a rising exchange which was bound to hit the export industries particularly hard; 2) falling prices, which were bound to hamper trade and industry in general; 3) a reduction of costs, which was bound to mean primarily a reduction of wages; and lastly, 4) general unemployment on a large scale, since this is the only known means by which wages can be forced down . . . and rentiers, as a class, have not had their money incomes reduced as abstract justice would have required" (1925, 414). Of course, revaluation was something that did benefit the parts of the population with savings and fixed salaries, such as members of the bourgeoisie like university professors.

22 As we shall see in chapter 6, funding the floating debt acquired a further important political purpose in Britain: to eliminate the exceptional postwar situation whereby, due to the excessive circulation of government bonds, the Bank of England's monetary sovereignty was being challenged. Indeed, creditors could evade the credit restrictions of the Bank by not renew-

ing their Treasury bonds at maturity. On the other hand, once debt was funded, the economic-political divide would once more achieve its force. The government would no longer be involved in monetary management.

23   While in Brussels the issue was not yet ripe for consensus, by 1922 the Genoa resolutions clearly stated that "It is *in the general interest* that European Governments should declare now that the establishment of a Gold Standard is their ultimate object" (Report of the Second Commission [Finance] Resolution VI, in Gordon and Montpetit 1922, 68, my italics).

24   Before the war the currency was based on the value of gold, and thus fluctuations of the rates of exchange were limited. These ideas had been clearly formulated in the meeting of the London experts, where Ralph Hawtrey had taken the floor (see chapter 6 for greater detail on his role and his theories). The main intuition was that it was only through anchoring the currency to a fixed parity with gold that it was possible to actually escape the inherent instability of national and international currency.

25   As the resolutions suggested, their key function was to regulate credit "with a view to maintaining the currencies at par" (Report of the Second Commission [Finance], Resolution 11, in Gordon and Montpetit 1922, 70).

26   According to our experts, a rise in interest rates reacted to the rates for money generally, and acted as a check in two ways. On the one hand, increased money rates tended directly to attract gold to Britain or to keep within the country gold that might otherwise have left. On the other hand, by lessening the demand for loans for business purposes, they tended to check expenditure and so to lower prices in Britain, with the result that imports were discouraged and exports encouraged, and the exchanges thereby turned in Britain's favor.

27   The precondition for the gold standard was to stop inflation, which required a balanced budget. In the words of Resolution VII: "So long as there is a deficiency in the annual budget of the State which is met by the creation of fiduciary money or bank credits, no currency reform is possible, and no approach to the establishment of the gold standard can be made. The most important reform of all must therefore be the balancing of the annual expenditure of the State without the creation of fresh credits unrepresented by new assets" (Report of the Second Commission [Finance], in Gordon and Montpetit 1922, 68–69). Having achieved the gold standard, the state was limited in its capacity to spend by losing the power to print money to finance its expenditure while having to maintain a balance of trade, as excessive imports would entail loss of gold.

28   Their firm commitment to gold was accompanied by an underlying fear of the extreme consequences of deflation, in particular "for countries where currency has fallen very far below the pre-war parity, a return to it must involve the social and economic dislocation attendant upon continuing readjustments of money-wages and prices, and a continual increase in the

burden of internal debt" (Reports of the Committee of Experts appointed by the currency and exchange sub-commissions of the financial commission, Annex A, in Gordon and Montpetit 1922, 73). Most experts believed that the transition to gold would be gradual, and would be done with caution.

29 R. H. Brand repeated this idea: "The inadequacy of capital and consequently of productive power is fundamental, and therefore, in my opinion, it is the necessity of increasing it as rapidly as possible that should be the main guide of Public Finance" (Brussels 1920, Verbatim Record, vol. 2, 16).

30 On Keynes's position regarding monetary policy after the war, see Howson's (1973) classic, "A 'Dear Money Man'?"

31 Keynes in February 1920, reprinted in Tooze (2014, 356).

32 The quote continues: "that is—to use the words of a statesman of my country, W. E. Gladstone—in favor of allowing money to fructify in the pockets of the people, then, except in the cases of clearest necessity, it is imperative that the Governments should restrict their expenditure within the smallest dimensions" (R. H. Brand, Brussels 1920, Verbatim Record, vol. 2, 17).

33 Pantaleoni specified: "Governments have everywhere, but in a different measure, taken into their management and away from private management, a very large series of services for which they are utterly unfit, as ancient and recent experience has proved, viz.: (a) They cannot manage railways; (b) They cannot manage shipping; (c) They cannot manage harbours; (d) They cannot manage international commerce; (e) They cannot manage the commerce in bills; (f) They cannot regulate prices of commodities; and (g) they cannot conserve and distribute commodities after requisition" (Brussels 1920, vol. 5, 102).

34 Haldane to Escher, December 26, 1918, in Johnson (1968, 245).

35 Our comparative analysis of the Italian and British cases does not do justice to all other countries in which austerity was implemented after World War I, including the United States, a country that implemented and pushed to implement austerity overseas. See for example Migone (2015, 1–27).

Chapter Six

1 Including the likes of Professor Pigou and Treasury officials such as John Bradbury and our protagonist, Basil Blackett.

2 HMSO 1918b, 5.

3 Austen Chamberlain, HC Deb 16 March 1920, vol. 126, cc 2069.

4 Ibid., cc 2071.

5 Mitchell (1998, 189, Table B4).

6 See Moggridge (1972) and Howson (1974) for a detailed documentation of all the steps involved in a return to the gold standard.

7 The Treasury's role had grown as a response to the wartime loss of control over inflationary government borrowing. "When the Cabinet decided to strengthen the Treasury in 1919, what seems to have been uppermost in ministers' minds was the need for a powerful central department to control the government machine and cut out waste. The permanent secretary of the Treasury was designated head of the civil service, and in 1920 an order-in-council consolidated the Treasury's authority over the civil service by stipulating that the Treasury could make regulations for controlling the conduct of departments" (Peden 1983b, 376; for direct documentation on these reforms see T 199/351). In general, for an account of the structure and functioning of the Treasury in those years see Peden (2000, 128–90).

8 The equivalent of the minister of finance in most countries.

9 For example, in T 172/144b fols. 322–33, we find evidence that the chancellor received the 1925 Gold Bill and Budget Speech written by Niemeyer.

10 The Oxford degree *Literae Humaniores* combined ancient history and philosophy, using Greek and Latin texts, with modern philosophy, including logic. In other words, Blackett and Niemeyer were not economists by training. See Peden (2000, 20–21). Blackett and Niemeyer were practical men; they did not write scientific papers. However, once at the Treasury, as widely recognized financial and monetary experts they had many contacts with the academic world. Blackett lectured at the American Academy of Political and Social Sciences. He died in 1934 in a car accident on his way to give a lecture at the University of Heidelberg. Niemeyer, on the other hand, was granted the prestigious task of writing the entry on "debt conversion" for the fourteenth edition of the *Encyclopedia Britannica* in 1930. He was chairman of the London School of Economics Court of Governors from 1941 to 1957, and a governor until 1965.

11 Also Robert Boyce, speaking of Chancellor Snowden in 1923, attests that "Snowden, dazzled by Norman, was also ready to defer to Sir Otto Niemeyer, his chief Treasury financial adviser, who soon dominated him as completely as he did other Chancellors after the war" (Boyce 1987, 51).

12 See *The Times*: "New Greek Loan," September 14, 1927, 10; "The Bulgarian Loan Negotiations," December 3, 1927, 12; "The Problem of Security," February 27, 1928, 13; and "End of Geneva Meeting," March 12, 1928, 13.

13 For a discussion of Niemeyer's understanding of the role of central banking in Argentina, see Sember (2012).

14 Daunton (2002, chapters 1–3) speaks about a "Gladstonian fiscal constitution." On the Victorian legacy see Peden (1985, 1–12).

15 For an exposition on the content of the Treasury view, see Skidelsky (1981) and Mattei (2016).

16 See article, "The Proposed Raise in the Bank Rate in the Near Future" by J. E. Norton, in T 176/5, part 2, fols. 2–4, June 1924.

17 For a secondary literature on Hawtrey's economic theory see Howson

(1978), Black (1977), Howson (1985), Deutscher (1990), Gaukroger (2008), Mattei (2017 and 2018a).

18   There have been extensive debates on the relation between economic ideas and practical knowledge: that is, on whether the Treasury view was primarily the outcome of economic theory or rather a product of traditions of public finance and of the city of London (see Howson and Winch 1977; Tomlinson 1981; Middleton 1985; Clarke 1988; Peden 1983b, 1984, 1996, 2000, 2004b; Mattei 2016, 2018a, 2018b). Our thesis provides an integration of the two: certainly the British Treasury did not adopt fiscal and monetary rigor *because of* Hawtrey's theory, yet his theory was central to refining austerity in its fullest form after the war. Hawtrey himself had been largely influenced by the practical wisdom of his senior colleagues at the Treasury, especially John Bradbury—the influential pro-austerity Treasury official who preceded Blackett and Niemeyer in steering the Treasury in his position as joint permanent secretary (1913–1919). Moreover, Hawtrey was something of an outsider to academic economic orthodoxy, which allowed him to offer original insights that escaped many of the bonds of conventional economic thinking. As Peden notes, when Hawtrey wrote his first books, he was "less than wholly conversant with the current literature" (Peden 1996). In Hawtrey's 1913 text the only reference to another economist was to Irving Fisher, and that reference was added after Hawtrey had finished the first draft. Moreover, Hawtrey denied that his theory on trade cycles was derived from that of Alfred Marshall (Deutscher 1990, 8, 247).

19   His position as in-house economist was not high enough to speak directly to the chancellor on his own initiative, however. Most often, Hawtrey would communicate his ideas through the controller: that is, through Blackett or Niemeyer.

20   Hawtrey's influence on the Treasury officials had waned in the 1930s (Howson 1978, 509–10). He was not involved in giving economic advice during the Second World War, by which time he was past the normal retirement age. He was employed keeping a record of financial policy.

21   Hawtrey was a prolific writer: between 1913 and 1940 he published twelve books and at least forty-four articles, not to mention the numerous book reviews that he regularly wrote for economics journals. Hawtrey became a fellow of the British Academy in 1935, and upon retirement he served as president of the Royal Economic Society from 1946 to 1948.

22   Hawtrey ultimately had an over-consumptionist monetary theory of the business cycle that differed from a standard monetarist reading. As he put it: "the quantity theory by itself is inadequate, and it leads up to the method of treatment based on what I have called the consumers' income and the consumers' outlay—that is to say, simply the aggregates of individual incomes and individual expenditures" (Hawtrey 1919a, Preface, v).

23 Conversations with Francis Spreng in 1973 and 1974, reprinted in Howson (1985a, 156).

24 On Hawtrey's optimistic views about returning to the gold standard without further monetary deflation see Mattei (2018b). It is worth noting that Hawtrey did not endorse a pure gold standard; rather, he proposed a gold exchange standard that would allow central banks to hold a limited amount of reserves in gold-related currencies as fully equivalent to gold, thus economizing on the use of gold and reducing the excess demand for it, which would further increase the necessity of deflation. Moreover, Hawtrey recommended that central banks, at least the Federal Reserve System and the Bank of England, should cooperate to control the supply of credit by reference to an index number of prices and other indicators of the state of trade. Hawtrey believed that the gold exchange standard scheme he proposed at Genoa was a marked improvement on the prewar conception: "the present resolutions improve upon the pre-war standard in two ways: 1) by adopting an exchange standard which will economize the actual use of gold; 2) by coordinating the value of gold as currency so as to stabilize its value in relation to commodities. (The second represents the most hopeful method for attaining stabilization)" (T 208/28, fol. 11).

25 Archival evidence of their exchanges is a basis for challenging the conventional account of Hawtrey as a man of respected intellect who was yet "kept at a distance from the main process of policy formulation" (Deutscher 1990, 3). This account caught on with Winston Churchill's claim that "the learned man be released from the dungeon in which we were said to have immured him" (cited in Black 1977, 379) and John Maynard Keynes's reference to "the Hawtrey backwater" (Howson and Winch 1977, 25). It has persisted despite Robert Black's attempted correction (Black 1977, 378).

26 One remarkable set of Niemeyer's files on monetary policy comprises mainly Hawtrey's memoranda (see T176/5). One example of how Niemeyer actively deployed Hawtreyan ideas is in his correspondence with the International Labour Office (ILO) official, Sir Llewellyn Smith. In order to formulate his replies, Niemeyer wrote to Hawtrey for advice on the relation between monetary policy and unemployment. The letters to Smith show that Niemeyer fully used Hawtrey's memo, the main theme being in fact the Hawtreyan concept of credit stabilization as the ultimate solution to unemployment (see T 208/95).

27 Again, on October 12, 1922, Norman wrote, "Dear Hawtrey, thank you for sending me your paper on the Genoa resolutions. I have read it with the appreciation of the lucidity of your argument and the compression of your thought and I would say that the Central Banks could in practice attain to the ideal that is set before them!"

28 Other participants of the Tuesday Club included economists Walter Layton, Hubert Henderson, and Dennis H. Roberton; City financers like

Charles Addis, Bob Brand, Reginald McKenna, and Henry Strakosch; public servants such as John Anderson and Josiah Stamp; and financial journalists like A. W. Kiddy and Hartley Withers (Skidelsky, 2003, 264).

29 The concept of currency was secondary to credit (or debt, debt being just the opposite of credit), as money was nothing but "the medium with which debts are legally payable" (Hawtrey 1925a, 232). This Hawtreyan perspective clearly differed from other monetary theories, such as those proposed by Marx and by Keynes (after 1936 in the General Theory), that understood money as a store of value. For Hawtrey, the initiative of production rested on the orders of the "dealer" or trader, i.e., the intermediary between the producer and the consumer. The subsequent process of production gives rise to a chain of debts: "The manufacturer or contractor becomes indebted day by day to his employees. The merchant becomes indebted to the manufacturer" (Hawtrey 1919a, 376).

30 Other passages point out to the relation between increased credit and an increase in effective demand: "So we reach the conclusion that an acceleration or retardation of the creation of credit means an equal increase or decrease in people's incomes" (Hawtrey 1919a, 40). And again: "Inflation consists in the spread of the infection of high prices through production to the consumers' income and thus to the consumers' outlay" (ibid., 114).

31 As Keynes did in 1930, as early as 1919 Hawtrey understood effective demand as made up of two components: the part of purchasing power applicable to consumption and the part applicable to investment. Hawtrey wrote "the purchasing power applicable to accumulation, as distinguished from consumption, comes from two sources, from savings and from banker's loans" (Hawtrey 1919a, 348). Keynes specified that effective demand is the point at which aggregate demand equals aggregate supply. Keynes understands this equilibrium point from the perspective of the entrepreneur such that aggregate demand is his expected proceeds from employing a certain number of men (which corresponds to the expectations about the amount society spends on consumption and the amount it spends on investment). Aggregate supply, on the other hand, is the benchmark: the amount of proceeds an entrepreneur needs to expect in order to justify his outlay in wages ("expectations of proceeds required to employ N men"). The innovation that explains why Keynes attached such an importance to government expenditure is his idea that, within free market capitalism, effective demand is usually deficient with respect to the level needed to achieve full employment. This is because, most of the time, entrepreneurs do not have sufficiently high expectations to actually invest. The problem of idle savings was not an issue for Hawtrey. Hawtrey believed that money which was saved would be spent "sooner or later" on fixed capital or invested abroad. Thus, while Hawtrey's models are primarily concerned with inflation due to over-consumption, Keynes's primary concern in the 1930s lies in a shortfall of investment (also motivated by under-consumption). It is interesting to note, however, that in 1919 Hawtrey did introduce a crucial insight for the later Keynesian framework: he points to the fact that supply is governed by effective demand. In his words: "The employment of the country's productive resources is governed by effective demand" (Hawtrey 1919a, 348) and again: "production feeds demand, demand stimulates production" (ibid., 376).

32 "An indefinite expansion of credit seems to be in the immediate interest of merchants and bankers alike. The continuous and progressive rise of prices makes it profitable to hold goods in stock, and the rate of interest which the merchant who holds such goods is prepared to pay is correspondingly high" (Hawtrey 1919a, 13). It is this self-propelling inflationary mechanism, driven by the rational reactions of economic agents, by which "there is an inherent tendency on the part of traders to borrow more and more and of bankers to lend more and more" (ibid., 30), that caused an increase in the velocity of circulation of the monetary unit and thus a depreciation of the currency. It followed that "the expansive tendencies of credit are in perpetual conflict with the maintenance of a fixed standard of value" (ibid., 16), since the currency "could be indefinitely depreciated" (ibid., 52).

33 Hawtrey explains: "As prices rise, the quantity of credit needed to finance a given consignment of goods increases in proportion, and the creation of credit is still further accelerated" (1919a, 43).

34 Hawtrey thought this was especially true in the war and postwar moment. See Hawtrey (1919a, 344–63).

35 In this sense, Hawtrey was amongst the first to introduce the income approach to international trade theory.

36 Together with his colleagues, Hawtrey uncritically adhered to the renowned Say's law, which pictures savings flowing smoothly into the stream of spending. Savings and investment were considered to be equated by variation in the rate of interest. In this sense, the problem of under-investment, which might also be called excessive savings, was not usually a concern. For Hawtrey such flows were kept equal by the workings of the investment market (see Davis 1981, 213–15). On Hawtrey's views see also Peden (1996, 75–81).

37 Hawtrey agreed and admonished: "If expenditure is directed too much to consumption and too little to investment, the process of economic recovery is retarded and the scarcity of commodities is intensified and prolonged" (Hawtrey 1919a, 350).

38 The "thrifty man" from the working class could "put his savings into a savings bank"; however, "he must first see to it that he has a little money in the house" (Hawtrey 1919a, 22).

39 In Hawtrey's economic model, the "consumer outlay" included two distinct

actions: consumption on expendable goods and services (unproductive consumption), and savings in the form of investments in assets, shares, and bonds (productive consumption). Deutscher (1990) suggests that Hawtrey's terminology does not distinguish between spending on goods and spending on securities. Both elements were part of the consumer outlay.

40 Middle classes, very broadly defined, included white-collar workers who lacked powerful trade unions to protect them against inflation. At a time when there were only means-tested state old age pensions, and not all private companies provided pensions (and these were not index-linked), such people relied on accumulating savings over their working lives to support them when they retired (personal communication with Peden).

41 Hawtrey endlessly repeated that "financial strain" was the main obstacle to currency reform. Budgetary rigor was crucial in controlling inflation—or better, it was a prerequisite for currency stabilization (Hawtrey 1919b, 435). His preaching found international acclamation. The Genoa resolutions directly transcribed Hawtrey's firsthand draft memos: "In each country, the first step towards re-establishing a gold standard will be the balancing of the annual expenditure of the State . . . [this] is the necessary and sufficient condition for gaining control of the currency" ("Financial Subjects," T 208/28, fol. 6). In March 1922, Niemeyer steadfastly reaffirmed the mandate for British citizens of being truthful to fiscal orthodoxy: "If we do not ourselves balance our budget, the whole movement for sounder financial and commercial conditions in Europe will receive a mortal setback" ("Note to the Chancellor of the Exchequer," T 171/202, 28).

42 The exemption limit was reduced from £160 to £130, which meant a threefold increase in taxpayers by 1918–1919 as compared with five years prior. By the summer of 1917 there was a full-blown movement in opposition to the reduction of the exemption limit, mainly led by miners and coal workers who often refused to pay income tax. Its basis was on the Clydeside, the Midlands, parts of London, and South Wales (see Whiting 1990).

43 In the words of Vernon Hartshorn, a leading figure in the South Wales Miners Federation and Labour MP: "All these people who have that pay increase and are brought under the tax are simply being taxed on the extra cost of living; they have simply to pay the tax with money that has been allowed them on account of the extra cost of living" (T 172/982, fols. 17–18, in Whiting 1990, 907).

44 Blackett's predecessor Bradbury held the same convictions: "Taxation for the purpose of repayment of domestic debt tends by a process of compulsory thrift to increase rather than diminish the capital resources of the nation" (John Bradbury, "Reconstruction Finance," T 170/125, fol. 4, 1918).

45 Herbert Samuel's presidential address to the Royal Statistical Society made clear that "The British system of taxation is regressive in the lower stages;

the classes with the smallest incomes pay a larger proportion of them in contributions to the revenue than the classes immediately above them. . . . Such regression is the consequence of relying for revenue to so large an extent as we do upon the taxation of alcohol, tobacco, tea and sugar, and of the fact that the consumption of these articles is larger in proportion to income among the poorer classes" (Samuel 1919, 180).

46 "A large part of the debt is held by the banks and in connection with the monetary system of the country; here the interest will in general be placed at industry's dispose. Another large part is held by joint stock companies, and the interest is a direct payment to industry; the same is true of interest paid to those individuals who will invest it in private businesses of their own" (HMSO 1927, 99).

47 For a brief history of the ideological footing of Labour's position on taxes, see Daunton (2002, 50–60).

48 "What trade needs," Niemeyer claimed, "is for taxation to be reduced as a consequence of reducing expenditure. A transfer of expenditure from taxation to borrowing is at any rate of much less use to trade and in so far as it reduces pressure for the reduction of expenditure [underlined in the original] maybe positively harmful to trade" ("The Burden of Taxation," T. 171/202, fol. 28).

49 These demands for economy persisted for years. A confidential circu-lar communication of 1923 "on the subject of economy" (also called "the economy letter" or "the Treasury circular on economy"), sent from the Treasury to all departments, including the board of Education, the Ministry of Labour, and the Ministry of Pensions asking for their expen-diture and aggregate savings estimates, communicated that "every effort in economy will therefore be needed in order to balance the budget in 1924/25" (N. F. Warren Fisher, June 1, 1923, T 160/159).

50 Not counting the demobilization periods immediately after each world war.

51 The committee worked in stages, delivering reports to the government at monthly intervals between December 1921 and February 1922 that were considered in cabinet committees before being published in February 1922. See First Interim Report of Committee on National Expenditure (Cmd. 1581), Second Interim Report of Committee on National Expenditure (Cmd. 1582), and Third Report of Committee on National Expenditure (Cmd. 1589). See also McDonald (1989).

52 Even prior to the Geddes Axe, the Treasury had been successful in imposing a decision "not on merits but on financial considerations only" (Finance Committee, 30 June 1921, TNA, CAB 27/71). The crusade of the Treasury against the ambitious postwar housing programs dated back to 1919. The Treasury had refused to allocate the resources needed to face capital shortages. It doubled down with high interest rates on Treasury bills

(6 percent) that disincentivized investment in local authorities' housing bonds (which were at 5.5 percent), thus draining sources of investment. In November 1920, Chamberlain had asked the Cabinet to restrict Addison's plan of building 800,000 public houses to 160,000. However, until that autumn the government's commitment to the "Land Fit for Heroes" prerogative remained intact. Treasury cavils were rejected on the grounds that the government could not afford to break its pledges on housing. Not until 1921, with the collapse of the postwar boom and the weakening of labor's power, were the political conditions ripe for the government to surrender to the Treasury's demands for economy.

53 In March 1921 the government transferred Christopher Addison from the Ministry of Health to the anomalous post of minister without portfolio. After he resigned, Addison wrote a fierce pamphlet, *The Betrayal of the Slums* (1922), to denounce the government's austerity moves.

54 See Thomas and Dimsdale (2017); for health and education, table A28a; and for data on public sector debt interest payments see table A28.

55 Unemployment insurance in Britain also fell victim to austerity. Throughout the 1920s mechanisms were constantly devised to reduce its coverage and costs, by enacting the requirement to "be genuinely searching for work" and harsh means tests that excluded married women from receiving benefits—see Thane (1982).

56 In its numerous memos to the Geddes Committee, the Treasury advocated for substantially reducing the staff of the various ministries and departments and even closing them down. See for example "Treasury Report to Geddes committee, Ministry of Transport estimates 1922/1923" (T 186/25).

57 On the Gairloch episode see Peden (1993).

58 Niemeyer had already expressed these thoughts clearly to the colonial secretary, Winston Churchill, in October 1921. Churchill had asked him to disclose the Treasury view concerning financial conduct and employment, and his reply was concise but effective: "The best assistance which the State can give to unemployment . . . is 1) to reduce its expenditure 2) to repay its debts" (T 176/5, part 2, fol. 39). Thus, he continued, "It is obvious that certain minimum immediate assistance must be given to the unemployed to prevent starvation but for the ultimate solution of the unemployment problem it is essential that this assistance should be kept at the minimum" (ibid., fol. 38).

59 According to this view, the crowding out occurs because savers invest in government bonds instead of other productive ventures and because in borrowing from the public the government competes for a limited pool of funds and thus increases the cost of borrowing money for other private investors. Their arguments were surely influential, since it was Churchill's budget speech of April 15, 1929 that provided the most clear-cut statement

of the crowding-out argument: "The orthodox Treasury view . . . is that when the Government borrow[s] in the money market it becomes a new competitor with industry and engrosses to itself resources which would otherwise have been employed by private enterprise, and in the process raises the rent of money to all that have need of it" (Winston Churchill, HC Deb 15 April 1929, vol. 227, 5s, 1928–29, fols. 53–54, cited in Peden 2004a, 57).

60 For an account of the evolution of Keynes's ideas see Moggridge (1976) and Howson (1973).

61 Hawtrey's most famous formulation of the crowding-out argument is in "Public Expenditure and the Demand for Labour" (Hawtrey 1925b), where he sought explicitly to refute the policy of public intervention through public works designed to alleviate the huge British unemployment problem. He had expressed these ideas repeatedly in his prior scholarly works (see for example Hawtrey 1919a, 208, and 1913) and in his Treasury memoranda. Hawtrey fundamentally thought that in moments of economic downturn the creation of bank credit alone would be sufficient to increase employment, and that public works would be "unnecessary." He put it strongly: "The public works are merely a piece of ritual, convenient to people who want to be able to say that they are doing something, but otherwise irrelevant. To stimulate an expansion of credit is usually only too easy. To resort for the purpose to the construction of expensive public works is to burn down the house for the sake of the roast pig" (Hawtrey 1925b, 44). For a good explanation of Hawtrey's crowding out argument see Peden (1996).

62 In his memorandum on "Unemployment," Baldwin's home secretary, Sir William Joynson-Hicks, made clear that the only way for the Conservative government to escape "vilification" at the general elections for "its insufficient unemployment policies" was a "comprehensive" stimulus through large publicly funded loans to extend the productive power of the dominions and "road construction on a fairly large scale" (HMSO 1929, 294–300) that could compete with the ambitious proposals of the Labour and Liberal parties.

63 The theoretical assumption was that monetary wages would be flexible downward as prices fell and that workers would price themselves into jobs.

64 Or in the words of Hawtrey: "Deflation therefore means a reduction of profits and wages. If wages resist the process and it falls unduly on profits, the result is unemployment" (Hawtrey 1919a, 361). Blackett warned the chancellor that any form of government expenditure would prevent wages and costs of living from going down. In his words, "So long as the British government is creating new credit to meet its expenditure or to replace maturing short debt, there is added difficulty in getting prices and wages and the cost of living down to reasonable figures" (August 6, 1921, T 175/6 part 1, fol. 15). Hence, as Niemeyer repeated, "Ambitious schemes

of expenditures or credits can only intensify the evils of unemployment by maintaining wages and prices and making its ultimate remedy more difficult" (T 176/5, part 2, fols. 38–39).

65 Also, Blackett displayed a sharp understanding of the political issues at stake: "Falling prices," he emphasized, "are disliked by all traders, and however much a worker as a consumer may dislike high prices, he dislikes still more reductions in wages and lack of employment" (T 176/5, part 2, fol. 50).

66 Another crucial aspect of the Trade Disputes and Trade Unions Act was the limits it placed on the political power of labor, striking at its party and unions. The Labour Party was robbed of much of its funding with the prohibition of "any contribution to the political fund of a trade union" unless a formal notice was sent out declaring the union members' "willingness to contribute to that fund." Instead of "contracting out," as stipulated by the 1913 Trade Union Act, union members now had to "contract in." As a result of this legislation, in just two years the Labour Party lost substantial financial resources (a quarter of its total income from affiliation funds) and a third of its subscriptions (Cole 1948, 195). Moreover, the British state barred civil servants from participation in labor organizations with the risk of "disqualification and discharge from the service." This law severely limited the political freedom of public employees. According to Millis, "of 300,000 or 400,000 civil servants, 130,000, a majority of whom were telephone and telegraph operators and others employed in the postal service, had membership in seven organizations affiliated to the Trade Union Congress and the Labour Party. In some instances this affiliation dated back to 1906" (Millis 1928, 326–27).

67 For Hawtrey's emphatic defense of an "orthodox theory of the money market" that "prescribes high money rates as the remedy for adverse exchanges and for the other symptoms of a too great expansion of credit," see his memo "Cheap or Dear Money" (February 4, 1920, T 176/5, part 2, fols. 71–76). This is a memo that both Niemeyer and Blackett studied closely.

68 For a discussion of Hawtrey's theory of the quick effectiveness of a change in bank rates for both deflationary and inflationary purposes, see Mattei (2018a, 477–79). It is noteworthy that the key difference between Keynes and Hawtrey in the 1920s was that Hawtrey attached enormous influence to the short-term interest rate (because short-term borrowing financed retailers' and wholesalers' stock), whereas for Keynes the long-term rate was more important (because private investment is eventually "funded" by stock issues). Hawtrey's critique of Keynes in *A Century of Bank Rate* (1938) was to show that the long-term rate did not vary much, and therefore could not be an explanation of volatile investment.

69 For an application of Hawtrey's model to the British situation, see his memo "The Credit Situation" (June 8, 1921, T 17/6 part 1, fols. 5–15).

70 For data on Bank rates and Treasury bill rates, see Howson (1975, table 3, p. 50, and Appendix 2, pp. 160–66). For banknote circulation see Mitchell (1998, table G1, p. 789).

71 Chamberlain was aware of Keynes's suggestion: "K. would go for a financial crisis (doesn't believe it would lead to unemployment). Would go to whatever rate is necessary—perhaps 10%—and keep it at that for three years" (February 4, 1920, T 172/1384). The Treasury file (T 172/1384) was collected during the Second World War at Keynes's request and includes a comment by him in 1942 which shows that he did not regret having given this advice at that time. He wrote: "What impresses me most is the complete hopelessness of the situation. All controls had been abandoned. . . . With all the methods of control, then so unorthodox, excluded, I feel myself that I should give today exactly the same advice that I gave then, namely a swift and severe dose of dear money, sufficient to break the market, and quick enough to prevent at least some of the disastrous consequences which would otherwise ensue. In fact, the remedies of the economists were taken, but too timidly" (T 172/1384, fol. 3). For further information on Keynes's views on monetary policy in 1920 and their relation to his later views, see Howson (1973).

72 "Keynes's Note of Interview with Chancellor" (February 15, 1920, T 172/1384, in Howson 1973, 459).

73 Falling prices increased the value of financial assets that were fixed in nominal terms, notably the war-swollen national debt, and thus increased the wealth of holders of these assets—mainly the better-off members of the community and financial institutions. The assumption was again of an immediate connection between savings and capital formation. In March 1920 Blackett shared with the chancellor an article by Pigou that reiterated the common dogma: "The country is in tremendous need for new capital. . . . It is imperative, therefore, that people should save. Cheap money does not encourage them to do this. Dear money does" (A. C. Pigou, "Dear Money," *The Times*, March 1, 1920, 10; also in T172/1384, fol. 50).

74 While economic historians may debate whether monetary austerity was the primary cause for the slump, there is no doubt that it was a central factor and that it contributed to the slump's "severity and length" (Peden 2000, 153).

75 High rates persisted throughout the decade, with the result that currency in circulation dropped impressively, falling by almost 21 percent from 1920 to 1929. One must consider that high bank rates in a time of falling prices were much higher in real terms, since they had a large deterrent effect on investment by creating expectations of falling prices and thus falling profits. This was the typical deflationary spiral that haunted Britain for the decade.

76 Hawtrey's criticism about the perpetuation of a dear money policy increased after 1925, once the gold standard was achieved (see Howson 1978, 507–8). Yet his fear of inflation continued to haunt him so that in the late 1930s, when revival and rearmament were threatening to produce a boom, Hawtrey argued for a dear money policy once more (ibid., 510).

77 "Under the Gold Standard the supply of legal tender was related to the supply of gold, all bank notes being backed by gold, apart from a certain amount, fixed by statute, known as the fiduciary issue" (Peden 2000, 151).

78 There has been an intense debate among British historians about the extent to which the decision to go back to the gold standard was benefiting financial interests over industrial interests. We do not intend to simplify the complex composition of capitalist dynamics and the structural conflicts among competing sectors of the capitalist class (see Harvey 1982, chapter 10). However, as chapter 9 will fully articulate, this book argues that austere discipline and the consequent defeat of the embattled British workers, emblematically represented in the defeat of the 1926 general strike, was beneficial not just to specific sectors of the capitalist class but to the preservation of capital order altogether.

79 The decline in volume of exports between 1925 and 1926 was soon recuperated with a substantial increase in 1927, leading to an improvement of the trade deficit in subsequent years. See Thomas and Dimsdale (2017, table A.36). The same drop in exports occurred with the harsh 1920 deflation. However, as early as 1922 the volume of exports was higher than in 1919 and 1920.

80 In fact, once the gold standard was in place, the avoidance of gold outflows required a favorable balance of trade. Toward this end, deflation of UK prices and incomes was crucial to offset the overvaluation of the currency and keep British exports competitive. In turn, low public and private consumption kept imports in check. If the country was importing too much, the drainage of gold would raise prices and restrict consumption. Furthermore, throughout the decade, austerity measures constituted the "proper economic barriers against the export of capital" (Bradbury in Howson 1974, 96). Indeed, high bank rates were the instrument to avoid capital flight to America, at a time when speculation in that country was high and London had been dethroned as the leading financial center. As a result of the way the war had been financed, the Bank of England had more short-term assets held by foreigners in London than short-term debts of foreigners to London. The ratio of the former to the latter became 2:1 in the 1920s, whereas in 1914 it was approximately 1:1. Thus, sterling was always vulnerable to movement of funds from London if interest rates were higher elsewhere or if fund-holders felt that sterling's exchange rate would fall (Peden, 1985, 72–73).

81 J. Bradbury, "Relations between the Treasury and the Bank of England: Testimony of Former Permanent Secretaries and Controllers of Finance" (T 176/13, fol. 23).

82 By 1922 its operational position was much stronger than the prewar years, with its new capacity to engage in active open market operations (see Moggridge 1972, 26).

83 On the other hand, as an expert body, the central bank played a direct part in the consultations by which the financial ministers made their decisions (see Hawtrey 1928).

84 These types of answers were given time and again to Parliament (see T 176/13, fols. 9–15).

Chapter Seven

1 Literally: "regime della lesina," where "lesinare" is an Italian word synonymous with the English verb "to economize."

2 All these sensational events have been widely documented by both contemporary observers and historians, and the classic work of Angelo Tasca (1965) is an unbeatable portrait of one of the tensest epochs of Italian history.

3 Italian Liberal governments made efforts to balance the budget in 1921–1922 (Frascani 1975; Toniolo 1980, chapter 2; Ciocca 2007, chapter 7), but it was only during the Fascist years that the country's economic agenda appeared to have the potential to embody austerity successfully. Many influential economists and politicians were ready to test Mussolini's ability to normalize the financial situation. Thus, prominent figures of the Liberal establishment (for example, the historian Salvemini, the politicians Nitti and Giolitti, and the economists Einaudi, Giretti, and De Viti De Marco) expressed vocal support for the new ministry's full powers.

4 The four economists were primary, though not alone, in their support for the regime. Support was widespread in the profession and included the most prominent economists of the time. Michelini (2011b, 47–50) documents how the majority of economic journals, including the two principal reviews of Italian economic theory—*Il Giornale degli Economisti* and *La Reforma Sociale*—published articles endorsing Mussolini's agenda.

5 See Rossi (1955), Salvemini (1966), Lyttelton (1973), Guarneri (1953).

6 A royal decree is synonymous with a presidential executive order—one that does not require a bill to be introduced in the parliament and subjected to scrutiny and debate. See "Legal Decree for the Delegation of Full Powers to Sir Majesty's Government for the Rearrangement of the Taxation System and of Public Administration," Law 1601, December 3, in GU 293 (December 15, 1922). For a detailed description of Fascist economic policies

see Gangemi (1929). Lello Gangemi collaborated with De Stefani at the Ministry of Finance.

7   Pantaleoni became full professor [*professore ordinario*] of science of finances [*scienze delle finanze*] in 1884. He then became full professor of political economy (the equivalent of economics today) in Naples, Geneva, and Pavia. From 1901 till his death in 1924 he held the prestigious chair of political economy at Rome La Sapienza. In 1921 De Stefani became professor of political economy at Scuola Superiore di Commercio of Venice (Ca' Foscari). In 1925 he became full professor of politics and financial legislation [*politica e legislazione finanziaria*], and in 1929 he was full professor of economic and financial policy in the department of political sciences at Rome La Sapienza. In 1954 he became emeritus professor. Umberto Ricci also had an extensive academic career: he became full professor of political economy in Macerata (1912–14), then professor of statistics in Parma (1915–18) and Pisa (1919–21), after which he became professor of political economy in Bologna (1922–24). Ricci succeeded Pantaleoni at the University of Rome La Sapienza (1924–28). Luigi Einaudi was full professor of science of finances [*scienze delle finanze*] at the University of Turin (1902); then he directed the Economics Institute at Bocconi University of Milan (1920–26). The secondary literature on Einaudi is endless; amongst many, see Del Vecchio (2011), Farese (2012), Faucci (1986), Forte (2009), Einaudi (2000). On Pantaleoni, see Augello and Michelini (1997), Bellanca (1995), Giocoli and Bellanca (1998), Bini (1995), Bini (2007), Bini (2013), De Cecco (1995), Marcoaldi (1980), Michelini (1992), Michelini (1998), Michelini (2011a), Mosca (2015). While the literature on Einaudi and Pantaleoni abounds, research on Ricci and De Stefani is more limited. On Ricci, the main references are Bini and Fusco (2004), Ciocca (1999), Fausto (2004), Busino (2000), Dominedò (1961). On De Stefani, see Perfetti in De Stefani and Perfetti (2013), Spaventa in De Stefani (1998), Gangemi (1929), Marcoaldi (1986), Banca d'Italia (1983), Parrillo (1984). For a broad picture of the four authors, within the wider context of Italian economics of the time, see Faucci (2014, chapters 6–7). Mattei (2017) expounds on some of the topics that this chapters delves deeper into. For an excellent reconstruction of the international economic debate in which the Italian authors participated, see Marchionatti (2021).

8   During and after World War I Pantaleoni published frequently in the press (especially *Il Mezzogiorno, Il Popolo d' Italia, Politica*, etc.). The Laterza publishing house collected many of his articles as books (Pantaleoni 1917, 1918, 1919, 1922). As Michelini notes, "In these writings Pantaleoni was clearly intent on offering an organic concatenation of economic theory and politics" (Michelini 2020, 32). Indeed, his political writings were imbued with his economic principles, displaying the interconnection between theory, economic policy, and political militancy; this link is also visible in

the publications of his colleagues. Ricci's numerous newspaper contributions are collected in several volumes (Ricci 1919, 1920, 1921, 1926). De Stefani's public speeches and press articles were collected by Treves (De Stefani 1926b, 1927, 1928, 1929). Einaudi's fervent activity as a journalist and press editor is well known. When he first began to work for the *Economist* in 1908, he was already co-editor of *La Riforma Sociale*, where in 1910 he became editor in chief. Einaudi also wrote for *La Stampa* (1896–1902), which he left to start a long collaboration with *Il corriere della sera* that lasted until the end of 1925. As the Italian correspondent for the *Economist*, between 1920 and 1935 Einaudi published more than 220 articles, an average of about 14 a year. The collection of his articles is republished in Einaudi (1959–1965) and Einaudi (2000).

9   See the preface by Perfetti in De Stefani and Perfetti (2013, 5).

10 Upon his resignation, De Stefani continued to teach in Italian universities while remaining deeply involved in politics, observing political events and writing in the main national press. In 1929 he was again nominated for the Fascist Grand Council (*Gran Consiglio del Fascismo*), the main governing body of Mussolini's Fascist government. He lived a very long life (1879–1969), and after the 1920s he abandoned his neoclassical-austere perspective—and ultimately, economic science altogether (see Marcoaldi 1986, 55). On De Stefani's life and career, see also the preface by Perfetti in De Stefani and Perfetti (2013, 5–26).

11 Pure economics was the term the authors used to indicate the neoclassical tradition of economics that stemmed from marginalism (what Dobb [1973] calls the "Jevonian revolution," from William Stanley Jevons). For a good historical-theoretical analysis of the neoclassical theory, see Lunghini and Lucarelli (2012).

12 Pareto is not one of the main figures in our story because he remained in Switzerland during the first years of the Fascist regime (he died on August 19, 1923). However, it goes without saying that, as a committed Fascist and a prominent exponent of pure economics, Pareto held ideological and theoretical sway over our economic experts and their austerity project, as well as others among the Fascist and Liberal elites.

13 In the early 1900s Pantaleoni sat as a socialist in Parliament. His brief honeymoon with the nascent socialist party was based on his belief that it was the sole organized social force that protected free trade (Michelini 2020, 29; see also Michelini 1998). These ideas were shared with Pareto and the other pure economists, like Enrico Barone. However, by the early 1900s, when the workers' movement gained strength, Pareto, Pantaleoni, and Barone stood fast in their objective to protect the bourgeois order and espoused the nationalist cause: "the three pure economists saw first in nationalism and then in fascism the political and social forces capable of engineering a final showdown with both the socialist movement, be it reformist or revo-

lutionary, and weak Italian liberalism, which very timidly was opening up to the logic of political and social democracy" (Michelini 2020, 30). Indeed, through his interventions on *La Politica*, the official nationalist journal, Pantaleoni worked to expel all the "Left" and "eversive" residues of the Fascist movement. On Pantaleoni's and Pareto's nationalism and their anti-Semitic ideology together with Pantaleoni's political career and journalistic activities, see Michelini (2011a, 2019, 2020). Michelini (2011a) convincingly argues that there was a continuity between Pantaleoni's anti-Semitic polemics and his anti-collectivist and anti-socialist polemics. Thus, the explanation of anti-Semitism and Fascism cannot be considered as an external component with respect to his theoretical economic analysis and especially his austere views.

14 Originally published in *Il Giornale degli Economisti*, April 1925.

15 ACS Segreteria Particolare del Duce, Carteggio Riservato, Cs b. 91, Umberto Ricci, June 1925.

16 Ricci began exposing the inefficiencies of the emerging corporativist economy and the consequent abandonment of the free market. For instance, in one of his first critical articles, "Sindacalismo giudicato da un economista" (Ricci 1926, 107–66). Ricci argued against both the role of unions in the labor market and the abolition of private property in the name of collective entities like Fascist corporations. His polemic reached its peak with the article "La scienza e la vita" (Ricci 1928) in the journal *Nuovi studi di diritto, economia e politica*, where he argued that the regime's economic reforms did not comply with "economic science" and especially austerity principles. In particular, he criticized the interventionist measures embodied by the "battle of wheat" whereby "farmers were forced to cultivate crops that were comparatively more expensive" (1928, 223). He also denounced the protectionist turn of the government that "prohibited industrialists from buying raw material from abroad." He further denounced rent control laws, "useless" public works, and unemployment subsidies as well as migration and population control policies.

17 "La finanza dello stato egiziano nell'ultimo decennio," in *Studi economici finanziari e corporativi* 19, no. 3 (October 1941), published in Rome by Edizioni Italiane [*Mi sembrò allora opportuno di illuminare l'opinione pubblica egiziana e tenni due conferenze, una alla società di economia politica e l'altra all'università*].

18 On June 10, 1924, Giacomo Matteotti, a young member of the Italian Parliament and secretary of the Italian Socialist Party, was kidnapped outside his house by agents of the Fascist secret police (*Ceka*) that were under Mussolini's command. Two months later Matteotti's body was found a few kilometers outside Rome. The so-called Matteotti Affair gave rise to events that resulted in the establishment of a totalitarian Fascist regime, forcing Mussolini to reveal his inherently totalitarian ambitions and abandon the pretense of "legality" that had marked the first two years of the Fascist government (1922–24). The so-called *fascistissime* laws that banned all political parties were the means by which Mussolini overcame the crisis the murder precipitated. The *Economist* noted: "It is hard to see how [a] constitutional Government—in the sense now generally accepted in Western society—can be more than a name in a country where one political leader is able to call up armed men, at a moment's notice, to do his bidding" ("The Crisis in Italy," *Economist*, July 5, 1924, 11).

19 On Einaudi's support of Fascism at least until 1924, see Faucci (1986, 194–211). Indeed, in the *Economist*, Einaudi's writings focused exclusively on Fascism's economic policies, without any regard for the wider political context. Still, in 1927 Einaudi was reporting positively on Italian economic factors, glossing over any aspects that could have exposed the real authoritarian face of Fascist austerity. Among the many articles that reveal this approach see "Italy—Mussolini's Policy—Population and the Lira—Stock Exchanges—Readjusting the Price Level—The Campaign for Reduction of Prices," *Economist*, June 11, 1927, 1236ff.; "Italy—Revaluation Policy and the State Revenue—Appeals for Economy—Treasury Cash Funds—Increasing Gold Reserves," *Economist*, July 2, 1927, 22ff.

20 See for example Alesina's influential intervention at the April 2010 Ecofin council of Madrid called "Fiscal Adjustments: Lessons from Recent History" (Alesina 2010). We will discuss these episodes at length in chapter 10. On the international political influence of the Bocconi graduates, see Helgadóttir (2016, 392–409).

21 "Il programma finanziario del partito Nazional-Fascista, lettera aperta al Senatore Luigi Einaudi," *Il popolo d'Italia*, January 14, 1922.

22 Ricci's scientific production takes three different forms: his reviews for *Il Giornale degli Economisti* (he wrote in the section called "Rassegna economica"); his lectures on political economy in Rome 1924–1925; and his theoretical pieces—in particular, his two most famous works: *Il Capitale* and *I saggi sul Risparmio*. Pantaleoni was a very prolific and complex scholar; much ink has been spilled studying his thought, and many interpretive controversies between scholars exist. The main point of divergence is between those who understand Pantaleoni's writings as substantially unitary, and those who see a theoretical shift from his *Principii* to the lectures he delivered in the early twentieth century (see Michelini 1998 and Bini 2007). De Stefani was not an original contributor to pure economic theory; his main contributions are cumbersome empirical studies (see for example De Stefani 1925 and 1926a). Einaudi's scientific work was more applied in nature, especially regarding taxation and financial science. However, he expressed full consensus with the meta-economic approach of pure economics.

23 For a critique of the newfound framework of the neoclassical school see Dobb (1973, 166–211).

24 A deductivist logic is based on a small set of "axioms" (such as the rational maximizing calculation) that produce an internally consistent framework for explaining observed economic phenomena. The outcomes of these abstract thought experiments lead to rigorous laws; given certain premises, the fundamental economic theorems follow (Pantaleoni 1898, 3).

25 "Savers are necessary for production?" [*I risparmiatori sono necessari alla produzione?*], *Il corriere della sera*, April 27, 1920, in Einaudi (1961, vol. 5, 720).

26 The *homo economicus* acquires this virtue of saving only as a matter of rational economic calculations aimed at maximizing personal pleasure: "We believe that the homo economicus compares present pleasure to future satisfaction, properly reduced and discounted" (Ricci 1999, 22).

27 Pantaleoni's elitist view is inseparable from his Social Darwinist perspective, by which in his lectures on political economy he teaches his students that the economic qualities are innate and cannot be compensated for with education or external factors. Inequality is explicitly a natural fact, and a very healthy one for society. As he bluntly put it: "the most complex of social organizations does not require any other condition than freedom of action and choice in order to proceed with increasing virtue for the selective elimination of the incapable" (Pantaleoni 1922, 197). On Pantaleoni's Social Darwinist perspective, see Bini (2013) and Mosca (2015).

28 In macroeconomics today the identity of savings = investments (private savings plus public savings) still holds true. In other words, there is no hoarding of capital, since the assumption is that everything the businessman invests finds a buyer. The debunking of Say's law is foundational to post-Keynesian and Marxian analysis today. See Blecker and Setterfield (2019) and Shaikh (2016).

29 Italian Bolshevism—an epithet that was the title of Pantaleoni's famous booklet published in 1922—was loosely used to denote *any* state intervention within the sphere of the market and any form of social redistribution. Einaudi agreed that "socialism of whatever type was inevitably synonymous with reckless and pleasure-loving spirit, of a run towards immediate consumption, with demands of larger wages for less work" (Faucci 1986, 176).

30 According to Einaudi, during the war the Italian people could easily have undertaken greater sacrifice than they did, especially through taxation, thus avoiding debt and monetary inflation. As he wrote: "Our people did not abandon immediately the arts of peace, did not renounce the habitual pleasures [*godimenti*], did not deprive itself of the large part of its income to throw it on the nation's altar for the salvation of the army and the grandeur of the nation" (Einaudi 1933, 32).

31 Einaudi spoke of himself and his fellow economists as "we, first apostles of

the Word of Abstinence" (Einaudi 1920, 173) [*apostoli della prima ora del verbo dell'astinenza*]. For Einaudi, both during and after the war, savings led to economic and moral redemption: "war imposes the necessity to observe temperance and teaches how it is possible to live soberly, in a much nobler manner than before" (Einaudi 1920, 120). Einaudi thought it "reasonable" and "necessary" to "inculcate . . . in the Italian people the virtue of sacrifice, the renunciation of all that is superfluous, of useless consumption" [*inculcare . . . agli italiani la virtù del sacrificio, della rinuncia a tutto cio' che e' superfluo, a tutti i consumi inutili*] ("Abolire i Vincoli!" *Il corriere della sera*, January 15, 1919, reprinted in Einaudi 1961, vol. 5, 43).

32 Pantaleoni (1922, 229). And again: "the traitors, the depressionists, the saboteurs have to get caught and shot without pity. Otherwise we will have the Soviets" [*i traditori, i depressionisti, i sabotatori vanno senza pietà acciuffati e fucilati: altrimenti avremo i Soviet*] (Pantaleoni 1917 in Michelini 2011a, 34). Referring to the heads of the Bolshevik movement, Pantaleoni says: "It is obvious that between people who have such a morality and us there cannot be but *extermination war*" (Pantaleoni 1918, 167, italics in original).

33 Pantaleoni's hatred toward socialism grew ever stronger after the Great War, especially with the occupation of the factories in 1920. It was in these years that *La Vita Italiana*—the nationalist-Fascist political journal that Pantaleoni co-directed with Giovanni Preziosi—geared up its anti-Semitic campaign. Michelini (2011a) shows how the anti-Semitism that many Fascist intellectuals espoused was not biological but based on political reasons: Jewish people were associated with an anti-capitalist conspiracy. For example, Giovanni Preziosi wrote: "the biggest and most influential demagogues and the most active agitators of the working classes are Jewish or under Jewish influence" (Preziosi, in Michelini 2011b, 96). On the intrinsic connection between anti-socialism, anti-Semitism, and pure economics, see Michelini (2011a).

34 Most scholars see De Stefani's ministerial action as the emblem of the normalization phase of Italian Fascism (Marcoaldi 1986, 18; Toniolo 1980, 50). However, the connection between austerity and an authoritarian government reveals a deep ideological continuity between the so-called normalizing austerity policies of the 1920s and the violent, anti-democratic insurgency of the Fascist movement.

35 On the Fascist squads and their violent actions, see Vivarelli (1967) and Tasca (1965).

36 Once he was appointed minister of finance in late November, De Stefani received a letter from Mussolini asking him to also take up the post of minister of treasury, pending the creation of a unified Ministry of Finance and Treasury. De Stefani gave him a firm and austere reply: "Dear Mussolini,

I obey and I arrange for the fusion of the two ministries. In accepting, I confide in your collaboration for the reduction of the expenditures of the State. Faithfully yours" (Rome, December 20, 1922, De Stefani Archive, reprinted in Marcoaldi 1986, 70). In the *Economist* Einaudi breathed a sigh of relief: "it was high time that from the Government bench a voice should be raised against the frenzied finance of the Bolshevist after-armistice period" ("Italy—Absolute Government in Italy—Taxes to Be Simplified—Working of the Succession Tax—A New Excise?" *Economist*, December 2, 1922, 1032ff.).

37 Certainly, Italy faced greater external constraints in debt repayment than Britain due to its utter dependence on imports of food and raw materials. On this dependence and how it exerted pressure in favor of austerity, see chapter 8.

38 The postwar progressive tax reform was based on the idea that "these necessary sacrifices will have to fall mainly on the shoulders of the wealthy classes, and mostly on those who have derived big profits from the war, while the new measures of taxation must weigh less heavily on the average and lower middle classes, and only lightly or not at all on the labouring classes" (Minister Carlo Schanzer's statement on the financial situation made in the Chamber of Deputies session of June 10, 1919, T 1/12367/35323, 24–25).

39 Giolitti announced the institution of a Parliamentary enquiry on war profits in 1919, and it was instituted in 1920. De Stefani eventually disbanded it and that prevented it from issuing an informative final report. Crocella et al. (2002) reproduce the minutes and the material of the enquiry.

40 In June 1920, the deputy of the socialist party, Filippo Turati, gave a long speech in Parliament in which he advocated for a system of inheritance taxation based on the radical proposals of the engineer Eugenio Rignano (1870–1930). Rignano adhered to the labor theory of value and argued that the existing inheritance systems "tended to perpetuate the deprivation of the working class and to confer an immortal character to the fortunes accumulated by the capitalist class." On Rignano's proposals and the debates that it sparked, see Erreygers and Di Bartolomeo (2007).

41 "Il manifesto dei fasci di combattimento," *Il popolo d'Italia*, June 6, 1919.

42 In that same budget speech, De Stefani could proudly assert that "the country is now in a much better situation than it was seven months ago. The country is at work, there are no labour disputes, unemployment is decreasing, the balance of trade is improving, the amount of paper money in circulation is tending to decrease. . . . The Government has shown that it respects labour but it does not intend to persecute capital" (Summary of Financial Statement, Milan, May 13, 1923, FO 371/8887, fol. 13).

43 Other measures encouraged foreign capital to invest in Italy: debts con-

tracted abroad now could be deducted from the *ricchezza mobile*; and the Ministry of Finance could grant exemptions on incomes subject to double taxation, at home and in foreign countries (Forsyth 1993, 275). For other measures in favor of capital such as the liberalization of financial markets, see Rossi (1955, 75–90) and Guarneri (1953).

44 The Italian taxation system was of course much more regressive than the British one, since the majority of the state revenue came from indirect taxes. De Stefani's reforms meant a further regressive push to an already regressive system. For details on the Italian fiscal system after World War I see Forsyth (1993).

45 The workers now had to pay 12.4 percent in tax on all their belongings, while farmers holding land on certain types of tenures [*coloni, coloni parziari*] started paying a 10 percent income tax rate (Royal Decree 16, January 14, 1923, in Toniolo 1980, 47). Public employees also became liable (Royal Decree 1660, December 16, 1922, in GU 305 [December 30, 1922], and Royal Decree 1661, December 21, 1922, in GU 305 [December 30, 1922], 9934).

46 In 1924, the British embassy transmitted two copies of the publications issued by the Ministry of Finance called "Fascist Financial Policy" which stated: "the number of income tax payers has increased from 600,000 to 700,000. The entry on the roll of contributors of labourers hereto exempt from taxation . . . has increased the number by another 100,000 to which must be added a further 1,250,000 through the application of this tax to incomes derived from farming" (Ettore Rosboch, Rome 1924, FO 371/9936, fol. 35 [p. 11]).

47 Tax breaks were granted also to the proceeds of administrators of joint stock companies; to the proceeds of directors and procurers of commercial firms; on dividends, interest, and bonuses of securities issued by non-government bodies; and on the *imposta complementare* on income above 10,000 lire (Toniolo 1980, 47).

48 The *nominatività dei titoli* was a measure approved in Italy after the Great War, to make it possible to link capital incomes to individual taxpayers and subject them to a personal, progressive income tax (Manestra 2010, 28).

49 Inheritance tax provided the state with revenue of 305 million in 1922–1923. When De Stefani's law exempted 65 percent of inheritance from taxation, the revenue went down to 72 million by 1925–1926 (La Francesca 1972, 10). With the new law, only transfers outside the family (defined as "ascendants, descendants, spouses, siblings, uncles/aunts, nephews/nieces") were taxed (Gabbuti 2020a, 16). Pantaleoni prepared the study of inheritance tax for De Stefani that reached the following conclusion: "it is desirable to arrive by degrees to the abolishment of inheritance tax" [*è perciò opportuno arrivare per gradi alla soppressione totale della imposta successoria*] (see Ricci 1939, 94). On the abolition of the inheritance tax and the support of the Fascist and liberal press, see Gabbuti (2021).

50 Brosio and Marchese (1986) provide data even more stark than those in Ragioneria Generale dello Stato (RGS, 2011). They show that redistributive expenditures dropped more than three times from 1922 to 1924 (from 6,664 million lire to 1,911 million lire). If after World War I redistributive expenditures had quickly increased to reach 26 percent of total public spending in 1921, they were cut back to 11 percent by 1923 (elaborations from the data in Brosio and Marchese 1986, tables 1A and 4A).

51 "In February 1923, the state raised the degree of disability that farm workers had to demonstrate in order to obtain compensation for work-related injuries from 10 percent to 15 percent. These measures had reversed the extension of Giolitti in 1921. The right to indemnity shrank to include workers age 12 to 65 instead of 9 to 75 as provided by the Gilittian reforms. The reform also made *mezzadri* and tenant farmers responsible for paying a portion of the contributions that up to then had been entirely covered by their employers. By 1925, the *Cassa Nazionale Infortuni* reported that their contributions fell by 43 percent" (Pavan 2019, 866).

52 By the end of 1923, the state's yearly contribution to unemployment insurance was suspended (Royal Decree 3184, December 30, 1923, in GU 40 [February 16, 1924]). Most importantly, its mandatory nature—the true achievement of the many popular movements just a few years prior—was trashed. Moreover, farm workers, domestic staff, and home workers were exempt from insurance obligations. Pavan comments: "The most innovative feature of the Italian laws, which were the first in the world to envision unemployment insurance even for farm workers, was erased" (Pavan 2019, 867).

53 *Rassegna della previdenza sociale* vol. 6 (1923): 120. The ministry would be rehabilitated only after 1945. In the 1920s the Fascist regime even abolished the Superior council of labor, a symbol of liberal reformism that since the beginning of the century guaranteed participation of workers' organizations in the activities of the State.

54 Elaborations from Ragioneria Generale dello Stato (RGS 2011). The primary surplus was maintained throughout the decade, and public expenditure (not counting expenditure defense and interest payment) lingered below 20 percent until the big escalation of the Ethiopian war in 1935.

55 Social expenditure lagged at around the 1931 level (1.2 percent of nominal GDP) until 1936, when it jumped up to almost 2 percent. These were the years of the Ethiopian war, when total public spending jumped to 37.9 percent in 1935 and 44.9 percent in 1936.

56 See Toniolo (1980, 53–58).

57 See for example OXFAM, October 12, 2020, "IMF Paves Way for New Era of Austerity post–COVID-19," https://www.oxfam.org/en/press-releases/imf-paves-way-new-era-austerity-post-covid-19.

58 This campaign against what Pantaleoni called "Italian Bolshevism" encom-

passed the formidable polemic against the so-called *bardature di guerra*, literally "war harnesses"—a term that purposefully signaled a cumbersome and nagging impediment. See for example Einaudi, "Abolire i Vincoli!" January 15, 1919, in Einaudi (1961, vol. 5, p. 43).

59 As Ricci put it, "it must be those men capable of producing and interested in producing are not chased away [*scacciati*] and tormented by government" (Ricci 1920a, 8).

60 In May 1923 the public works budget was cut by a quarter, and De Stefani could announce that it would be "limited to those works that cannot be deferred, to avoid the deterioration of works already begun" (De Stefani 1926b, 214).

61 These policies widely satisfied the spirit of retaliation of Liberal public opinion. In the words of Federico Flora, who would join the board of directors of the State Railways in 1925, the personnel had been "ruined" [*rovinato*] by "the factious propaganda of thousands of agents: Russian and Red" [*propaganda faziosa di centinaia di agenti, russi e rossi*] (Flora 1923, 28). Among many other economists, Giorgio Mortara was of the same opinion: "performance has diminished due to the spirit of indiscipline and negligence that looms over the railway workers" [*ma ancora più il rendimento è diminuito per lo spirito di indisciplina e di negligenza che aleggia fra gli agenti ferroviari*] (Mortara 1922, 298).

62 Letter of Sir R. Graham to Marques Kurzon of Kedleston, December 22, 1922, FO 371/7651, fol. 265 [p. 2]; on austerity in the railways see also report received on November 5, 1922, FO 371/8886, fol. 57.

63 Third-class ticket prices increased 15 percent, and second-class prices increased by 6 percent, while first-class tickets were unchanged (Toniolo 1980, 50). The state reduced investment in railway track maintenance, thereby dismissing the least profitable lines and impeding their modernization. All these measures helped to improve the budget: in 1924–1925 railways realized a profit of 175.8 million lire compared to the year ending June 30, 1922, in which they had a deficit of 1,258 million lire (ibid., 49–50). The priority of orthodox finance implied that the state gave up on a crucial task of improving the country's infrastructure.

64 Our experts undertook a ferocious campaign against municipal companies for the management of public utilities. Speaking about his experience as finance minister in the city of Fiume, Pantaleoni suggested that "the services of drinking water, tramways, gas and electrical lighting were in deficit and *only because [they were] managed by the state*" (Pantaleoni 1922, Preface, xxx).

65 "Postal strikes would become impossible if the government stopped defending state monopoly and prohibiting the private sector, i.e., the associations of merchants and industrialists, from organizing a private postal service, an organization that would be in place in less than 24 hours and in much more perfect form than the public one" (Pantaleoni 1922, 233).

66 "Labour has a final degree of utility of its own, just like any other direct commodity . . . and as to the causes affecting its disposable quantity, are intimately connected with the merceological [commodified] nature of labour" (Pantaleoni 1898, 285).

67 Legal protection of labor was obviously the primary threat to the optimal and harmonious model. "If by law or any other artifice one could make it such that the worker could work 8 instead of 9 hours, there would be no obstacle that could impede the reduction of the working day and the increase of wages" (Pantaleoni 1910, 212). In the *Economist* Einaudi had lamented that "An application of the policy of the eight-hours' day, and of the weekly rest, by which the hours of effective work were sometimes reduced to two or three hours a day, is largely responsible for this lamentable state of affairs; but lack of discipline contributed no less to it" (December 31, 1923, in Einaudi 2000, 270).

68 Writing in the *Economist* in 1926, Einaudi explained the details of the Bill on Industrial Disputes that followed the pact of Palazzo Vidoni, extolling "its far-reaching importance." Einaudi laid bare the features of the corporatist authoritarian state, but he did so without any critical tone. He instead offered a sober description that pointed to a fundamental success: strikes had been defeated. "One of the cardinal principles of the Fascist program was indeed the elimination of industrial disputes. In fact, strikes, which were rampant in the postwar years (18,887,917 days lost in industry in 1919 and 16,398,227 in 1920), had diminished to 7,772,870 days lost in 1921 and 6,276,565 in the first ten months of 1922. But if the decrease in the spirit of unrest was already sensible, it is only after October 1922 that the number of days lost became almost negligible: 309,670 in the last two months of 1922, 295,929 in 1923, and 1,159,271 in 1924. In agriculture strikes have almost disappeared. Fascism has always aimed at suppressing class-feuds and replacing industrial struggles with co-operation between capital and labor. The Bill . . . will put on the statute-book the principles which were hitherto the practical policy of the present government. . . . Only those employers or employees can be admitted as members of the recognized associations who have a good political record from the national point of view. This aims at excluding from membership followers of subversive political and social creeds" ("Italy—The Bill on Industrial Disputes—Its Far-Reaching Importance—Reform of the Senate," *Economist*, January 9, 1926, 64).

69 Chamberlain received a summary of the Labour Charter on February 21, 1927 (FO 371/12202, fol. 80). (On corporativism and the functions of the new labor magistracy, see ibid., fol. 89.)

70 "According to the [corporative] system, denoted as 'corporativismo,' the conflicting interests of employers and employees had to be reconciled with the supreme interests of the state." Corporativism was initially created through an agreement signed on October 2, 1925, between the representa-

tives of Italian industrialists and the representatives of Fascist trade unions and was then codified in a series of laws approved in 1926. (These laws are Law no. 563, April 3, 1926, in GU 87 [April 14, 1926]; Royal Decree 1130, July 1, 1926, in GU 155 [July 7, 1926], 2930; and Royal Decree 1131, July 2, 1926, in GU 155 [July 7, 1926], 2941.) For the legal aspects of the system see Balandi and Vardaro (1988). The Fascist regime was an authoritarian corporativism where the representation of workers' interests was only formal, not substantial, given the absence of freedom of association and the state's power to nominate the representatives of the Fascist union. The relation between capital and labor moreover was regulated within the fixed objectives of the regime's austerity policies. On the other hand, the employer's association [*confindustria*] was capable of maintaining its autonomy at least till the mid-1930s.

71   "La carta del lavoro di 1927," Article 6, *Gazzetta ufficiale* 68, no. 100 (April 30, 1927): 1795.

72   He explicitly wrote: "it is enough to start from the non-controversial premise in pure economics that the hypothesis of unlimited free competition gives the optimal wage solution. Starting from such a premise, the policy-maker can legitimately try to achieve with different means (a judge's decision, an agreement between associations, etc.) this same optimal solution in the cases where the hypothesis of free unlimited competition does not operate and thus cannot deliver the optimal effects."

73   "La carta del lavoro di 1927," Article 2, *Gazzetta ufficiale* 68, no. 100 (April 30, 1927): 1794.

74   The Bedaux system had already been extensively experimented with in Britain. By 1937, 49 Italian and 225 British firms had incorporated this practice (Kreis 1990, 280). The Bedaux system consisted of a wage incentive scheme "based upon the scientific measurement of human labor" (ibid., 324) that could track effort expended by the worker and could rank their efficiency, speed up production, and eliminate idle time.

75   Michelini (2019 and 2020) provides a good overview of the two main strands that characterize the economic culture of Fascism: the one inspired by Pantaleoni's pure economics, and the other inspired by Alfredo Rocco's New-Mercantilist/Corporativist school. The two schools of thought shared an anti-democratic and anti-socialist stance, and a rebuttal of any autonomy of workers' organizations in production, thus marginalizing the revolutionary syndicalist component of early Fascism. While the latter corporativist strand became more prominent in the late 1920s, the pure economics strand of Pantaleoni remained influential, even within the corporativist tradition itself, as is evident in the debates on the significance of the 1927 Labour Charter. For example, Michelini (2020) points to the fact that the pure economist Gustavo Del Vecchio opposed those who saw the Labour Charter as giving real power to the Fascist trade union. Instead, he

greeted it "as a historical embodiment of the economic principles enunci-
ated by Pantaleoni focused on the exaltation of innovative entrepreneurs"
(Del Vecchio 1929; Michelini 2020, 26). Many Fascist intellectuals agreed.
The Fascist and corporativist theoretician Carlo Costamagna, for example,
insistently underlined how the Labour Charter safeguarded private initiative (see Costamagna 1931). Corporativisim, he remarked, "is an instrument, not an end." Most importantly, "the premise of the new national economic order rests within the individual, within private initiative," which is
the "cornerstone of the Fascist constitution" (Costamagna 1933, 1–3). Gino
Arias, another Fascist corporativist, firmly distinguished Fascist corporativism from state socialism. The former understood private initiative as the
"strongest . . . basis for any productive initiative" and implied "a spontaneous self-discipline" of the workers to achieve "economic equilibrium"
(Arias 1929, 371). Indeed, "to the corporation can be assigned the serious
and efficacious protection of the superior interest of production against
the egoisms of the unions" (ibid.). The Fascist politician and economist
Ettore Rosboch, who had worked closely with De Stefani's ministry, also
agreed. In 1930, Rosboch noted that the increasing public intervention in
economics was still about prioritizing private property, and not at all about
subordinating it to separate priorities of the state: "The economic function
of the Fascist state has the well-defined task of integrating and developing
as much as possible the productive activity of the private sector" (Rosboch
1930, 254). This evidence further corroborates our thesis of continuity between austerity and corporativist institutions such as the Labour Charter.

76 In the *Economist* Einaudi commented that "the most interesting sections
of the Charter are those which aim at giving a practical scope to general
principles," with the principle of the conciliation of "capital and labor under the supreme authority of the state, in the interest of the nation at large,"
taking precedence. He quoted: "Private initiative and labor are forces which
must be guided and conciliated by the state in the interest of maximum
production. But the state, and the Fascist state primarily, cannot recognize
as legal organizations of employers and employed which aim at subverting it." Thus, the expulsion of non-Fascist unions ("Italy's Labour Charter,"
Economist, May 14, 1927, 1008ff.).

77 "La carta del lavoro di 1927," Article 7, in GU 68, no. 100 (April 30, 1927):
1795.

78 The historian Jon S. Cohen concludes his classic article on the battle of the
lira with the following remarks: "When the [Fascist] government became
directly involved in the private sector in the 1920s and 1930s, the motivation was to protect and support private interests, not to usurp their control.
There was no conflict of interest between Italian fascism and Italian capitalism" (Cohen 1972, 654). In line with this argument, Michelini (2020, 41–49)
demonstrates that many economists writing in the Fascist journals inter-

preted state interventionism in labor relations and state interventionism in production to boost economic growth as measures that would protect capitalism from socialist and redistributive ideas.

79 Contemporaries believed the drop in wages was even greater. Buozzi remarked that by the 1930s "the overall nation-wide reduction of real wages could be considered to be 15-40% with respect to 1920–1921" (Buozzi 1972, 428). Gaetano Salvemini also wrote "we arrive at the conclusion that between 1926 and 1934 workers in industry lost an average of 40 to 50% of their wages" (Salvemini 1936, 253). Real annual wages reached their historical minimum in 1936 due to the inflationary wave sparked by the war against Ethiopia and the international sanctions that followed. In 1936 real wages dropped by almost 20 percent from 1921 levels—decreasing from 17.34 lire in 1921 to 13.98 lire in 1936 (daily real wages at lira 1938; Zamagni 1975, Table 1 and 3). Scholars have discussed how the introduction of the family check starting from 1934 had very little effect on the worker's living standard (see Zamagni 1975, 541).

80 In Cotula and Spaventa (1993, 579).

81 Pantaleoni (1922, 38).

82 Restrictive debt management policy was indispensable to diminishing the liquidity in the economy. On November 6, 1926, the bills outstanding at that date were long-term government bonds with no maturity which paid 5 percent. Between June 1926 and May 1927, the state reduced the value of short-term debt held by the public and the banking system from 27 billion lire to 6 billion lire. The refunding operation was successful, and liquidity was cut (Cohen 1972, 649). Following the British procedure, the Fascist regime introduced a sinking fund in August 1927 (FO 371/12947, fol. 162). This permitted consolidation of the floating debt whereby the five- and seven-year Treasury bonds were converted into the longer-term "*littorio* loans" (on November 6, 1926, "conversione forzosa"). The *littorio* loans represented a popular "effort" [*sforzo*] that attracted the small savers for the national "economic battle" [*battaglia economica*] (Volpi, in Cotula and Spaventa 1993, 588).

83 "Italian Finance," *The Times*, April 9, 1925, 9. See also "Ministerial Changes in Italy," *The Times*, July 13, 1925, 15.

84 For a similar diagnosis stressing the solidity of the Italian fundamentals, see "Italian Finance," *The Times*, April 9, 1925, 9; "Fall of the Lira," *The Times*, June 19, 1925, 15; "Italian Bank Rate Increased," *The Times*, June 18, 1925, in OV 36/22. On speculation as a reason for a drop in the value of the lira during the exchange rate crisis of summer 1925, see also Einaudi's account, "Italy—The Foreign Exchanges Scare—Extraordinary Payments for Wheat—Paper Issues Stationary—The Inter-Allied Debt Problem" *Economist*, July 18, 1925, 107ff.

85 De Stefani, *The Times* notes, had acted egregiously in moving toward fulfill-

ment of his financial promises: "Two of the first promises of the Fascist government on its accession to power were to balance the budget and to improve by 50 percent the value of the lira. The advance made during the last two years towards the fulfilment of the first promise has been sufficient to dispel all doubt as to the possibility of its ultimate attainment" ("Italian Finance," *The Times*, April 9, 1925, 9). The excessive monetary rigor and "Bourse regulations and measures" with which De Stefani confronted the fall in the value of the lira had the opposite impact of aggravating the financial crisis and the depreciation of the lira, and he was thus forced to resign ("Italian Ministers Resign," *The Times*, July 9, 1925, 14). De Stefani resigned on July 9, 1925. Einaudi, who reported the resignation in the *Economist*, paid high tribute to his colleague for his impressive austerity record, and even noted how his resignation had to do with "a well-meant endeavor to revalue the lira" that "shook financial markets" (see "Italy—Resignation of Signor De Stefani—Public Finance—Stock Markets—Duty on Cereals—Wholesale Prices," *Economist*, August 15, 1925, 270ff.). Volpi praised De Stefani as a name to be "written in the annals of Italian finance as the restorer of budget equilibrium" ("Italian Financial Policy," *The Times*, July 14, 1925, 13; also see OV 36/22, fol. 36).

86 For example, the difficulty in selling grain abroad caused independent farmers of the Padania plain to suffer from hunger, thus forcing them to adhere to the centralized migration plan of the regime to recolonize the area of the Agro-Pontino in the Lazio Region. Pennacchi's historical novel, *Canale Mussolini*, provides a vivid picture of such a dramatic episode.

87 "Italy—Stock Exchange Situation—Unemployment—Foreign Trade—New Issues and Savings—Bank Balance Sheets," *Economist*, January 8, 1927, 68ff.

88 See *Daily Telegraph*, "Italy's War Debt," June 19, 1925, in OV 36/22, fol. 30. The official discount rates were fixed by decree by the minister of treasury and finance.

89 "Italian Finance," *The Times*, April 9, 1925, 9, or see OV 36/22, fol. 23. The article reported on the deflationary measures that were undertaken to halt devaluation. In De Stefani's own words: "It is essential that Italy, by taking adequate precautions and at the cost of inevitable though temporary sacrifices, should recover the control of her own currency . . . and it is towards the accomplishment of this end that the financial policy of the Government is now directed."

90 This same speech was also reported in the *Economist*: "The Stabilisation of the Lira," *Economist*, December 31, 1927, 1179ff.

91 "Everyone must be convinced that re-evaluation has exigencies that are so vast as to require financial policy to be subordinated to them in order to avoid the assessment crisis that re-evaluation may entail" (De Stefani 1928, 151).

92 The immediate action for revaluation consisted in increasing the demand

for the lira on the international market. To this end the Italian state purchased lira with its international currency. Exports were therefore crucial to generate a reserve inflow to maintain Italian foreign monetary reserves.

93   "Financial and Economic Situation in Italy," August 6, 1926, FO 371/11387, fol. 153.

94   By July 1926 Volpi could write to Mussolini satisfied that "the budget of the state clear and devoid of any possibility of criticism will at the end of the financial year 1925-1926 triplie the estimated surplus, bringing it up to beyond one billion two million lire" (July 13, 1926, FO 371/11387, fol. 129). Volpi exceeded his own expectations. The League of Nations and the Bank of England were quickly informed that he had realized a surplus of 417 million lira in 1924–25 and a surplus of 2,268 million lira in 1925–26 (January 27, 1928, OV 36/22, fol.123A, 2).

95   For example, the letter that the representatives of the cotton industry sent to Mussolini on December 20, 1926, read: "The industrialists find themselves facing a crisis and have suspended any new plant or technical improvement, or more generally, any expense that is not strictly pertinent to production. They have already been forced to reduce the weekly wages of their workers significantly. They now present to the government the need to decrease, by January, the basis of pay in the amount necessary to adjust the new monetary basis with the cost of production, and thus of the prices of sale" (ACS, Carte Volpi, fase. 49, in Cotula and Spaventa 1993, 597).

96   As Einaudi put it in the *Economist*: "A rearrangement, however, of internal costs of production is clearly due if Italian industry wishes to hold its hard-won ground in foreign markets. Hence the campaign started by the government, the corporations (employers' and employees' syndicates), and the press for the reduction of salaries, wages, rents, and prices" ("Italy—Mussolini's Policy—Population and the Lira—Stock Exchanges—Readjusting the Price Level—The Campaign for Reduction of Prices," *Economist*, June 11, 1927, 1236ff.). Similarly, in September 1927 Einaudi spoke of a good balance of payments and of the nonexistence of idle savings thanks to the fact that, unlike Britain, the corporativist state was already established. He wrote: "The real point of interest in the economic policy of Italy is the method adopted for reaching the new equilibrium of price, incomes, wages, public revenue, &c. . . . The true agency working for a new equilibrium is the idea of the 'Corporate State'" that amongst other things was setting the price of labor ("Italy—Sinking Fund for Public Debt—Imports and Exports Figures—Towards a New Economic Equilibrium," *Economist*, September 17, 1927, 482ff.).

97   Favero (2010) stresses that the decision of the Fascist state to fix a 20 percent generalized reduction in the country's nominal wages was based on a calculation of the consumer price index (CPI) by ISTAT (Italian National Institute of Statistics) that was manipulated downward. The use of

ISTAT's data was the result of an agreement between the government and Confindustria whereby the government committed to calculating a CPI based on the prices of the industries' own stores [*spacci operai contenuti nella fabbrica*], which were lower than market prices. Favero notes how this technique justified a further state-enforced wage cut of 8 percent in November 1930 (2010, 328).

98 In May 1927, the General Fascist Confederation of Industry spoke clearly of the perpetual relation between the gold standard and industrial austerity. It announced to "the Italian workmen, with a praiseworthy spirit of discipline," a "general reduction of industrial wages—a step which seems indeed to be unavoidable if the exchange value of the lira is to be maintained at a rate about 30 percent higher than recent averages" (May 20, 1927, FO 371/12202, fol. 128).

99 Increases in unemployment were also attested in a document from the Bank of England (OV 9/440, fol. 30). The British embassy reported that the revaluation of the lira "caused general dislocation in nearly all branches of trade and industry," and that this depression had begun in 1926 and progressed in 1927 (Summary of Board of Trade Report on the Economic Situation in Italy during 1927, April 1928, OV 36/1). Even with the recovery of 1929, the index of industrial employment was still 3 percent below the level of 1925–26 (Toniolo 1980, 131). Official unemployment was at 10 percent of the industrial labor force (Cohen 1972, 649).

100 For example, the corporativist economist Gino Arias described the 1929 episode as "a crisis of overconsumption" (Arias 1931) brought about by high salaries, the "unpredictability of the working classes," financial speculation, and "the unlimited increase in production and wealth" with "the most open violation of all the most elementary norms of public and private morality" (Arias 1933, 216, in Michelini 2020, 42–43). The editorial board of the Fascist journal *Lo Stato* composed of prominent economists agreed that the crisis was brought upon by an international "abuse of credit." By contrast, the economic policy of Fascism stood out, as it "adopted from the beginning a policy of austere realism" (Direzione 1931, in Michelini 2020, 49). On those pages Giuseppe Ugo Papi argued that that the economic policy of the corporativist "controlled economy" would translate into a rapid reduction of all revenues, taking care to also reduce public spending and to maintain the state budget in balance (Papi 1931, in Michelini 2020, 49).

Chapter Eight

1 Like many others, Niemeyer knew that British loans to Italy would provide the country with the means to buy British commodities, and thus that the economic impact of such loans should not be underestimated. He was

well aware of the connection between loans to Italy and increased British exports to Italy when he reported to the Macmillan Committee in June 1930, "I am inclined to believe that on the whole foreign lending does not seriously outrun the constable, and in that case is greatly to our advantage. For the greater part loans mean orders direct or indirect . . . even stabilization loans which preserve order are fairly in the interest of British trade" (G1/428). In 1919 Rodney Rodd of the British embassy was of the same opinion: "But generally it seems to me that the question of extending further credits to Italy in a moment of great financial difficulty should be considered not only from the point of view of liquidating debts already incurred towards Great Britain, but also from the point of view of the future development of British trade in this country, in the interest of which the stability of Italian finance cannot be disregarded" (February 7, 1919, FO 371/3808).

2   For an analysis of the trade figures see Luigi Einaudi, "Italy—The Direction of Foreign Trade—Revival of Trade Unions Movement—Fascist Corporations and Class Federations," *Economist*, December 13, 1924, 964.

3   See Carlo Schanzer, "Statement on the Financial Situation," made in the chamber of deputies sitting in June 10, 1919, Rome in T1/12367/35323.

4   James Rennell Rodd's letter to Earl George Nathaniel Curzon on April 2, 1919, FO 608/38/15, fol. 449.

5   The February loan was used primarily for paying all outstanding debts to British departments for services rendered to the Italian government prior to February 1, 1919. On the February agreements see also T 1/12343/8035/19. It is worth noting that monetary austerity in Britain could affect the amount of the Italian loan. On June 16, 1920, the Italian chargé d'affaires, Gabriele Preziosi, wrote in a preoccupied tone to Chancellor Neville Chamberlain: "When the agreement of 8th of August 1919 was negotiated the bank rate had kept steady for a long time at 5 percent. Afterwards it rose to 6 percent and recently to 7 percent, causing a considerably larger increase of the debt of the Italian Treasury" (T 160/10/12, fol. 3). The British government consented to fix a uniform rate at 5 percent interest for all renewals of Italian bills.

6   The commercial counselor ended the report with this bleak judgment: "I can only say that it is my firm belief, after more than 30 years of close study of this country, that the Italians are, at the moment, not exaggerating their necessities and that the dangers which confront this country are of the most serious nature possible" (T 1/12551, 7).

7   Hambling's memo, which was kept by the British Treasury, read: "Responsible people in Italy are convinced (and from my knowledge of Italy, which I have visited on several occasions during the War, I feel certain they are right) that there is very serious risk owing to the present conditions in

Italy of an enormous political upheaval unless they are allowed in some way to obtain the essential imports for their industries in order that their people may continue in employment. The cost of living there has reached such limits that the people are extremely restive and any lack of employment would probably result in revolution and bolshevism. This country has already lent Italy about 400 million sterling and it would seem almost a necessity for us to give them the further assistance they now require for a period of two years, in order to protect the amount we have already at stake. I am aware that in the city of London at the present time there are certain prominent people who are of opinion that England cannot afford now to give long credits to other countries but the danger of unrest among peoples is very great and any trouble in Italy might quickly spread. . . . I do think our refusal to assist Italy at the present time might have serious consequences" (T 1/12367/35323, memorandum from Sir Herbert Hambling).

8   Political pressures that opposed welfare cuts were especially troubling: "the head of an English bank had told me," Capel-Cure reported, "the adverse point which made a special impression on financial circles in the city of London was that the Italian government had been forced to yield to the clamour of the socialists in their attempt to take off the subsidy now given on bread" (April 12, 1920, T 1/12551/4).

9   Similar lamentations against the government's financial and economic policy sparked from the Italian Confederation of Industry. The motion of the executive committee "pointed out that the policy of the financial authorities, of the Treasury, and of the Public Services, would appear to render the situation more difficult by taxation, unequalled in any other country, which absorbs capital as well as interest, rendering saving impossible and thereby thwarting the flow of new capital into productive channels" ("Industry and Production: Motion of Executive Committee on the Confederation of Industry," April 6, 1922, FO 371/7656, fol. 156).

10   Internal actors of course agreed. Nitti, for example, on March 12, 1922, urged the implementation of the principles of British legislation "by renouncing all adventurous policies" (FO 371/7669, fol. 201). "Everyone recognizes," he continued, "that there is only one means of salvation, to return to the habit of saving." Just like those of his fellow economists we studied in chapter 7, Nitti bemoaned the lack of austere virtue: "neither the state, nor the local bodies, nor private individuals, save. The State, indeed, sets the bad example of squandering" (ibid., fol. 198).

11   See for example "Investment of Foreign Capital in Italy," dispatch by Ambassador Graham, November 11, 1922, FO 371/7656, fols. 292–293. A month later, the *Economist* reported that the royal decree of December 16, 1922 (Royal Decree Law 1660, in GU 305 [December 30, 1922]) exempted from income tax all loans issued in foreign countries for the purpose of import-

ing new capital into Italy. See also: "Italy—Restriction on Sale of Occupied Houses—Exemption from Taxes to Foreign Loans—Succession Duty—Increase of Failures," *Economist*, August 25, 1923, 298.

12 The estimated reduction was 254 million lire. "Succession Duty in Italy," *The Times*, August 21, 1923, 7.

13 December 27, 1923, FO 371/8887, fols. 76–77. The dispatch reported the words of the minister of national economy, Orso Mario Corbino.

14 Another article in *The Times*, titled "Bold Italian Finance," praised the pledge of the Fascist government to reduce the deficit to zero by 1925, a hard task which was possible given that the Italian people were now "guided by a firm hand and by a man [De Stefani] who knows how to act," a man who was implementing the formula "more money and less spending" ("Bold Italian Finance," *The Times*, May 14, 1923, 11).

15 As we know from chapter 7, in his post at the *Economist*, Einaudi had only praise for the Fascist economic policies of the 1920s.

16 "Italy—Signor De Stefani's Speech—An Italian Geddes Committee—The Deficit for 1923–24—New Debts after 1914—Treasury Control—Economic Improvement," *Economist*, May 26, 1923, 1194ff. Not only was the government diligently applying a Geddes Axe; the application was also bearing its fruits, since "the economic conditions" were "improving," as De Stefani noted in his speech. In particular, imports had decreased, and exports had gone up.

17 "Fascismo," *The Times*, July 2, 1923, 13.

18 Ibid. In another article, titled "Signor De Stefani and London Italians" (*The Times*, July 28, 1924, 15), De Stefani's speech in London to the Italian Cooperative Club at Greek Street was reported. He addressed a large audience which included Italians from all districts of London: "the Italians, he said, were steadily at work and through patient sacrifice had rebuilt and restored the economic and financial structure of the country."

19 "Fascismo," *The Times*, July 2, 1923, 13.

20 "Signor Mussolini's Policy," *The Times*, November 17, 1922; also, in FO 371/7660, fol. 236.

21 Mr. Harvey, second secretary of the Embassy, reiterated the words of his colleague when, a year later, he reported about the further postponement of the Italian elections. Harvey put it bluntly: "the members of the present chamber are little better than caretakers. . . . The abject attitude of the Chamber, moreover, is justified to some extent by the obvious fact that it is no longer representative of the country" (FO 371/8886, fol. 46).

22 Graham reported that the "bill of full powers" was the "only means of affecting economies." He explained that, "having been granted 'full powers' by Parliament in November 1922 for the period of one year, Signor Mussolini was independent of the Chamber and he governed as a dictator" (Annual Report for 1923, FO 371/9946, fol. 246, p. 16). There were long reports

on the functioning of the bill of full powers (see chapter 7) remarking that "according to various Ministerial declarations, there would appear to be practically no limits to the scope of the powers conferred by the new law" (November 21, 1922, FO 371/7660).

23 In November 1922 the *Economist* had noted that "Apparently the object of Signor Mussolini is to form a Government of the best men of his own choice, not at the dictation of the groups from which they come, and one of the first planks in his programme is drastic cutting down of public expenditure. . . . The attempt to perform it will be watched with sympathy by observers of whatever nationality, who realise the crying need for sane finance in Europe" ("The Fascisti in Power," *Economist*, November 4, 1922, 840ff.).

24 For example, the *Economist* was jubilant: "Signor Mussolini has restored order, and eliminated the chief factors of disturbance." In particular, "wages reached their upper limits, strikes multiplied." These were the factors of disturbance, and "no government was strong enough to attempt a remedy" ("The Results of Fascism," *Economist*, March 22, 1924, 623ff.). And in 1924 *The Times* praised Fascism as a solution to the ambitions of the "Bolshevist peasantry" in "Novara, Montara, and Alessandria" and "the brutal stupidity of these folk." The article continued, "For two years and a half, agricultural strikes, so virulent that the crops were left to perish in the ground, were the order of the day. The petty leaders of the Communists, more stupid even than their followers, desired to make here the first experiments in so-called collective management" ("The Dissident Fascisti," *The Times*, June 17, 1924, 15).

25 In August 1928 Graham wrote to Chamberlain and spoke of a tradeoff between liberty and order in which the second prevailed: "There is the question of liberty, which exercises so many minds. There is no doubt that the restraints are actually or potentially harsh, and are often unfair. But there are very many Italians who ask themselves if they were better off, spiritually, in the days when Giolitti held sway, or when Nitti failed to govern, when strike succeeded strike and violence followed violence, when Italy's claims were impatiently regarded by other Powers, and her international position politely, or impolitely, questioned" (FO 371/13679, fol. 97, 7).

26 The chairman of the bank, Beaumont Pease, reported that "Nothing but a return to lofty ideals, to the highest conception of State authority, to stern civic discipline and self-sacrifice, to strenuous work and thrift, could save the nation from complete moral and economic disruption" ("The British Italian Banking Corporation, Limited," *Economist*, March 22, 1924, 640ff.). And again: "the achievements of this remarkable ruler's administration in less than 15 months of plenary powers are astonishing, more especially in matters that count from the economic and financial point of view" (ibid.). In 1927 the line was much the same; the chairman of the British National

Provincial Bank, Sir Henry Goschen, reported that "In Italy, owing to the firm administration of Signor Mussolini, the economic position is being strengthened" ("National Provincial Bank, Limited—Rubber Securities, Ltd.," *Economist*, January 29, 1927, 225ff.).

27 The reform of the new Italian penal code contributed to the authoritarian consolidation. It reversed "the previous direction of Italian criminal legislation. It is based on a retributed as against a preventive or curative view of punishment . . . capital punishment is reintroduced. Punishments are increased and new crimes are created . . . usury is to be a crime and so are economic or political strikes, boycotts or lock-outs" ("The New Italian Penal Code," 1927, OV 9/440, fol. 34, in the Bank of England Archives).

28 On the Fascist militia's integration with the state apparatus, see for example "Celebration of Rome's Foundation Day: Fascista Military Organization," April 25, 1923, FO 371/8885, fols. 1–4.

29 In November 1922 Graham told his compatriots that "for him [Mussolini] it is the black shirts not the Chamber that represent Italy, and his rule is to be based on the former, the latter only continuing to sit on suffrance" (November 16, 1922, FO 371/7660, fol. 235).

30 For example, a dispatch of December 28, 1923 (FO 371/8886, fol. 174) reported about the Fascisti's attack on the journalist and politician Giovanni Amendola in the streets of Rome. On June 13, 1924, the embassy reported about the attack on Signor Misuri after he had condemned Fascista extremist measures in the Chamber (FO 371/9938, fol. 176). On the Fascist persecutions of Nitti see Ambassador Graham's "General Report," 1923 (FO 371/9946, fol. 246, 24).

31 A fascinating document of the foreign office called "The Reasons for the Success of the Fascisti in the Municipal Elections of Milan" reveals that the British government was well aware of the anti-democratic tendencies of the Fascist party from the very beginning. It explains that the sudden defeat of the Socialist and Communist parties in the Milan election of December 10, 1922, by the "constitutional bloc" (Fascisti with all the other parties of order—i.e., the nationalists, liberals, and other constitutional parties) was achieved via violence and electoral fraud: "by 5 a.m. on the Sunday morning the various polling booths were occupied by parties of the Fascisti, armed with sticks and revolvers. Any efforts on the part of the socialists to encourage socialist votes, such as propaganda in the form of leaflets, distribution of socialist ballot papers, etc., were at once suppressed by the Fascisti, and the culprits generally had to be taken to the infirmary. The socialist voters found themselves in a somewhat difficult situation" (FO 371/7673, fol. 248).

32 A dispatch for example read: "Italian authorities have recently conducted a round-up of communists on a large scale, the number of arrests for the

whole country being given as over a thousand" (September 25, 1925, FO 371/10784, fol. 162). In 1928 the British embassy reported on the trial by the Italian special tribunal of "persons accused of communistic activities" (February 8, 1928, FO 371/12949, fol. 235).

33 On the Matteotti Affair, see chapter 7, note 18. For further dispatches on the Matteotti affair, see FO 371/7660, fols. 176, 178, and 187.

34 Graham to Ramsay MacDonald, June 23, 1924, FO 371/9938, fol. 214; for a similar line, see "The Crisis in Italy," *Economist*, July 5, 1924, 11.

35 "Achievements of Fascismo," *The Times*, October 31, 1923, 13.

36 Migone points out that even someone like Walter Lippmann, the director of the *New York World*—the only daily paper with national-level political influence to maintain a consistently critical stance toward the Fascist regime—had specified to Thomas William Lamont of Morgan Bank that he did not "fail to recognize the progress that has been made on the financial front" (Migone 2015, 60). As Migone writes: "One might expect that the destruction of that constitutional order which was supposed to be the hallmark of the liberal democratic order would elicit some reaction in the nation founded on one of the world's great liberal revolutions. Instead critiques and negative evaluations were utterly marginalized, nearly completely confined to Marxist and extreme factions, often within minority ethnic communities. . . . This editorial and diplomatic interpretation on the rise of Fascism constitutes significant early evidence of what would become an American historical tendency: ever more frequent toleration of exceptions to democratic rule, in the name of ever more imposing American interests" (ibid., 47–48). The attitude of the American diplomatic and financial circles matched the attitudes I have explored for Britain. For the American reception of the Matteotti affair, see Migone (2015, 50–68).

37 "The British-Italian Banking Corporation, Limited," *Economist*, March 21, 1925, 559ff.

38 Winston Churchill's remarks are an exemplary illustration of this way of thinking: "Different nations have different ways of doing the same thing. . . . Had I been an Italian, I am sure that I should have been with you from start to finish in your victorious struggle against . . . Leninism. But in Britain we have not yet had to face this danger in the same poisonous form . . . but I do not have the least doubt that, in our struggle, we shall be able to strangle communism" ("Churchill Parla dell'Italia e del Fascismo," *Il corriere della sera*, January 21, 1927; De Felice 1966, 330).

39 FROM OUR ROME CORRESPONDENT, "The Italian Elections," *The Times*, April 4, 1924, 11.

40 Personal cable to Benjamin Strong, October 26, 1927, reprinted in https://fraser.stlouisfed.org/archival-collection/papers-benjamin-strong-jr-1160/correspondence-great-britain-473618/fulltext. Plenty of documents in the hands of the Bank of England spoke of the suppression of freedom of the

press. See for example, the letter by Monsieur Louis Franck to Governor Norman: "There is no free press, or public opinion, or liberal criticism and comment, nor even personal liberty, which the methods of the administration tend more and more to curtail" (November 9, 1926, OV 36/1, fol. 19).

41 The words of the governor of the Federal Reserve of the US, Benjamin Strong, were paramount to those of his colleague. He wrote to Norman to express his pleasure about the collaboration between the central banks of the three countries, remarking that "Whatever may be our views in regard to democracy and individual freedom (which frequently means liberty and sometimes license) I think we can both agree that the present regime in Italy has been little short of miraculous in promoting the welfare of the Italian people. We may not entirely agree, speaking from the standards of liberal democracy, with the methods, but we certainly cannot disagree as to the results accomplished" (Letter of November 9, 1927, G1/307, fol. 47A). Once more the alleged benefit for the Italian people was associated with the resumption of capital accumulation and the people's subjugation under its economic laws.

42 For example, in 1924 Graham sent a telegram congratulating the "sweeping Fascista victory" ("Italian Election Results," April 11, 1924, FO 371/9938, fol. 50). The electoral violence was largely downplayed ("there were relatively few serious cases of violence and bloodshed," April 18, 1924, ibid., fol. 61) and once more understood as a typical trait in Italian affairs: "That the sweeping Fascista victory was due in some degree to improper measures of coercion is no doubt the case, but it must be born in mind that violence and corruption have always been widely prevalent in Italian elections, particularly in the south" (April 11, 1924, FO 371/9938, fol. 51). Ultimately what mattered was that Mussolini represented political stability. He commented that, if the English electoral system (i.e., a majoritarian voting system) were adopted, "practically the whole chamber would be Fascista" (ibid.).

43 In this article Einaudi expressed concern for the institutionalization of the new corporativist state and the lack of political liberty. In the same breath, however, he reminded the reader that "there exists among us, also, a full recognition of the work Signor Mussolini has done for his country and admiration for his high ideals" ("The Corporative State in Italy," *Economist*, June 23, 1928, 1273ff.).

44 That year Graham also wrote that "the question as to what would happen if Signor Mussolini was suddenly to disappear is one that nobody can answer." In August 1929, when the first plebiscite went overwhelmingly in favor of Mussolini, Graham would gladly report to Minister Austen Chamberlain that "the outward 'Fascistisation' of the country has proceeded with undiminished speed and with every appearance of success" (Ambassador Graham's confidential letter to A. Henderson, August 1, 1929, FO 371/13679, fol. 96, 2).

45 *The Times* commented that "an offensive against the lira has been started in foreign markets by creditor countries with a view to exerting pressure on

Italy to induce her to pay her debts" ("Fall of the Lira," *The Times*, June 19, 1925, 15; also in OV 36/22, fol. 31).

46 Italy's financial weakness, negative balance of trade, and reliance on British finance for imports of munitions and food, made it a war debtor, owing, at the time of the armistice, most of its money to Great Britain ($1.855 billion, adjusted for gold shipments and credits to Great Britain amounting to $152,314,000) and to the United States ($1.31 billion). Foreign capital was at the country's throat. To finance the war effort Britain was also forced to borrow from the US (£1.027 billion by the end of the armistice—Morgan 1952, 320). High indebtedness to the new American hegemony had a strong impact on British and Italian postwar politics. The United States adopted an intransigent stance toward war loans that forced all countries to be rigorous in their expectations for payment in order to in turn meet their own liabilities. This was especially the case for Britain, which required Italy, among many other countries, to pay back its debts.

47 British financier Sir Felix Schuster to the governor of the Bank of Italy, Bonaldo Stringher, April 23, 1923, G 30/11.

48 The British embassy translated and commented on the Italian budgetary estimate for each year. (See for example the year 1927–28 in FO 371/12198, fol. 84.) Similarly, the Bank of England kept many files to monitor financial maneuvers, trade balance, and monetary circulation in Italy throughout the 1920s (see for example OV 36/1, fols. 13–14). For similar financial monitoring on the part of the US, see Migone (2015).

49 The June 1925 report of the Bank of England largely made the same points (see OV 36/1, fol. 3).

50 On November 14, 1925, Count Volpi and Mr. A. W. Mellon, United States secretary of treasury and president of the American Foreign Debt Commission, signed in Washington "an agreement consolidating Italy's debt to the United States, which, on June 15th, 1925, including capital and interest, less certain sums in respect of payments already effected, had amounted to 2,042 million dollars" (OV 36/22, 2); on January 7, 1926, an agreement was concluded in London between Count Volpi and Mr. Churchill that settled Italy's debt to the United Kingdom (OV 36/22, 14).

51 The stabilization of the lira could only occur with the help of international credit—partially private, partially furnished by the issuing institutions under the jurisdiction of the head of the Federal Reserve, Benjamin Strong, and the bankers of the house of Morgan with the concurrence of the Bank of England. Since May 1926 these foreign financiers had pushed Italy to return to the gold standard. The American banker Thomas William Lamont, representing J. P. Morgan, had been in the business of "urging Italy at any rate as being in the strongest position to consider seriously an early return to the gold basis . . . it met with immediate approval of Montagu Norman and Governor Strong" (May 21, 1926; OV 36/1, fol. 14).

52 Two other important loans in support of stabilization occurred in 1927 concomitantly with the return to the gold standard: the governor of the Bank of Italy, Bonaldo Stringher, obtained a loan of $75 million from private British and American banks (Hambro Bank and Rothschild Bank) and $75 million from the reserve banks.

53 By 1924 the embassy had compiled many reports on De Stefani's doings, discussing the consolidation of the floating debt (letter from Graham to Prime Minister James Ramsay MacDonald, July 3, 1924, FO 371/9936, fol. 42; see also OV 36/1, fol. 21); the payment of internal debt; the decline in the country's trade deficit; and increases in savings and in employment (Summary of Financial Statement, June 27, 1924, FO 371/9936, fol. 44). The frequency of these reports monitoring Italy only increased during the time of the stabilization of the lira. See for example the report of September 3, 1926 (OV 36/22, fol. 83 and OV 36/1, fol. 16).

54 Letter from Volpi to Mussolini, October 20, 1926, in Cotula and Spaventa (1993, 575) [*I tecnici inglesi che sono i nostri critici più avveduti*].

55 For example, a comparison of the economic fundamentals of Britain and of Italy written in 1927 reported a great decline in Italian floating debt and an improvement of the balance of trade. It also remarked that Italy's burden of domestic debt was much less pronounced than that of Britain given its large increase in industrial production (OV 9/440, 6–7; see also OV 9/440, fol. 21).

56 As documented in chapter 7, curtailment of wages by law became a regular practice of Fascist industrial austerity. Starting in 1925, the British embassy widely reported on the subordination of labor to the Fascist state (October 9, 1925, FO 371/9936, fol. 257) through the outlawing of strikes, lockouts, and unions—except for the Fascist Syndicate—which were reduced to a "state of complete impotence, so far as negotiations with the employers are concerned" (December 1, 1925, FO 371/9936, fol. 259). Fascist syndicalism, Graham specified, "was a factor for collaboration in production" (December 21, 1925, FO 371/9936, fol. 276).

57 The most important leaders of the dissolved CGdL were reported to have signed a declaration supporting corporativism (see FO 371/12202, fol. 77).

58 "The Stabilisation of the Lira," *Economist*, December 31, 1927, 1179ff.

59 A memorandum from the Bank of England reads: "the Bank of Italy is a joint stock company, and was formed by the fusion of the National Bank of Italy with the National Bank of Tuscany and the Tuscan Bank of Credit under the law of August 1893" (OV 36/22, fol. 76). See also "Italian Bank-Note Reform," *The Times*, May 25, 1926, 13.

60 The doings of the Bank of England were constantly in the minds of Italian technocrats. Finance Minister Volpi, for example, announced: "the Bank of Italy, following the example set by the Bank of England when the British government had decided to revert to the gold parity in 1924, had exerted itself to obtain the co-operation of international banking circles, partly to

strengthen the defence of the exchange as definitely fixed, and partly because it thought that credits form the central banks and big bankers would testify to cordial co-operation with and universal approval of the government's decisions" (OV 36/22, fol. 123A, 13–14).

61 G14/95, fol. 1, extracts from the minutes of the committee of the Treasury.

62 Norman's concerns were grounded in the conviction that "a measure of independence in fact is essential for the conduct of any Central Bank on financial (rather than political) lines" (Letter to Strong, October 29, 1926, fol. 9, 2). He also wrote to the Dutch central banker Gerard Vissering to say: "the existing regime is fatal to independence, and I cannot co-operate with a partner whose hands are tied" (December 28, 1926, G1/307, fol. 37, 2). On Norman's insistence on the "complete autonomy and freedom from political control" regarding Italy, see Letter to Dr. H, Schacht, November 5, 1926, G1/307; and Letter to Sir Arthur Salter, November 8, 1926, G1/307).

63 Norman also reminded the Bank of Italy that "in the case of Austria, Hungary, Germany and Belgium, legal independence has been obtained for the Central Bank," and that the other central bankers wished nothing more than "to cooperate with an independent Stringher" (October 25, 1926, G14/95, 2–3).

64 In another letter to Dr. Schacht, Governor Strong wrote: "I have not examined the position in detail, but according to Stringher the budget is balanced; there is no floating debt; the necessary economic adjustments have taken place; the balance of trade is satisfactorily adjusted; and the Bank of Italy not only accepts the general principles of co-operation among central banks on a financial basis but is established in a position of independence and financial control" (December 5, 1927, OV 9/440).

65 FO 371/12947, fol. 176A, 49.

66 "Italian Internal Situation and Policy," FO 371/8885, fol. 88, June 9, 1923.

67 "Achievements of Fascismo," *The Times*, October 31, 1923, 13.

68 The IMF's imposition of austerity has not stopped even under the COVID-19-pandemic crisis and even once the IMF's own research shows that austerity worsens poverty and inequality. See "IMF Paves Way for New Era of Austerity Post-COVID-19," Oxfam, October 12, 2020, https://www.oxfam .org/en/press-releases/imf-paves-way-new-era-austerity-post-covid-19.

Chapter Nine

1 The wage shares in both Britain and Italy saw a brief upturn during the early 1930s, at the peak of the recession. This was not a political outcome but a mechanical one due to the anti-cyclical nature of labor shares, as profits are lower in times of crisis. However, after 1933 in both countries the recovery disproportionately accrued to profits, and wage shares declined.

In Britain, the series reached a new minimum in 1938 (73 percent), while in Italy the wage share saw its lowest level in 1942–1944 (41 percent).

2 This working measure of exploitation does not consider "unproductive labor," i.e., all the work of domestic servants and the like which in those years was a significant part of the labor force in both countries. In principle the wages of unproductive labor ought to be added into the measure of surplus value; thus our working measure understates the rate of exploitation. In Britain, the rate of exploitation increased from 0.29 in 1921 to 0.36 in 1929. In Italy, in 1918 the rate of exploitation was 0.82 and in 1928 it was 1.25. (Note that these numbers are not immediately depicted in figure 9.2 given that the chart shows a two-year moving average.)

3 Thomas and Dimsdale (2017, table A56). Note that here 2013 is used as the base year (or 2013 = 100).

4 Total Labor Productivity Net of Housing and PA, Giordano and Zollino (2020).

5 The renewed favorable environment for investment is visible in the remarkable growth of share prices. In Britain these prices increased by 63 percent from 1923 to 1928. In Italy the index of stock and dividend yield too made an astounding recovery after a bad setback during the red biennium. Indeed, as we know from chapter 7, privatization, tax breaks, and bank rescues provided "excellent profit opportunities for financial intermediaries" (Toniolo 1995, 300–302). It guaranteed a total yield of stocks and dividends that almost tripled over the course of the decade. From 1923 to the end of the decade, the new publicly traded companies increased their value by almost 40 percent. This rise indicates how austerity created favorable conditions for the Italian financial world (see Siciliano 2001, figure 1.1).

6 Even if the class implications of austerity are embodied in the profit rate itself, regardless of the secondary question of how much of the profit rate the capitalists wind up investing, it is interesting to note that in our case high profit rates favored greater capital accumulation, evidenced by the impressive growth of industrial production starting in 1921. In both countries, industrial production almost doubled over the decade (Mitchell 1998, 422). Capital stock also grew substantially. In Italy it rose by 18 percent between 1922 and 1929. This is an impressive spike given that the British capital stock increased only 4.8 percent during the same time. For the Italian data on nominal capital stock see Bank of Italy's LABCAP 3.0 (2010). For British data see Thomas and Dimsdale (2017).

7 "The average 1922–1929 real growth rate in Italy was 4% (compared to 1.7% in 1861–1896 and 2.2% in 1896–1913)" (Gabbuti 2020b, 256).

8 As we know from chapter 6, in Britain monetary austerity hit starting in the spring of 1920, producing a slump that was followed by a decade of "doldrums." In Pigou's words: "The Doldrums was a period of relative stability and quasi-equilibrium. But the equilibrium was not a healthy one,

because it was characterised throughout by a very large amount of involuntary idleness" (Pigou 1947, 42). In general, historians agree that "the British economy remained for the whole 1920s in a condition of underutilization of resources and elevated unemployment" (Toniolo 1980, 22–23).

9 Official unemployment statistics by definition downplay the actual level of unemployment. For instance, they do not count those who have given up looking for work, those who never succeeded in finding jobs in the first place, and those who do not enter the work force because of the hopelessness of it. Therefore, many scholars estimate "real unemployment" to be significantly higher than the official figure, even double. For the contemporary case of the United States, see the Bureau of Labor Statistics, "Labor Force Statistics from the Current Population Survey," https://www.bls.gov/cps/cps_htgm.htm. For a detailed study of British unemployment statistics and their shortcomings, see W. R. Garside (1990).

10 The national average downplays the extent of the crisis in the staple industries (steel, coal, textile, etc.) located largely in the north of England, which suffered the most from the revaluation of the pound. For example, the mining industry, which employed 1.3 million workers in 1920, lost over 200,000 workers by the end of the decade. With the Great Depression the picture only got worse. Unemployment reached a peak of 3.4 million in 1932, and then averaged slightly less than 2.5 million until the start of World War II. It was indeed the war that provided the stimulus and ultimate solution to this endemic social problem.

11 The interpretation of strike data cannot be universalized. In different moments of the history of capitalism low strike rates may indicate different power dynamics. A low strike rate may reflect dominance on either side. In the 1920s as well as in the 1980s, the decrease in the number of strikes can certainly be attributed to the attacks on organized labor that are typical of industrial austerity.

12 Our findings correspond to the majority of empirical studies on strikes, which show how strike frequency is associated with the business cycle: when unemployment decreases, or inflation increases, the number of strikes tends to increase. Similarly, unions' greater organizational strength is correlated with a greater number of strikes. See Franzosi (1989, 358).

13 Of which 1,046,000 were in agriculture. See Ministero dell' Economia Nazionale (1924, 278).

14 Including industry, construction, agriculture, mining, etcetera. See Toniolo (2013, table A5 for number of workers in total industry and in the total economy).

15 The industrial reserve army also increased because of the tightening of immigration laws in the United States and the pressure to work experienced by the downtrodden rural population with exceedingly low living standards.

16 The consequences of the Great Depression on the Italian labor market were dramatic, even worse than for Britain: between 1929 and 1932 the number of people registered at the employment offices quadrupled (Mattesini and Quintieri 2006, 417). The government's efforts to remain on the gold standard drastically diminished the measures and resources mobilized to cure unemployment, which soared during the years of the Great Depression, peaking at more than 1 million in 1933, or 36.6 percent of the industrial workforce. (Note that this is an estimate arrived at by averaging the maximum and minimum employment figures for 1933.) See the Italian bollettino del lavoro of 1925–35, later called "Sindacato e corporazione." For the data on the industrial workforce see Toniolo (2013, table A5).

17 Note that the discussion of wages applies only to those that are still employed. Real wages partly reflect a compensatory upward effect, given that lower-paid workers are the first to be thrown into unemployment.

18 Federico et al. (2019) provide empirical evidence of the exceptionally low real wages of Italian unskilled workers in the period 1861–1913 with respect to workers in other European countries, such as Britain, Germany, and the Netherlands. This is especially the case for workers in the south of Italy.

19 In those two years metal workers lost almost 30 percent of their nominal daily wages. This downward trend in Italy continued up until the Ethiopian war of 1935, when daily nominal wages reached their ultimate low for the average industrial worker (45 percent lower than the 1926 level, dropping to 14.9 lire from 26.34 lire). With respect to the "red years" this represented a fall of more than one third in daily compensation. (All figures from Scholliers and Zamagni 1995, 231–32, table A6.)

20 For data on Italian nominal daily industrial wages, see Scholliers and Zamagni (1995, table A6). Note that Mitchell's (1998) historical statistics show a sevenfold increase for all industrial workers.

21 Cohen (1979) shows similar data for Italy: a decline in foodstuff consumption throughout the 1920s, especially of protein-rich food and fresh fruits, on the part of the lower classes. The author concludes that "fascist policy objectives were achieved in part through reduced food consumption by Italian workers" (1979, 83). Tellingly, the only class of consumption expenditures that did increase was rent, which rose from 1926 onward, resulting in an increase in its proportion of total household expenditures (see Vecchi 2017).

22 Favero (2010, 337) uncovers a telling anecdote: in publishing the proceedings of its first scientific meeting in October 1939 in Pisa, the Italian Statistical Society excluded only one intervention, namely a paper that set out to prove empirically that the relationship between earnings and needs of working-class families was below subsistence level.

23 During the Fascist years "many distressed households approached asylums as poor houses, to temporarily relieve them from expenses for dependent

members" (Gabbuti 2020b, 272). The "increase in confinements in Italy (from 60,000 to 100,000 between 1925 and 1941—Moraglio 2006) would therefore be another, rather disturbing sign of the worsening condition of the poor" (Gabbuti 2020b, 271–72). Indeed, the situation for the poor did not improve in the 1930s. Contrary to what the Fascist propaganda declared, "assistance funding was even cut by 4.5 million between 1929-1930 and 1930-1931" (Melis 2018, 468), resulting in a contraction of poverty relief (Preti and Venturoli 2000, 744). On the ineptness of social redistributive measures during the inter-war period, see also Giorgi and Pavan (2021).

24 Gabbuti (2020b, 263–72) documents how the deterioration in living conditions of the Italian population continued into the 1930s, visible in the increase of malnutrition, the spread of deaths due to malaria and other diseases, and higher mortality rates.

25 For an analysis of income concentration in Britain in the 1920s, see León and de Jong (2018).

26 These numbers that assess income by means of fiscal source fail to account for the large profits that were exempt from taxation (illicit profits, the incomes of the high state bureaucracy, etc.) and especially for the large-scale tax evasion that took place overwhelmingly at the top. As we know from chapter 7, such evasion was largely facilitated by the Fascist regime's tax reforms (see Gabbuti 2020a, 21–24). Gabbuti points out that the war on tax evasion had the effect of increasing the fiscal burden on small taxpayers. Also, Gabbuti and Gómez-León (2021) reveal a steep rise in inequality throughout the 1920s.

27 This term emerged out of a conversation with Duncan Foley, and I thank him for it.

28 For a recent Kaleckian-inspired model that formally illustrates the consequences of welfare measures and of full employment for economic growth—especially the negative impact of a rising rate of employment on the rate of capital accumulation and the consequent mechanisms of political reaction, see Flaschel et al. (2008).

29 Austerity's negative effect on aggregate demand has been highlighted by Keynesians as the madness of current austerity, but also by many Marxists, particularly those of the Monopoly Capital or Monthly Review school (see, for example, Foster and McChesney 2012). Indeed, the 1929 crisis, interpreted by some as a crisis of overproduction, was certainly exacerbated by the precariousness of an economic growth that depended so heavily on exports in an over-flooded international market, given the forced "abstinence" of British and Italian workers, among others. Moreover, the perseverance of austerity policies throughout the 1930s contributed heavily to worsening the Great Depression (for British policies in Britain during the Great Depression, see Howson 1975, chapter 4).

Chapter Ten

1 For example, Semmler (2013) argues how an "austerity-driven reduction in spending has a stronger negative effect on output and employment when there is severe financial stress, which in turn reduces consumption and investment, feeding a downward spiral" (2013, 899). These models suggest that the impacts of fiscal consolidation are worse (to the point of causing a recession) in a state of financial fragility, low growth, low propensity to consume, and high indebtedness such as was the case in Europe after 2008. For an assessment of austerity in Europe after the 2008 crisis, see also Mittnik and Semmler (2012) and Semmler and Haider (2016).

2 For a discussion on the trend of Argentina's interest rates and the country's macroeconomic crisis of 2001–2002, see Damill and Frenkel (2003).

3 For a comprehensive account of austerity in various countries around the globe starting from the 1970s, see Shefner and Blad (2019).

4 In both Britain and Italy, the 1970s were years of social protection that extended well beyond the factory floor. The British national health system reorganized in 1974, in favor of greater centralization and accessibility. In those same years the Italian welfare state undertook a substantial qualitative and quantitative expansion with, among other things, a centralized healthcare system and a generalized unemployment scheme. The state regulation of the labor market rested on three main pillars: a) a general unemployment insurance scheme, b) centralized employment services, and c) a scheme for short-term earnings replacement in case of temporary redundancies [*Cassa integrazione guadagni ordinaria*]. In the mid-1950s, total Italian social expenditures (including income maintenance, healthcare, and social assistance) absorbed around 10 percent of GDP; in 1970 this percentage had risen to 17.4 percent, and it reached 22.6 percent in 1975—a level in line with that of France or Belgium and higher than that of Britain (Ferrera and Gualmini 2004, 35). On the evolution of the Italian social welfare system, see Giorgi and Pavan (2021); on the British system see Peden (1985).

5 Greater unionization mirrored greater contestation, which had already exploded in Italy during the hot autumn of 1969 when a season of strikes, factory occupations, student protests, and mass demonstrations spread throughout northern Italy, with its epicenter at Fiat in Turin. Most stoppages were unofficial, led by workers' factory committees or militant leftist groups rather than by the (party-linked) trade unions. The demands echoed those of the "red biennium" of 1919–1920: for example, active participation in industrial management, "egalitarianism" (i.e., reduction of wage differentials among genders, categories, and qualifications), and greater control on income policies (see Ferrera and Gualmini 2004, 43). An important victory came with the signing of the Statute of the Workers

in May 1970, which represented a legal and political turning point for labor rights. For example, the statute reinforced the power of trade unions in the workplace, giving them a central role on factory planning bodies. It also instituted the rule of compulsory re-hiring in the case of no "justified reason" in all enterprises with more than fifteen employees, abolishing the option of paying the penalty instead. In 1975, *Confindustria* even had to accept an agreement that established a new system to index wages to inflation, which would push up wages. These material gains did not prevent further protests from emerging that year: in 1977 an extremely radical student movement united with the growing sector of precarious workers and the most radical sections of the unionized working classes (for example, the metal workers of the *Federazione Lavoratori Metalmeccanici*, FLM) in polemic with the moderatism of CGIL and in favor of a non-capitalist society. For a comprehensive recent reconstruction of the 1977 movement, see Falciola (2015).

6 Thomas and Dimsdale (2017).

7 Ibid.

8 On the Mont Pelerin Society, see Mirowski and Plehwe (2015). Note that the Mont Pelerin economist Friedrich Hayek had a frequent correspondence with Prime Minister Thatcher, who was vastly influenced by him.

9 The "Statement of Aims" of the newly formed Mont Pelerin Society begins with a warning: "The central values of civilization are in danger. Over large stretches of the Earth's surface the essential conditions of human dignity and freedom have already disappeared. In others they are under constant menace from the development of current tendencies of policy. The position of the individual and the voluntary group are progressively undermined by extensions of arbitrary power. Even that most precious possession of Western Man, freedom of thought and expression, is threatened by the spread of creeds which, claiming the privilege of tolerance when in the position of a minority, seek only to establish a position of power in which they can suppress and obliterate all views but their own." See "Statement of Aims," the Mont Pelerin Society, https://www.montpelerin.org/statement-of-aims/.

10 The chancellor spoke the following words: "I propose to raise the excise duties as a whole broadly in line with inflation, but to make some modest adjustments within the total. The duty on cigarettes and hand-rolling tobacco will be increased, by the equivalent, including VAT, of between threepence and fourpence for a packet of 20 cigarettes. This will take effect from midnight on Thursday. The duty on a packet of five small cigars will rise by twopence, but that on pipe tobacco will remain unchanged. As to the alcohol duties, I propose increases which, including VAT, will put about a penny on the price of a pint of average-strength beer and cider, fourpence on a bottle of table wine, and sixpence on a bottle of sparkling or fortified wine. There will once again be no increase in the duty on spirits. These

changes will take effect from 6 o'clock tonight" ("Taxes on Spending," HC Deb 15 March 1988, vol. 129, cc 1003).

11 For a short history of privatizations in Britain that continue unabated after the Thatcher epoch, see Seymour (2012).

12 On anti-union legislation between 1980 and 2000 see the report by the British Trades Union Congress (TUC), http://www.unionhistory.info/timeline/1960_2000_Narr_Display.php?Where=NarTitle+contains+%27Anti-Union+Legislation%3A+1980-2000%27.

13 Author's calculations. The rate of exploitation has been calculated as the ratio of the profit share and the wage share. The data is taken from Thomas and Dimsdale (2017).

14 Council of European Communities (1992, 25).

15 See EU membership criteria: https://ec.europa.eu/neighbourhood-enlargement/policy/conditions-membership_en.

16 About the European integration process, especially after Maastricht, Dyson and Featherstone (1996) comment: "The domestic policy agenda has shifted more decisively to budget retrenchment, reform of the welfare state and privatization; wage and price flexibility have taken on a new importance in a policy framework that rules out devaluation; and constitutional questions have been raised about the performance of the political system and the type of political structure that can best support domestic discipline. There is also a shift in the balance of power between domestic actors, upgrading the role of technocrats and the Banca d'Italia (with, post-Maastricht, two senior Banca d'Italia officials holding office as prime minister)" (1996, 273).

17 For data on public expenditures see Ragioneria Generale dello Stato (RGS 2011). On the wage share dynamics in Italy see Gabbuti (2020a).

18 Mario Monti, interview on the RAI television show *Che tempo che fa*, November 25, 2012, available on YouTube at https://www.youtube.com/watch?v=2L88XcsQvNo.

19 Ibid. Monti stated: "[Regarding the cuts to health care provided for ALS patients] We get to things that are heavy, sometimes very negative, but the answer is simple, it goes so far because it has been considered a petty crime for decades to evade taxation it was considered that individual interest and cunningness had the right of citizenship in all fields, because everyone has protected their privileges."

20 Jepsen (2019). See also data reported in Magnani (2019).

21 For data on real per capita consumption in Italy see Jordà, Schularick, and Taylor (2017).

22 Apart from positions as professors at prestigious universities in the US and Europe (Harvard, Chicago, Stanford, MIT, Bocconi, etc.) and editorial roles with the top economic journals (such as the *Quarterly Journal of Economics*, the *European Economic Review*, etc.), these experts held seats in

prominent institutions for the dissemination of policy-relevant economic research. Alesina, for example, directed the Political Economic Program of the National Bureau of Economic Research (NBER) from its formation in 2006. The professors also worked as consultants for the World Bank, European Central Bank, and International Monetary Fund, and advised government agencies such as the French Treasury, the New York Federal Reserve, the Italian Treasury, and the Italian central bank. They also directly advised Italian governments. Tabellini advised the government of Romano Prodi (2006–2008) and Matteo Renzi (2014–2016); Giavazzi advised Mario Monti (2011–2013) and as of 2021 is currently an advisor for Mario Draghi. The experts also regularly write in the main Italian press. For details on these experts' national and international networks of power, see Helgadóttir (2016).

23 As Alesina astutely summarized: "What keeps an economy from slumping when government spending, a major component of aggregate demand, goes down? . . . The answer: private investment. Our research found that private-sector capital accumulation rose after the spending-cut deficit reductions, with firms investing more in productive activities—for example, buying machinery and opening new plants. . . . After the tax-hike deficit reductions, capital accumulation dropped" (Alesina 2012). Furthermore, Alesina and Perotti (1995) claim that "the main theoretical reasons which suggest that fiscal adjustments may not be contradictory is the 'crowding in' argument: a reduction in the government borrowing requirement, by reducing interest rates, may 'crowd in' private investments" (1995, 21). For a reframing of these arguments, see also Alesina et al. (2019).

24 Alesina, Tabellini, and Perotti have repeated this argument, in favor of austerity based on entrepreneurs' expectations, over reams and reams in the past decades (see for example: Alesina and Ardagna 2010, 2013; Alesina, Ardagna, and Galí 1998; Alesina and Perotti 1995, 1997; Alesina and de Rugy 2013; and Alesina, Favero, and Giavazzi 2015).

25 Indeed, the austere experts displayed a constant anxiety for the potential disruption of the orderly basis of capital accumulation. To them, "debt-financed increases of public employment, wages of public sector employees, unemployment benefits and labor taxes put pressure on unions' wage claims, leading to higher private sector wages, lower employment, capital and output" (Alesina and Ardagna 2013).

26 On supply-side reforms, see Alesina (2012) and Alesina and Rugy (2013).

27 To the point that there exists a large discrepancy between the national electoral results and the representation on the ECB board. In particular, the European Left is vastly underrepresented on the ECB board (see Alesina and Grilli 1991, 29).

28 A central bank is understood to be politically independent if it has the capacity to choose the final goal of monetary policy. Economic indepen-

dence, on the other hand, is the freedom to choose the instruments with which to pursue these goals. See Grilli et al. (1991, 366–67) and Alesina and Grilli (1991). For a detailed analysis of the ECB's institutional characteristics and how they guarantee the highest degree of independence, see Alesina and Grilli (1991). As the former governor of the Central Bank of Cyprus, Athanasios Orphanides, notes: "it [the ECB] is considerably more independent and arguably less accountable than the Fed. In the United States, the Federal Reserve reports to Congress and its powers are subject to change by law. By contrast the European Parliament has relatively little power over the ECB. The legal framework of the ECB is governed by the Treaties of the European Union and as such cannot be modified by any single government or by the European Parliament" (Statement by Athanasios Orphanides before the Subcommittee on Monetary Policy and Trade of the Committee on Financial Services, United States House of Representatives, November 13, 2013, 62–67).

29 "Art 21.1 forbids the ECB to open [new] lines of credit to community or national public institutions, not even on a temporary basis. The same article bans the ECB from participating on the primary market for national government bonds" (Alesina and Grilli 1991, 14–15).

30 Functional Distribution of Income (Percent), Table 2, base 1977 in Agacino and Madrigal (2003, 47). Here the rate of exploitation is calculated as net profits/wages. The authors show that the trend continues, even if at lower rates, after the fall of Pinochet. The change in regime does not mean a change in the underlying austerity agenda. For a brief discussion on how successive governments in Chile preserved Pinochet's economic and institutional model, and on the current struggles to gain back citizens' role, see Vergara (2021).

31 On the estimation of poverty in Latin America, see Económicas, NU CEPAL División de Estadística y Proyecciones (1990).

32 "The World's Worst Central Banker," *Economist*, October 16, 1993, 108.

33 "On Monday, he [Yelstin] shut down several newspapers partial to parliament and banned some political organizations that have opposed him. And he continued a pattern of harassing prominent political opponents— cutting their phone lines, taking away their cars, removing their security details" (Elliott and McKay 1993).

34 "Yeltsin regrets," *Economist*, October 9, 1993, 15ff.

35 In Russia unemployment was 5 percent in 1991 and 13 percent in 1998 (see https://www.macrotrends.net/countries/RUS/russia/unemployment-rate). Real wages declined 40 to 60 percent between 1987 and 1996, catalyzing a major reduction of wage shares, which dropped from 41 percent of GDP in 1987–88 to 26 percent in 1993–94 (see Milanovic 1998, 29).

36 Milanovic (1998, 68, table 5.1, for household budget surveys [HBS]). Klein (2008, 237–38) gives a good picture of the decline in the living conditions

of Russians in those years, which were reflected in higher addiction, suicide, and homicide rates.

37 Non-wage private sector income equals income from sales of agricultural products, entrepreneurial income, interest and dividends, income from abroad, gifts, and income (or consumption).

38 Lawrence H. Summers, "Comment," in Blanchard et al. (1994, 253).

39 See for example "Borrowed Time," *Economist*, May 22, 1993, 66.

40 See breakdown of the $2.3 trillion in: "A Breakdown of the CARES Act," J. P. Morgan, April 14, 2020, https://www.jpmorgan.com/insights/research/cares-act.

41 The ILO's World Employment and Social Outlook Trends 2021, p. 12 (https://www.ilo.org/wcmsp5/groups/public/---dgreports/---dcomm/---publ/documents/publication/wcms_795453.pdf). The report further reads: "Projected employment in 2021, however, will still fall short of its pre-crisis level. In addition, it is likely that there will be fewer jobs than would have been created in the absence of the pandemic. Taking this forgone employment growth into account, the crisis-induced global shortfall in jobs is projected to stand at 75 million in 2021 and at 23 million in 2022. . . . The corresponding shortfall in working hours in 2021 amounts to 3.5 per cent—equivalent to 100 million full-time jobs."

42 The 2021 ILO report tells us that "global labour income, which does not include government transfers and benefits, was US$3.7 trillion (8.3 per cent) lower in 2020 than it would have been in the absence of the pandemic. For the first two quarters of 2021, this shortfall amounts to a reduction in global labour income of 5.3 per cent, or US$1.3 trillion" ("World Employment and Social Outlook Trends," 12). Moreover, the World Bank estimates that in 2020 an additional 78 million people were living in extreme poverty, defined as households with a per capita income of less than US$1.90 per day in PPP terms (Lakner et al. 2021).

43 The combined wealth of these billionaires rose from $8.04 trillion to $12.39 trillion between March 18, 2020, and March 18, 2021. In that year there were 179 more billionaires (see Collins and Ocampo 2021). For a more general perspective on this trend, see Zucman (2019).

44 "A Conversation with Lawrence H. Summers and Paul Krugman," *Princeton Bendheim Center for Finance*, video recording, February 12, 2021, minute 45, https://www.youtube.com/watch?v=EbZ3_LZxs54&t=121s.

Bibliography

Archival Sources

Archivio Centrale dello Stato [Central Archives of the State] (ACS), Piazza degli Archivi, Rome, Italy. Citations of items in this collection will be made by item title or description, date, ACS, collection name, box or folder number, and item number. Catalogue and some digitized items available online at https://www.acs.beniculturali.it.

Bank of England Archives (BoEA), Threadneedle Street, London, UK. Citations of items in this archive will be made by item title or description, date, department code (OV9 = Overseas Department, Papers of Otto Ernst Niemeyer; OV36 = Overseas Department, Italy; G1 = Governor's files, G14 = Committee of Treasury files), collection number, piece and/or item number, and page, folder, or folio numbers. Catalogue and digitized items available online at https://www.bankofengland.co.uk/archive.

Churchill Archive Center, Papers of Sir Ralph Hawtrey (RGH), Churchill College, Cambridge, UK. Citations of items in this collection will be made by item title or description, date, GBR/0014/HTRY, followed by box/folder number and item number. Catalogue and some digitized items available online at https://www.chu.cam.ac.uk/archives/collections/.

Gazzetta Ufficiale del Regno d'Italia, 1917–1926 (GU). Rome: Stabilimento Poligrafico dello Stato. Cited as Law, Regent's Decree [*Decreto luogotenenziale*], Regent's Decree Law [*Decreto-legge luogotenenziale*], Royal Decree [*Regio decreto*], or Royal Decree Law [*Regio decreto legge*], in GU, followed by volume number, date, and page number. Available and searchable online at https://www.gazzettaufficiale.it/homePostLogin.

National Archives of the UK (TNA), Kew, Richmond, UK. Citations of items in this archive will be made by item title or description, date, department code (IR = Inland Revenue, FO = Foreign Office, T = Treasury), collection number,

piece and/or item number, and page, folder, or folio numbers. Some records
and catalogues available online at https://www.nationalarchives.gov.uk.
Proceedings of Parliament, UK. Hansard report of all parliamentary debates.
Cited in text by speaker's name, HC (House of Commons) or HL (House of
Lords), volume number, column number(s), date. Available and searchable
online at https://hansard.parliament.uk.

Published Sources

Addison, Christopher. *The Betrayal of the Slums*. London: H. Jenkins, 1922.

Agacino, Rafael, and María Madrigal. "Chile Thirty Years after the Coup: Chiaro-
scuro, Illusions, and Cracks in a Mature Counterrevolution." *Latin American
Perspectives* 30, no. 5 (2003): 41–69. https://www.jstor.org/stable/3184958.

Alber, Jens. "L'espanzione del welfare state in Europa Occidentale: 1900–1975."
Rivista italiana di scienza politica 13, no. 2 (1983): 203.

Alberti, Manfredi. *Senza lavoro: La disoccupazione in Italia dall'unità a oggi*. First
edition. Bari: GLF Editori Laterza, 2016.

Alesina, Alberto. "Macroeconomic Policy in a Two-Party System as a Repeated
Game." *Quarterly Journal of Economics* 102, no. 3 (1987): 651–78. https://doi
.org/10.2307/1884222.

———. "Macroeconomics and Politics." In *NBER Macroeconomics Annual 1988*,
vol. 3, ed. Stanley Fischer, 13–62. Cambridge, MA: National Bureau of Economic Research, Inc., 1988.

———. "Fiscal Adjustments: Lessons from Recent History." Prepared for the Ecofin Meeting in Madrid, April 15, 2010.

———. "The Kindest Cuts." *City Journal* (Autumn 2012). https://www.city-journal
.org/html/kindest-cuts-13503.html.

Alesina, Alberto, and Silvia Ardagna. "Large Changes in Fiscal Policy: Taxes
versus Spending." *Tax Policy and the Economy* 24, no. 1 (2010): 35–68. https://
doi.org/10.1086/649828.

———. "The Design of Fiscal Adjustments." *Tax Policy and the Economy* 27, no. 1
(2013): 19–68. https://doi.org/10.1086/671243.

Alesina, Alberto, Silvia Ardagna, and Jordi Galí. "Tales of Fiscal Adjustment." *Economic Policy* 13, no. 27 (1998): 489–545. https://www.jstor.org/stable/1344762.

Alesina, Alberto, Silvia Ardagna, Roberto Perotti, et al. "Fiscal Policy, Profits, and
Investment." *American Economic Review* 92, no. 3 (2002): 571–89. https://www
.jstor.org/stable/3083355.

Alesina, Alberto, Omar Barbiero, Carlo Favero, et al. "Austerity in 2009–13." *Economic Policy* 30, no. 83 (July 2015): 383–437. https://doi.org/10.1093/epolic/eiv006.

Alesina, Alberto, and Geoffrey Carliner. *Politics and Economics in the Eighties*.
Chicago: University of Chicago Press, 1991.

Alesina, Alberto, Gerald D. Cohen, and Nouriel Roubini. "Macroeconomic Policy and Elections in OECD Democracies*." *Economics & Politics* 4, no. 1 (1992): 1–30. https://doi.org/10.1111/j.1468-0343.1b00.

Alesina, Alberto, and Veronique de Rugy. *Austerity: The Relative Effects of Tax Increases versus Spending Cuts*. Arlington, VA: Mercatus Center at George Mason University, 2013. https://www.hks.harvard.edu/centers/mrcbg/programs/growthpolicy/austeritythe-relative-effects-tax-increases-versus-spending.

Alesina, Alberto, Carlo Favero, and Francesco Giavazzi. "The Output Effect of Fiscal Consolidation Plans." *Journal of International Economics* 96, 37th Annual NBER International Seminar on Macroeconomics (July 1, 2015): S19–42. https://doi.org/10.1016/j.jinteco.2014.11.003.

Alesina, Alberto, Carlo Favero, et al. *Austerity*. Princeton, NJ: Princeton University Press, 2019.

Alesina, Alberto, and Vittorio Grilli. *The European Central Bank: Reshaping Monetary Politics in Europe*. Working Paper 3860. Cambridge, MA: National Bureau of Economic Research, 1991. https://doi.org/10.3386/w3860.

Alesina, Alberto, James Mirrlees, and Manfred J. M. Neumann. "Politics and Business Cycles in Industrial Democracies." *Economic Policy* 4, no. 8 (1989): 57–98. https://doi.org/10.2307/1344464.

Alesina, Alberto, and Roberto Perotti. *The Political Economy of Budget Deficits*. Working Paper 4637. Cambridge, MA: National Bureau of Economic Research, 1994. https://doi.org/10.3386/w4637.

———. "Reducing Budget Deficits." Paper prepared for the conference "Growing Government Debt—International Experiences," Stockholm, June 12, 1995. https://doi.org/10.7916/D87P95XP.

———. "The Welfare State and Competitiveness." *The American Economic Review* 87, no. 5 (1997): 921–39. https://www.jstor.org/stable/2951333.

Alesina, Alberto, and Howard Rosenthal. "Partisan Cycles in Congressional Elections and the Macroeconomy." *American Political Science Review* 83, no. 2 (1989): 373–98. https://doi.org/10.2307/1962396.

Alesina, Alberto, and Nouriel Roubini. "Political Cycles in OECD Economies." *Review of Economic Studies* 59, no. 4 (1992): 663–88. https://doi.org/10.2307/2297992.

Alesina, Alberto, and Jeffrey Sachs. "Political Parties and the Business Cycle in the United States, 1948–1984." *Journal of Money, Credit and Banking* 20, no. 1 (1988): 63–82. https://doi.org/10.2307/1992667.

Alesina, A., and L. H. Summers. "Central Bank Independence and Macroeconomic Performance: Some Comparative Evidence." *Journal of Money, Credit and Banking* 25, no. 2 (1993), 151–62.

Alesina, Alberto, and Guido Tabellini. "External Debt, Capital Flight and Political Risk." *Journal of International Economics* 27, nos. 3–4 (November 1989): 199–220. https://doi.org/10.1016/0022-1996(89)90052-4.

———. "A Positive Theory of Fiscal Deficits and Government Debt." *The Review of Economic Studies* 57, no. 3 (1990): 403–14. https://doi.org/10.2307/2298021.

——. "Positive and Normative Theories of Public Debt and Inflation in Historical Perspective." *European Economic Review* 36, nos. 2–3 (April 1992): 337–44. https://doi.org/10.1016/0014-2921(92)90089-F.

Arendt, Hannah. "What Is Authority?" In *Between Past and Future: Eight Exercises in Political Thought.* New York: Viking Press, 1961.

Arias, Gino. "Il consiglio delle corporazioni e l'economia corporativa." *Gerarchia* 7, no. 5 (1929): 367–73.

——. "Problemi economici mondiali." *Gerarchia* 10, no. 8 (1931): 643–50.

——. "La crisi bancaria americana." *Gerarchia* 12, no. 3 (1933): 215–19.

Armitage, Susan H. *The Politics of Decontrol of Industry: Britain and the United States.* London: Weidenfeld & Nicolson, 1969.

Arnot, Robert. *Further Facts from the Coal Commission: Being a History of the Second Stage of the Coal Industry Commission; with Excerpts from the Evidence.* London: George Allen and Unwin, 1919.

Augello, Massimo M., et al., eds. *L'economia divulgata: Stili e percorsi Italiani, 1840–1922.* Milan: FrancoAngeli, 2007.

Augello, Massimo, and Luca Michelini. "Maffeo Pantaleoni (1857–1924). Biografia scientifica, storiografia e bibliografia." *Il pensiero economico Italiano* 5, no. 1 (1997): 119–50.

Baccini, Alberto, Fausto Domenicantonio, Giuseppe Felicetti, Andrea Ripa di Meana, Giancarlo Salvemini, and Vera Zamagni. *Banca d'Italia II: Ricerche per la storia della Banca d'Italia.* Rome: Banca d'Italia, 1993. https://www .bancaditalia.it/pubblicazioni/collana-storica/contributi/contributi-02/index .html.

Bachi, Riccardo. *Italia economica nell'anno 1915: Annuario della vita commerciale, industriale, agraria, bancaria, finanziaria e della politica economica.* Città di Castello: S. Lapi, 1916. https://babel.hathitrust.org/cgi/pt?id=njp .32101064528845&view=1up&seq=12&q1=imprenditore.

——. *L'Italia economica nel 1916.* Città di Castello: S. Lapi, 1917.

——. *Italia economica nell'anno 1920: Annuario della vita commerciale, industriale, agraria, bancaria, finanziaria e della politica economica.* Città di Castello: S. Lapi, 1921. https://babel.hathitrust.org/cgi/pt?id=njp.3210106452 8886&view=1up&seq=7&q1=Confederazione%20Generale%20dell%E2%80 %99Agricoltura.

——. *L'alimentazione e la politica annonaria in Italia, con una appendice su "Il rifornimento dei viveri dell'esercito italiano" di Gaetano Zingali.* New Haven, CT: Yale University Press, 1926.

Balandi, Gian Guido, and Gaetano Vardaro, eds. *Diritto del lavoro e corporativismi in Europa, ieri e oggi.* Facoltà di Economia e Commercio di Urbino 6. Milan: F. Angeli, 1988.

Banca d'Italia. *L'archivio di Alberto de' Stefani.* Rome: Banca d'Italia, 1983. https:// www.bancaditalia.it/pubblicazioni/altre-pubblicazioni-asbi/1983-de-stefani/ index.html.

Barbagallo, Francesco. *Francesco S. Nitti*. Turin: Unione tipografico-editrice torinese, 1984.

Bartocci, Enzo. *Le politiche sociali nell'Italia liberale: 1861–1919*. Rome: Donzelli, 1999.

Barucci, P. "La diffusione del marginalismo, 1870–1890." In *Il pensiero economico italiano, 1850–1950*, ed. M. Finoia. Bologna: Cappelli, 1980.

Bel, Germà. "The First Privatisation: Selling SOEs and Privatising Public Monopolies in Fascist Italy (1922–1925)." *Cambridge Journal of Economics* 35, no. 5 (2011): 937–56. https://www.jstor.org/stable/24232431.

Bellanca, N. "'Dai principii' agli 'erotemi.' Un'interpretazione unitaria." *Rivista di politica economica* 85 (1995).

Bezza, Bruno. "La mobilitazione industriale: Nuova classe operaia e contrattazione collettiva." In *Storia della società Italiana*, vol. 21, *La disgregazione dello stato liberale*, 71–102. Milan: Nicola Teti Editore, 1982.

Bini, Piero. "Quando l'economia parlava alla società. La vita, il pensiero e le opere." *Rivista di politica economica* 85 (1995).

———. "'Esiste l'*Homo economicus*? La didattica di Maffeo Pantaleoni: Dai principii di pura alle lezioni di economia politica. In economia divulgata stili e percorsi (1840–1922)." *Manuali e trattati* 1 (2007).

———. *Captains of Industry and Masters of Thought: The Entrepreneur and the Tradition of Italian Liberal Economists from Francesco Ferrara to Sergio Ricossa*. SSRN Scholarly Paper, ID 2718541, Social Science Research Network, April 2013. https://papers.ssrn.com/abstract=2718541.

Bini, Piero, and Antonio Maria Fusco. *Umberto Ricci (1879–1946): Economista militante e uomo combattivo*. Florence: Polistampa, 2004.

Black, R. D. C. "Ralph George Hawtrey 1879–1975." In *Proceedings of the British Academy*. London: British Academy, 1977.

Blackett, Basil. *War Savings in Great Britain, or, The Gospel of Goods and Services, Addresses*. New York: Liberty Loan Committee, 1918a.

———. "Thinking in Terms of Money the Cause of Many Financial Fallacies." *The Annals of the American Academy of Political and Social Science* 75 (1918b): 207–16.

———. "What I Would Do with the World." *The Listener* 6, no. 150 (1931).

———. "The Practical Limits of Taxable Capacity." *Public Administration* 10, no. 3 (1932): 232–41. https://doi.org/10.1111/j.1467-9299.1b01.

Blanchard, Olivier, et al., eds. *The Transition in Eastern Europe*, vol. 1: *Country Studies*. Chicago: University of Chicago Press, 1994.

Blecker, Robert A., and Mark Setterfield. *Heterodox Macroeconomics*. Cheltenham, UK: Edward Elgar, 2019.

Blyth, Mark. *Austerity: The History of a Dangerous Idea*. New York: Oxford University Press, 2013.

Bordogna, Lorenzo. "Le relazioni industriali in Italia dall'accordo Lama-Agnelli alla riforma della scala mobile." In *L'Italia repubblicana nella crisi degli anni settanta. Partiti ed organizzazioni di massa*, ed. Francesco Margeri and Paggi Leonardo, vol. 3, 189–221. Soveria Mannelli: Rubbettino, 2003.

Bortolotti, Lando. "Origine e primordi della rete autostradale in Italia, 1922–1933." *Storia urbana* 16, no. 59 (1992).

Boyce, Robert W. D. *British Capitalism at the Crossroads, 1919–1932: A Study in Politics, Economics, and International Relations.* Cambridge: Cambridge University Press, 1987.

Boyle, Andrew. *Montagu Norman: A Biography.* New York: Weybright and Talley, 1968.

Brosio, Giorgio, and Carla Marchese. *Il potere di spendere: Economia e storia della spesa pubblica dall'unificazione ad oggi.* Bologna: Il Mulino, 1986.

Buffetti, Ferdinando. *Manuale della cooperativa di lavoro e di produzione.* Rome: Buffetti, 1921. https://catalog.hathitrust.org/Record/010694376/Home.

Buozzi, Bruno. "L'Occupazione delle fabbriche." *Almanacco socialista Italiano.* Rome: Partito Socialista Italiano, 1935.

———. "Le condizioni della classe lavoratrice in Italia (1922–1943)." *Annali, Fondazione Giangiacomo Feltrinelli* 14 (1972): 382.

Burgess, Keith. *The Challenge of Labour: Shaping British Society, 1850–1930.* London: Croom Helm, 1980.

Burk, Kathleen, ed. *War and the State: The Transformation of British Government, 1914–1919.* Boston: Allen & Unwin, 1982.

Busino, G. "La riscoperta di Umberto Ricci economista." *Rivista storica Italiana* 112, no. 3 (2000): 1166–74.

Camarda, Alessandro, and Santo Peli. *L'altro esercito: La classe operaia durante la prima guerra mondiale.* First edition. Milan: Feltrinelli Economica, 1980.

Camera dei deputati, Segretariato generale. *La legislazione fascista 1922–1928.* 7 vols. Rome: Typography of the Chamber of Deputies [Tipografia della Camera dei deputati], 1929.

Canzoneri, Matthew B., et al., eds. *Establishing a Central Bank: Issues in Europe and Lessons from the US.* Cambridge: Cambridge University Press, 1992.

Caracciolo, Alberto. "La grande industria nella Prima Guerra Mondiale." In *La formazione dell'Italia industriale*, 163–219. Bari: Laterza, 1963.

———. *Il trauma dell'intervento: 1914/1919.* Florence: Vallecchi, 1968.

———. *La formazione dell'Italia industriale.* Bari: Laterza, 1969.

Cassel, Gustav. "The Economic and Financial Decisions of the Genoa Conference." *Manchester Guardian Commercial*, June 15, 1922, 140.

Castronovo, Valerio. *L'industria Italiana dall'ottocento a oggi.* 2nd edition. Milan: A. Mondadori, 1982.

———. *Storia economica d'Italia: Dall'ottocento ai giorni nostri.* Turin: Einaudi, 1995.

Cecini, S. "Il finanziamento dei lavori pubblici in Italia: Un confronto tra età liberale ed epoca fascista." *Rivista di storia economica* 27, no. 3 (2011): 325–64.

Cherubini, Arnaldo. *Storia della previdenza sociale in Italia 1860–1960.* First edition. Rome: Editori Riuniti, 1977.

Chiozza Money, L. G. *The Triumph of Nationalization.* London and New York:

Cassell and Co., 1920. https://babel.hathitrust.org/cgi/pt?id=aeu.ark:/13960/
t00z8dx5z&view=1up&seq=1.

Ciocca, Pierluigi. *Umberto Ricci: L'uomo l'economista*. Lanciano: Carabba, 1999.

———. "Einaudi e le turbolenze economiche fra le due guerre." *Rivista di storia
economica* 3 (2004): 279–308. https://doi.org/10.1410/18779.

———. *Ricchi per sempre? Una storia economica d'Italia, 1796—2005*. First edition.
Turin: Bollati Boringhieri, 2007.

Clarke, John Joseph. *The Housing Problem: Its History, Growth, Legislation and
Procedure*. New York: Sir I. Pitman & Sons, 1920. https://babel.hathitrust.org/
cgi/pt?id=uc2.ark:/13960/t53f4wz5t&view=1up&seq=7.

Clarke, Simon. *Keynesianism, Monetarism, and the Crisis of the State*. Aldershot,
UK: Gower Publishing, 1988.

Clyne, P. K. "Reopening the Case of the Lloyd George Coalition and the Post-War
Economic Transition." *Journal of British Studies* 10, no. 1 (1970): 162–75.

Coates, Ken, and Anthony Topham, eds. *Industrial Democracy in Great Britain: A
Book of Readings and Witnesses for Workers' Control*. London: Macgibbon &
Kee, 1968.

Cohen, Jon S. "The 1927 Revaluation of the Lira: A Study in Political Economy." *Economic History Review* 25, no. 4 (1972): 642–54. https://doi.org/10.2307/2593953.

———. "Fascism and Agriculture in Italy: Policies and Consequences." *Economic
History Review* 32, no. 1 (1979): 70. https://doi.org/10.2307/2595966.

Cole, G. D. H. *Labour in War Time*. London: George Bell & Sons, 1915.

———. *Chaos and Order in Industry: G. D. H. Cole*. London: Methuen, 1920a.

———. *The World of Labour: A Discussion of the Present and Future of Trade
Unionism*. 4th edition. London: George Bell & Sons, 1920b.

———. "The British Building Guild: An Important Development of Policy." *Journal of the American Institute of Architects* 9, no. 1 (1921a): 289–91.

———. "The Great Building Adventure: The English Building Guilds at Work."
Journal of the American Institute of Architects 9, no. 1 (1921b): 17–19.

———. *Trade Unionism and Munitions*. New York: H. Milford, 1923.

———. *A History of the Labour Party from 1914*. First edition. London: Routledge,
1948. https://doi.org/10.4324/9780429446009.

———. *A History of Socialist Thought, Vol. 4*. New York: St. Martin's Press, 1958.

Collins, Chuck, and Omar Ocampo. "Global Billionaire Wealth Surges $4 Trillion
over Pandemic." Institute for Policy Studies, March 31, 2021. https://ips-dc.org/
global-billionaire-wealth-surges-4-trillion-over-pandemic/.

Comitato Centrale di Mobilitazione. "Le ricerche statistiche per la mobilitazione
industriale e gli ammaestramenti per il dopo-guerra." *Il bollettino del comitato
centrale di mobilitazione* 4 (October 1917): 130–32.

———. "Il problema sociale dell'infortunio sul lavoro." *Il bollettino del comitato
centrale di mobilitazione* 8-9 (February-March 1918): 96–103. https://catalog
.hathitrust.org/Record/012511927.

Committee on Financial Services. *House Hearing, 113th Congress—What Is Central about Central Banking? A Study of International Models*. Washington, DC: US Government Printing Office, 2013. https://www.govinfo.gov/content/pkg/CHRG-113hhrg86685/pdf/CHRG-113hhrg86685.pdf.

Costamagna, Carlo. "La validità della carta del lavoro." *Lo stato* 2, no. 11 (1931).

———. "Direttive di azione economica." *Lo stato* 4, no. 1 (1933): 1–5.

Cotula, F., and L. Spaventa. "La politica monetaria tra le due guerre: 1919–1935." In *La Banca d'Italia: Sintesi della ricercar storica 1893–1960*, ed. F. Cotula, M. De Cecco, and G. Toniolo. Rome and Bari: Laterza, 1993. https://www.semanticscholar.org/paper/La-Politica-monetaria-tra-le-due-guerre-%3A-1919-1935-Cotula-Spaventa/9cf7f455ec7c916874bb19d9e7c9d0ca3b7d7dc2.

Council of European Communities, Commission of the European Communities. "Treaty on European Union." Luxembourg: Office for Official Publications of the European Communities, 1992.

Cox, Garfield V. "The English Building Guilds: An Experiment in Industrial Self-Government." *Journal of Political Economy* 29, no. 10 (December 1921): 777–90.

Coy, Peter. "Why are Fast Food Workers Signing Noncompete Agreements?" *New York Times*, September 29, 2021. https://www.nytimes.com/2021/09/29/opinion/noncompete-agreement-workers.html.

Critchley, T. A. *A History of Police in England and Wales*. Revised edition. London: Constable, 1978.

Crocella, Carlo, et al., eds. *L'inchiesta parlamentare sulle spese di guerra (1920–1923)*. Rome: Camera dei deputati, Archivio storico, 2002.

Cronin, James E. *Industrial Conflict in Modern Britain*. Lanham, MD: Rowman and Littlefield, 1979.

———. *Labour and Society in Britain, 1918–1979*. London: Batsford Academic and Educational, 1984.

Damill, Mario, and Roberto Frenkel. "Argentina: Macroeconomic Performance and Crisis." Paper prepared for the Macroeconomic Policy Task Force of the International Policy Dialogue (IPD), 2003. https://doi.org/10.7916/D8862P4D.

Danninger, Stephan, Alberto Alesina, and Massimo Rostagno. "Redistribution through Public Employment: The Case of Italy." *International Monetary Fund Working Papers* 1999, no. 177 (1999): 44pp. https://doi.org/10.5089/9781451858853.001/.

Daunton, M. J. *Just Taxes: The Politics of Taxation in Britain, 1914–1979*. New York: Cambridge University Press, 2002.

Davis, E. G. "R. G. Hawtrey, 1879–1975." In *Pioneers of Modern Economics in Britain*, 203–33. London: Palgrave Macmillan, 1981.

Davis, Joseph S. "World Currency and Banking: The First Brussels Financial Conference." *Review of Economics and Statistics* 2, no. 12 (1920): 349–60.

Dawson, William Harbutt, ed. *After-War Problems*. London: George Allen & Unwin, 1917. https://babel.hathitrust.org/cgi/pt?id=inu.30000127800187.

De Cecco, M. "Il ruolo delle istituzioni nel pensiero di Pantaleoni." *Rivista di politica economica* 3 (1995).

De Felice, Renzo. *Mussolini il fascista: La conquista del potere (1921–1925)*. Turin: Einaudi, 1966.

De Luca, Giuseppe. "La costruzione della rete autostradale Italiana: L'autostrada Firenze-Mare, 1927–1940." *Storia urbana* 16, no. 59 (1992).

De Stefani, Alberto. *Lezioni di economia politica: Appunti: Anno accademico 1919–20*. Padua: La Litotipo, 1919.

———. "Vilfredo Pareto." *Gerarchia* (1923): 1187–89.

———. *L'azione dello Stato Italiano per le opere pubbliche (1862–1924)*. Rome: Libreria dello Stato, 1925.

———. *La legislazione economia della guerra*. Bari: Laterza; New Haven, CT: Yale University Press, 1926a.

———. *La restaurazione finanziaria 1922–1925*. Modena: N. Zanichelli, 1926b.

———. *Vie maestre: Commenti sulla finanza del 1926*. Trieste: Fratelli Treves, 1927.

———. *Colpi di vaglio: Commenti sulla finanza del 1927*. Milan: Fratelli Treves, 1928.

———. *L'oro e l'aratro*. Milan: Treves, 1929.

———. *Quota 90: La rivalutazione della lira: 1926–1928*. Edited by Marco di Mico; translated by L. Spaventa. Turin: UTET Università, 1998.

De Stefani, Alberto, and Francesco Perfetti. *Gran consiglio, ultima seduta: 24-25 luglio 1943*. Florence: Le Lettere, 2013.

Del Vecchio, Gustavo. "Prefazione." In M. Pavesi, *Economia corporativa e dottrine realiste*, 5–18. Bologna: Stabilimento Poligrafico Riuniti, 1929.

———. "Einaudi Economista." *Giornale degli economisti e annali di economia* 23, no. 3/4 (1964): 136–44. https://www.jstor.org/stable/23238553.

———. "Einaudi economista." In *Einaudi*, ed. M. Achille Romani. Milan: Bocconi Press, 2011.

Deutscher, Patrick. *R. G. Hawtrey and the Development of Macroeconomics*. London: Macmillan, 1990.

———. "Ralph George Hawtrey (1879–1975)." In *The Palgrave Companion to Cambridge Economics*, ed. Robert A. Cord, 477–93. London: Palgrave Macmillan UK, 2017. https://doi.org/10.1057/978-1-137-41233-1_21.

Dingley, Tom. *The Shop Stewards and Workers' Committee Movement*. Coventry: Shop Stewards & Workers' Committee, 1918.

Dobb, Maurice Herbert. *Theories of Value and Distribution since Adam Smith; Ideology and Economic Theory*. Cambridge: Cambridge University Press, 1973.

Dominedò, V. "Umberto Ricci economista." *Economia internazionale* 14, no. 1 (1961): 1–20.

Dyson, Kenneth, and Kevin Featherstone. "Italy and EMU as a 'Vincolo Esterno': Empowering the Technocrats, Transforming the State." *South European Society and Politics* 1, no. 2 (June 1996): 272–99. https://doi.org/10.1080/1360874960 8539475.

Económicas, UN CEPAL División de Estadística y Proyecciones. *Magnitud de la pobreza en América Latina en los años ochenta.* Santiago de Chile: CEPAL, 1990. https://repositorio.cepal.org/handle/11362/33451.

Eichengreen, Barry J. *Golden Fetters: The Gold Standard and the Great Depression, 1919–1939.* New York: Oxford University Press, 1992.

Einaudi, Luigi. *Prediche.* Bari: G. Laterza, 1920.

——. *La guerra e il sistema tributario italiano.* Bari: G. Laterza; New Haven, CT: Yale University Press, 1927.

——. "Le premesse del salario dettate dal giudice." *La riforma sociale* 42 (1931): 311–16.

——. *La condotta economica e gli effetti sociali della guerra italiana.* New Haven, CT: Yale University Press, 1933.

——. *Cronache economiche e politiche di un trentennio (1893–1925).* Turin: Einaudi, 1959–65.

——. *From Our Italian Correspondent: Luigi Einaudi's Articles in* The Economist, *1908–1946.* Edited by Roberto Marchionatti. Florence: L. S. Olschki, 2000.

Elliott, Dorinda, and Betsy McKay. "Yeltsin's Free-Market Offensive." *Newsweek*, October 17, 1993. https://www.newsweek.com/yeltsins-free-market-offensive -194394.

Ermacora, Matteo. *Cantieri di guerra: Il lavoro dei civili nelle retrovie del fronte Italiano 1915–1918.* Bologna: Il Mulino, 2005.

——. "Labour, Labour Movements, Trade Unions and Strikes (Italy)." Translated by Benjamin Ginsborg. In *1914–1918 Online: International Encyclopedia of the First World War,* ed. Ute Daniel, Peter Catrell, Oliver Janz, Heather Jones, Jennifer Keene, Alan Kramer, and Bill Nasson. Berlin: Freie Universität Berlin, 2014. https://doi.org/10.15463/ie1418.10268.

Erreygers, Guido, and Giovanni Di Bartolomeo. "The Debates on Eugenio Rignano's Inheritance Tax Proposals." *History of Political Economy* 39, no. 4 (November 2007): 605–38. https://doi.org/10.1215/00182702-2007-034.

Espuelas, Sergio. "The Inequality Trap: A Comparative Analysis of Social Spending between 1880 and 1930." *Economic History Review* 68, no. 2 (2015): 683–706. https://www.jstor.org/stable/43910359.

Falciola, Luca. *Il movimento del 1977 in Italia.* First edition. Rome: Carocci Editore, 2015.

Farese, Giovanni. *Luigi Einaudi: Un economista nella vita pubblica.* Soveria Mannelli: Rubbettino, 2012.

Faucci, Riccardo. *Luigi Einaudi.* Turin: Unione tipografico-Editrice Torinese, 1986.

——. *A History of Italian Economic Thought.* First edition. London: Routledge, 2014. https://doi.org/10.4324/9781315780993.

Fausto, Domenicantonio. "I contributi di Umberto Ricci alla scienza delle finanze." In *Umberto Ricci (1879–1946): Economista militante e uomo combattivo,* 217–43. Florence: Polistampa, 2004.

Fava, Andrea. "Assistenza e propaganda nel regime di guerra." *Operai e contadini nella Grande Guerra,* ed. Mario Isnenghi. Bologna: Cappelli Editore, 1982.

Favero, Giovanni. "Le statistiche dei salari industriali in periodo fascista." *Quaderni Storici*(new series) 45, no. 134, 2 (2010): 319–57. https://www.jstor.org/stable/43780007.

Federico, Giovanni, et al. "The Origins of the Italian Regional Divide: Evidence from Real Wages, 1861–1913." *Journal of Economic History* 79, no. 1 (March 2019): 63–98. https://doi.org/10.1017/S0022050718000712.

Feinstein, C. H. *National Income, Expenditure and Output of the United Kingdom, 1855–1965.* Cambridge: Cambridge University Press, 1972.

Ferrera, Maurizio, and Elisabetta Gualmini. *Rescued by Europe? Social and Labour Market Reforms in Italy from Maastricht to Berlusconi.* Amsterdam: Amsterdam University Press, 2004.

Ferré-Sadurní, Luis, and Jesse McKinley. "N.Y. Hospitals Face $400 Million in Cuts Even as Virus Battle Rages." *New York Times*, March 30, 2020. https://www.nytimes.com/2020/03/30/nyregion/coronavirus-hospitals-medicaid-budget.html.

Flaschel, Peter, et al. "Kaleckian Investment and Employment Cycles in Post-War Industrialized Economies." In *Mathematical Economics and the Dynamics of Capitalism*, ed. Peter Flaschel and Michael Landesmann. New York: Routledge, 2008.

Flora, Federico. *La politica economica e finanziaria del fascismo (ottobre 1922–giugno 1923).* Milan: Imperia, 1923. https://catalog.hathitrust.org/Record/000959311.

Foley, Duncan K. *Understanding Capital: Marx's Economic Theory.* Cambridge, MA: Harvard University Press, 1986.

Forsyth, Douglas J. *The Crisis of Liberal Italy: Monetary and Financial Policy, 1914–1922.* New York: Cambridge University Press, 1993.

Forte, Francesco. *L'economia liberale di Luigi Einaudi: Saggi.* Florence: L. S. Olschki, 2009.

Foster, John Bellamy, and Robert W. McChesney. *The Endless Crisis: How Monopoly-Finance Capital Produces Stagnation and Upheaval from the USA to China.* New York: Monthly Review Press, 2012.

Franchini, Vittorio. *I comitati regionali per la mobilitazione industriale 1915–1918.* Milan: Alfieri, 1928.

———. *La mobilitazione industriale dell'Italia in guerra: Contributo alla storia economica della guerra 1915–1918.* Rome: Istituto Poligrafico e Zecca dello Stato, 1932.

Franzosi, Roberto. "One Hundred Years of Strike Statistics: Methodological and Theoretical Issues in Quantitative Strike Research." *Industrial and Labor Relations Review* 42, no. 3 (1989): 348–62. https://doi.org/10.2307/2523393.

Frascani, Paolo. *Politica economica e finanza pubblica in Italia nel primo dopoguerra (1918–1922).* Naples: Giannini, 1975.

Gabbuti, Giacomo. *A Noi! Income Inequality and Italian Fascism: Evidence from Labour and Top Income Shares.* Oxford Social History and Economics

Working Papers 177, University of Oxford, Department of Economics, 2020a. https://econpapers.repec.org/paper/oxfesohwp/_5f177.htm.

———. "When We Were Worse Off: The Economy, Living Standards and Inequality in Fascist Italy." *Rivista di storia economica* no. 3 (2020b): 253–98. https://doi.org/10.1410/100485.

———. "Il fascismo 'liberista' e la 'quasi abolizione' dell'imposta di successione del 1923." In *Le sirene del corporativismo e l'isolamento dei dissidenti durante il fascismo*, ed. Piero Barucci et al. Florence: Firenze University Press, 2021. https://doi.org/10.36253/978-88-5518-455-7.07.

Gabbuti, Giacomo, and Maria Gómez-León. "Wars, Depression, and Fascism: Income Inequality in Italy, 1900–1950." Working paper D. T. 2104, Departamento de Economía, Universidad Pública de Navarra, 2021.

Gallacher, William, and J. R. Campbell. *Direct Action: An Outline of Workshop and Social Organization*. London: Pluto Press, 1972. First published December 1919 by the National Council of the Scottish Workers' Committees, 1919.

Gallacher, William, and J. Paton. *Toward Industrial Democracy—A Memorandum on Workshop Control*. Paisley, UK: Paisley Trades and Labour Council, 1918.

Gangemi, Lello. *La politica finanziaria del governo Fascista (1922–1928)*. Florence: R. Sandron, 1929.

Garside, W. R. *British Unemployment, 1919–1939: A Study in Public Policy*. Cambridge and New York: Cambridge University Press, 1990.

Gaukroger, Alan. "The Director of Financial Enquiries." PhD thesis, University of Huddersfield, 2008.

Giachetti, Diego. *La FIAT in mano agli operai: L'autunno caldo del 1969*. Pisa: BFS Edizioni, 1999.

Giasi, Francesco, ed. *Gramsci nel suo tempo*. Rome: Carocci, 2008.

Giocoli, Nicola, and Nicolò Bellanca. *Maffeo Pantaleoni: Il principe degli economisti Italiani*. Florence: Polistampa, 1998.

Giordano, Claire, and Francesco Zollino. "Long-Run Factor Accumulation and Productivity Trends in Italy." *Journal of Economic Surveys* 35, no. 1 (June 2020). https://doi.org/10.1111/joes.12361.

Giorgi, Chiara, and Ilaria Pavan. *Storia dello stato sociale in Italia*. Bologna: Il Mulino, 2021.

Gleason, Arthur. *What the Workers Want: A Study of British Labor*. New York: Harcourt, Brace and Howe, 1920.

Gómez León, María, and Herman J. de Jong. "Inequality in Turbulent Times: Income Distribution in Germany and Britain, 1900–50." *Economic History Review* 72, no. 3 (2018): 1073–98. https://doi.org/10.1111/ehr.12770.

Gordon, Charles, and Edouard Montpetit. *The Genoa Conference for the Economic and Financial Reconstruction of Europe: Joint Report of the Canadian Delegates*. Ottawa, Ont.: F. A. Acland, 1922.

Gramsci, Antonio. "To the Commissars of the Workshop of Fiat Centro and

Brevetti" [Ai Commissari di reparto delle Officine Fiat Centro e Brevetti]. *L'Ordine nuovo* 1, no. 18 (September 13, 1919a): 140.

———. "The Problem of the Internal Commission" [Il problema della Commissioni interne]. *L'Ordine nuovo* 1, no. 15 (August 23, 1919b): 117–18.

———. "Syndicalism and the Councils" [Sindacalismo e Consigli]. *L'Ordine nuovo* 1, no. 25 (November 8, 1919c): 191–92.

———. "The Conquest of the State" [La conquista dello Stato]. *L'Ordine nuovo* 1, no. 9 (July 12, 1919d): 64.

———. "Postilla." *L'Ordine nuovo* 1, no. 15 (August 23, 1919e): 117.

———. "The Programme of *L'Ordine nuovo*" [il programma dell'Ordine nuovo]. *L'Ordine nuovo* 1, no. 12 (August 14, 1920a): 95.

———. "Soviet and Workers' Councils" [Soviet e Consigli di fabbrica]. *L'Ordine nuovo* 1, no. 43 (April 3–10, 1920b): 340.

———. "Chronicles of the New Order" [Cronache dell'*Ordine Nuovo*]. *L'Ordine nuovo* 2, no. 16 (October 2, 1920c): 121.

———. "The Factory Council" [Il consiglio di fabbrica]. *L'Ordine nuovo* 2, no. 5 (June 5, 1920d): 25.

———. "Socialism and Economics" [Socialismo ed economia]. *L'Ordine nuovo* 1, no. 34 (January 17, 1920e): 265.

———. "Superstition and Reality" [Superstizione e realtà]. *L'Ordine nuovo* 2, no. 1 (May 8, 1920f): 2.

———. "Toward a Renewal of the Socialist Party" [Per un rinnovamento del partito socialista]. *L'Ordine nuovo* 2, no. 1 (May 8, 1920g): 3.

———. "The Turin Factory Council Movement." *L'Ordine nuovo*, March 14, 1921. Translated by Michael Carley. https://www.marxists.org/archive/gramsci/1921/03/turin_councils.htm.

Gramsci, Antonio, with Palmiro Togliatti. "Workers' democracy" [Democrazia operaia]. *L'Ordine nuovo* 1, no. 7 (June 21, 1919: 47–48).

Gramsci, Antonio, et al. *Pre-Prison Writings*. Cambridge: Cambridge University Press, 1994.

Great Britain, Royal Commission on Coal Industry. *Reports and Minutes of Evidence, Vol. 1: On the First Stage of the Inquiry*. London: HMSO, 1919a.

———. *Reports and Minutes of Evidence, Vol. 2: On the Second Stage of the Inquiry*. London: HMSO, 1919b.

Grifone, Pietro. *Il capitale finanziario in Italia*. Turin: Einaudi, 1971.

Grilli, Vittorio, et al. "Political and Monetary Institutions and Public Financial Policies in the Industrial Countries." *Economic Policy* 6, no. 13 (1991): 342–92. https://doi.org/10.2307/1344630.

Guarneri, Felice. *Battaglie economiche tra le due grandi guerre*. Milan: Garzanti, 1953.

Hamon, A. "The Workers' Council in Britain" [I consigli degli operai in inghilterra]. *L'Ordine nuovo* 1, no. 19 (September 20–27, 1919): 145.

Hannington, Wal. *Industrial History in Wartime Including a Record of the Shop Stewards' Movement*. London: Lawrence & Wishart Ltd., 1941.

Hargrave, John. *Montagu Norman*. New York: The Greystone Press, 1942.

Harvey, David. *The Limits to Capital*. Oxford: B. Blackwell, 1982.

Hawtrey, R. G. *Good and Bad Trade*. London: Constable & Co., 1913. https://catalog.hathitrust.org/Record/001311354.

——. *Currency and Credit*. London: Longmans, Green & Co., 1919a. https://babel.hathitrust.org/cgi/pt?id=uc1.$b37816&view=1up&seq=7.

——. "The Gold Standard." *Economic Journal* 29, no. 116 (December 1919b): 428–42. https://doi.org/10.2307/2223352.

——. *Currency and Credit*. 2nd edition. London: Longmans, Green & Co., 1923. https://catalog.hathitrust.org/Record/006646138.

——. "Currency and Public Administration." *Public Administration* 3, no. 3 (1925a): 232–45. https://doi.org/10.1111/j.1467-9299.1b02.

——. "Public Expenditure and the Demand for Labour." *Economica* 13 (March 1925b): 38–48. https://www.jstor.org/stable/2548008?seq=1.

——. "Review of *Central Banks*, by C. H. Kisch and W. A. Elkin." *Economic Journal* 38, no. 151 (September 1928): 439–42.

——. *A Century of Bank Rate*. London: Longmans, Green, 1938.

Helgadóttir, Oddný. "The Bocconi Boys Go to Brussels: Italian Economic Ideas, Professional Networks and European Austerity." *Journal of European Public Policy* 23, no. 3 (March 2016): 392–409. https://doi.org/10.1080/13501763.2015.1106573.

Henderson, H. D. "The Reports of the Coal Industry Commission." *Economic Journal* 29, no. 115 (1919): 265–79.

Henwood, Doug. *After the New Economy*. New York: New Press, 2003.

Hinton, James. *The First Shop Stewards' Movement*. London: G. Allen & Unwin, 1973.

His Majesty's Stationery Office. *War Cabinet Report for the Year 1917*. Cmd. 9005, 1918a. House of Commons Parliamentary Papers online.

——. *First Interim Report of the Committee on Currency and Foreign Exchange after the War*. Cmd. 9182. London: HMSO, 1918b.

——. *War Cabinet Report for the Year 1918*. Cmd. 325, 1919a. House of Commons Parliamentary Papers online.

——. *Report of the Provisional Joint Committee Presented to Meeting of Industrial Conference*. Cmd. 501, 1919b. House of Commons Parliamentary Papers online.

——. *Final Report of the Committee on Currency and Foreign Exchange after the War*. Cmd. 464, 1919c.

——. "Draft Resolutions on Economy." Cab 23/23. Meeting of the Cabinet, December 8, 1920, 10 Downing Street. http://filestore.nationalarchives.gov.uk/pdfs/small/cab-23-23-cc-67-20-12.pdf.

——. Finance: Minutes, Records of Cabinet Committees, 1919–1922. Finance Committee, June 30, 1921. Cab 24/201/27, fols. 58–65.

——. "Reports of the Committee of Experts Appointed by the Currency and Exchange Sub-commission of the Financial Commission." Cmd. 1650, 1922a.

———. *First Interim Report of the Committee on National Expenditure.* Cmd. 1581, 1922b.

———. *Second Interim Report of the Committee on National Expenditure.* Cmd. 1582, 1922c.

———. *Third Report of the Committee on National Expenditure.* Cmd. 1589, 1922d.

———. *Report of the Committee on National Debt and Taxation.* Cmd. 2800, 1927. http://hdl.handle.net/2027/mdp.39015036796954.

———. "Memorandum on Unemployment," by Sir William Joynson-Hicks. Cab 24/201, June 13 to July 9, 1929. http://filestore.nationalarchives.gov.uk/pdfs/large/cab-24-204.pdf.

Hobsbawm, E. J. *Industry and Empire: From 1750 to the Present Day.* New York: Penguin Books, 1999.

Hodges, Frank. *Nationalization of the Mines.* New York: Thomas Seltzer, Inc., 1920.

Hood, Christopher, and Rozana Himaz. "The UK Geddes Axe of the 1920s in Perspective." In *When the Party's Over: The Politics of Fiscal Squeeze in Perspective,* ed. Christopher Hood, David Heald, and Rozana Himaz. Oxford: British Academy, 2014. British Academy Scholarship Online, 2015. https://doi.org/10.5871/bacad/9780197265734.003.0004.

Howson, Susan. "'A Dear Money Man'?: Keynes on Monetary Policy, 1920." *Economic Journal* 83, no. 330 (1973): 456–64. https://doi.org/10.2307/2231181.

———. "The Origins of Dear Money, 1919–20." *Economic History Review* 27, no. 1 (1974): 88–107.

———. *Domestic Monetary Management in Britain, 1919–38.* Cambridge: Cambridge University Press, 1975.

———. "Monetary Theory and Policy in the Twentieth Century: The Career of R. G. Hawtrey." In *Proceedings of the Seventh International Economic History Conference,* ed. M. Flinn, 505–12. Edinburgh: Edinburgh University Press, 1978.

———. "Hawtrey and the Real World." In *Keynes and His Contemporaries,* ed. G. C. Harcourt, 142–88. London: Macmillan, 1985a.

———. "Review of *The Making of Keynes' General Theory,* by Richard F. Kahn." *Journal of Economic History* 45, no. 4 (1985b): 1023–24. https://doi.org/10.1017/S0022050700035610.

Howson, Susan, and Donald Winch. *The Economic Advisory Council, 1930–1939: A Study in Economic Advice during Depression and Recovery.* Cambridge: Cambridge University Press, 1977.

Hurwitz, Samuel Justin. *State Intervention in Great Britain: A Study of Economic Control and Social Response, 1914–1919.* New York: Columbia University Press, 1949.

Inman, Phillip, and Robert Booth. "Poverty Increases among Children and Pensioners across UK." *The Guardian* (US edition), March 28, 2019. https://www.theguardian.com/society/2019/mar/28/poverty-increases-among-children-and-pensioners-across-uk.

International Labor Organization. *World Employment and Social Outlook Trends 2021.* 2021. https://www.ilo.org/global/research/global-reports/weso/trends 2021/lang--en/index.htm.

Invernizzi-Accetti, Carlo. *What Is Christian Democracy? Politics, Religion and Ideology.* Cambridge: Cambridge University Press, 2019.

Isnenghi, Mario, ed. *Operai e contadini nella grande guerra.* Bologna: Cappelli, 1982.

Istituto Nazionale di Statistica. "Calcolo della soglia di povertà assoluta." Dati analisi e prodotti. Last updated February 2, 2021. https://www.istat.it/it/dati -analisi-e-prodotti/contenuti-interattivi/soglia-di-poverta.

———. "Le statistiche dell'istat sulla povertà, anno 2020: Torna a crescere la povertà assoluta." Statistiche report, la povertà in Italia. June 16, 2021. https:// www.istat.it/it/files/2021/06/REPORT_POVERTA_2020.pdf.

Istituto Nazionale Fascista Infortuni. *Rassegna della previdenza sociale* 10, no. 6 (1923): 120. Rome: Cassa Nazionale Fascista Infortuni.

Ives, Martyn. *Reform, Revolution and Direct Action amongst British Miners: The Struggle for the Charter in 1919.* Leiden: Brill, 2016.

Jacchia, Arturo. "Workers' Life" [Vita Operaia]. *L'Ordine nuovo* 1, no. 9 (July 12, 1919): 66.

Jason (Pseud.). *Past and Future.* London: Chatto & Windus, 1918.

Jepsen, Maria, ed. *Benchmarking Working Europe 2019.* Brussels: European Trade Union Institute, 2019. https://www.etui.org/publications/books/benchmarking -working-europe-2019.

Johnson, Paul Barton. *Land Fit for Heroes: The Planning of British Reconstruction, 1916–1919.* Chicago: University of Chicago Press, 1968.

Jones, Thomas. *Whitehall Diary.* Oxford: Oxford University Press, 1969.

Jordà, Òscar, Moritz Schularick, and Alan M. Taylor. 2017. "Macrofinancial History and the New Business Cycle Facts." In *NBER Macroeconomics Annual 2016*, vol. 31, ed. Martin Eichenbaum and Jonathan A. Parker. Chicago: University of Chicago Press, 2017.

Joslyn, Carl S. "The British Building Guilds: A Critical Survey of Two Years' Work." *Quarterly Journal of Economics* 37, no. 1 (1922): 75–133. https://doi.org/ 10.2307/1885910.

Kalecki, M. "Political Aspects of Full Employment." *Political Quarterly* 14, no. 4 (1943): 322–30. https://doi.org/10.1111/j.1467-923X.1b01.

Kelton, Stephanie. *The Deficit Myth: Modern Monetary Theory and the Birth of the People's Economy.* New York: Public Affairs, 2020.

Kendall, Walter. *The Revolutionary Movement in Britain 1900–1921: The Origins of British Communism.* London: Weidenfeld and Nicolson, 1969.

Keynes, John Maynard. *The General Theory of Employment, Interest, and Money.* London: Palgrave Macmillan, 1964.

———. *The Collected Writings of John Maynard Keynes.* New York: St. Martin's Press, for the Royal Economic Society, 1971.

———. *The Economic Consequences of the Peace*. London: Taylor and Francis, Ltd.; New York: Routledge, 2017.

Kirby, M. W. *The British Coal Mining Industry, 1870–1946: A Political and Economic History*. London: Macmillan, 1977.

Klein, Naomi. *The Shock Doctrine: The Rise of Disaster Capitalism*. London: Picador, 2008.

Kreis, Steven. *The Diffusion of an Idea: A History of Scientific Management in Britain, 1890–1945*. PhD diss., University of Missouri-Columbia, 1990.

Krugman, Paul. "The Case for Cuts Was a Lie. Why Does Britain Still Believe It? The Austerity Delusion." *The Guardian* (US edition), April 29, 2015. https://www.theguardian.com/business/ng-interactive/2015/apr/29/the-austerity-delusion

Labanca, Nicola, and Giovanna Procacci. *Caporetto. Esercito, stato e società*. Florence: Giunti Editore, 2018.

Labour Party (Great Britain), Executive Committee. Labour and the New Social Order: A Report on Reconstruction. London: Labour Party, 1918.

———. *Report of the Nineteenth Annual Conference of the Labour Party,* June 25, 1919. Nottingham and London: Labour Party, 1919.

La Francesca, Salvatore. *La politica economica del Fascismo*. Bari: Laterza, 1972.

Laidler, David. "Hawtrey and the Origins of the Chicago Tradition." *Journal of Political Economy* 10, no. 6 (1993): 1068–1103.

Lakner, Christoph, et al. *Updated Estimates of the Impact of COVID-19 on Global Poverty: Looking Back at 2020 and the Outlook for 2021*. World Bank blogs, January 11, 2021. https://blogs.worldbank.org/opendata/updated-estimates-impact-covid-19-global-poverty-looking-back-2020-and-outlook-2021.

Lay, Adriana, Dora Marucco, and Maria Luisa Pesante. "Classe operaia e scioperi: Ipotesi per il periodo 1880–1923." *Quaderni storici* 8, no. 22/1 (1973): 87–147.

League of Nations. *Brussels Financial Conference 1920*. 5 vols. London: Printed for the League of Nations by Harrison and Sons, Ltd., 1920–1921. [Cited in text as Brussels 1920, followed by volume and page numbers.]

———. *Three Months of the League of Nations*. Boston: World Peace Foundation, 1920.

———. *Report of the Advisory Committee, International Financial Conference 1920*. London: Printed for the League of Nations by Harrison & Sons, 1920.

Levrero, E., and Antonella Stirati. "Real Wages in Italy 1970–2000: Elements for an Interpretation." *Economia & lavoro* 38, no. 1 (2004): 65–89. https://www.semanticscholar.org/paper/Real-Wages-in-Italy-1970-2000%3A-Elements-for-an-Levrero-Stirati/e9c0e323e752d32e326b4d19a1ce93e0da19bd18.

Lloyd, E. M. H. *Experiments in State Control at the War Office and the Ministry of Food*. London: H. Milford, 1924.

———. "Gold and Coal." *New Statesman* 25, no. 639 (July 25, 1925).

Lunghini, G., and Stefano Lucarelli. *The Resistible Rise of Mainstream Econom-*

ics: The Dominant Theory and the Alternative Economic Theories. Bergamo: University of Bergamo Press, 2012.

Lyttelton, Adrian. *The Seizure of Power: Fascism in Italy, 1919–1929.* New York: Scribner, 1973.

Macfarlane, L. J. "Hands off Russia: British Labour and the Russo-Polish War, 1920." *Past & Present* 38 (December 1967): 126–52.

Macnicol, John. *The Politics of Retirement in Britain, 1878–1948.* Cambridge: Cambridge University Press, 2002.

MacRae, C. Duncan. "A Political Model of the Business Cycle." *Journal of Political Economy* 85, no. 2 (1977): 239–63. https://www.jstor.org/stable/1830790.

Magnani, Alberto. "Retribuzioni, calo del 4,3% in 7 anni. Perché il problema dell'Italia sono gli stipendi." *Il Sole 24 Ore*, February 17, 2019. https://www .ilsole24ore.com/art/retribuzioni--calo-43percento-7-anni-perche-problema -dell-italia-sono-stipendi--ABWtwpSB?refresh_ce=1.

Maione, Giuseppe. *Il Biennio Rosso: Autonomia e spontaneità operaia nel 1919– 1920.* Bologna: Il Mulino, 1975.

Manestra, Stefano. *A Short History of Tax Compliance in Italy.* Questioni di Economia e Finanza 81, December 2010. https://www.bancaditalia.it/pubblicazioni/ qef/2010-0081/QEF_81.pdf.

Mankiw, N. Gregory. *Principles of Microeconomics.* 5th edition. Boston: South-Western Cengage Learning, 2009.

Mann, Geoff. *In the Long Run We Are All Dead: Keynesianism, Political Economy, and Revolution.* New York: Verso, 2017.

Marchionatti, Roberto. *Economic Theory in the Twentieth Century: An Intellectual History*, Vol. 2. Cham, Switzerland: Palgrave Macmillan, 2021.

Marcoaldi, Franco. "Maffeo Pantaleoni, la riforma finanziaria e il governo fascista nel periodo dei pieni poteri, attraverso le lettere ad Alberto De' Stefani." *Annali della Fondazione Luigi Einaudi* 14 (1980): 609–66.

———. *Vent'anni di economia e politica: Le carte De' Stefani, 1922–1941.* Milan: FrancoAngeli, 1986.

Marucco, Dora. "Alle origini del Ministero del Lavoro e della Previdenza Sociale in Italia [Electronic Resource]." *Il Mulino (The Mill)* (2008): 179–90. https://doi .org/10.1411/27173.

Marx, Karl, and Friedrich Engels. *Selected Works.* Moscow: Progress Publishers, 1969–1970. First published in 1888.

Mattei, Clara Elisabetta. "The Conceptual Roots of Contemporary Austerity Doctrine: A New Perspective on the 'British Treasury View.'" *New School Economic Review (NSER)* 8 (2016). https://nsereview.org/index.php/NSER/issue/view/8.

———. "Austerity and Repressive Politics: Italian Economists in the Early Years of the Fascist Government." *European Journal of the History of Economic Thought* 24, no. 5 (September 2017): 998–1026. https://doi.org/10.1080/09672567.2017 .1301510.

———. "Hawtrey, Austerity, and the 'Treasury View,' 1918 to 1925." *Journal of the*

History of Economic Thought 40, no. 4 (2018a): 471–92. https://doi.org/10.1017/ S1053837218000068.

———. "Treasury View and Post-WWI British Austerity: Basil Blackett, Otto Niemeyer and Ralph Hawtrey." *Cambridge Journal of Economics* 42, no. 4 (July 2018b): 1123–44. https://doi.org/10.1093/cje/bex061.

Matteotti, G. "La questione tributaria." Critica Sociale 29, nos. 6-7 (1919): 82–83.

Mattesini, F., and B. Quintieri. "Does a Reduction in the Length of the Working Week Reduce Unemployment? Some Evidence from the Italian Economy during the Great Depression." *Explorations in Economic History* 43, no. 3 (July 2006): 413–37. https://doi.org/10.1016/j.eeh.2005.04.001.

McDonald, Andrew. "The Geddes Committee and the Formulation of Public Expenditure Policy, 1921–1922." *The Historical Journal* 32, no. 3 (1989): 643–74.

McKibbin, Ross. *The Evolution of the Labour Party, 1910–1924.* Oxford: Oxford University Press, 1974.

———. *The Ideologies of Class: Social Relations in Britain, 1880–1950.* New York: Oxford University Press, 1990.

Medlicott, W. N., et al., eds. *Documents on British Foreign Policy, 1919–1939.* London: His Majesty's Stationery Office, 1974.

Melis, G. *La macchina imperfetta. Immagine e realtà dello Stato fascista.* Bologna: Il Mulino, 2018.

Menozzi, Daniele, et al., eds. *Un paese in guerra: La mobilitazione civile in Italia, 1914–1918.* First edition. Milan: Edizioni Unicopli, 2010.

Michelini, Luca. "Il pensiero di Maffeo Pantaleoni tra economia politica e politica militante." *Societá e storia* 58 (1992).

———. *Marginalismo e socialismo: Maffeo Pantaleoni, 1882–1904.* Milan: FrancoAngeli, 1998.

———. *Alle origini dell'antisemitismo nazional-fascista: Maffeo Pantaleoni e 'la vita Italiana' di Giovanni Preziosi, 1915–1924.* Venice: Marsilio, 2011a. https://www .academia.edu/42658223/Alle_origini_dellantisemitismo_nazional_fascista _Maffeo_Pantaleoni_e_La_Vita_italiana_di_Giovanni_Preziosi_1915_1924.

———. *Marxismo, liberismo, rivoluzione: Saggio sul Giovane Gramsci, 1915–1920.* Milan: La Città del Sole, 2011b.

———. *Il nazionalismo economico Italiano: Corporativismo, liberismo, fascismo: (1900–23).* Rome: Carocci Editore, 2019.

———. "From Nationalism to Fascism: Protagonists and Journals." In *An Institutional History of Italian Economics in the Interwar Period—Volume II,* ed. Massimo M. Augello et al., 21–57. New York: Springer International Publishing, 2020. https://doi.org/10.1007/978-3-030-38331-2_2.

Middlemas, Keith. *Politics in Industrial Society: The Experience of the British System since 1911.* London: A. Deutsch, 1979.

Middleton, Roger. *Towards the Managed Economy.* New York: Routledge, 1985. https://doi.org/10.4324/9781315019567.

Migone, Gian Giacomo. *The United States and Fascist Italy: The Rise of American*

Finance in Europe. First English edition. Cambridge: Cambridge University Press, 2015.

Milanovic, Branko. *Income, Inequality, and Poverty during the Transition from Planned to Market Economy (English)*. World Bank Regional and Sectoral Studies. Washington, DC: World Bank Group, 1998. https://documents .worldbank.org/en/publication/documents-reports/documentdetail/ 229251468767984676/Income-inequality-and-poverty-during-the-transition -from-planned-to-market-economy.

———. *Capitalism, Alone: The Future of the System that Rules the World*. Cambridge, MA: The Belknap Press of Harvard University Press, 2019.

Miliband, Ralph. *Parliamentary Socialism: A Study in the Politics of Labour*. London: Allen & Unwin, 1961.

———. *The State in Capitalist Society*. London: Weidenfeld & Nicolson, 1969.

Miller, Earl Joyce. "Workmen's Representation in Industrial Government." PhD thesis, University of Illinois, 1922. Reprinted in *University of Illinois Studies in the Social Sciences* 10, nos. 3–4 (1924).

Millis, H. A. "The British Trade Disputes and Trade Unions Act, 1927." *Journal of Political Economy* 36, no. 3 (1928): 305–29. https://www.jstor.org/stable/ 1822749.

Ministero dell'Economia Nazionale. *I conflitti del lavoro in Italia nel decennio 1914–1923 (dati statistici)*. Rome: "Grafia" SAI industrie grafiche, 1924.

Ministero delle Finanze. *L'azione dello stato Italiano per le opere pubbliche (1862–1924)*. Rome: Libreria dello stato, 1925.

Ministero per il Lavoro e la Previdenza Sociale. *Bollettino del lavoro e della previdenza sociale*, vol. 39, no. 1. Rome: Tipografia Cooperativa Sociale, 1923.

Ministero per l'Assistenza Militare e le Pensioni di Guerra, ed. *L'assistenza di guerra in Italia: assistenza militare, pensioni di guerra*. Rome: Società Anonima Poligrafica Italiana, 1919.

Ministry of Labour. *Industrial Councils. The Whitley Report*. London: HMSO, 1917.

———. *Report of the Committee of Enquiry on the Employment Exchanges*. Cmd. 1054, 1920.

Ministry of Reconstruction. *Interim Report of the Committee on Adult Education*. Cd. 9107. London: HMSO, 1918. https://archive.org/details/cu31924032188751.

———. *Adult Education Committee Final Report*. Cmd. 321. London: HMSO, 1919a.

———. *Report of the Women's Employment Committee*. Cd. 9239, 1919b.

Ministry of Reconstruction Advisory Council. *Women's Housing Sub-Committee Final Report*. Cd. 9232. London: HMSO, 1919.

Miozzi, U. Massimo. *La mobilitazione industriale italiana (1915–1918)*. Rome: La Goliardica, 1980.

Mirowski, Philip, and Dieter Plehwe, eds. *The Road from Mont Pèlerin: The Making of the Neoliberal Thought Collective, with a New Preface*. First Harvard University Press paperback edition. Cambridge, MA: Harvard University Press, 2015.

Missiroli, Mario. *Una battaglia perduta*. Milan: Corbaccio, 1924.

Mitchell, B. R. *International Historical Statistics: Europe, 1750–1993*. 14th edition. London: Palgrave Macmillan, 1998.

Mittnik, Stefan, and Willi Semmler. "Regime Dependence of the Fiscal Multiplier." *Journal of Economic Behavior & Organization* 83, no. 3, The Great Recession: Motivation for Re-thinking Paradigms in Macroeconomic Modeling (August 1, 2012): 502–22. https://doi.org/10.1016/j.jebo.2012.02.005.

Moggridge, D. E. (Donald Edward). *British Monetary Policy, 1924–1931, the Norman Conquest of $4.86*. Cambridge: Cambridge University Press, 1972.

———. *John Maynard Keynes*. New York: Penguin Books, 1976.

Montagna, Mario. "The Reverse of the Medal" [Il rovescio della medaglia]. *L'Ordine nuovo* 1, no. 26 (November 15, 1919): 202–3.

Montgomery, David. *The Fall of the House of Labor: The Workplace, the State, and American Labor Activism, 1865–1925*. First edition. Cambridge: Cambridge University Press, 1987. https://doi.org/10.1017/CBO9780511528774.

Monthly Labour Review. "The Housing Situation in England." *Monthly Labor Review* 12, no. 1 (January 1921): 213–21. https://www.jstor.org/stable/41827945.

Moraglio, M. "Dentro e fuori il manicomio. L'assistenza psichiatrica in Italia tra le due guerre." *Contemporanea* 9 (2006): 15–34.

Moreolo, Carlo Svaluto. "Carlo Cottarelli: 'There's No Spending Your Way out of Debt.'" *IPE Magazine* (July/August 2018). https://www.ipe.com/carlo-cottarelli-theres-no-spending-your-way-out-of-debt/10025492.article.

Morgan, E. Victor. *Studies in British Financial Policy, 1914–25*. London: Macmillan, 1952.

Morgan, Jane. *Conflict and Order: The Police and Labor Disputes in England and Wales, 1900–1939*. New York: Clarendon Press, 1987.

Morgan, Kenneth. *Consensus and Disunity: The Lloyd George Coalition Government 1918–1922*. Oxford: Oxford University Press, 1979.

Morgan, Kenneth O., and Jane Morgan. *Portrait of a Progressive: The Political Career of Christopher, Viscount Addison*. New York: Oxford University Press, 1980.

Mortara, Giorgio. *Prospettive economiche*. Città di Castello: Societá Tipografica "Leonardo da Vinci," 1922.

Mosca, Manuela. "'Io che sono Darwinista.' La visione di Maffeo Pantaleoni" ("I Am a Darwinist." Maffeo Pantaleoni's Vision). *Il pensiero economico Italiano* 23, no. 1 (2015): 23–45. https://ideas.repec.org/a/pei/journl/v23y201512p23-45.html.

Mowat, Charles Loch. *Britain between the Wars, 1918–1940*. London: Methuen, 1955.

Murphy, John Thomas. *The Workers' Committee, An Outline of Its Principles and Structure*. Sheffield: Sheffield Workers' Committee, 1917.

———. *New Horizons*. London: John Lane The Bodley Head, 1941.

Musso, Stefano. *Storia del lavoro in Italia: Dall'unità a oggi*. Venice: Marsilio, 2002.

Mussolini, Benito. *Discorsi sulla politica economica Italiana nel primo decennio.* Rome: Edito a cura dell'Istituto italiano di credito marittimo, 1933.

Natoli, Claudio. "Primo settembre, occupazione delle fabbriche." In *Calendario civile, per una memoria laica, popolare e democratica degli Italiani,* ed. Alessandro Portelli, 189–201. Rome: Donzelli Editore, 2017.

Nenni, Pietro. *Storia di quattro anni: 1919–1922.* 2nd edition. Turin: G. Einaudi, 1946.

Niemeyer, Otto Ernst. *Report Submitted to the Brazilian Government.* Rio de Janeiro: S. I., 1931.

Nordhaus, William D. "The Political Business Cycle." *Review of Economic Studies* 42, no. 2 (1975): 169–90. https://doi.org/10.2307/2296528.

North, Douglass C., and Robert Paul Thomas. *The Rise of the Western World: A New Economic History.* Cambridge: Cambridge University Press, 1973.

Ostergaard, Geoffrey. *The Tradition of Workers' Control: Selected Writings.* London: Freedom Press, 1997.

Oxfam. "IMF Paves Way for New Era of Austerity Post-COVID-19." *Oxfam International,* 11 December 2020. https://www.oxfam.org/en/press-releases/imf -paves-way-new-era-austerity-post-covid-19.

Paggi, Leonardo. *Le strategie del potere in Gramsci: Tra fascismo e socialismo in un solo paese, 1923–1926.* Rome: Editori Riuniti, 1984.

Pantaleoni, Maffeo. *Pure Economics.* London: Macmillan, 1898.

———. *Corso di economia politica: Lezioni dell'anno 1909–1910 redatte dal Dott. Carlo Manes.* Rome: Associazione Universitaria Romana, 1910.

———. "Note." In *Margine alla guerra.* Bari: Laterza, 1917.

———. *Politica: Criteri ed eventi.* Bari: G. Laterza, 1918.

———. *La fine provvisoria di un'Epopea.* Bari: Laterza, 1919.

———. *Bolcevismo Italiano.* Bari: G. Laterza, 1922. http://archive.org/details/ BolscevismoItaliano.

———. "Finanza fascista." *Politica* 15, nos. 44–45 (1923): 159–87.

Park, Emma, Derek R. Peterson, Anne Pitcher, and Keith Breckenridge. "Intellectual and Cultural Work in Times of Austerity." *Africa* 91, no. 4 (2021).

Parrillo, F. "Profilo di Alberto De Stefani." *Rivista bancaria* 12 (1984): 586–89.

Pavan, Ilaria. "'Nelle Trincee e sui campi.' Guerra, dopoguerra e stato sociale in Italia (1917–1921)." In *La libertà del lavoro: Storia, diritto, società,* ed. Laura Cerasi. Palermo: New Digital frontiers, 2016.

———. "War and the Welfare State: The Case of Italy, from WWI to Fascism." *Historia contemporanea* 61 (2019): 835–72.

Peden, G. C. "Sir Richard Hopkins and the 'Keynesian Revolution' in Employment Policy, 1929–45." *Economic History Review* 36, no. 2 (1983a): 281–96.

———. "The Treasury as the Central Department of Government, 1919–1939." *Citation Public Administration* 61, no. 4 (1983b): 371–85.

———. "The 'Treasury View' on Public Works and Employment in the Interwar Period." *Economic History Review* 37, no. 2 (1984): 167–81. https://doi.org/10 .2307/2596879.

——. *British Economic and Social Policy: Lloyd George to Margaret Thatcher.* Deddington, Oxfordshire: P. Allan, 1985.

——. "The Road to and from Gairloch: Lloyd George, Unemployment, Inflation, and the 'Treasury View' in 1921." *Twentieth Century British History* 4, no. 3 (1993): 224–49. https://doi.org/10.1093/tcbh/4.3.224.

——. "The Treasury View in the Interwar Period: An Example of Political Economy?" In *Unemployment and the Economists*, ed. Bernard Corry. Cheltenham, UK: Edward Elgar, 1996.

——. *The Treasury and British Public Policy, 1906–1959.* Oxford: Oxford University Press, 2000.

——, ed. *Keynes and His Critics: Treasury Responses to the Keynesian Revolution, 1925–1946.* Oxford: Oxford University Press, 2004a.

——. "The Treasury and the City." In *The British Government and the City of London in the Twentieth Century*, by Philip Williamson and R. C. Michie. Cambridge: Cambridge University Press, 2004b.

Pedersen, Susan. "Gender, Welfare, and Citizenship in Britain during the Great War." *American Historical Review* 95, no. 4 (1990): 983–1006. https://doi.org/10.2307/2163475.

——. *Family, Dependence, and the Origins of the Welfare State: Britain and France, 1914–1945.* New York: Cambridge University Press, 1993.

Peli, Santo. "La fabbrica militarizzata." In *Gli Italiani in guerra: Conflitti, identità, memorie dal risorgimento ai nostri giorni*, ed. Mario Isnenghi and Daniele Ceschin, vol. 3, 662–69. Turin: UTET, 2008.

Pelling, Henry. *History of British Trade Unionism.* London: Palgrave Macmillan, 1987.

Pennacchi, Antonio. *Canale Mussolini: Romanzo.* Milan: Mondadori, 2010.

Perotti, Roberto. *The "Austerity Myth": Gain without Pain?* Working Paper 17571, National Bureau of Economic Research, November 2011. https://doi.org/10.3386/w17571.

Pietravalle, Michele. "Per un ministero della sanità ed assistenza pubblica in Italia." *Nuova antologia* 54, no. 1131 (March 1919): 103–17.

Pigou, A. C. *Aspects of British Economic History: 1918–1925.* London: Routledge, 1947. https://doi.org/10.4324/9781315409979.

Piketty, Thomas, and Arthur Goldhammer. *Capital in the Twenty-First Century.* Cambridge, MA: The Belknap Press of Harvard University Press, 2014.

Polanyi, Karl. *The Great Transformation: The Political and Economic Origins of Our Time.* Boston: Beacon Press, 1944.

Pollard, Sidney. *The Development of the British Economy, 1914–1967.* 2nd edition, revised. London: Edward Arnold, 1969.

Porisini, Giorgio. *Il capitalismo Italiano nella prima guerra mondiale.* First edition. Florence: La Nuova Italia, 1975.

Pratt, E. L. *Industrial Unionism.* London: Solidarity Press, 1917.

Preti, A., and C. Venturoli. "Fascismo e stato sociale." In *Povertà e innovazioni istituzionali in Italia. Dal Medioevo ad oggi*, ed. V. Zamagni, 729–49. Bologna: Il Mulino, 2000.

Pribićević, Branko. *The Shop Stewards' Movement and Workers' Control, 1910–1922*. Oxford: Blackwell, 1959.

Price, Carter C., and Kathryn A. Edwards. "Trends in Income from 1975 to 2018." RAND Corporation Working Paper WR-A516-1, 2020. https://www.rand.org/pubs/working_papers/WRA516-1.html.

Procacci, G., ed. *Stato e classe operaia in Italia durante la prima guerra mondiale*. Milan: FrancoAngeli, 1983.

———. *Dalla rassegnazione alla rivolta: Mentalità e comportamenti popolari nella grande guerra*. Rome: Bulzoni, 1999.

———. *Warfare-Welfare: Intervento dello stato e diritti dei cittadini (1914–18)*. Rome: Carocci, 2013.

Procacci, Giovanna, and P. Corner. "The Italian Experience of Total Mobilization 1915–1920." In *State Society and Mobilization in Europe during the First World War*, ed. John Horne, 223–41. Cambridge: Cambridge University Press, 1997.

Ragioneria Generale dello Stato (RGS). "La spesa del balancio dello stato dall'unità d'Italia, anni 1862–2009." Excel spreadsheet, 2011, included in Ministero dell'Economia e della Finanze, 1500 Anniversario RGS, "La spesa dello stato dall'unità d'Italia." https://www.rgs.mef.gov.it/VERSIONE-I/pubblicazioni/pubblicazioni_statistiche/la_spesa_dello_stato_dallunit_dItalia/.

Rattner, Steven. "Volcker Asserts US Must Trim Living Standard." Special to the *New York Times*, October 18, 1979. https://www.nytimes.com/1979/10/18/archives/volcker-asserts-us-must-trim-living-standard-warns-of-inflation.html.

Redmayne, R. A. S. *The British Coal-Mining Industry during the War*. Oxford: Clarendon Press and H. Milford, 1923.

Ricci, Umberto. "Rassegna del movimento scientifico: Economia." *Giornale degli economisti* 34 (February 1907, series II): 152–63.

———. "Rassegna del movimento scientifico: Economia." *Giornale degli economisti* 36 (May 1908, series II): 385–405. https://babel.hathitrust.org/cgi/pt?id=umn.319510019080341&view=1up&seq=16.

———. *Politica ed economia*. Rome: Società Anonima Editrice "La Voce," 1919.

———. *La politica economica del ministero Nitti: Gli effetti dell'intervento economico dello stato*. Rome: Società Anonima Editrice "La Voce," 1920.

———. *Il fallimento della politica annonaria*. Rome: Società Anonima Editrice "La Voce," 1921.

———. "Il miglioramento del bilancio dello stato." *Rivista di politica economica* 13, no. 6 (1923): 593–612.

———. *Dal protezionismo al sindacalismo*. Bari: Laterza, 1926.

———. "La scienza e la vita." *Nuovi studi di diritto, economia e politica* 6, no. 3 (1928): 220–25.

———. *Tre economisti Italiani: Pantaleoni, Pareto, Loria*. Bari: Laterza, 1939.

———. *La finanza dello stato egiziano nell'ultimo decennio*. Estratto da "studi economici finanziari e corporativi" 19, no. 3 (October). Rome: Edizioni Italiane, 1941.

———. *Saggi sul risparmio*. Lanciano: Carabba, 1999.

Ricciardi, Mario. *Lezioni di storia sindacale Italia, 1945–1985*. Bologna: CLUEB, 1986.

Rigola, Rinaldo. "Le classi operaie e le assicurazioni sociali." *Rassegna sociale. Rivista mensile della cassa nazionale d'assicurazione per gli infortuni degli operai sul lavoro* 5, no. 1 (1918): 1–13.

Rocca, G. "L'occupazione delle terre 'incolte.'" *La riforma sociale* (May-June 1920): 221–52.

Romeo, Rosario. *Breve storia della grande industria in Italia: 1861–1961*. 4th edition, revised and expanded. Bologna: Cappelli, 1972.

Rosboch, Ettore. "L'azionariato di stato nell'economia fascista." *Lo stato* 1, no. 3 (1930): 253–58.

Rossi, Ernesto. *I padroni del vapore*. Bari: Laterza, 1955.

Rubin, Gerry R. *War, Law, and Labour: The Munition Acts, State Regulation, and the Unions, 1915–1921*. New York: Oxford University Press, 1987.

Saez, Emmanuel, and Gabriel Zucman. *The Triumph of Injustice: How the Rich Dodge Taxes and How to Make Them Pay*. First edition. New York: W. W. Norton, 2019.

Salter, J. Arthur. *Allied Shipping Control: An Experiment in International Administration*. Oxford: Clarendon Press, 1921.

Salvemini, Gaetano. *La dittatura fascista in Italia*. New York: Libreria del Nuovo mondo, 1929.

———. *Under the Axe of Fascism*. New York: Viking Press, 1936.

———. *Le origini del fascismo in Italia: "Lezioni di Harvard."* First edition. Milan: Feltrinelli, 1966.

Samuel, Herbert. "The Taxation of the Various Classes of the People." *Journal of the Royal Statistical Society* 82, no. 2 (1919).

Santhià, Battista. *Con Gramsci all'Ordine nuovo*. Biblioteca della Resistenza 7. Rome: Editori Riuniti, 1956.

Sayers, R. S. *The Bank of England, 1891–1944*. Cambridge: Cambridge University Press, 1976.

Scholliers, Peter, and Vera Zamagni, eds. *Labour's Reward: Real Wages and Economic Change in 19th- and 20th-Century Europe*. Cheltenham, UK: Edward Elgar, 1995.

Seassaro, Cesare. "The Teachings of the Struggle of the Engineers" [Gli insegnamenti della lotta dei metallurgici]. *L'Ordine nuovo* 2, no. 16 (October 2, 1920): 133–34.

Sefton, James, and Martin Weale. *Reconciliation of National Income and Expenditure: Balanced Estimates of National Income for the United Kingdom, 1920–1990*.

Studies in the National Income and Expenditure of the United Kingdom 7. Cambridge and New York: Cambridge University Press, 1995.

Segreto, Luciano. "Armi e munizioni. Lo sforzo bellico tra speculazione e progresso tecnico." *Italia contemporanea* 146 (1982): 35–66.

Sember, Florencia. "El papel de Raúl Prebisch en la creación del Banco Central de la República Argentina." *Estudios críticos del desarrollo* 2, no. 3 (2012): 133–57. https://estudiosdeldesarrollo.mx/estudioscriticosdeldesarrollo/wp-content/uploads/2019/01/ECD3-6.pdf.

Semmler, Willi. "The Macroeconomics of Austerity in the European Union." *Social Research* 80, no. 3 (2013): 883–914. https://www.jstor.org/stable/24385696.

Semmler, Willi, and Alexander Haider. "The Perils of Debt Deflation in the Euro Area: A Multi-Regime Model." *Empirica* 43, no. 2 (May 1, 2016): 257–78. https://doi.org/10.1007/s10663-016-9327-5.

Serpieri, Arrigo. *La guerra e le classi rurali Italiane.* New Haven, CT: Yale University Press, 1930.

Serri, Niccolò. "Review of *Senza lavoro. La disoccupazione in Italia dall'unità ad oggi*, by Manfredi Alberti." *Modern Italy* 22, no. 3 (August 2017): 339–40. https://doi.org/10.1017/mit.2017.11.

Seymour, Richard. "A Short History of Privatisation in the UK: 1979–2012." *The Guardian*, March 29, 2012. https://www.theguardian.com/commentisfree/2012/mar/29/short-history-of-privatisation.

Shaikh, Anwar. *Capitalism: Competition, Conflict, Crises.* Oxford: Oxford University Press, 2016.

Shefner, Jon, and Cory Blad. *Why Austerity Persists.* First edition. Cambridge: Polity Press, 2019.

Siciliano, Giovanni. *Cento anni di borsa in Italia: Mercato, imprese e rendimenti azionari nel ventesimo secolo.* Bologna: Il Mulino, 2001.

Siepmann, H. A. "The International Financial Conference at Brussels." *Economic Journal* 30, no. 120 (1920): 436–59.

Skidelsky, Robert. "Keynes and the Treasury View: The Case for and against an Active Unemployment Policy, 1920–1929." In *The Emergence of the Welfare State in Britain and Germany, 1850–1950*, ed. Wolfgang Mommsen. London: Routledge, 1981.

———. *John Maynard Keynes: Economist, Philosopher, Statesman.* Abridged edition. London: Macmillan, 2003.

———. *Keynes: The Return of the Master.* First edition. New York: PublicAffairs, 2009.

Slobodian, Quinn. *Globalists: The End of Empire and the Birth of Neoliberalism.* Cambridge, MA: Harvard University Press, 2018.

Spriano, Paolo. *Torino operaia nella grande guerra (1914–1918).* Turin: G. Einaudi, 1960.

———. *L'Ordine nuovo e i consigli di fabbrica.* Turin: Einaudi, 1971.

———. *The Occupation of the Factories: Italy 1920.* London: Pluto Press, 1975.

Stein, Ben. "In Class Warfare, Guess Which Class Is Winning?" *New York Times*, November 26, 2006.

Storm, Servaas. "Lost in Deflation: Why Italy's Woes Are a Warning to the Whole Eurozone." *International Journal of Political Economy* 48, no. 3 (July 2019): 195–237. https://doi.org/10.1080/08911916.2019.1655943.

Summers, Lawrence H. "Inflation Caused by Fed Dismissing Concerns as Transient." Interview with *Bloomberg Wall Street Week*, March 5, 2021. https://www.youtube.com/watch?v=dni9TbqIwqo.

Sylos Labini, Paolo. *Saggio sulle classi sociali.* Bari: Laterza, 1975.

Tabellini, Guido, and Alberto Alesina. "Voting on the Budget Deficit." *American Economic Review* 80, no. 1 (1990): 37–49. https://www.jstor.org/stable/2006732.

Tasca, Angelo. "An Episode of Working-Class Struggle at the Eve of Revolution: The Invasion of the Lands of Medicina" [Un episodio della lotta di classe alla vigilia della rivoluzione]. *L'Ordine nuovo* 2, no. 9 (July 10, 1920): 69–70.

———. *Nascita e avvento del fascismo.* Bari: Laterza, 1965.

Tawney, R. H. "The Abolition of Economic Controls, 1918–1921." *Economic History Review* 13, no. 1/2 (1943): 1–30. https://doi.org/10.2307/2590512. JSTOR.

Taylor, Lance. "Not So Modern Monetary Theory." *Institute for New Economic Thinking*, October 31, 2019. https://www.ineteconomics.org/perspectives/blog/not-so-modern-monetary-theory.

Taylor, Lance, with Özlem Ömer. *Macroeconomic Inequality from Reagan to Trump: Market Power, Wage Repression, Asset Price Inflation, and Industrial Decline.* Cambridge: Cambridge University Press, 2020.

Terry, George Percy Warner. *The Representation of the People Act 1918.* London: C. Knight & Co., 1918.

Terzi, Alessio. "The Great Fiscal Lever: An Italian Economic Obsession." *Bruegel* (blog post), August 21, 2018. https://www.bruegel.org/2018/08/the-great-fiscal-lever-an-italian-economic-obsession/.

Thane, Pat. *Foundations of the Welfare State.* Second edition. Longman Social Policy in Britain Series. New York and London: Addison-Wesley Longman, 1996.

Thomas, Peter D. *The Gramscian Moment: Philosophy, Hegemony and Marxism.* Leiden: Brill, 2009.

Thomas, R., and N. Dimsdale. *"A Millennium of UK Data": Bank of England OBRA Dataset.* Bank of England, 2017. https://www.bankofengland.co.uk/statistics/research-datasets.

Titmuss, Richard. "Essays on the Welfare State." *University Press Scholarship Online*, 2018.

Titmuss, Richard Morris. *Essays on "The Welfare State."* London: Allen & Unwin, (1958) 2018.

Tittoni, Tommaso. *Nuovi scritti di politica interna ed estera.* Milan: Treves, 1930.

Togliatti, Palmiro. "Labor's State" [Lo stato del lavoro]. *L'Ordine nuovo* 1, no. 10 (July 19, 1919a): 71–72.

———. "The Battle of Ideas" [La battaglia delle idee]. *L'Ordine nuovo* 1, no. 24 (November 1, 1919b): 190.

———. "The Assembly of the Turin Metallurgical Department" [L'assemblea della sezione metallurgica Torinese]. *L'Ordine nuovo* 1, no. 25 (November 8, 1919c): 195–96.

———. "Class Control" [Controllo di classe]. *L'Ordine nuovo* 1, no. 32 (January 3, 1920): 249–50.

Tomassini, Luigi. "Industrial Mobilization and the Labour Market in Italy during the First World War." *Social History* 16, no. 1 (1991): 59–87. https://doi.org/10 .1080/03071029108567789.

Tomlinson, Jim. *Problems of British Economic Policy, 1870–1945.* London: Rout- ledge, 1981. https://doi.org/10.4324/9781315019666.

Toniolo, Gianni. *L'economia dell'Italia fascista.* Bari: Laterza, 1980.

———. "Italian Banking, 1919–1936." In *Banking, Currency, and Finance in Europe between the Wars.* Oxford: Oxford University Press, 1995. https://doi.org/10 .1093/0198288034.003.0011.

———, ed. *The Oxford Handbook of the Italian Economy since Unification.* Oxford: Oxford University Press, 2013.

Tooze, J. Adam. *The Deluge: The Great War, America and the Remaking of the Global Order, 1916–1931.* New York: Viking Adult, 2014.

———. "Neoliberalism's World Order." *Dissent Magazine* (Summer 2018). https:// www.dissentmagazine.org/article/neoliberalism-world-order-review-quinn -slobodian-globalists.

Trentin, Bruno. *Autunno caldo: Il secondo biennio rosso 1968–1969.* Rome: Editori Riuniti, 1999.

Ufficio Municipale del Lavoro. *Bollettino mensile*, vol. 3. Rome (Italy), 1920. https://catalog.hathitrust.org/Record/012392095.

US Department of Labor. "Industrial Unrest in Great Britain: Reports of the Commission of Inquiry into Industrial Unrest." *Bulletin of the United States Bureau of Labor Statistics* 237 (October 1917): 7–227.

Vecchi, Giovanni. *Measuring Wellbeing: A History of Italian Living Standards.* Oxford: Oxford University Press, 2017.

Vergara, Camila. "The Meaning of Chile's Explosion." *Jacobin Magazine*, October 29, 2019.

———. "Burying Pinochet." *Sidecar*, 2021. https://newleftreview.org/sidecar/posts/ burying-pinochet.

Viglongo, Andrea. "The Experiment of Cooperative Management of the Caste- naso Workers" [L'esperimento di gestione cooperativa degli operai di caste- naso]. *L'Ordine nuovo* 2, no. 10 (July 17, 1920): 75–76.

Vivarelli, Roberto. *Il dopoguerra in Italia e l'avvento del fascismo (1918–1922).* Naples: Istituto Italiano per Gli Studi Storici, 1967.

Walsh, Tom. *What Is the Shop Steward Movement? A Survey with Diagrams.* Lon- don: The Agenda Press, 1920.

Wartzman, Rick. "'We Were Shocked': RAND Study Uncovers Massive Income Shift to the Top 1%." *Fast Company*, September 14, 2020. https://www .fastcompany.com/90550015/we-were-shocked-rand-study-uncovers-massive -income-shift-to-the-top-1.

Whetham, William Cecil Dampier. *The War and the Nation: A Study in Constructive Politics*. London: John Murray, 1917.

Whiteside, Noelle. "Welfare Legislation and the Unions during the First World War." *Historical Journal* 23, no. 4 (1980): 857–74. https://www.jstor.org/stable/ 2638729. JSTOR.

Whiting, R. C. "Taxation and the Working Class, 1915–24." *Historical Journal* 33, no. 4 (1990): 895–916. https://www.jstor.org/stable/2639803.

Wolfe, Humbert. *Labour Supply and Regulation*. New York: H. Milford, 1923.

Wood, Ellen Miskin. *The Origin of Capitalism*. New York: Monthly Review Press, 1999.

Wrigley, Chris. *A History of British Industrial Relations 1914–1939*. Brighton, Sussex, UK: Harvester Press, 1987.

———. *Lloyd George and the Challenge of Labour: The Post-War Coalition, 1918– 1922*. Hemel Hempstead, UK: Harvester Wheatsheaf, 1991.

Zaganella, Mario. "La mobilitazione industriale: Un pilastro nella evoluzione del modello Italiano di intervento pubblico in economia." In *Istituzioni e società in Francia e in Italia nella prima guerra mondiale*. Rome: Edizioni Nuova Cultura, 2017. https://www.pucrs.br/humanidades/wp-content/uploads/sites/ 30/2016/03/La-mobilitazione-industriale.pdf.

Zamagni, Vera. "La dinamica dei salari nel settore industriale, 1921–1939." *Quaderni storici* 10, nos. 29/30 (2/3) (1975): 530–49.

———. *Dalla periferia al centro: La seconda rinascita economica dell'Italia, 1861– 1981*. Bologna: Il Mulino, 1990.

———. "Industrial Wages and Workers' Protest in Italy during the 'Biennio Rosso' (1919–1920)." *Journal of European Economic History* 20, no. 1 (Spring 1991): 137–153.

Zevin, Alexander. *Liberalism at Large: The World According to the Economist*. London: Verso, 2019.

Zini, Zino. "From Citizen to Producer" [Da cittadino a produttore]. *L'Ordine nuovo* 1, no. 38 (February 21, 1920): 301–2.

Zucaro, Domenico. *La rivolta di Torino del 1917 nella sentenza del tribunale militare territoriale*. Milan: Rivista Storica del Socialismo, 1960.

Zucman, Gabriel. "Global Wealth Inequality." *Annual Review of Economics* 11, no. 1 (August 2019): 109–38. https://doi.org/10.1146/annurev-economics -080218-025852.

Index

canteens, 326n33

Capel-Cure, Sir Edward Henry, 251–53, 389n8

capital, 21–22, 130; accumulation, 5, 8, 12–14, 21, 30, 35, 42–43, 49, 51, 53–54, 57, 58, 76, 93, 99–100, 114, 127, 128, 132, 134, 136, 141, 144–46, 149, 152–54, 158, 163, 177–78, 182, 183, 187, 189, 196–98, 205, 213, 221, 225, 230, 244, 247, 254, 258, 269–71, 273, 285, 286, 287, 299, 308, 310, 355n17, 394n41, 398n6, 401n28, 405n23, 405n25; duties, 291; and labor, 234, 282; rehabilitation, and lower wages, 191

capitalism, 3–7, 9–10, 12–13, 14, 15, 21–28, 33, 35, 66, 82, 91, 96, 99–102, 108–11, 125, 131–34, 217, 287, 289, 309; alternatives to, 301, 305, 307; and austerity, 3–4, 271; class relations between owners and workers, 23; coercion under, 22–23; crisis of, 3, 25, 53–54, 74, 116, 127, 158, 249; and exploitation (*see* exploitation); free-market, 45, 51, 85, 361n31; laissez-faire, 42, 54, 57, 72, 73, 156, 167, 321n2; monetary economy, 32–33; private property, 35; and pure economics (*see* pure economics); structural flaws, 86; vertical relationship of powers, 136

capitalist civilization, 252, 320n17

capital order, 4, 5, 7, 13, 25, 157, 228, 237, 262, 272, 287, 289, 290, 296, 297, 300–303, 307–8

Caporetto, Battle of, 59, 338n6

CARES Act (US), 303

Cassa Nationale Infortuni (CNI), 69

Cassel, Gustav, 136, 138–39, 353n4

Castenaso co-op, 92–93, 94

central banks, 8, 15, 141, 151, 201–2, 265–66, 360n24, 405n28; freedom of, 151–52, 165, 199–200, 266–68, 300

Central Labour College, 186

Cermenati, Mario, 68, 335n38

Chalmers, Lord Robert, 134–35, 140–41, 144, 146, 355n16

Chamberlain, Austen, 162, 176, 179–81, 193, 201, 365n52, 381n69, 394n44

Chamberlain, Neville, 180–81, 193, 201, 368n71, 388n5, 391n25

Chamber of Commerce, 67, 69, 90, 169

Chamber of Labour of Bologna and Turin, 71

Chambers of Labour, 332n19

chemical industry, 119, 329n56

Cherubini, Arnaldo, 331n15, 335n36, 335n41, 335n43

"Chicago Boys," 301

Chile, 1, 301, 406n30

Chiozza Money, Leo George, 28–29, 31, 45–46, 85, 156, 322n4, 324n19, 327n43, 342n31

Churchill, Winston, 46, 166, 172–73, 201–2, 264–65, 327n45, 340n20, 360n25, 365nn58–59, 393n38, 395n50

Ciampi, Carlo Azeglio, 292–93

Ciocca, Pierluigi, 30, 311, 370n3, 371n7

Ciuffelli, Augusto, 69

Clarke, Simon, 81, 320n18, 333n24, 359n18

class(es), 4, 10, 12, 163, 176, 179; capitalist, 12, 16, 17, 23, 102, 131, 152, 183, 249, 273, 278, 305, 345n4, 369n78; conflict, 12–13, 19, 20, 308; differences, 177; division, 342n29; middle classes, 76, 166, 272, 304, 338n3, 363n40, 377n38; repression, 308; shares, 272; struggle, 147; tensions, in postwar Britain, 78; upper, 8; working classes, 4, 8, 9, 11–12, 15–17, 20, 25, 35, 36, 40, 47, 49–50, 59, 61–63, 65, 67, 69–70, 76, 77, 79, 83, 92, 96, 99, 100, 106, 110, 112, 116, 118, 127, 129, 130, 133, 158, 182, 219, 225, 231, 263, 299, 329n58, 341n22

classless society, 100, 139, 243, 345n2

Clinton, Bill, 302

Clydeside region, 99, 104, 105, 339n12

Clyde Workers Committee, 50

Clynes, John R., 343n33

coal, 72, 323n11, 342n31; miners (*see* miners)

coercion strategy, 8, 22, 38, 114, 127, 143, 147–48, 151, 163, 197, 237, 245, 278, 286, 311

Cohen, Jon S., 383n78, 384n82, 387n99, 400n21

Cokayne, Brien (Baron Cullen of Ashbourne), 150–51

Cole, G. D. H., 29, 41, 49, 74–76, 80–81, 82, 88, 90–91, 95, 97, 98, 289, 326n37, 337n1, 337n3, 367n66

colonies, austerity in, 7, 186, 320n12

Commission on Currency and Exchange, 143, 150–54

Commission on Finance, 144

Commission on Public Finance, 140, 142–44, 146, 159

Committee of Enquiry (1920), 326n35

Committee of National Expenditure (Geddes Committee), 184